OTHERWORLDLY IZA...

NOBO

ENGLISH EDITION
Translation: CALEB D. COOK
Typesetting: MIYOKO HOSOYAMA
Sound Effects: EK WEAVER
Associate Editor: M. CHANDLER

UDON STAFF
Chief of Operations: ERIK KO
Director of Publishing: MATT MOYLAN
VP of Business Development: CORY CASONI
Director of Marketing: MEGAN MAIDEN
Japanese Liaisons: STEVEN CUMMINGS
ANNA KAWASHIMA

Original Story
NATSUYA SEMIKAWA

Manga
VIRGINIA NITOUHEI

Character Design
KURURI

ISEKAI IZAKAYA "NOBU" Volume 8

©Virginia-Nitouhei 2019
©Natsuya Semikawa,Kururi/TAKARAJIMASHA

First published in Japan in 2019 by KADOKAWA CORPORATION, Tokyo.
English translation rights arranged with KADOKAWA CORPORATION, Tokyo
through TUTTLE–MORI AGENCY, INC., Tokyo.

English language version published by UDON Entertainment Inc.
118 Tower Hill Road, C1, PO Box 20008
Richmond Hill, Ontario, L4K 0K0 CANADA

www.UDONentertainment.com

First Printing: October 2021
ISBN: 978-1-77294-214-9

Printed in Canada

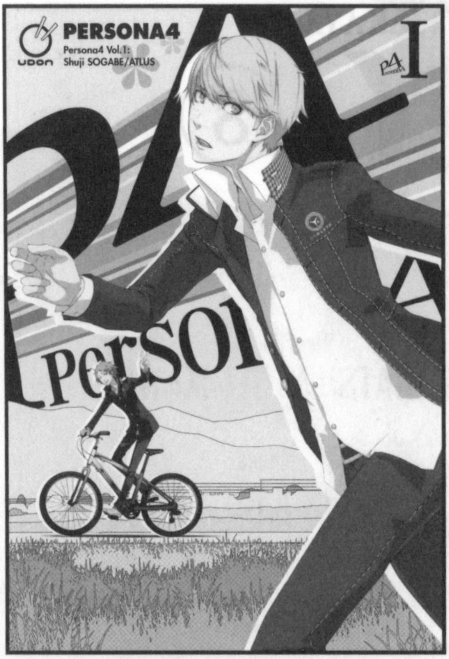
PERSONA4
Persona4 Vol.1:
Shuji SOGABE/ATLUS
UDON
I

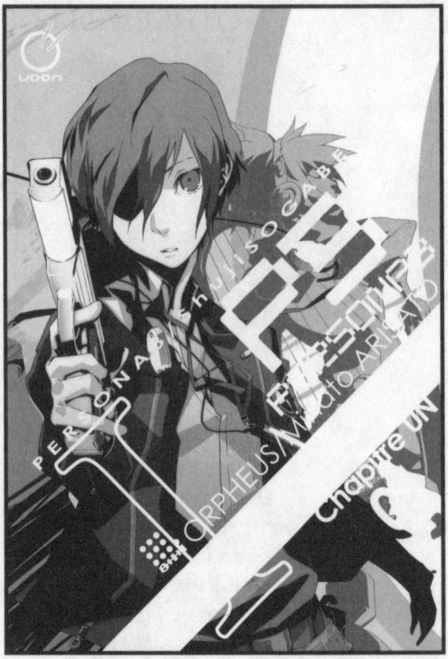
UDON
ORPHEUS
Chapitre UN

PERSONA 4 VOL.1
ISBN: 978-1927925577

PERSONA 3 VOL.1
ISBN: 978-1927925850

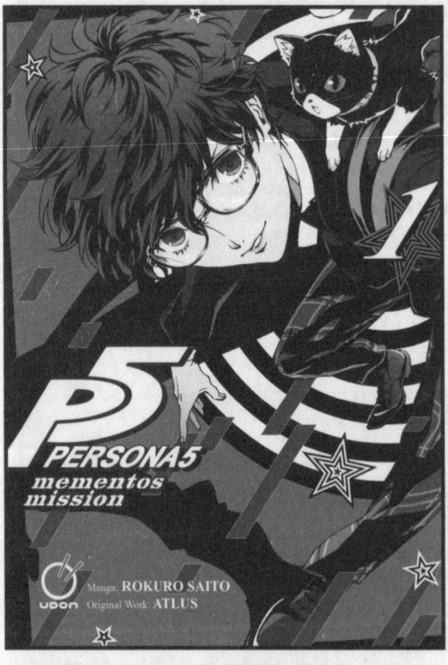
1
PERSONA5
mementos
mission
Manga: ROKURO SAITO
Original Work: ATLUS
UDON

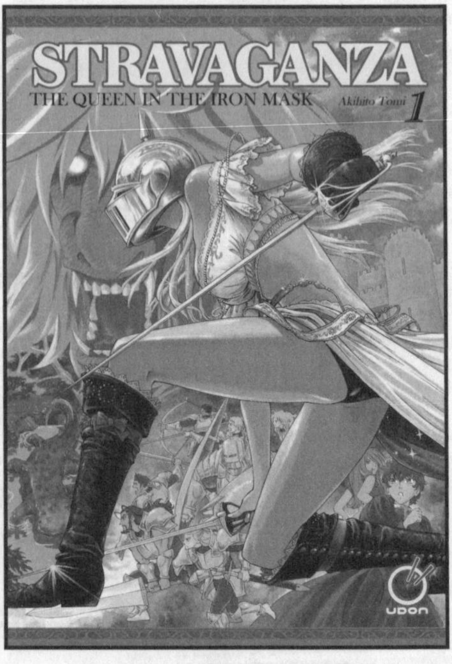
STRAVAGANZA
THE QUEEN IN THE IRON MASK
Akihito Tomi 1
UDON

PERSONA 5: MOMENTOS MISSION VOL.1
ISBN: 978-1772942200

STRAVAGANZA VOL.1
ISBN: 978-1772941036

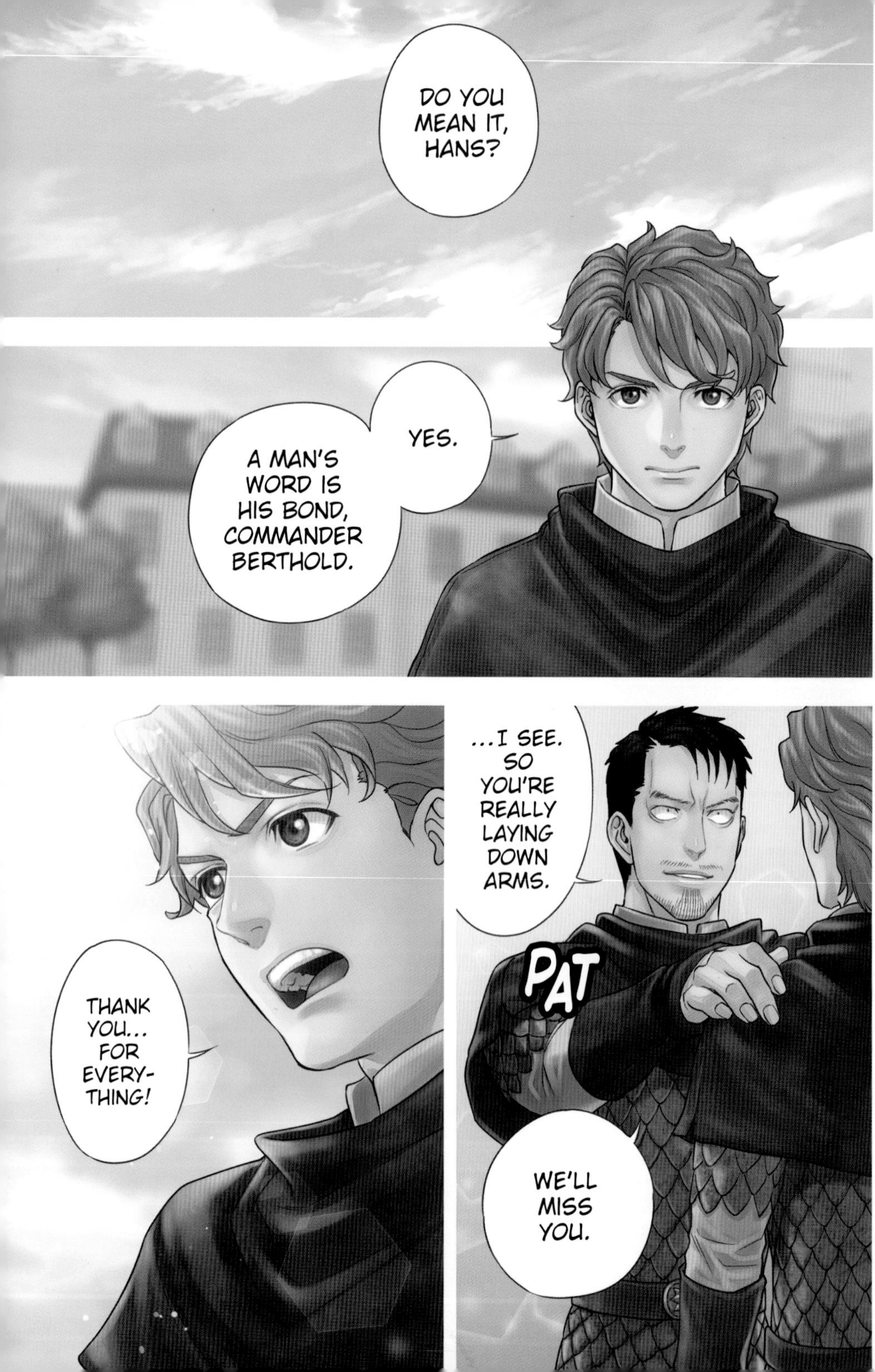
DO YOU MEAN IT, HANS?
YES.
A MAN'S WORD IS HIS BOND, COMMANDER BERTHOLD.
...I SEE. SO YOU'RE REALLY LAYING DOWN ARMS.
PAT
WE'LL MISS YOU.
THANK YOU... FOR EVERY-THING!

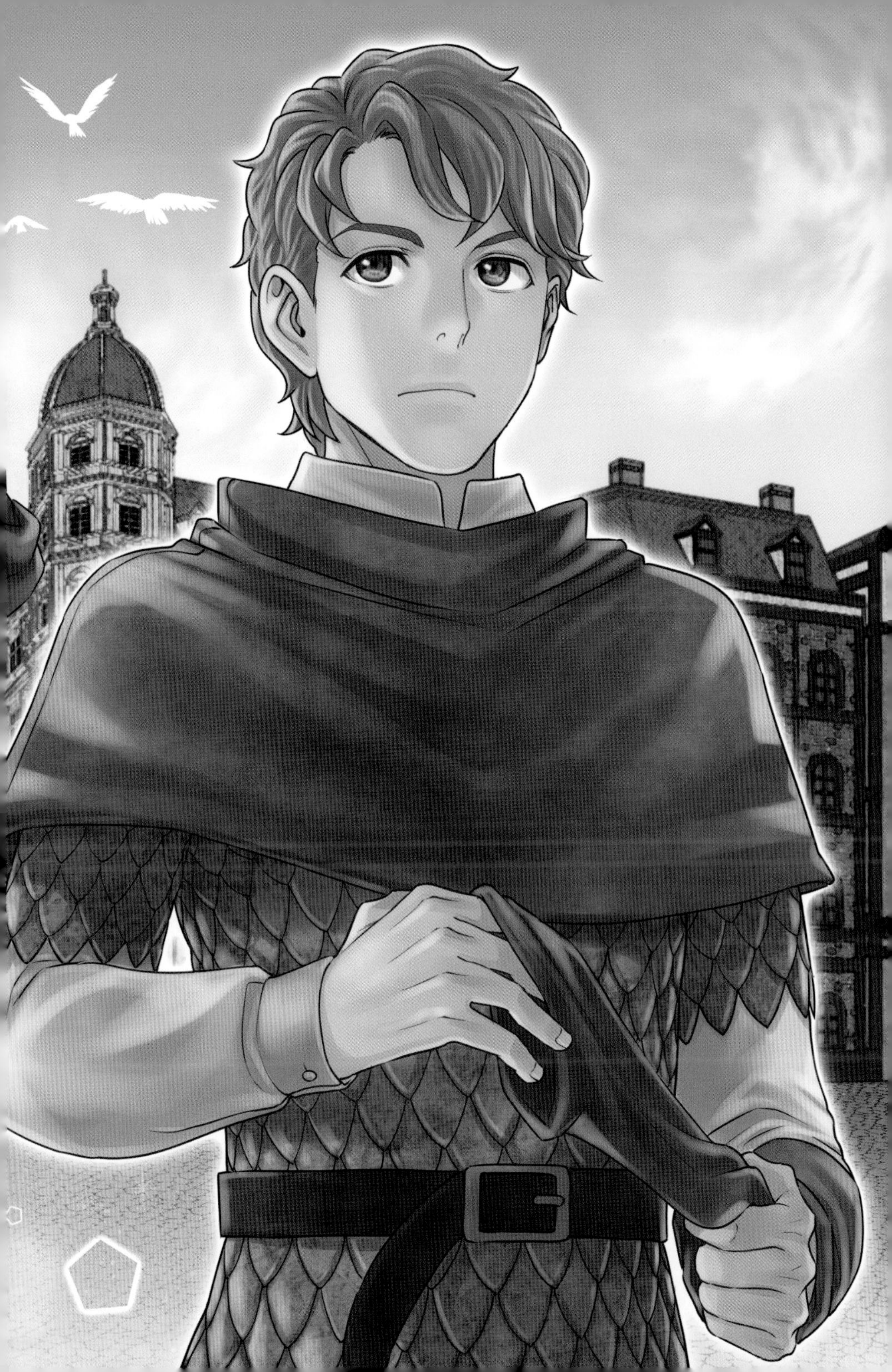

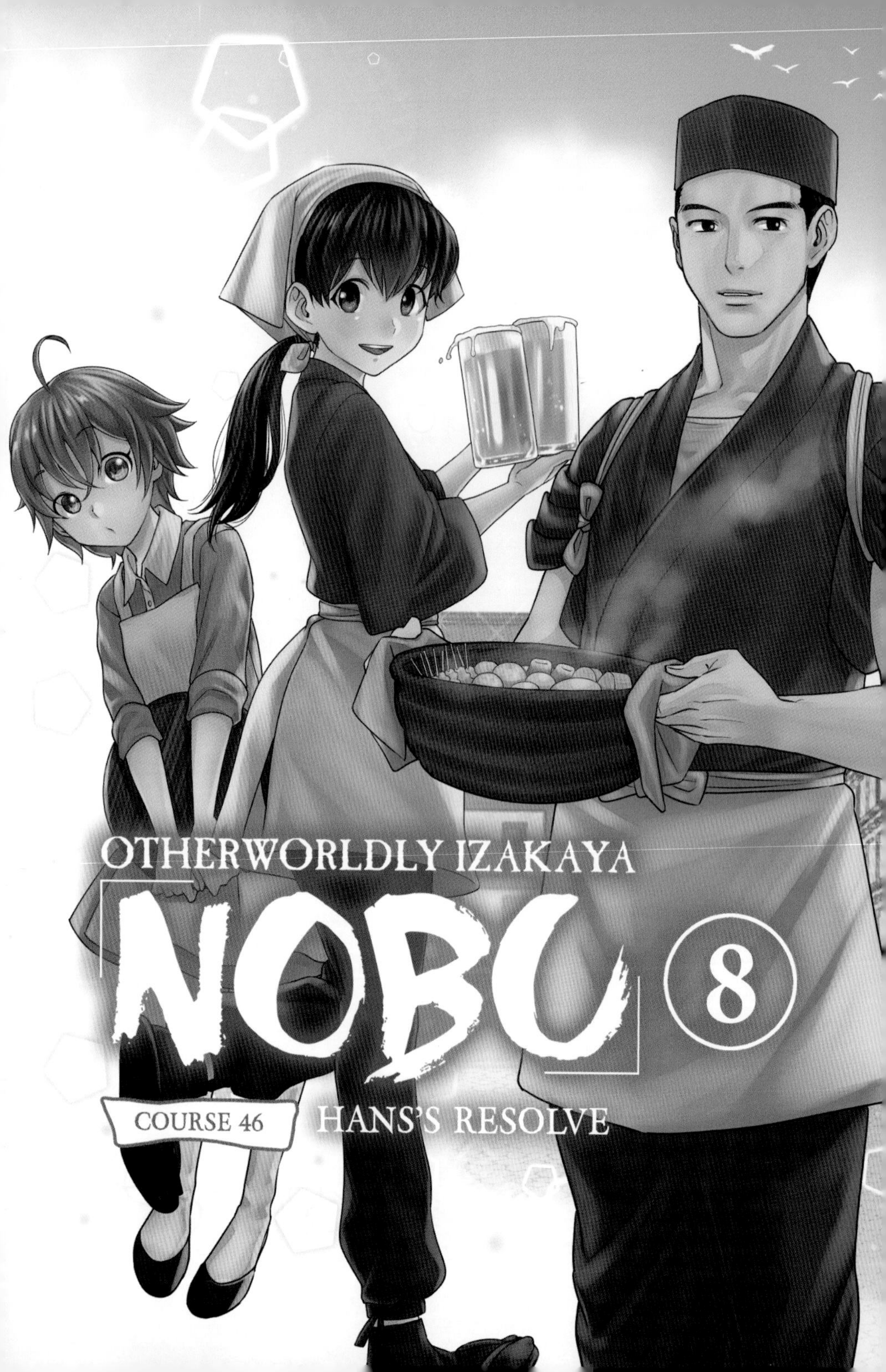
OTHERWORLDLY IZAKAYA
NOBU
8
COURSE 46
HANS'S RESOLVE

MENU

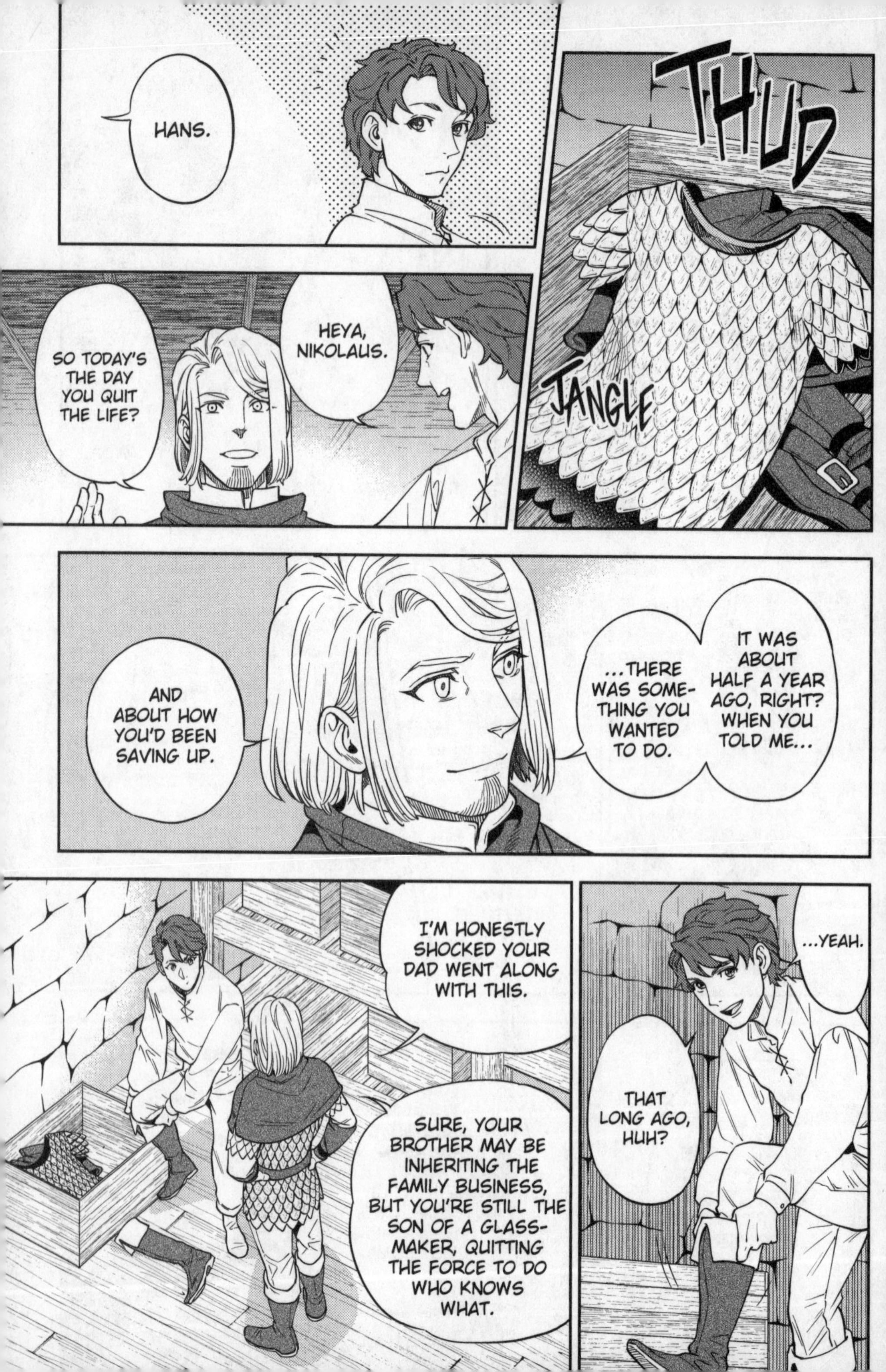
THUD
JANGLE
HANS.
HEYA, NIKOLAUS.
SO TODAY'S THE DAY YOU QUIT THE LIFE?
IT WAS ABOUT HALF A YEAR AGO, RIGHT? WHEN YOU TOLD ME...
...THERE WAS SOME-THING YOU WANTED TO DO.
AND ABOUT HOW YOU'D BEEN SAVING UP.
...YEAH.
THAT LONG AGO, HUH?
I'M HONESTLY SHOCKED YOUR DAD WENT ALONG WITH THIS.
SURE, YOUR BROTHER MAY BE INHERITING THE FAMILY BUSINESS, BUT YOU'RE STILL THE SON OF A GLASS-MAKER, QUITTING THE FORCE TO DO WHO KNOWS WHAT.

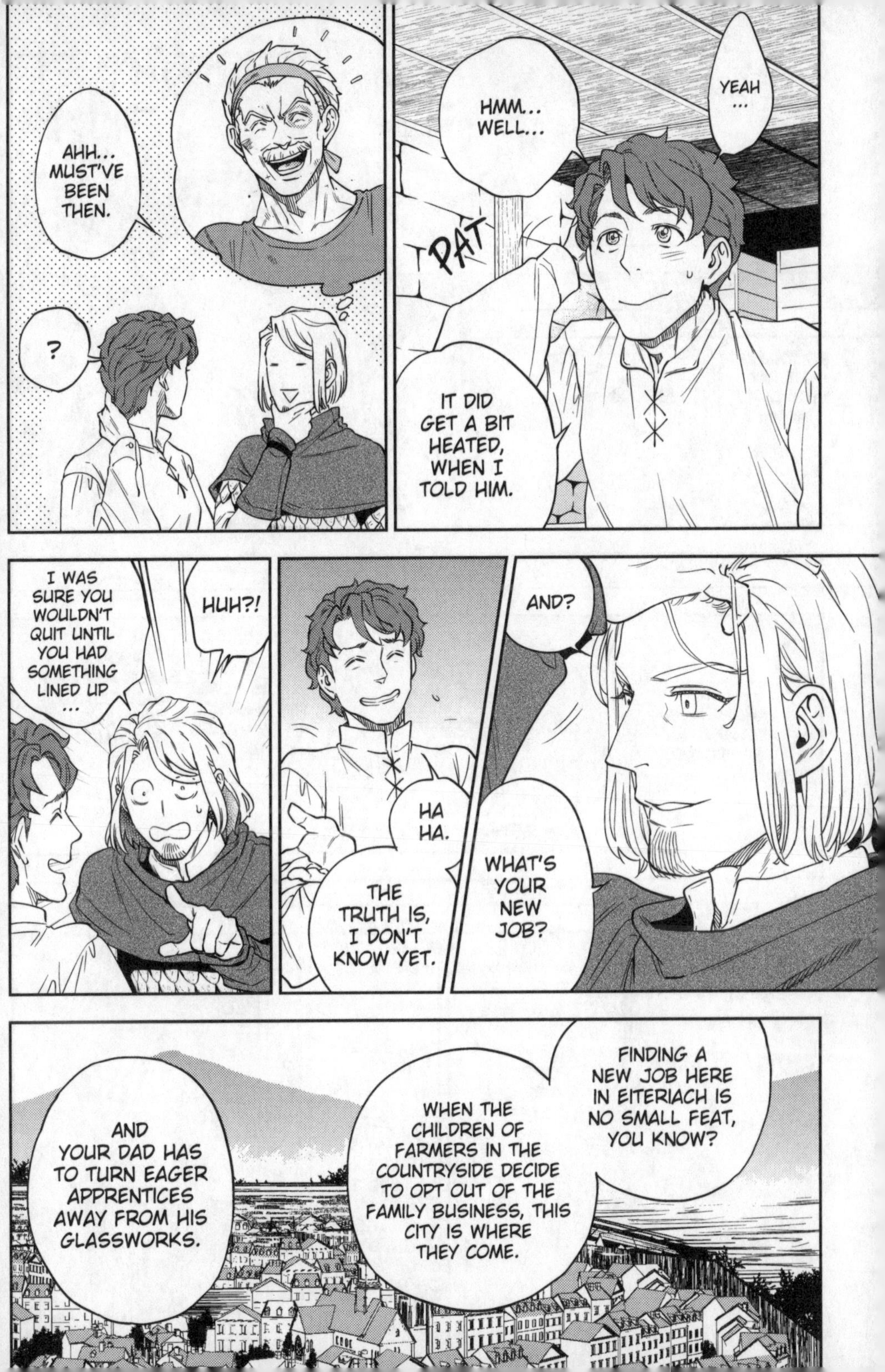
YEAH ...
HMM... WELL...
PAT
IT DID GET A BIT HEATED, WHEN I TOLD HIM.
AHH... MUST'VE BEEN THEN.
?
AND?
WHAT'S YOUR NEW JOB?
HA HA.
THE TRUTH IS, I DON'T KNOW YET.
HUH?!
I WAS SURE YOU WOULDN'T QUIT UNTIL YOU HAD SOMETHING LINED UP ...
FINDING A NEW JOB HERE IN EITERIACH IS NO SMALL FEAT, YOU KNOW?
WHEN THE CHILDREN OF FARMERS IN THE COUNTRYSIDE DECIDE TO OPT OUT OF THE FAMILY BUSINESS, THIS CITY IS WHERE THEY COME.
AND YOUR DAD HAS TO TURN EAGER APPRENTICES AWAY FROM HIS GLASSWORKS.

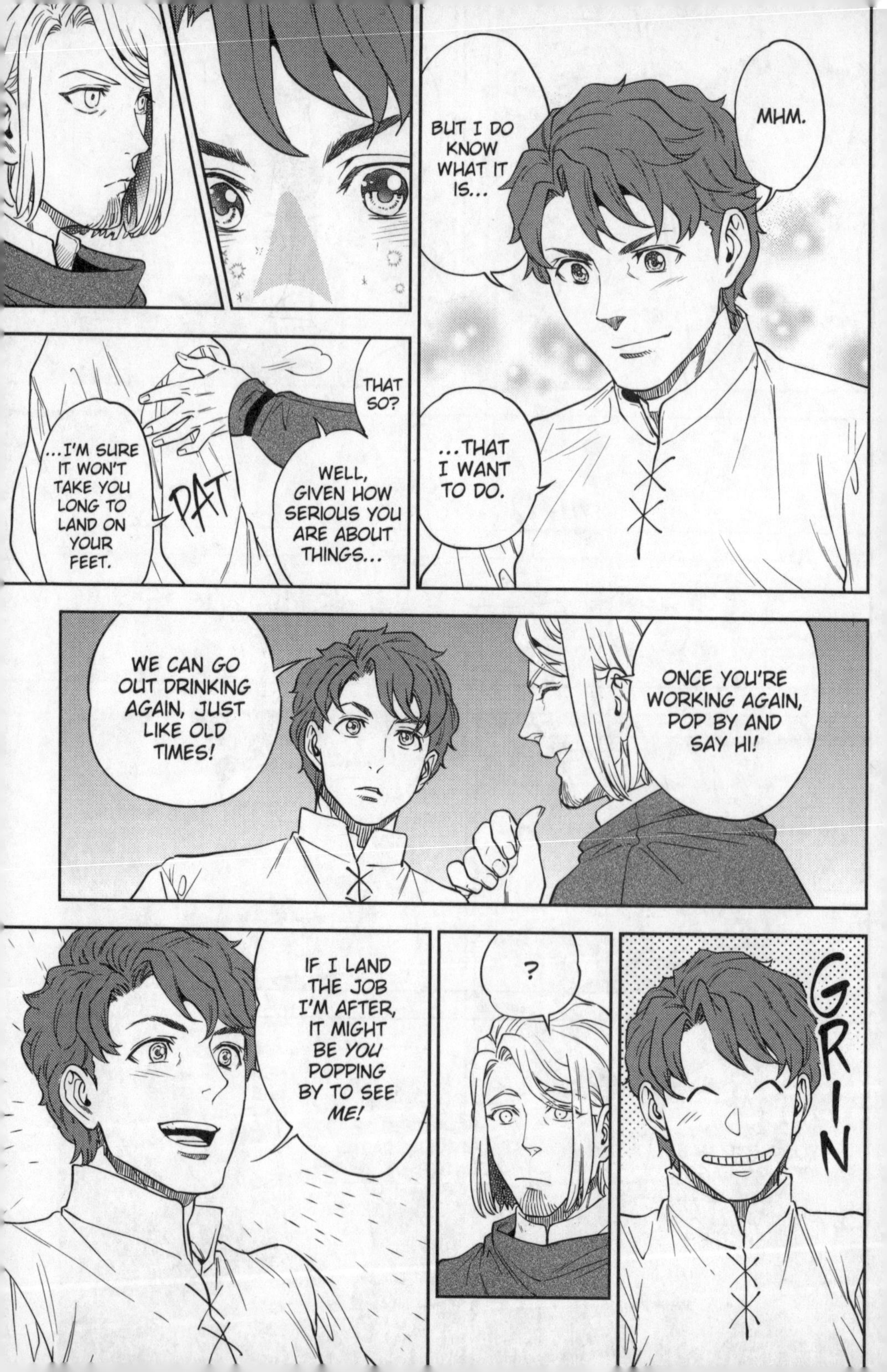
MHM.
BUT I DO KNOW WHAT IT IS...
...THAT I WANT TO DO.
THAT SO?
WELL, GIVEN HOW SERIOUS YOU ARE ABOUT THINGS...
PAT
...I'M SURE IT WON'T TAKE YOU LONG TO LAND ON YOUR FEET.
ONCE YOU'RE WORKING AGAIN, POP BY AND SAY HI!
WE CAN GO OUT DRINKING AGAIN, JUST LIKE OLD TIMES!
GRIN
?
IF I LAND THE JOB I'M AFTER, IT MIGHT BE *YOU* POPPING BY TO SEE *ME*!

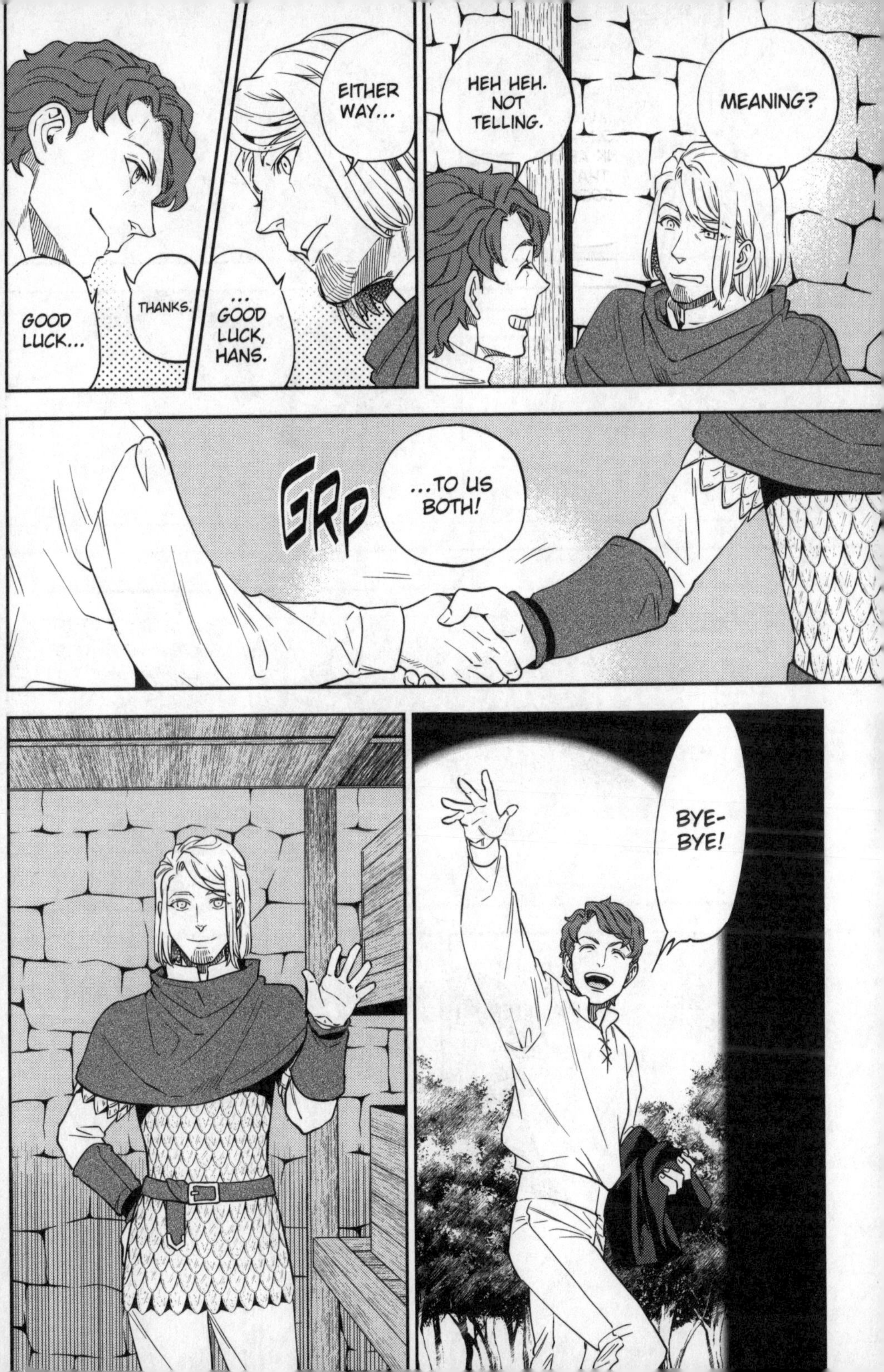
MEANING?
HEH HEH. NOT TELLING.
EITHER WAY...
...GOOD LUCK, HANS.
THANKS.
GOOD LUCK...
...TO US BOTH!
GRP
BYE-BYE!

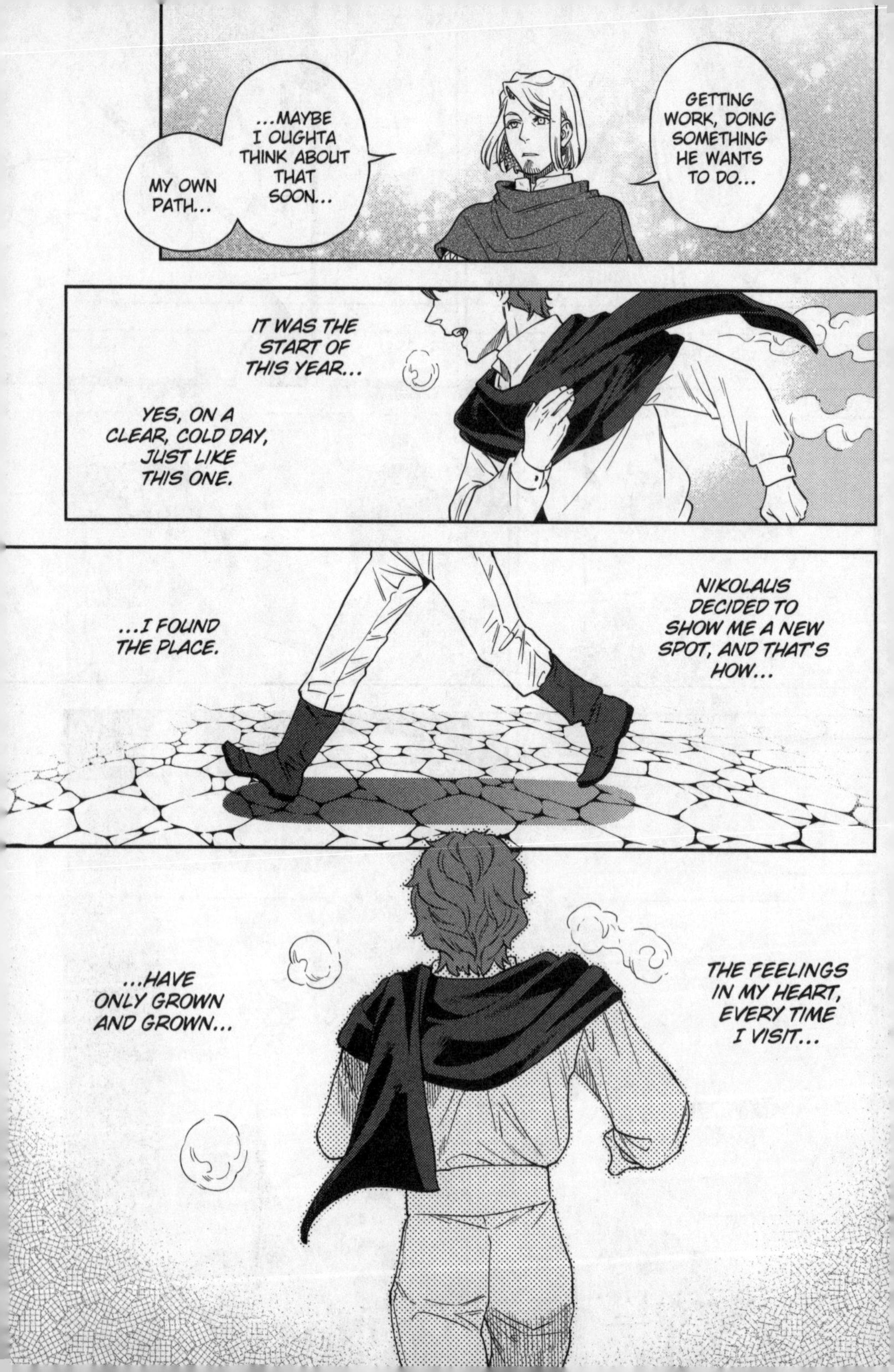
GETTING WORK, DOING SOMETHING HE WANTS TO DO...
...MAYBE I OUGHTA THINK ABOUT THAT SOON...
MY OWN PATH...
IT WAS THE START OF THIS YEAR...
YES, ON A CLEAR, COLD DAY, JUST LIKE THIS ONE.
NIKOLAUS DECIDED TO SHOW ME A NEW SPOT, AND THAT'S HOW...
...I FOUND THE PLACE.
THE FEELINGS IN MY HEART, EVERY TIME I VISIT...
...HAVE ONLY GROWN AND GROWN...

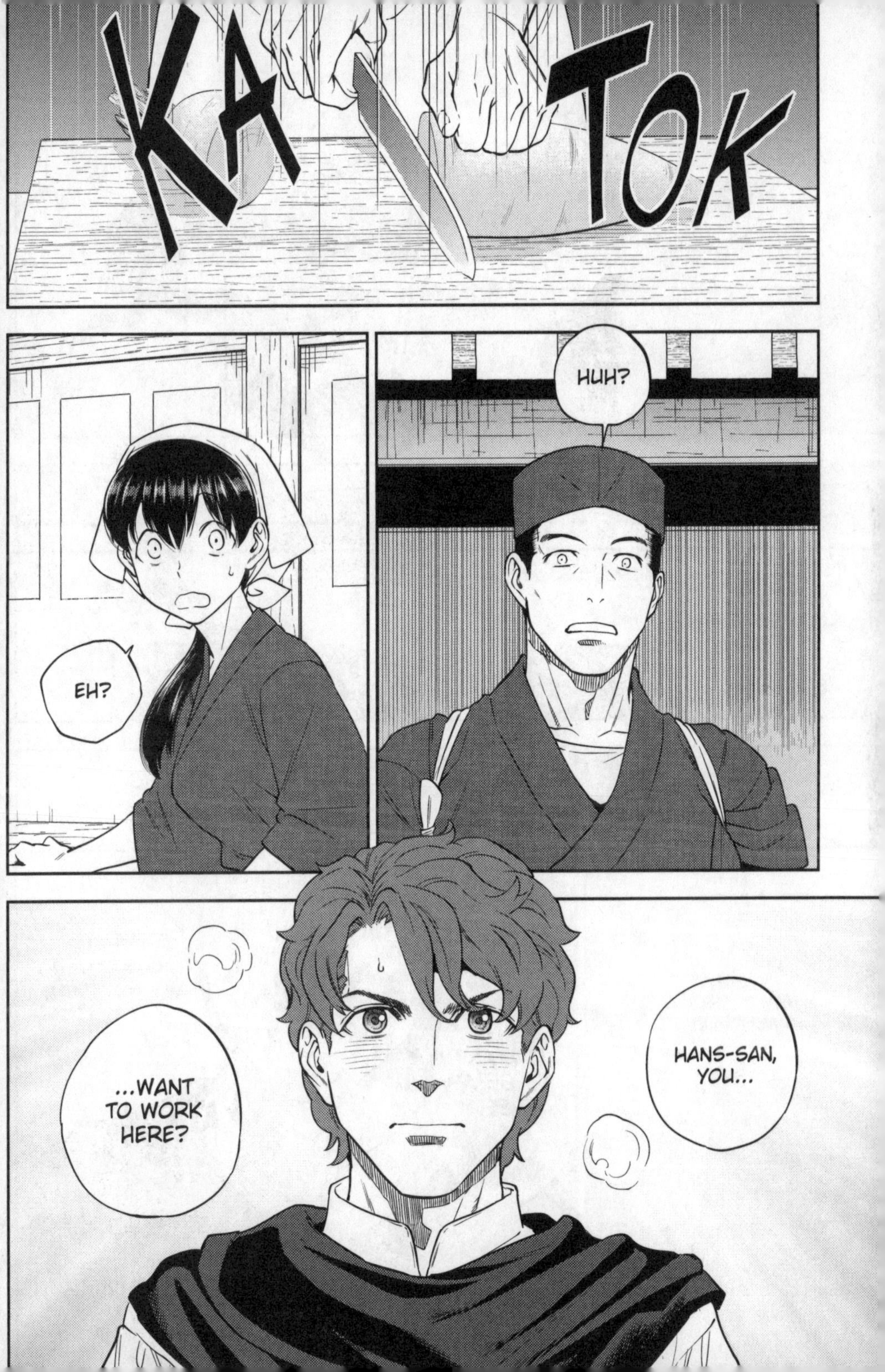
KA TOK
HUH?
EH?
HANS-SAN, YOU...
...WANT TO WORK HERE?

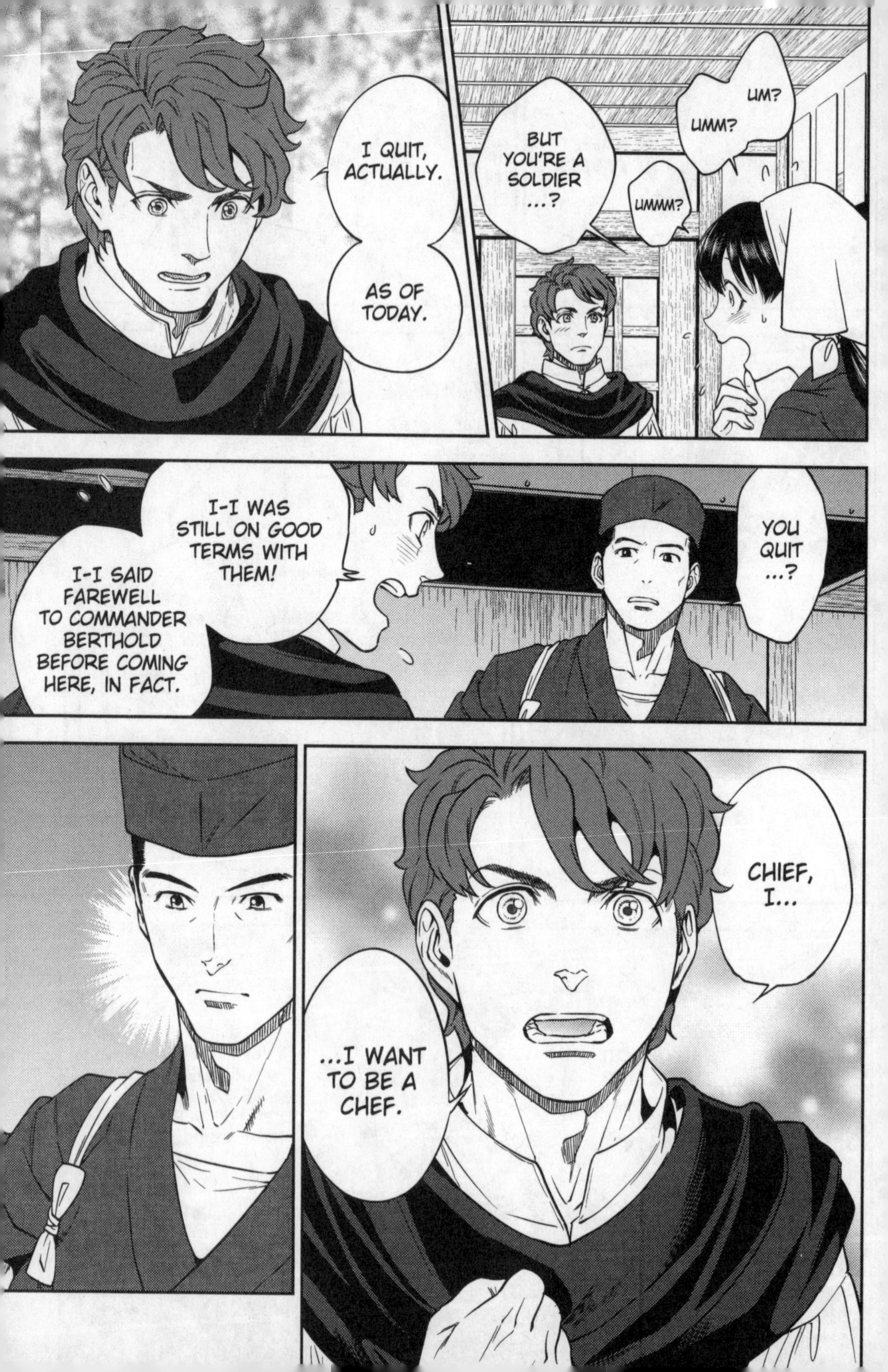
UM?
UMM?
BUT YOU'RE A SOLDIER ...?
UMMM?
I QUIT, ACTUALLY.
AS OF TODAY.
YOU QUIT ...?
I-I WAS STILL ON GOOD TERMS WITH THEM!
I-I SAID FAREWELL TO COMMANDER BERTHOLD BEFORE COMING HERE, IN FACT.
CHIEF, I...
...I WANT TO BE A CHEF.

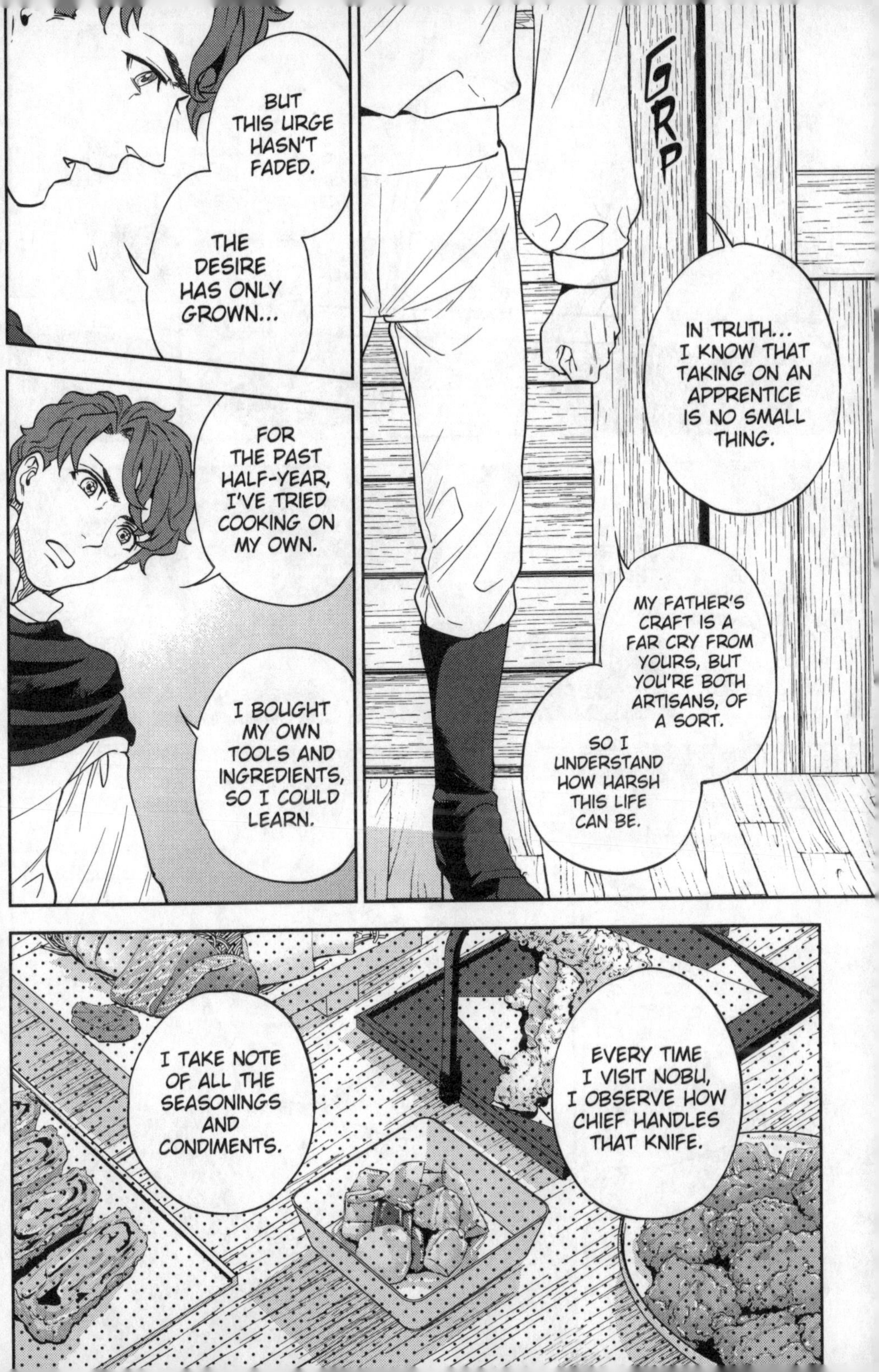
GRP
IN TRUTH... I KNOW THAT TAKING ON AN APPRENTICE IS NO SMALL THING.
MY FATHER'S CRAFT IS A FAR CRY FROM YOURS, BUT YOU'RE BOTH ARTISANS, OF A SORT.
SO I UNDERSTAND HOW HARSH THIS LIFE CAN BE.
BUT THIS URGE HASN'T FADED.
THE DESIRE HAS ONLY GROWN...
FOR THE PAST HALF-YEAR, I'VE TRIED COOKING ON MY OWN.
I BOUGHT MY OWN TOOLS AND INGREDIENTS, SO I COULD LEARN.
EVERY TIME I VISIT NOBU, I OBSERVE HOW CHIEF HANDLES THAT KNIFE.
I TAKE NOTE OF ALL THE SEASONINGS AND CONDIMENTS.

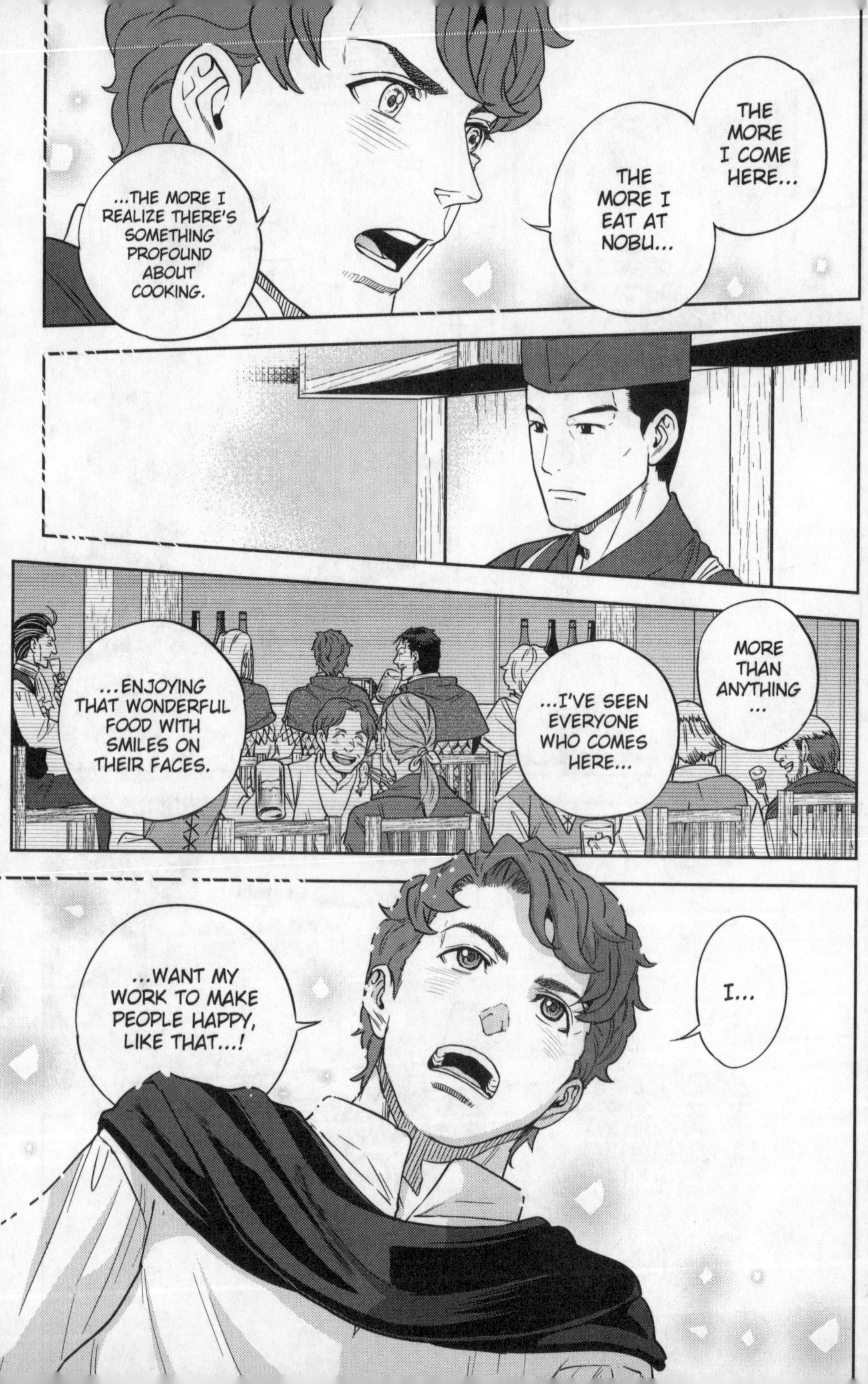
THE MORE I COME HERE...
THE MORE I EAT AT NOBU...
...THE MORE I REALIZE THERE'S SOMETHING PROFOUND ABOUT COOKING.
MORE THAN ANYTHING...
...I'VE SEEN EVERYONE WHO COMES HERE...
...ENJOYING THAT WONDERFUL FOOD WITH SMILES ON THEIR FACES.
I...
...WANT MY WORK TO MAKE PEOPLE HAPPY, LIKE THAT...!

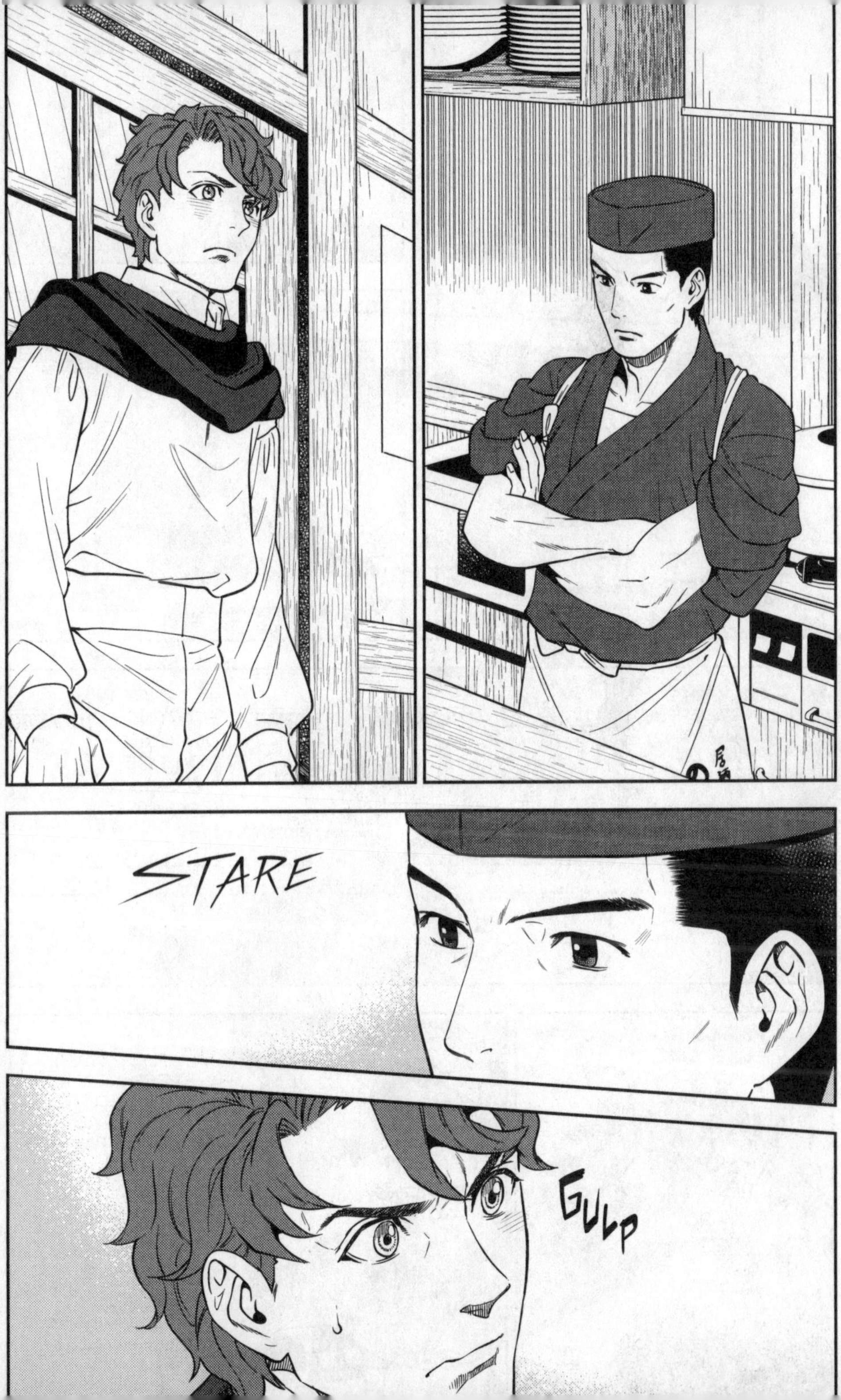
STARE
GULP

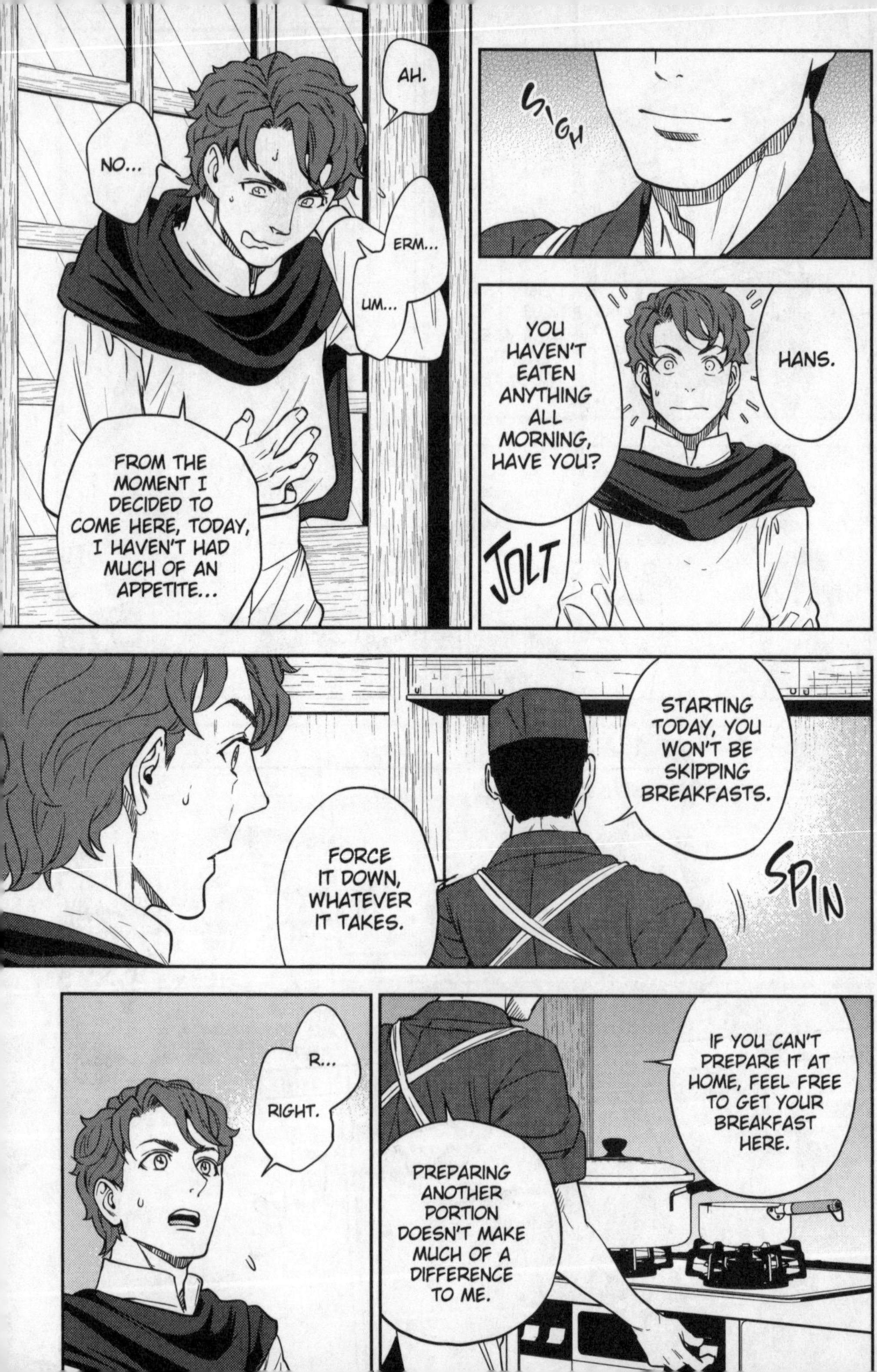
SIGH
HANS.
YOU HAVEN'T EATEN ANYTHING ALL MORNING, HAVE YOU?
JOLT
AH.
NO...
ERM...
UM...
FROM THE MOMENT I DECIDED TO COME HERE, TODAY, I HAVEN'T HAD MUCH OF AN APPETITE...
STARTING TODAY, YOU WON'T BE SKIPPING BREAKFASTS.
SPIN
FORCE IT DOWN, WHATEVER IT TAKES.
IF YOU CAN'T PREPARE IT AT HOME, FEEL FREE TO GET YOUR BREAKFAST HERE.
PREPARING ANOTHER PORTION DOESN'T MAKE MUCH OF A DIFFERENCE TO ME.
R...
RIGHT.

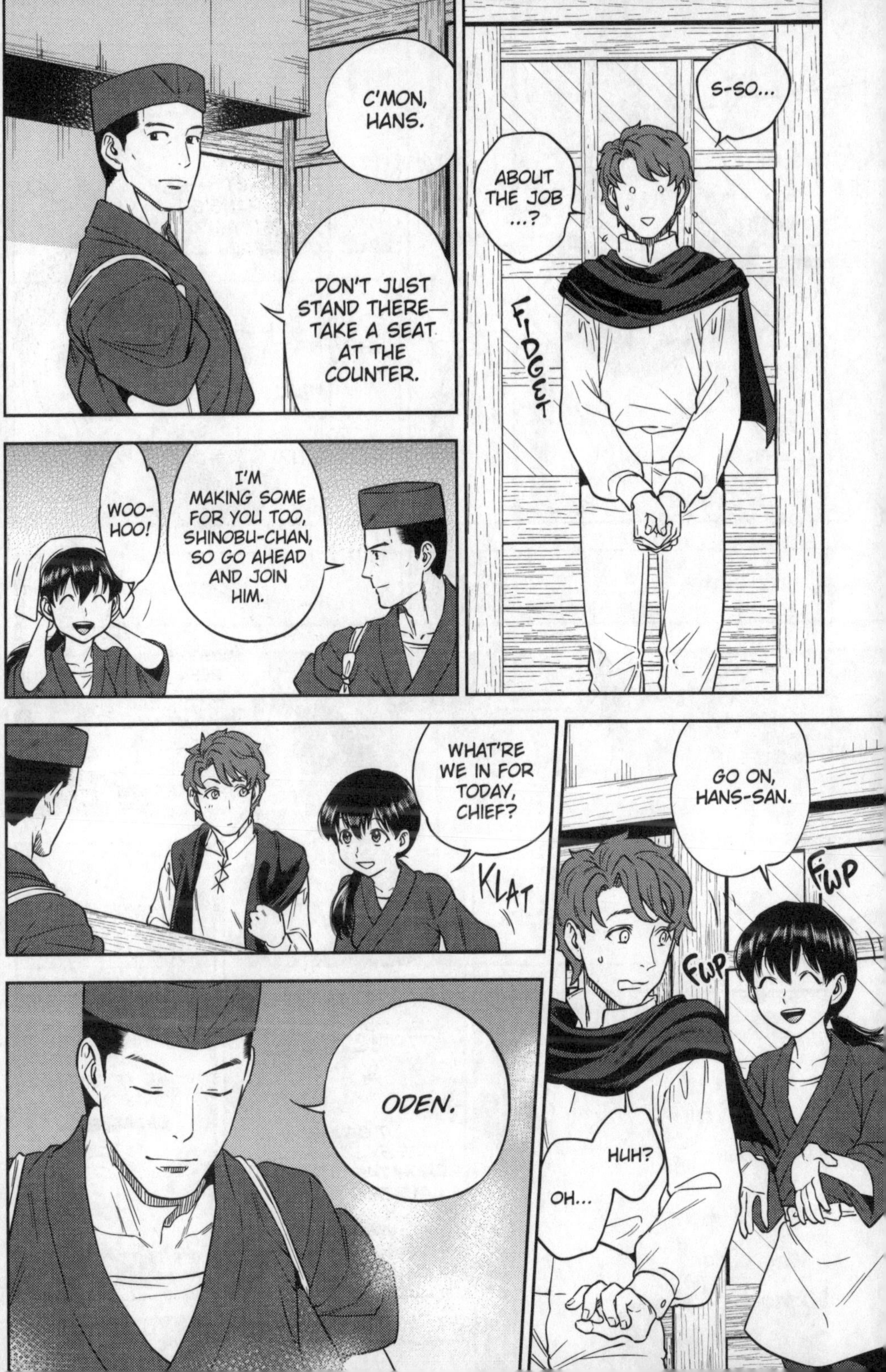
S-SO...
ABOUT THE JOB ...?
FIDGET
C'MON, HANS.
DON'T JUST STAND THERE—TAKE A SEAT AT THE COUNTER.
I'M MAKING SOME FOR YOU TOO, SHINOBU-CHAN, SO GO AHEAD AND JOIN HIM.
WOO-HOO!
GO ON, HANS-SAN.
FWP
FWP
HUH?
OH...
WHAT'RE WE IN FOR TODAY, CHIEF?
KLAT
ODEN.

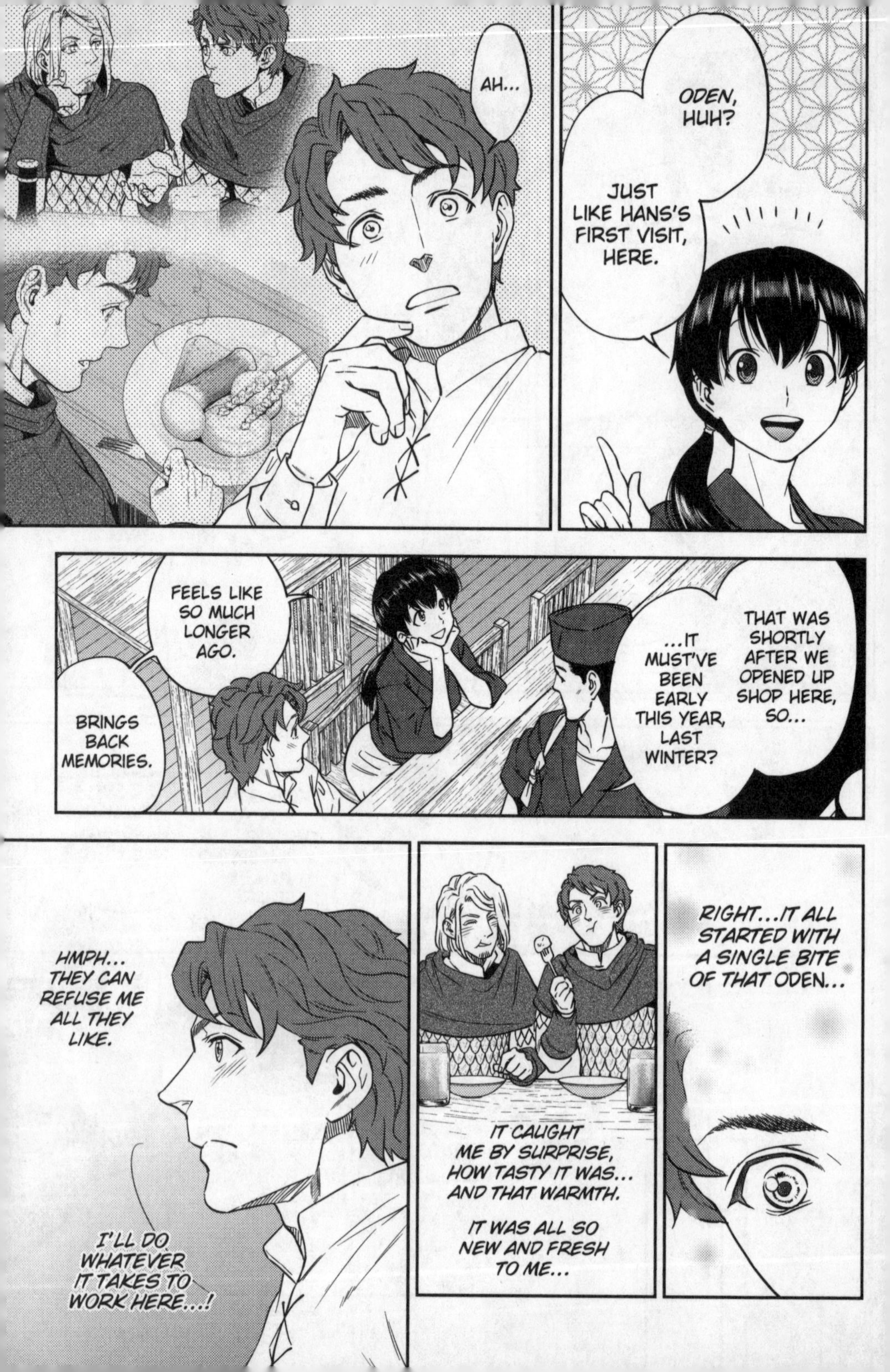
ODEN, HUH?
JUST LIKE HANS'S FIRST VISIT, HERE.
AH...
THAT WAS SHORTLY AFTER WE OPENED UP SHOP HERE, SO...
...IT MUST'VE BEEN EARLY THIS YEAR, LAST WINTER?
FEELS LIKE SO MUCH LONGER AGO.
BRINGS BACK MEMORIES.
RIGHT...IT ALL STARTED WITH A SINGLE BITE OF THAT ODEN...
IT CAUGHT ME BY SURPRISE, HOW TASTY IT WAS... AND THAT WARMTH.
IT WAS ALL SO NEW AND FRESH TO ME...
HMPH... THEY CAN REFUSE ME ALL THEY LIKE.
I'LL DO WHATEVER IT TAKES TO WORK HERE...!

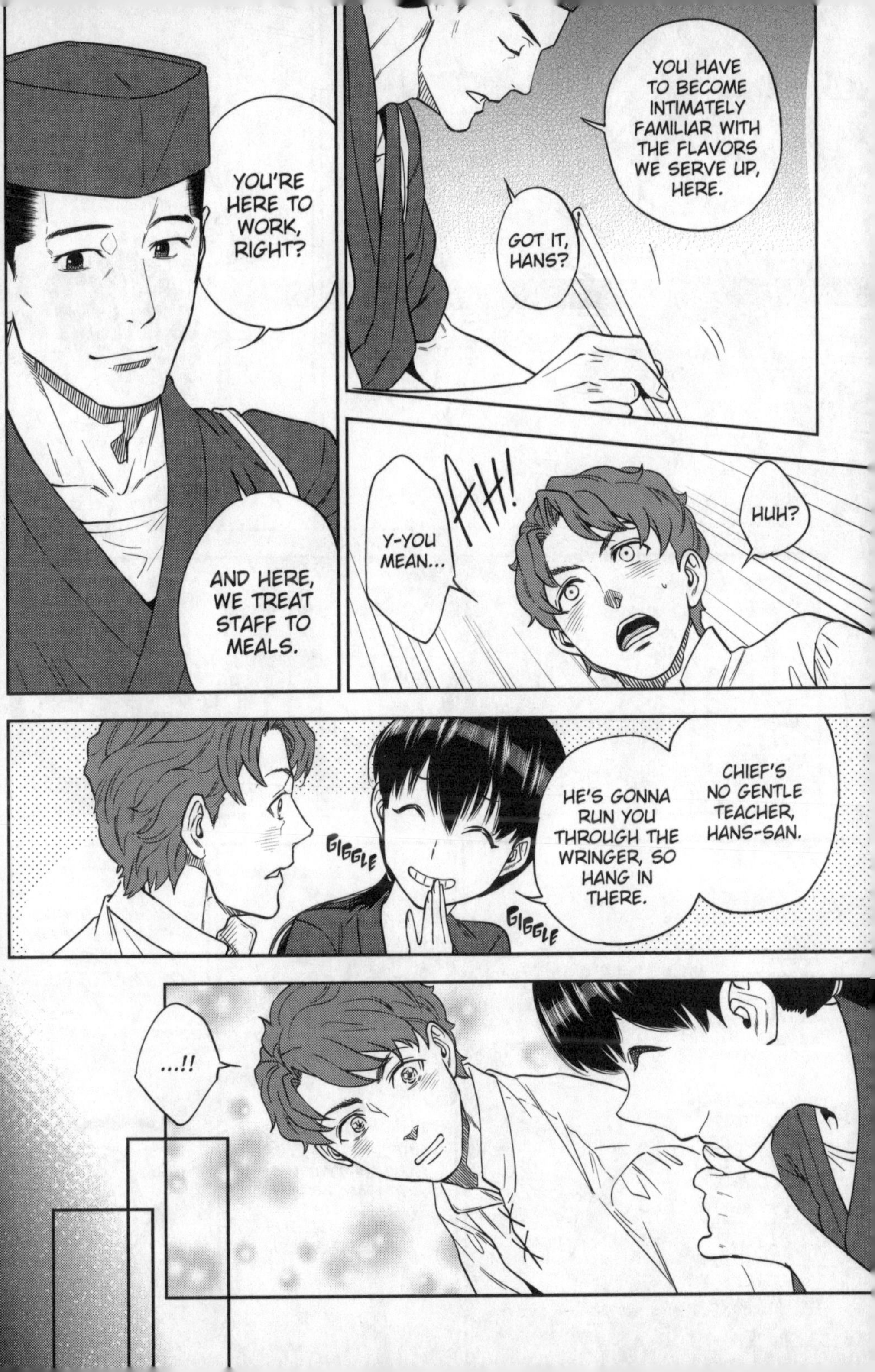
YOU HAVE TO BECOME INTIMATELY FAMILIAR WITH THE FLAVORS WE SERVE UP, HERE.
GOT IT, HANS?
HUH?
AH!
Y-YOU MEAN...
YOU'RE HERE TO WORK, RIGHT?
AND HERE, WE TREAT STAFF TO MEALS.
CHIEF'S NO GENTLE TEACHER, HANS-SAN.
HE'S GONNA RUN YOU THROUGH THE WRINGER, SO HANG IN THERE.
GIGGLE
GIGGLE
...!!

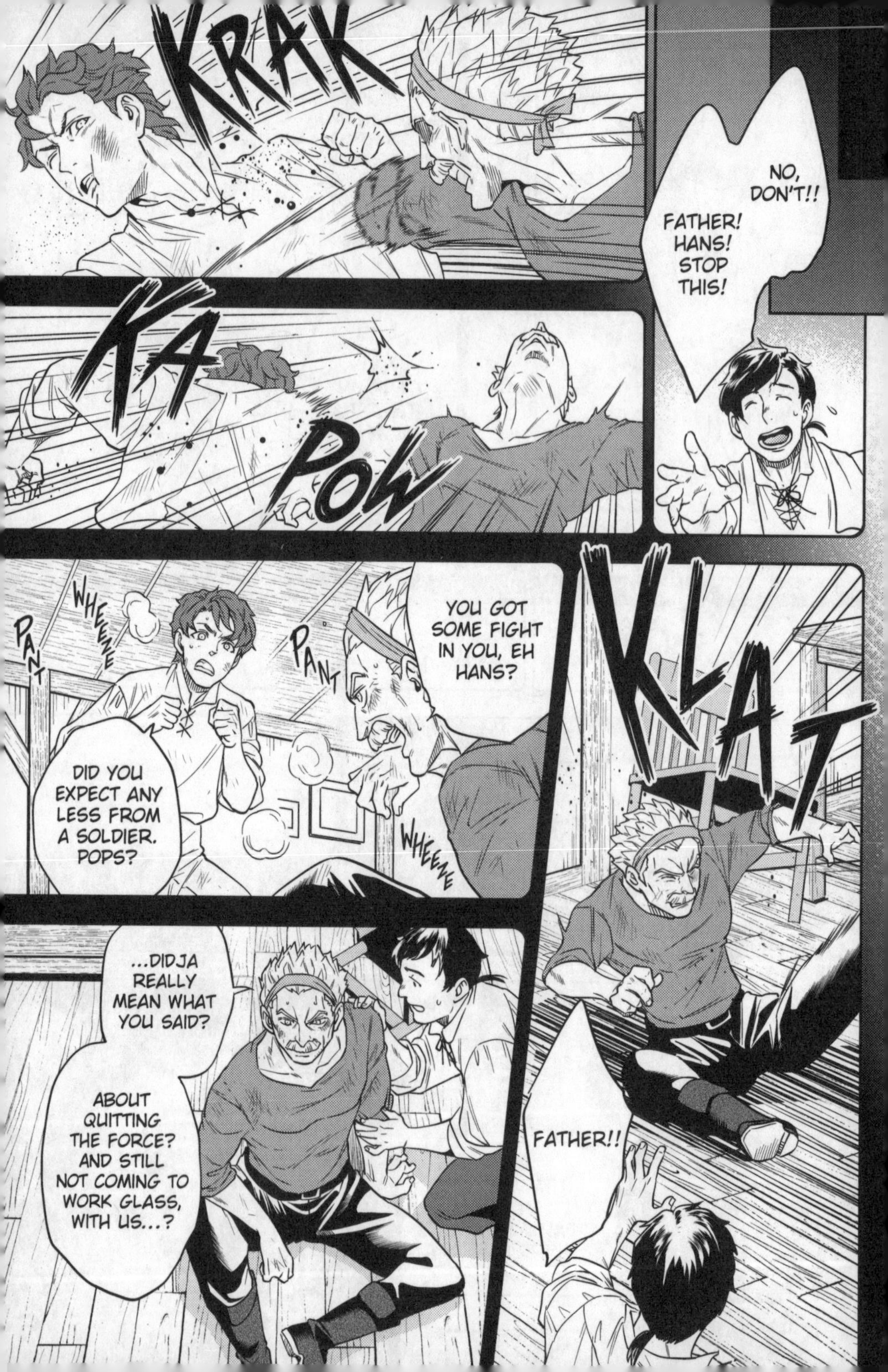
NO, DON'T!!
FATHER! HANS! STOP THIS!
KRAK
KA POW
KLAT
FATHER!!
YOU GOT SOME FIGHT IN YOU, EH HANS?
PANT
WHEEZE
PANT
DID YOU EXPECT ANY LESS FROM A SOLDIER. POPS?
WHEEZE
...DIDJA REALLY MEAN WHAT YOU SAID?
ABOUT QUITTING THE FORCE? AND STILL NOT COMING TO WORK GLASS, WITH US...?

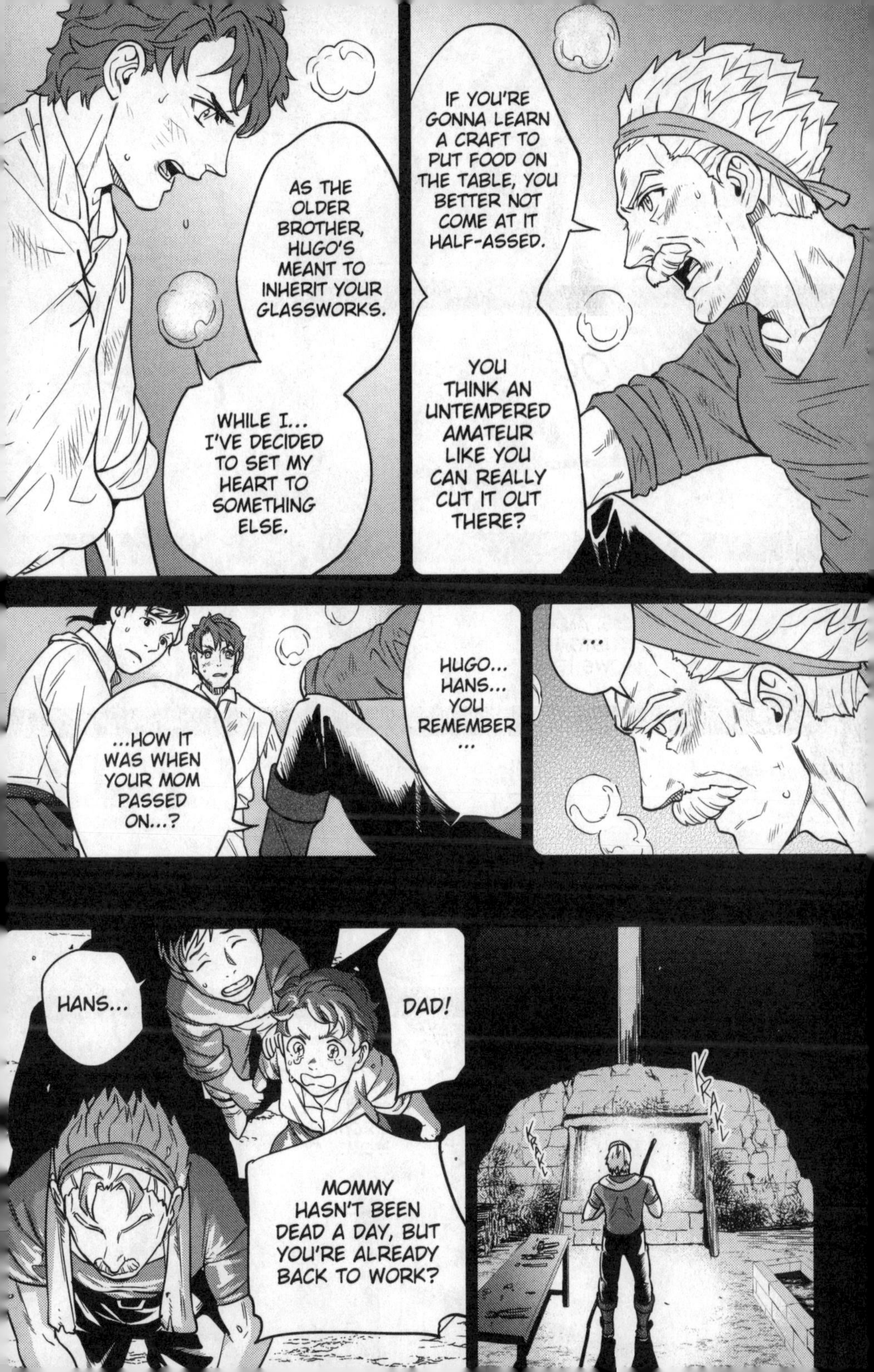
IF YOU'RE GONNA LEARN A CRAFT TO PUT FOOD ON THE TABLE, YOU BETTER NOT COME AT IT HALF-ASSED.
YOU THINK AN UNTEMPERED AMATEUR LIKE YOU CAN REALLY CUT IT OUT THERE?
AS THE OLDER BROTHER, HUGO'S MEANT TO INHERIT YOUR GLASSWORKS.
WHILE I... I'VE DECIDED TO SET MY HEART TO SOMETHING ELSE.
...
HUGO... HANS... YOU REMEMBER ...
...HOW IT WAS WHEN YOUR MOM PASSED ON...?
KRAK
KRAK
DAD!
HANS...
MOMMY HASN'T BEEN DEAD A DAY, BUT YOU'RE ALREADY BACK TO WORK?

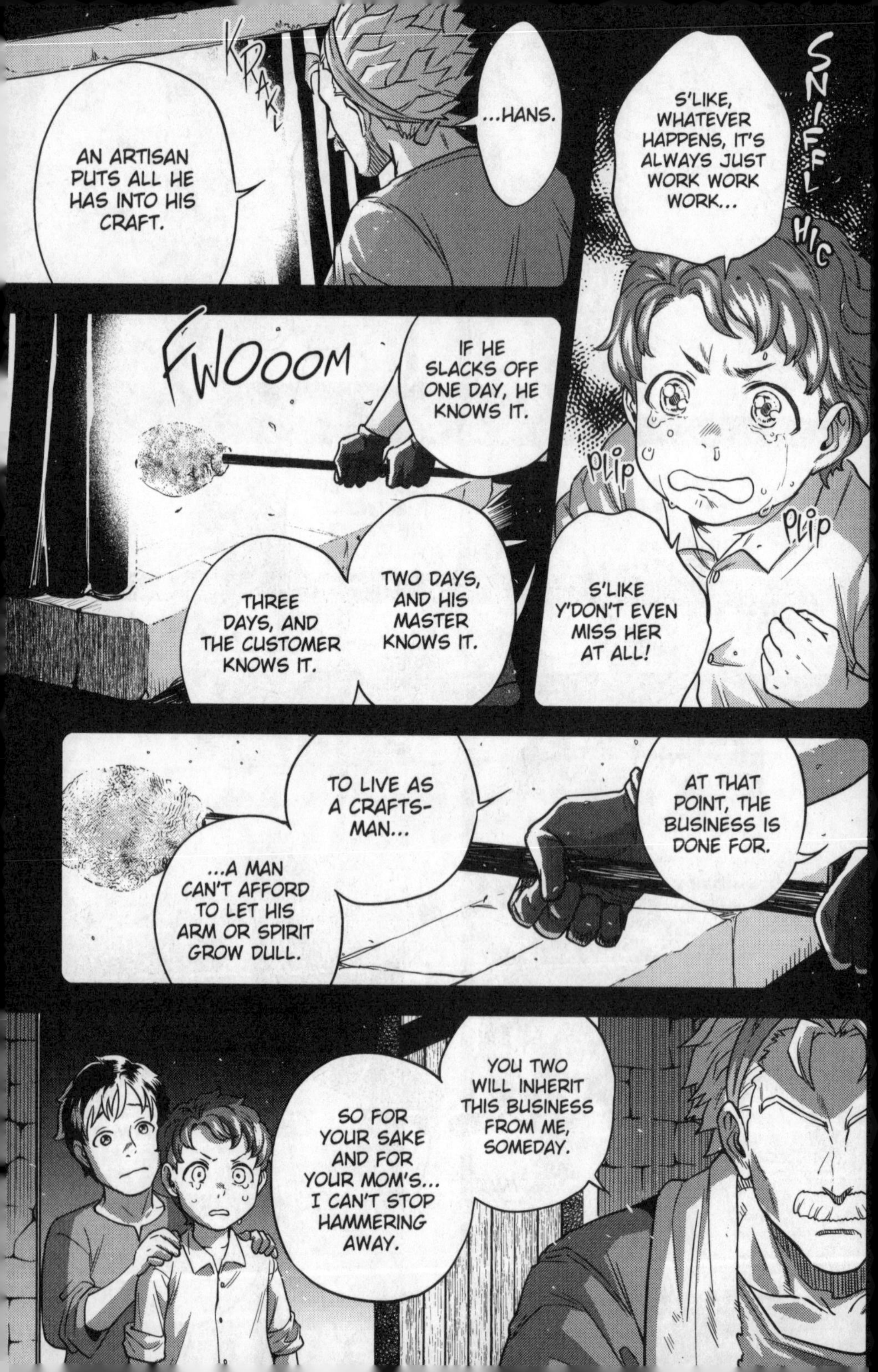
SNIFFL
S'LIKE, WHATEVER HAPPENS, IT'S ALWAYS JUST WORK WORK WORK...
HIC
PLIP
PLIP
S'LIKE Y'DON'T EVEN MISS HER AT ALL!
KRAKL
...HANS.
AN ARTISAN PUTS ALL HE HAS INTO HIS CRAFT.
FWOOOM
IF HE SLACKS OFF ONE DAY, HE KNOWS IT.
TWO DAYS, AND HIS MASTER KNOWS IT.
THREE DAYS, AND THE CUSTOMER KNOWS IT.
AT THAT POINT, THE BUSINESS IS DONE FOR.
TO LIVE AS A CRAFTS-MAN...
...A MAN CAN'T AFFORD TO LET HIS ARM OR SPIRIT GROW DULL.
YOU TWO WILL INHERIT THIS BUSINESS FROM ME, SOMEDAY.
SO FOR YOUR SAKE AND FOR YOUR MOM'S... I CAN'T STOP HAMMERING AWAY.

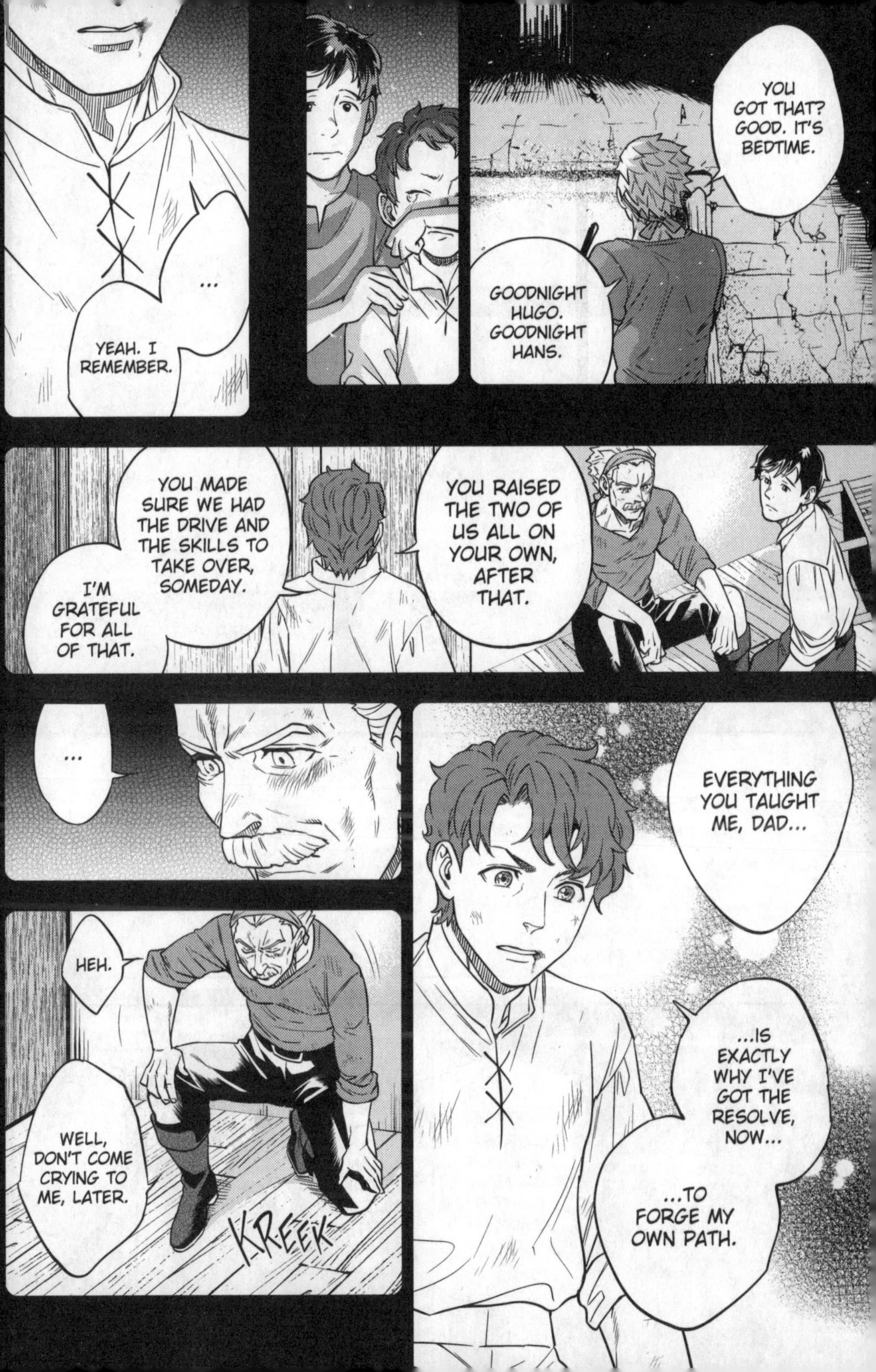
YOU GOT THAT? GOOD. IT'S BEDTIME.
GOODNIGHT HUGO. GOODNIGHT HANS.
...
YEAH. I REMEMBER.
YOU RAISED THE TWO OF US ALL ON YOUR OWN, AFTER THAT.
YOU MADE SURE WE HAD THE DRIVE AND THE SKILLS TO TAKE OVER, SOMEDAY.
I'M GRATEFUL FOR ALL OF THAT.
EVERYTHING YOU TAUGHT ME, DAD...
...IS EXACTLY WHY I'VE GOT THE RESOLVE, NOW...
...TO FORGE MY OWN PATH.
...
HEH.
WELL, DON'T COME CRYING TO ME, LATER.
KREEK

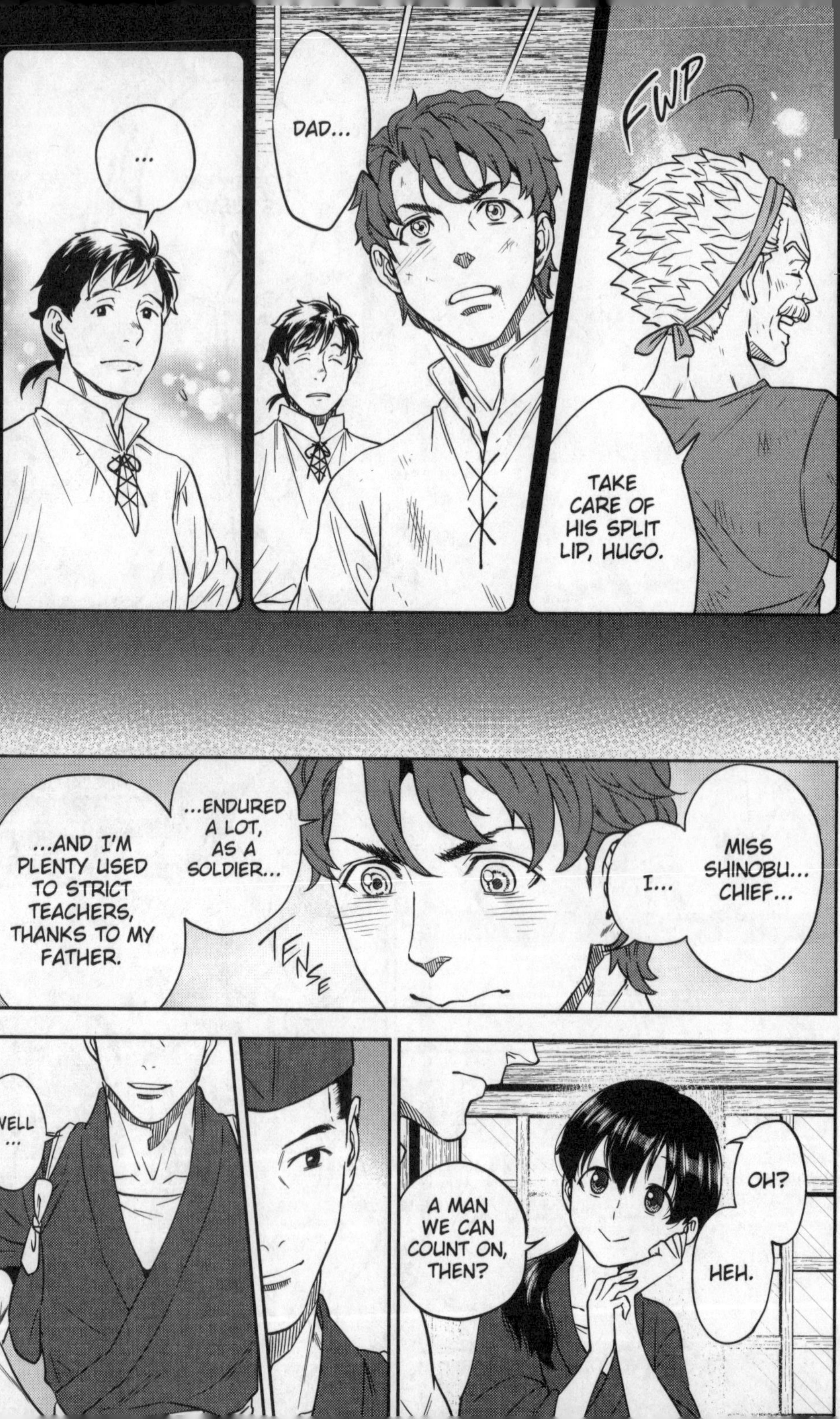
FWP
TAKE CARE OF HIS SPLIT LIP, HUGO.
DAD...
...
MISS SHINOBU... CHIEF...
I...
...ENDURED A LOT, AS A SOLDIER...
TENSE
...AND I'M PLENTY USED TO STRICT TEACHERS, THANKS TO MY FATHER.
OH?
HEH.
A MAN WE CAN COUNT ON, THEN?
WELL...

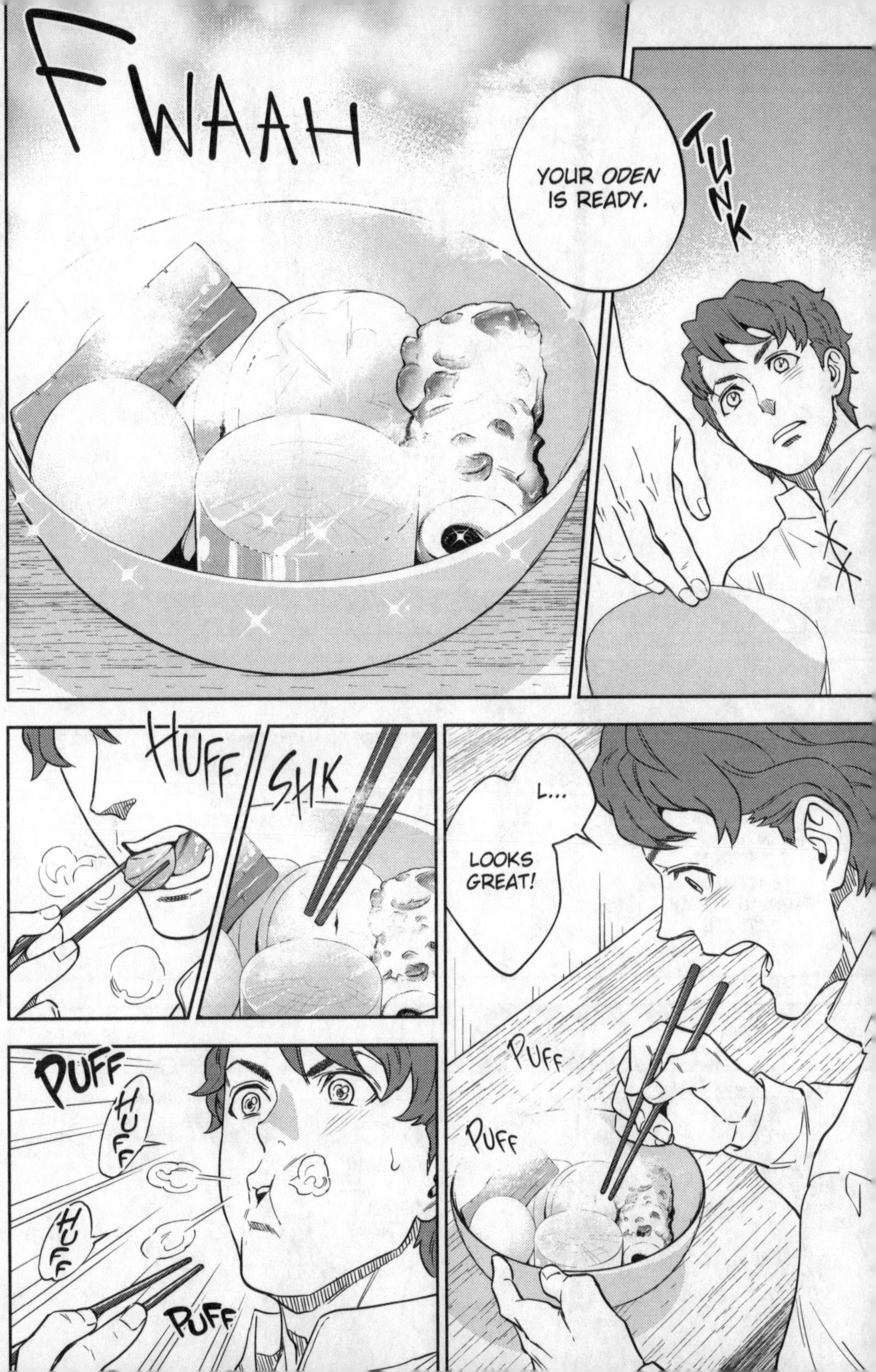
YOUR ODEN IS READY.
TUNK
FWAAH
L...
LOOKS GREAT!
PUFF
PUFF
SHK
HUFF
PUFF
HUFF
HUFF
PUFF

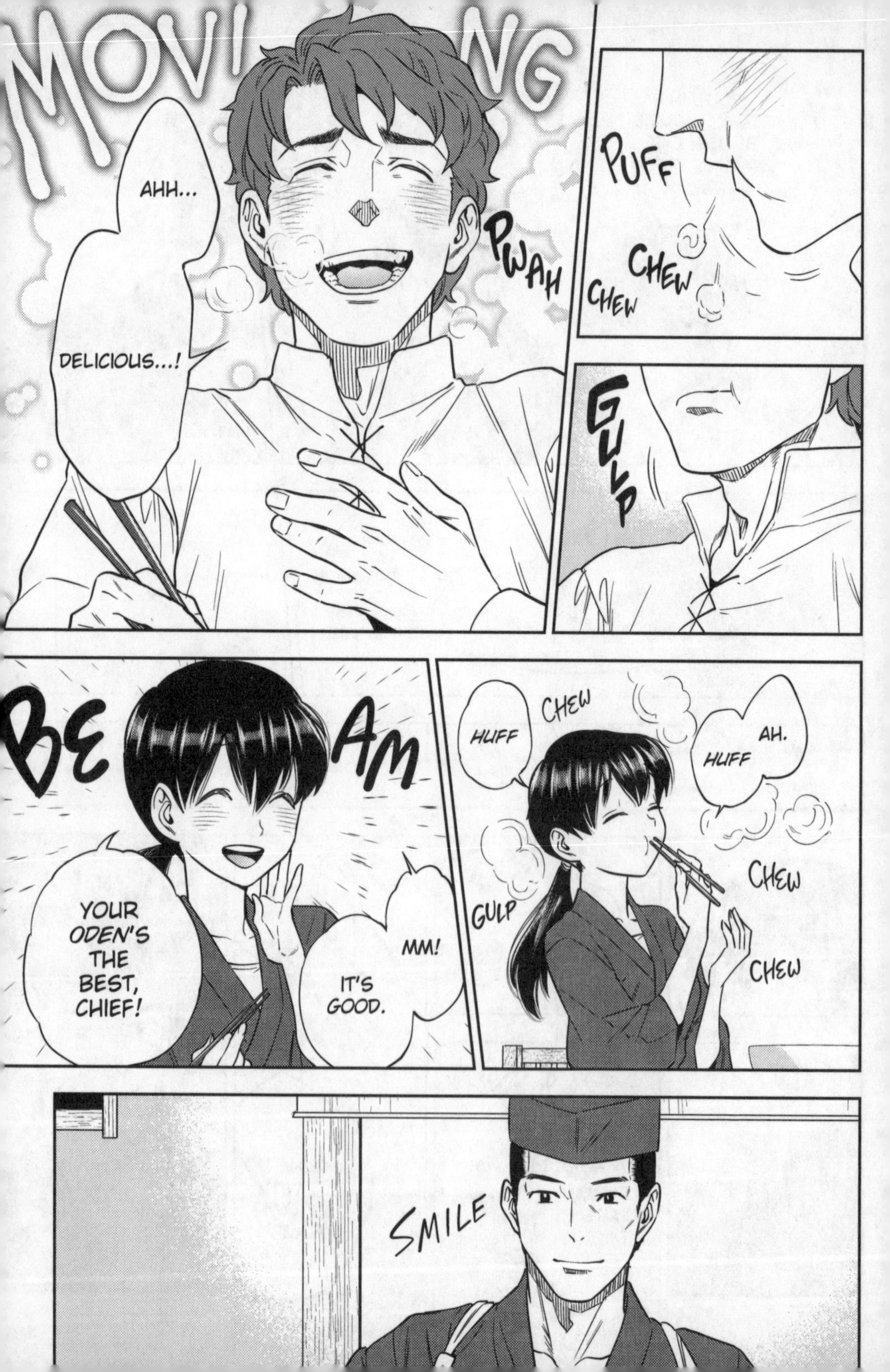
PUFF
CHEW
CHEW
GULP
MOVI
NG
PWAH
AHH...
DELICIOUS...!
CHEW
AH.
HUFF
HUFF
CHEW
GULP
CHEW
BE
AM
MM!
IT'S GOOD.
YOUR ODEN'S THE BEST, CHIEF!
SMILE

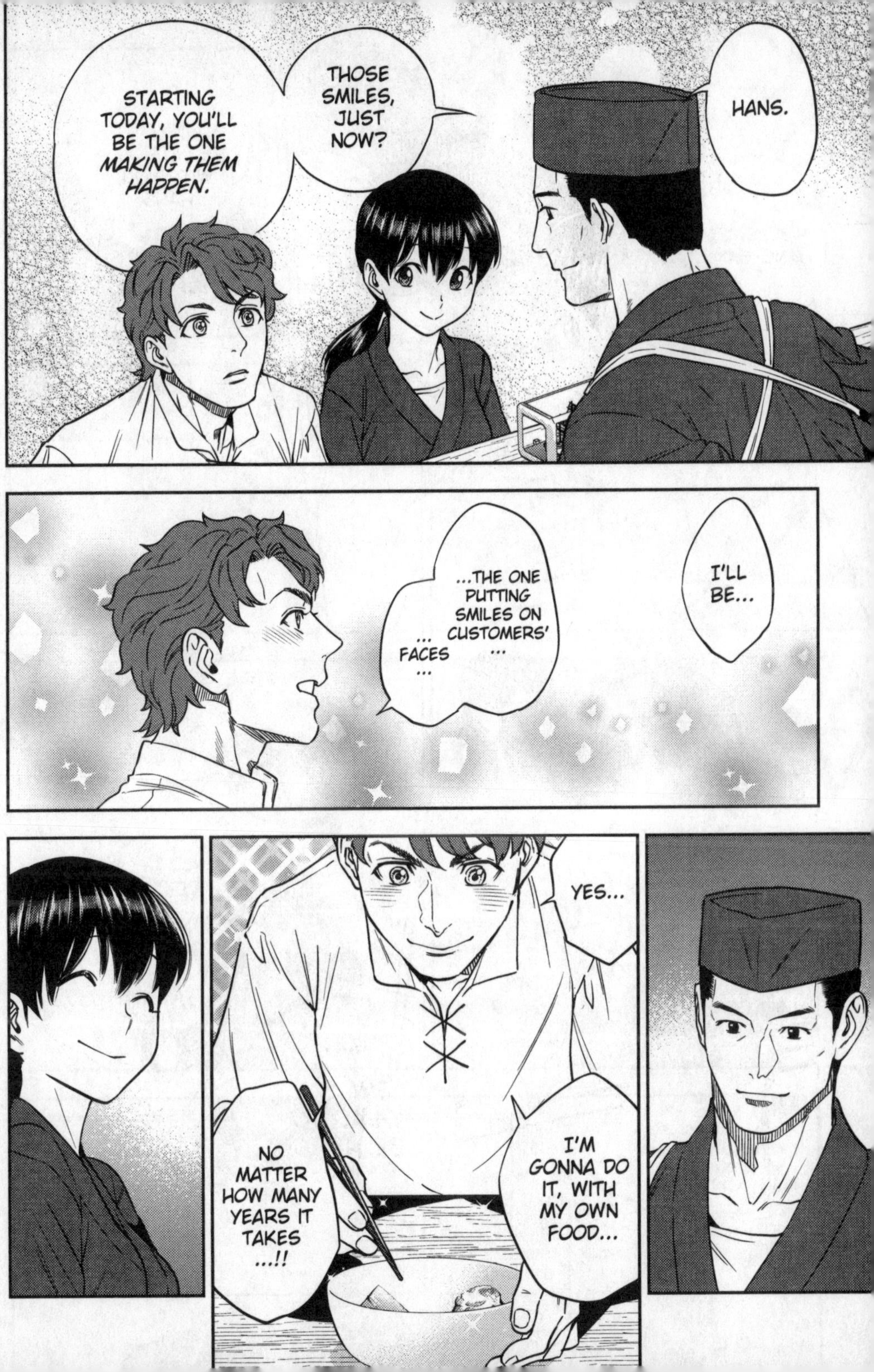
HANS.
THOSE SMILES, JUST NOW?
STARTING TODAY, YOU'LL BE THE ONE *MAKING THEM HAPPEN.*
I'LL BE...
...THE ONE PUTTING SMILES ON CUSTOMERS' ... ... FACES ...
YES...
I'M GONNA DO IT, WITH MY OWN FOOD...
NO MATTER HOW MANY YEARS IT TAKES ...!!

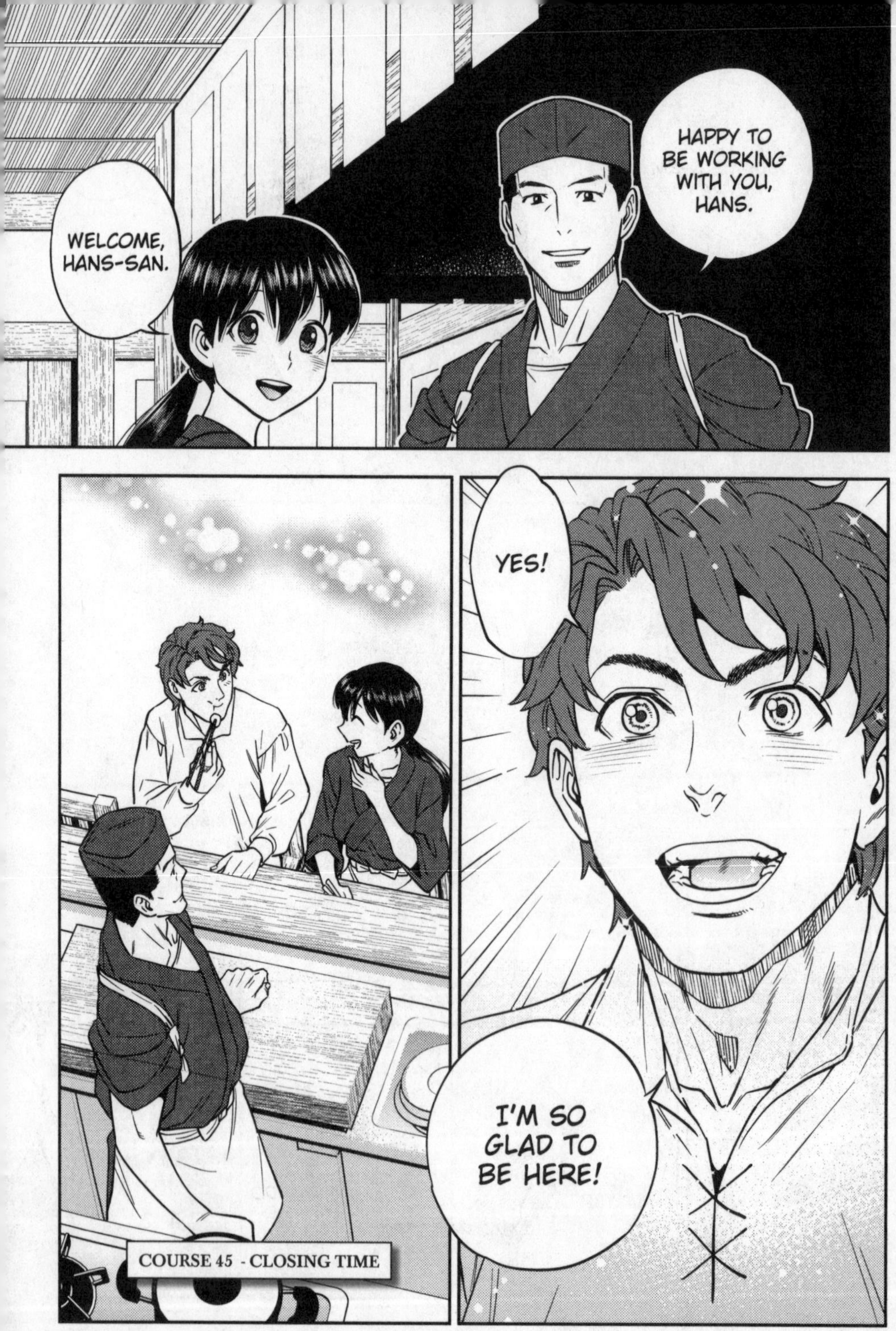
HAPPY TO BE WORKING WITH YOU, HANS.
WELCOME, HANS-SAN.
YES!
I'M SO GLAD TO BE HERE!
COURSE 45 - CLOSING TIME

Oden

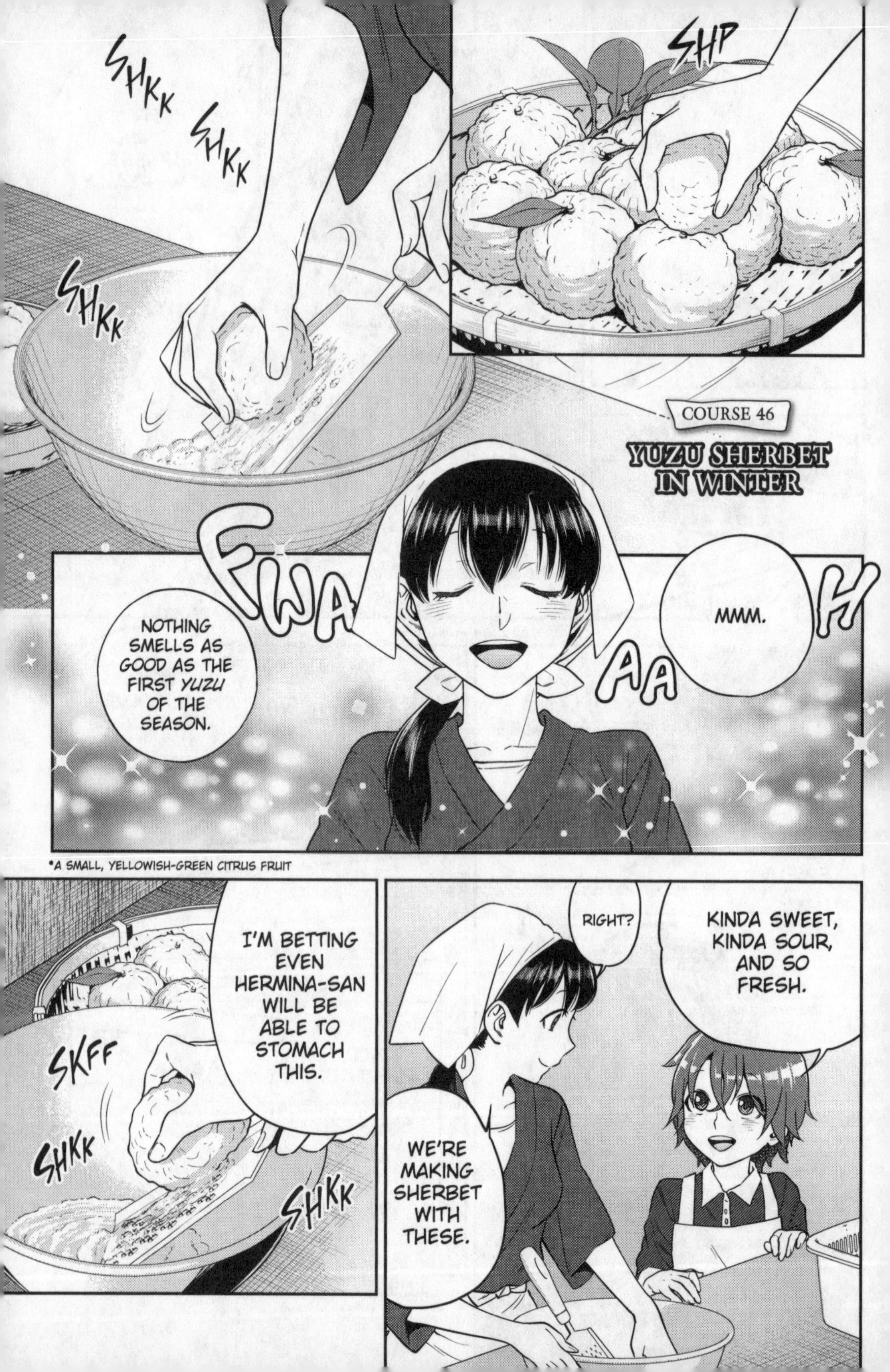
SHP
SHKK
SHKK
SHKK
COURSE 46
YUZU SHERBET IN WINTER
FWAAAH
MMM.
NOTHING SMELLS AS GOOD AS THE FIRST *YUZU* OF THE SEASON.
KINDA SWEET, KINDA SOUR, AND SO FRESH.
RIGHT?
WE'RE MAKING SHERBET WITH THESE.
I'M BETTING EVEN HERMINA-SAN WILL BE ABLE TO STOMACH THIS.
SKFF
SHKK
SHKK

*A SMALL, YELLOWISH-GREEN CITRUS FRUIT

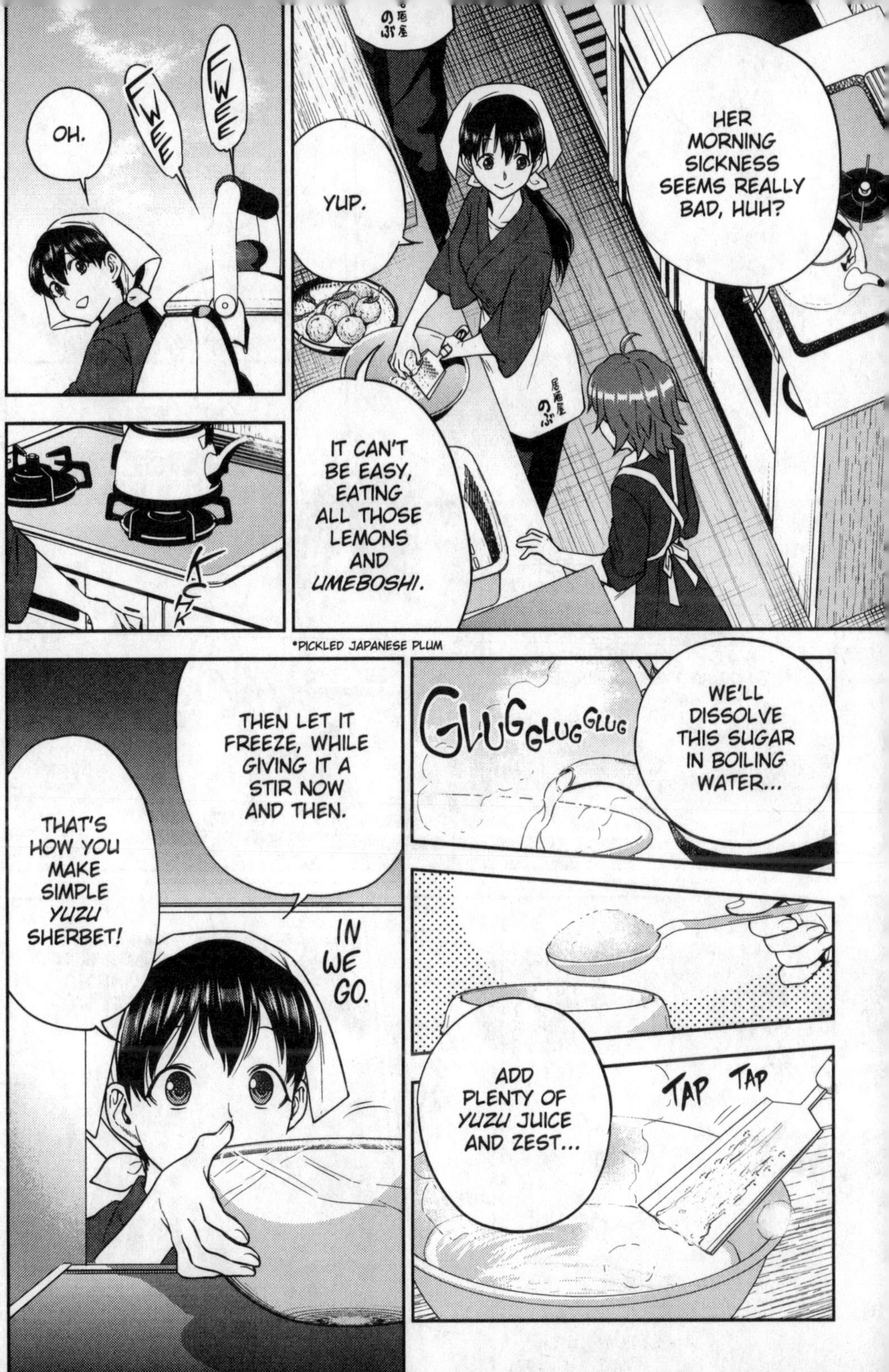
HER MORNING SICKNESS SEEMS REALLY BAD, HUH?
YUP.
IT CAN'T BE EASY, EATING ALL THOSE LEMONS AND *UMEBOSHI*.
居酒屋 のぶ
FWEE
FWEE
OH.
KACHK
*PICKLED JAPANESE PLUM
WE'LL DISSOLVE THIS SUGAR IN BOILING WATER...
GLUG GLUG GLUG
ADD PLENTY OF *YUZU* JUICE AND ZEST...
TAP TAP
THEN LET IT FREEZE, WHILE GIVING IT A STIR NOW AND THEN.
THAT'S HOW YOU MAKE SIMPLE *YUZU* SHERBET!
IN WE GO.

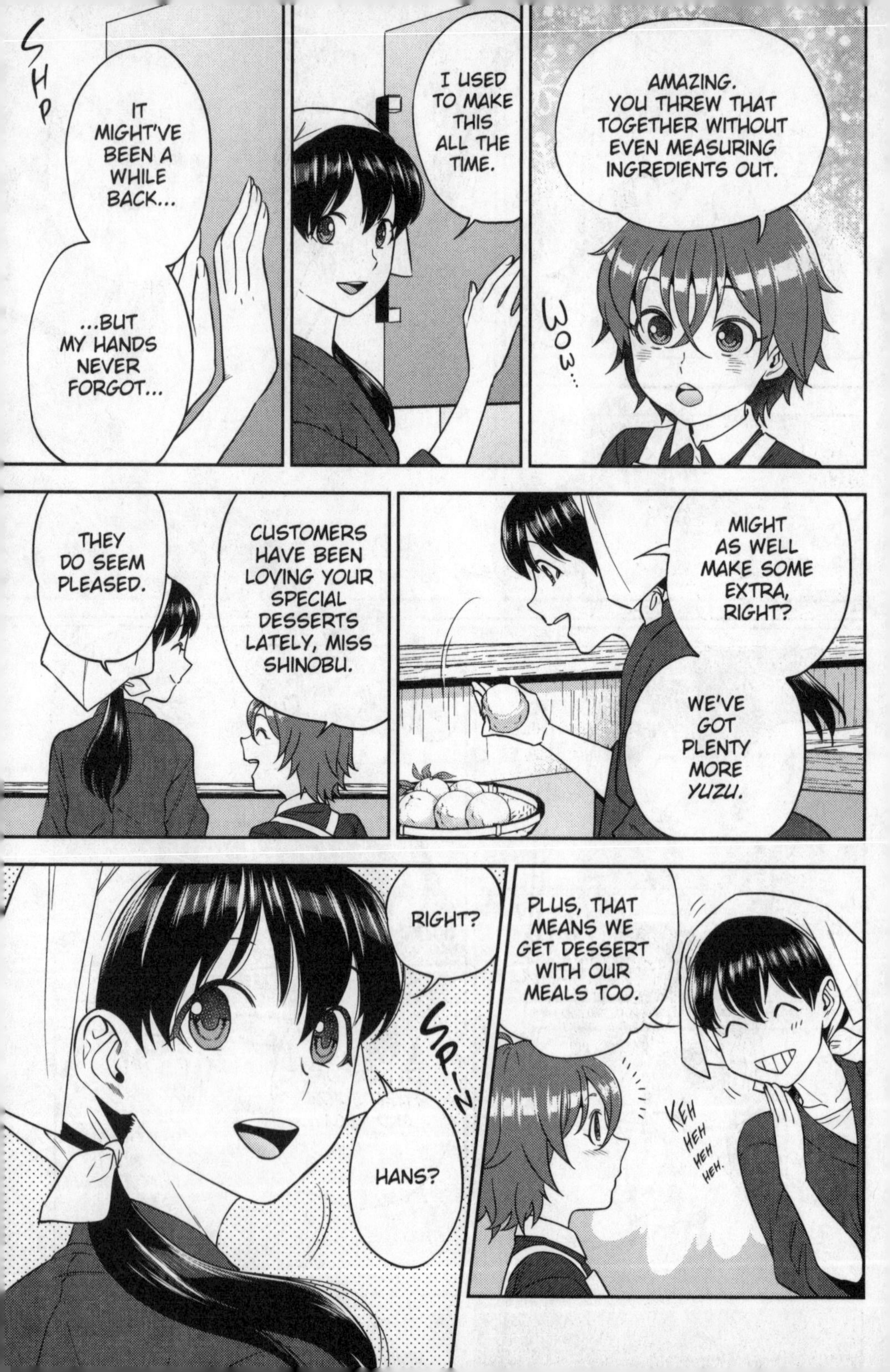
AMAZING. YOU THREW THAT TOGETHER WITHOUT EVEN MEASURING INGREDIENTS OUT.
WOW...
I USED TO MAKE THIS ALL THE TIME.
SHP
IT MIGHT'VE BEEN A WHILE BACK...
...BUT MY HANDS NEVER FORGOT...
MIGHT AS WELL MAKE SOME EXTRA, RIGHT?
WE'VE GOT PLENTY MORE YUZU.
CUSTOMERS HAVE BEEN LOVING YOUR SPECIAL DESSERTS LATELY, MISS SHINOBU.
THEY DO SEEM PLEASED.
PLUS, THAT MEANS WE GET DESSERT WITH OUR MEALS TOO.
KEH HEH HEH HEH.
RIGHT?
SPIN
HANS?

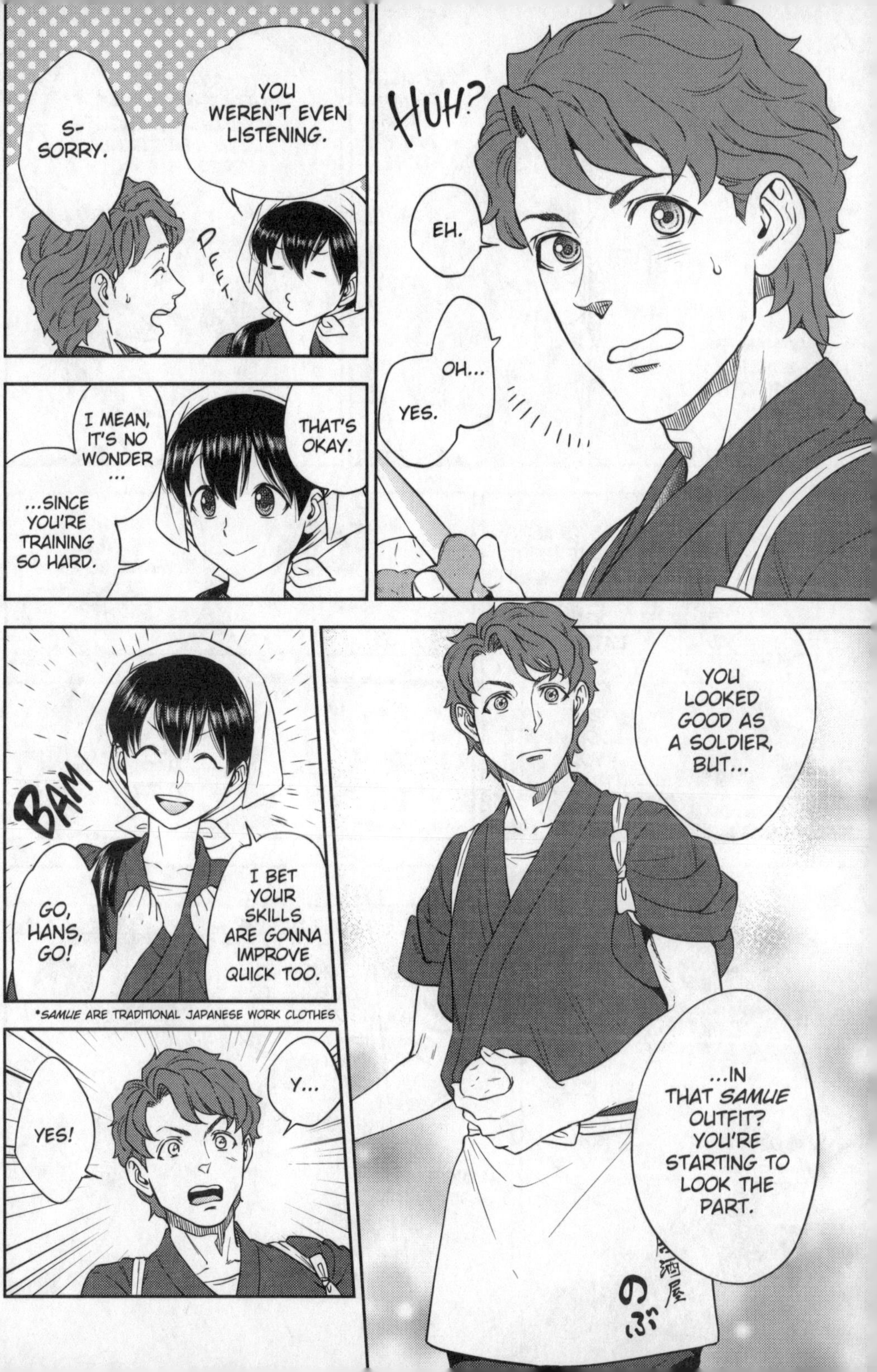
HUH?
EH.
OH...
YES.
YOU WEREN'T EVEN LISTENING.
S-SORRY.
PFFT.
THAT'S OKAY.
I MEAN, IT'S NO WONDER...
...SINCE YOU'RE TRAINING SO HARD.
YOU LOOKED GOOD AS A SOLDIER, BUT...
...IN THAT *SAMUE* OUTFIT? YOU'RE STARTING TO LOOK THE PART.
酒屋
のぶ
BAM
I BET YOUR SKILLS ARE GONNA IMPROVE QUICK TOO.
GO, HANS, GO!
Y...
YES!

**SAMUE* ARE TRADITIONAL JAPANESE WORK CLOTHES

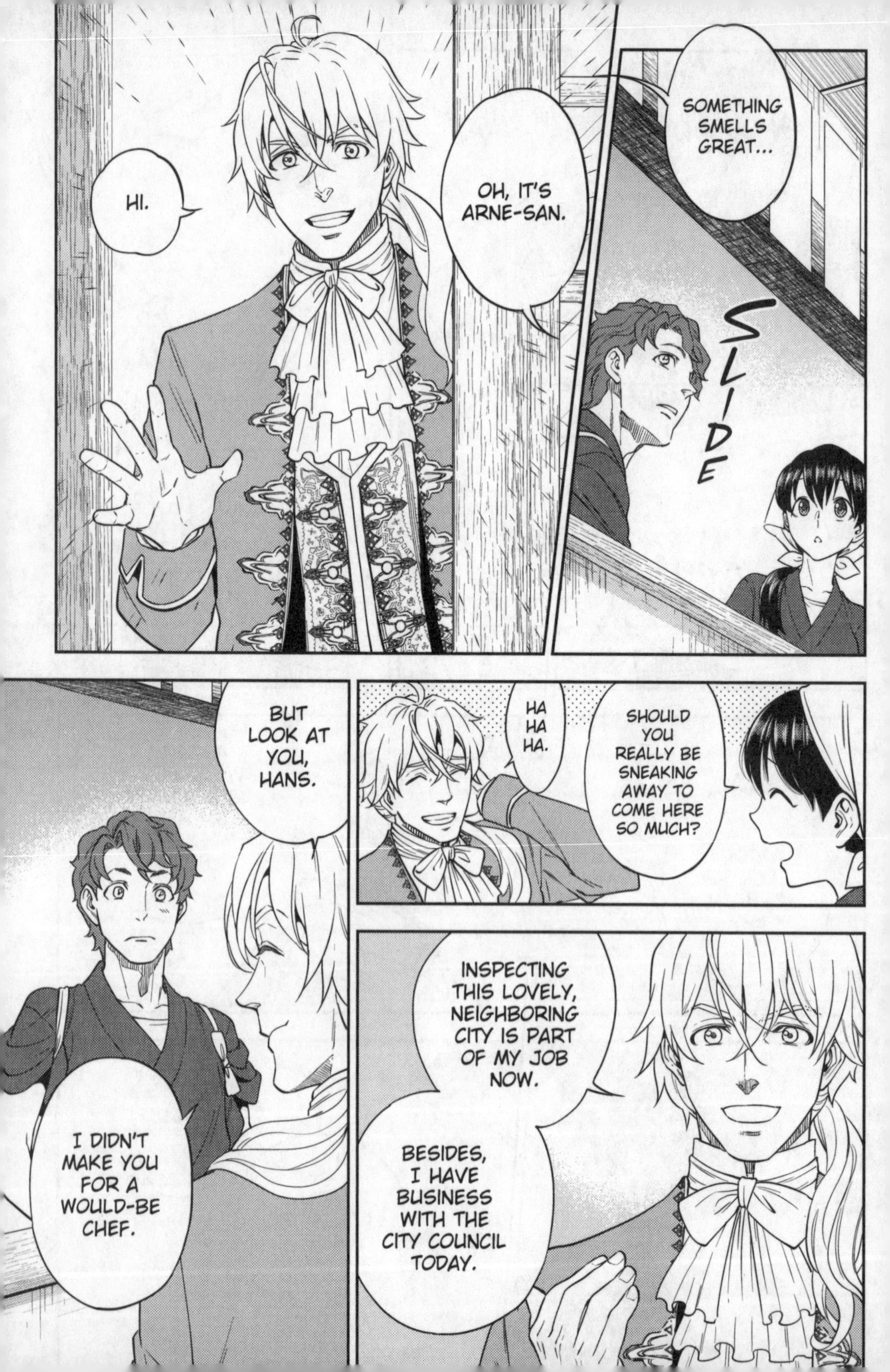
SOMETHING SMELLS GREAT...
SLIDE
OH, IT'S ARNE-SAN.
HI.
SHOULD YOU REALLY BE SNEAKING AWAY TO COME HERE SO MUCH?
HA HA HA.
INSPECTING THIS LOVELY, NEIGHBORING CITY IS PART OF MY JOB NOW.
BESIDES, I HAVE BUSINESS WITH THE CITY COUNCIL TODAY.
BUT LOOK AT YOU, HANS.
I DIDN'T MAKE YOU FOR A WOULD-BE CHEF.

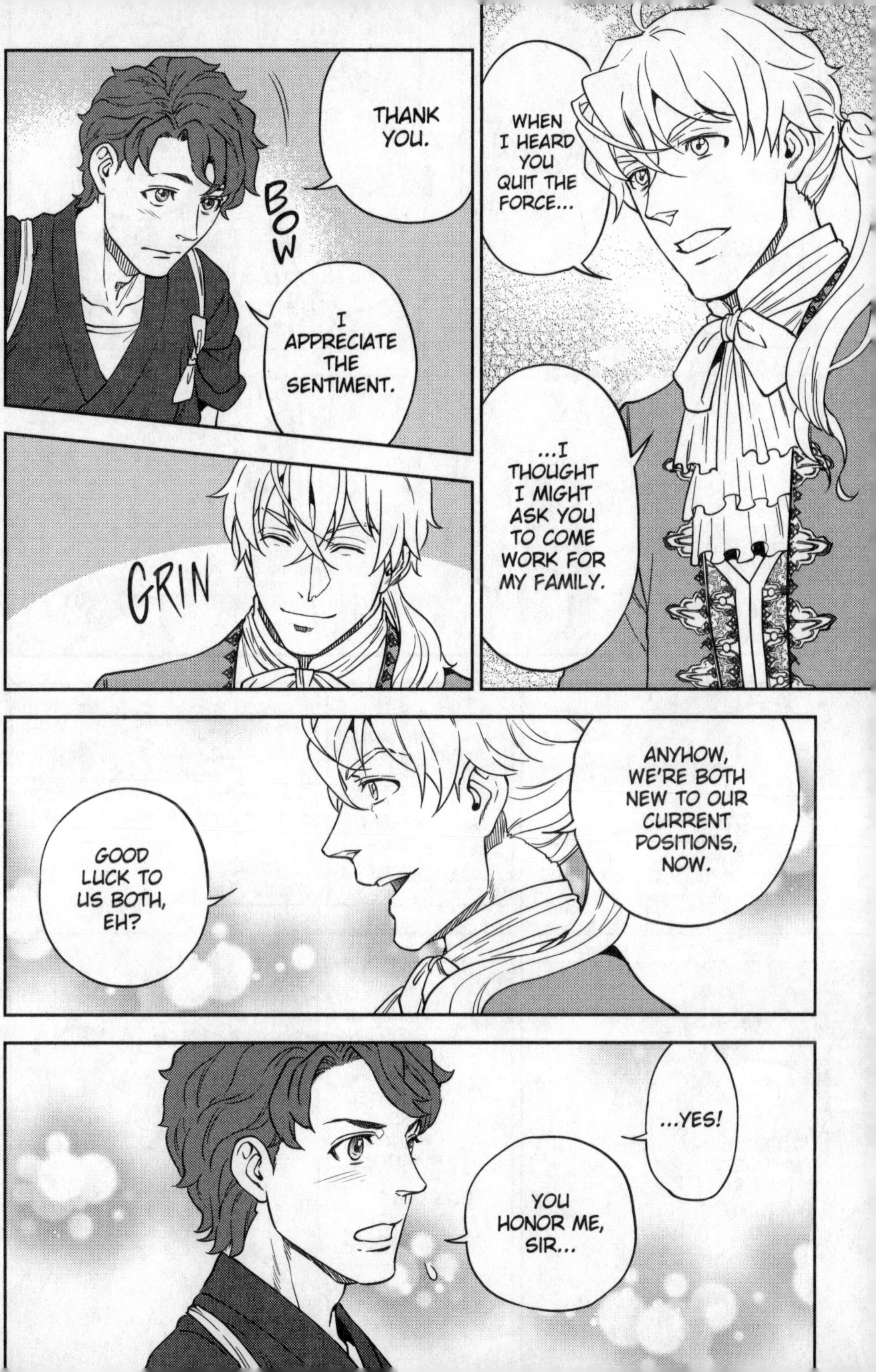
WHEN I HEARD YOU QUIT THE FORCE...
...I THOUGHT I MIGHT ASK YOU TO COME WORK FOR MY FAMILY.
THANK YOU.
BOW
I APPRECIATE THE SENTIMENT.
GRIN
ANYHOW, WE'RE BOTH NEW TO OUR CURRENT POSITIONS, NOW.
GOOD LUCK TO US BOTH, EH?
...YES!
YOU HONOR ME, SIR...

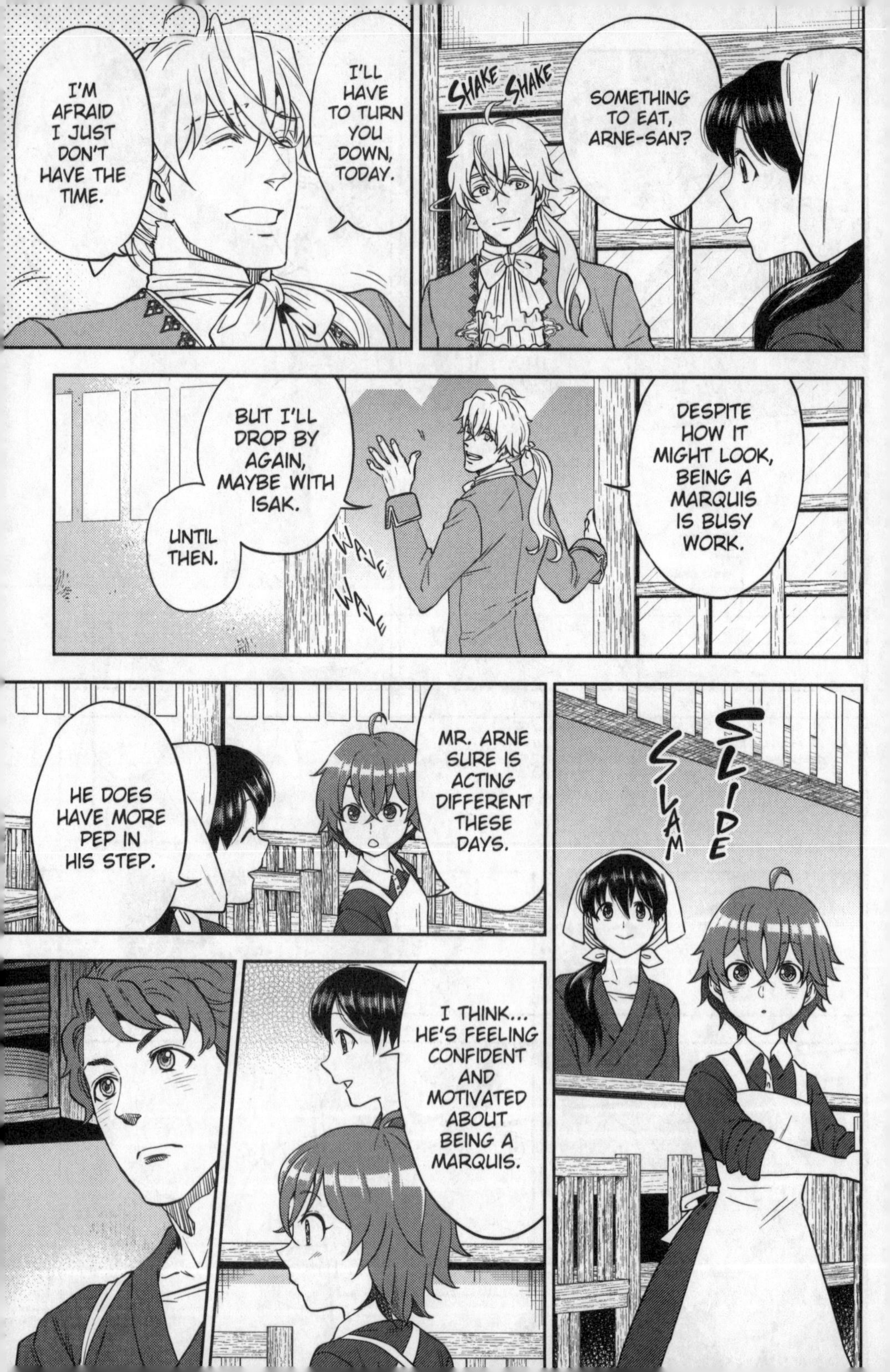
SHAKE SHAKE
SOMETHING TO EAT, ARNE-SAN?
I'LL HAVE TO TURN YOU DOWN, TODAY.
I'M AFRAID I JUST DON'T HAVE THE TIME.
DESPITE HOW IT MIGHT LOOK, BEING A MARQUIS IS BUSY WORK.
BUT I'LL DROP BY AGAIN, MAYBE WITH ISAK.
UNTIL THEN.
WAVE WAVE
SLIDE
SLAM
MR. ARNE SURE IS ACTING DIFFERENT THESE DAYS.
HE DOES HAVE MORE PEP IN HIS STEP.
I THINK... HE'S FEELING CONFIDENT AND MOTIVATED ABOUT BEING A MARQUIS.

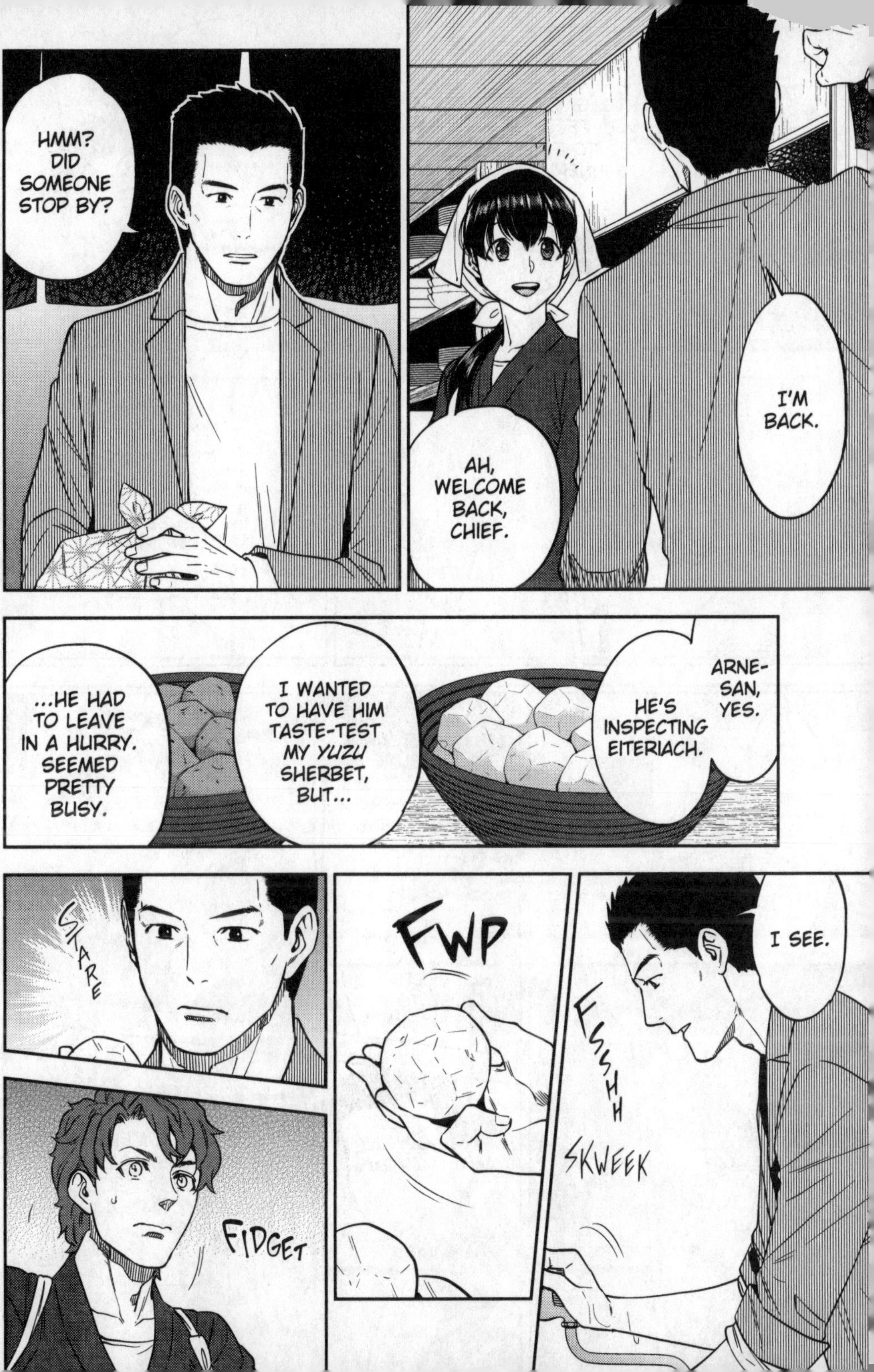
I'M BACK.
AH, WELCOME BACK, CHIEF.
HMM? DID SOMEONE STOP BY?
ARNE-SAN, YES.
HE'S INSPECTING EITERIACH.
I WANTED TO HAVE HIM TASTE-TEST MY *YUZU* SHERBET, BUT...
...HE HAD TO LEAVE IN A HURRY. SEEMED PRETTY BUSY.
I SEE.
FSSHH
SKWEEK
FWP
STARE
FIDGET

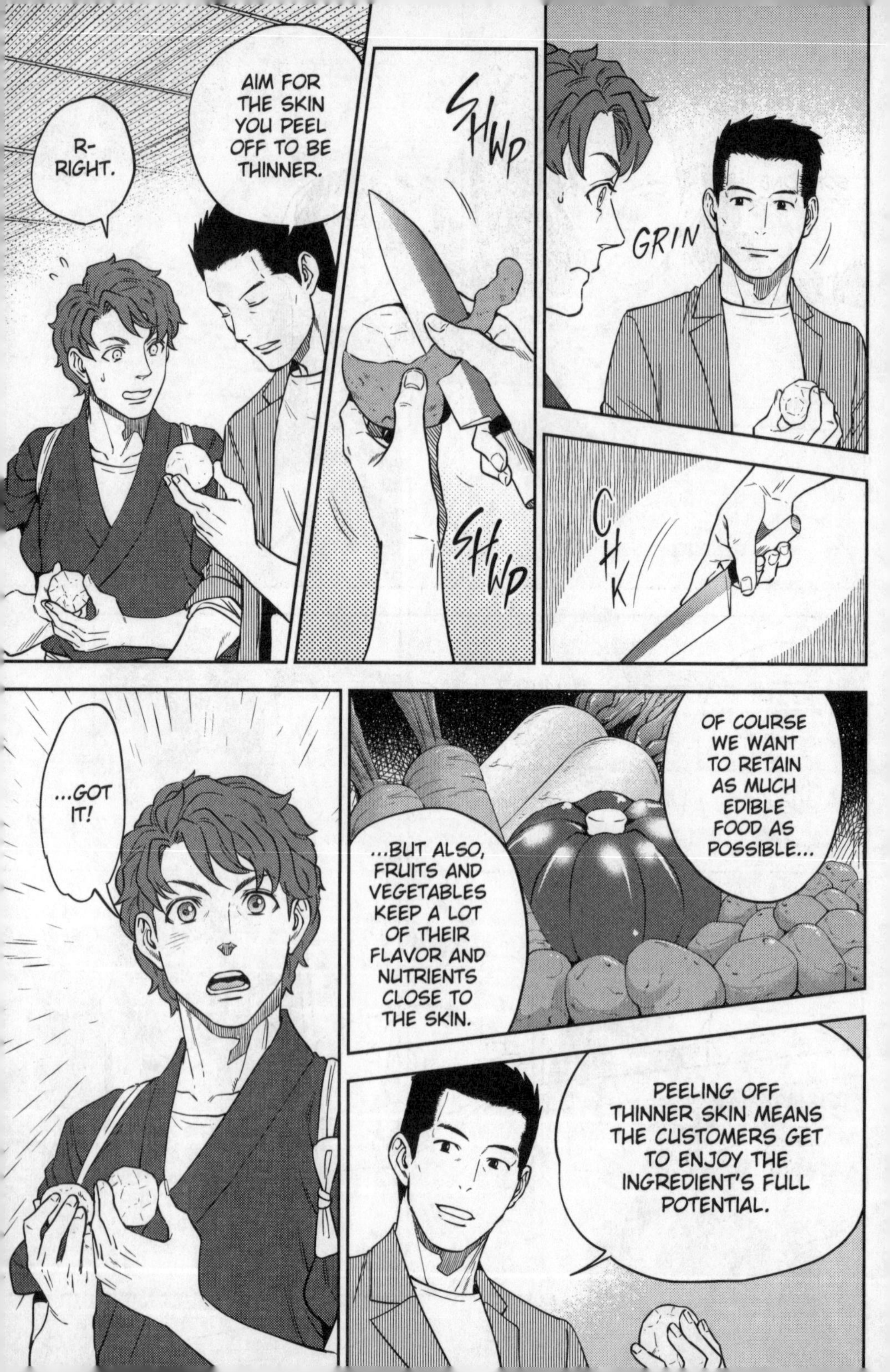
GRIN
CHK
SHWP
SHWP
AIM FOR THE SKIN YOU PEEL OFF TO BE THINNER.
R-RIGHT.
OF COURSE WE WANT TO RETAIN AS MUCH EDIBLE FOOD AS POSSIBLE...
...BUT ALSO, FRUITS AND VEGETABLES KEEP A LOT OF THEIR FLAVOR AND NUTRIENTS CLOSE TO THE SKIN.
PEELING OFF THINNER SKIN MEANS THE CUSTOMERS GET TO ENJOY THE INGREDIENT'S FULL POTENTIAL.
...GOT IT!

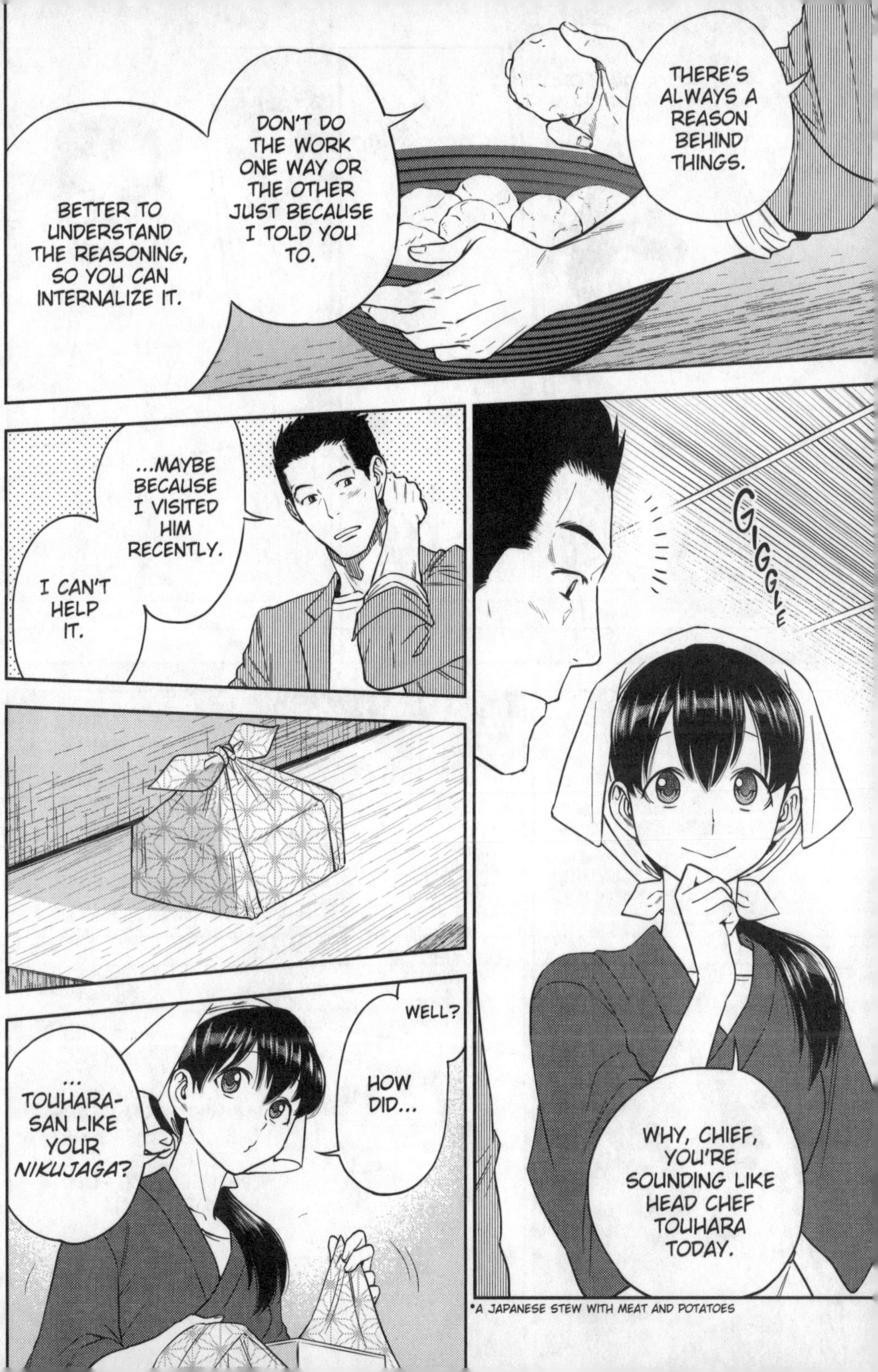
THERE'S ALWAYS A REASON BEHIND THINGS.
DON'T DO THE WORK ONE WAY OR THE OTHER JUST BECAUSE I TOLD YOU TO.
BETTER TO UNDERSTAND THE REASONING, SO YOU CAN INTERNALIZE IT.
GIGGLE
WHY, CHIEF, YOU'RE SOUNDING LIKE HEAD CHEF TOUHARA TODAY.
...MAYBE BECAUSE I VISITED HIM RECENTLY.
I CAN'T HELP IT.
WELL?
HOW DID...
...TOUHARA-SAN LIKE YOUR NIKUJAGA?

*A JAPANESE STEW WITH MEAT AND POTATOES

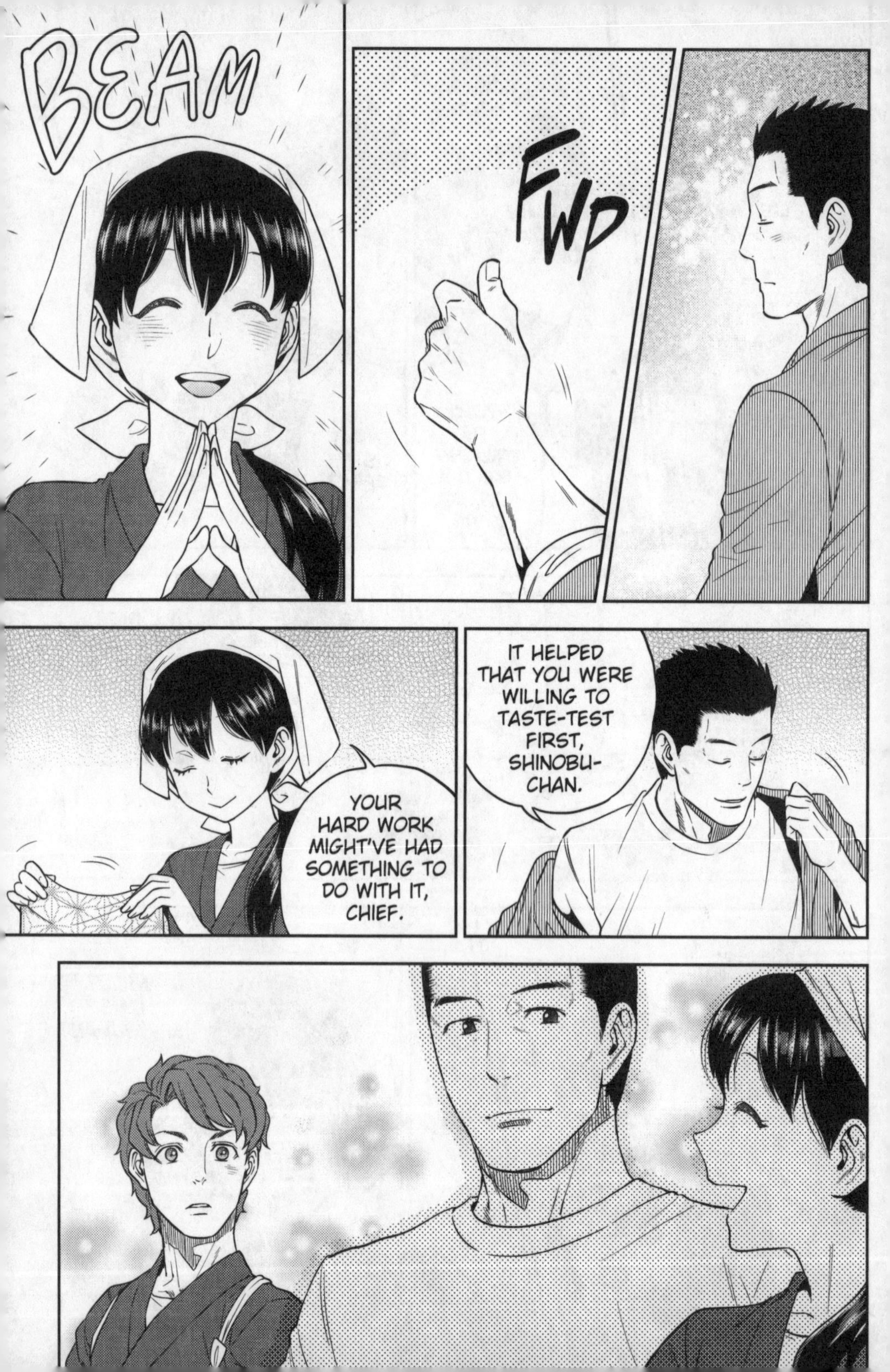
FWP
BEAM
IT HELPED THAT YOU WERE WILLING TO TASTE-TEST FIRST, SHINOBU-CHAN.
YOUR HARD WORK MIGHT'VE HAD SOMETHING TO DO WITH IT, CHIEF.

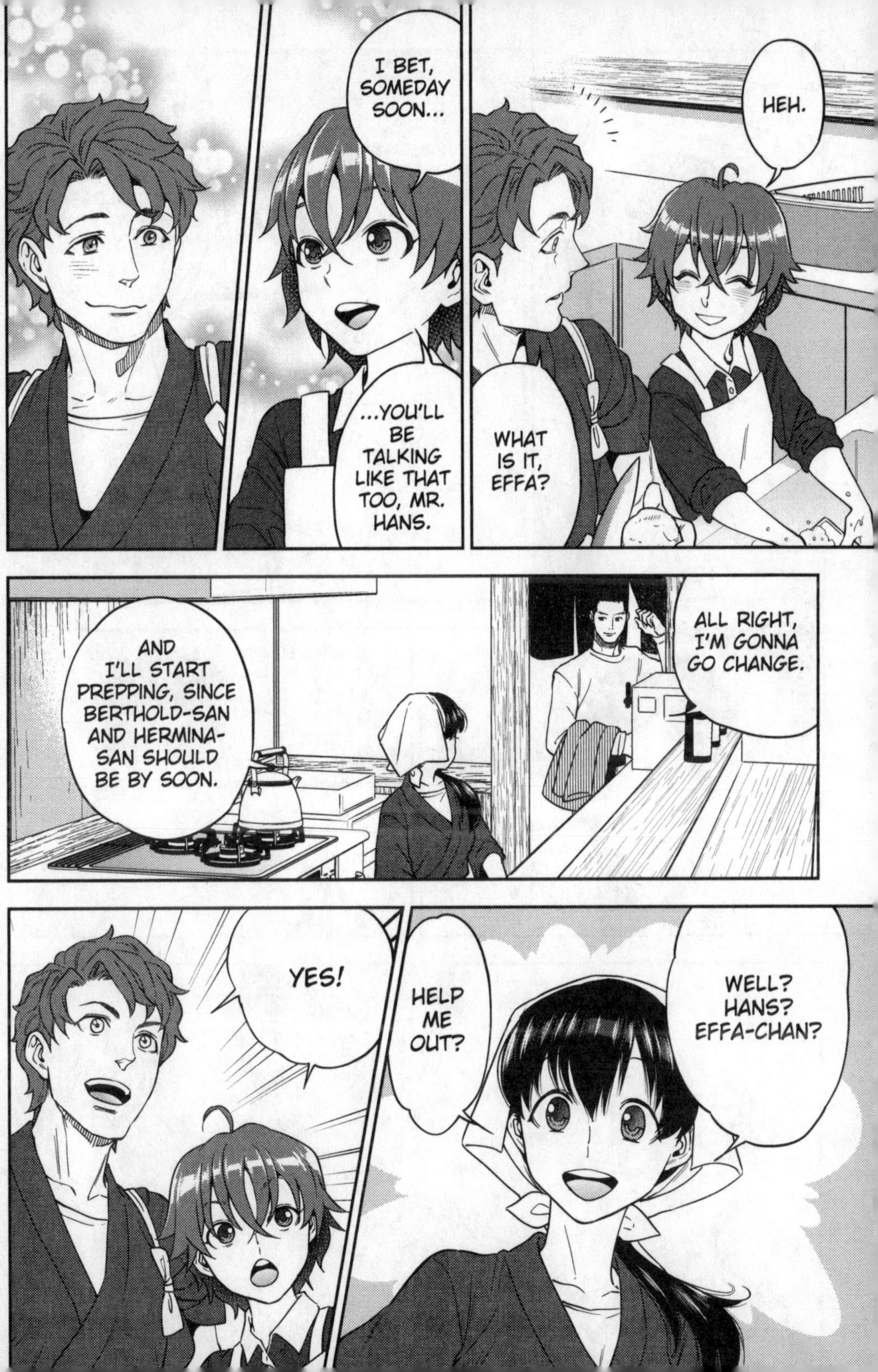
HEH.
WHAT IS IT, EFFA?
I BET, SOMEDAY SOON...
...YOU'LL BE TALKING LIKE THAT TOO, MR. HANS.
ALL RIGHT, I'M GONNA GO CHANGE.
AND I'LL START PREPPING, SINCE BERTHOLD-SAN AND HERMINA-SAN SHOULD BE BY SOON.
WELL? HANS? EFFA-CHAN?
HELP ME OUT?
YES!

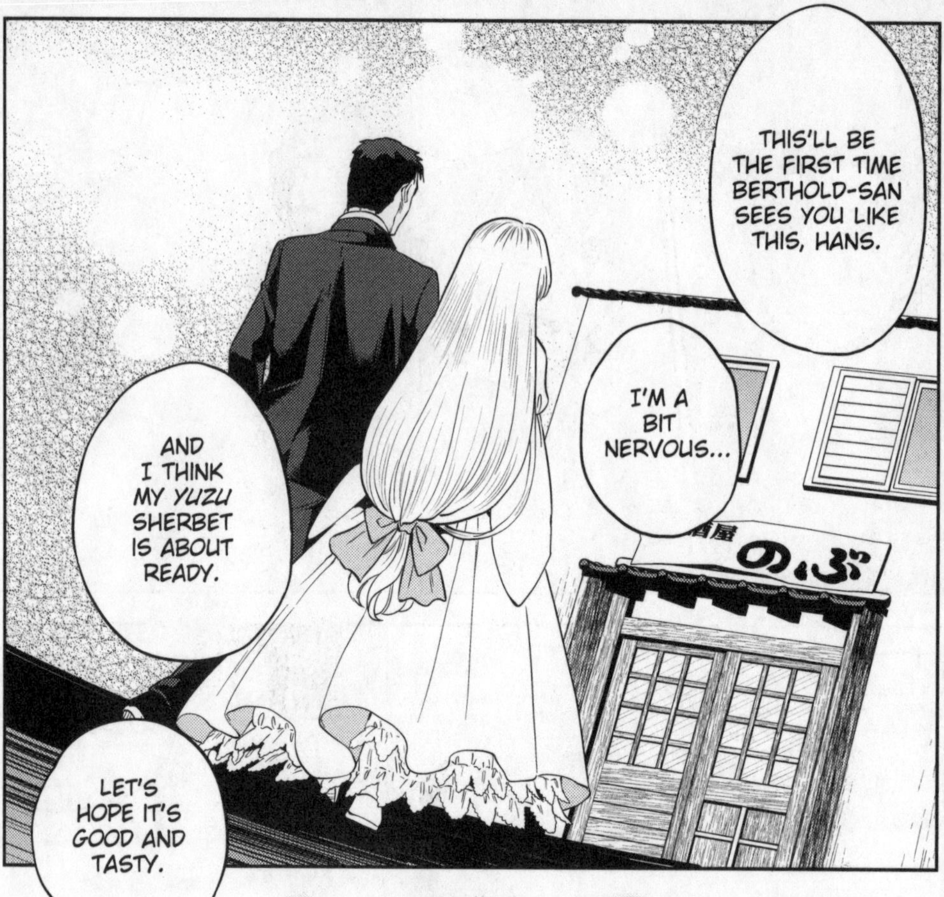
THIS'LL BE THE FIRST TIME BERTHOLD-SAN SEES YOU LIKE THIS, HANS.
I'M A BIT NERVOUS...
AND I THINK MY *YUZU* SHERBET IS ABOUT READY.
LET'S HOPE IT'S GOOD AND TASTY.

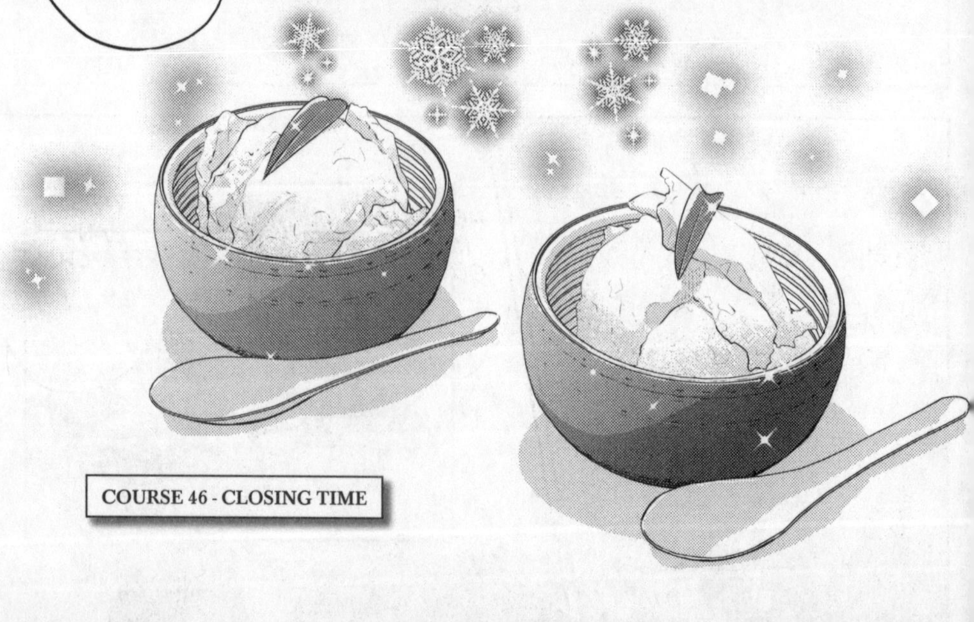

COURSE 46 - CLOSING TIME

Yuzu Sherbet

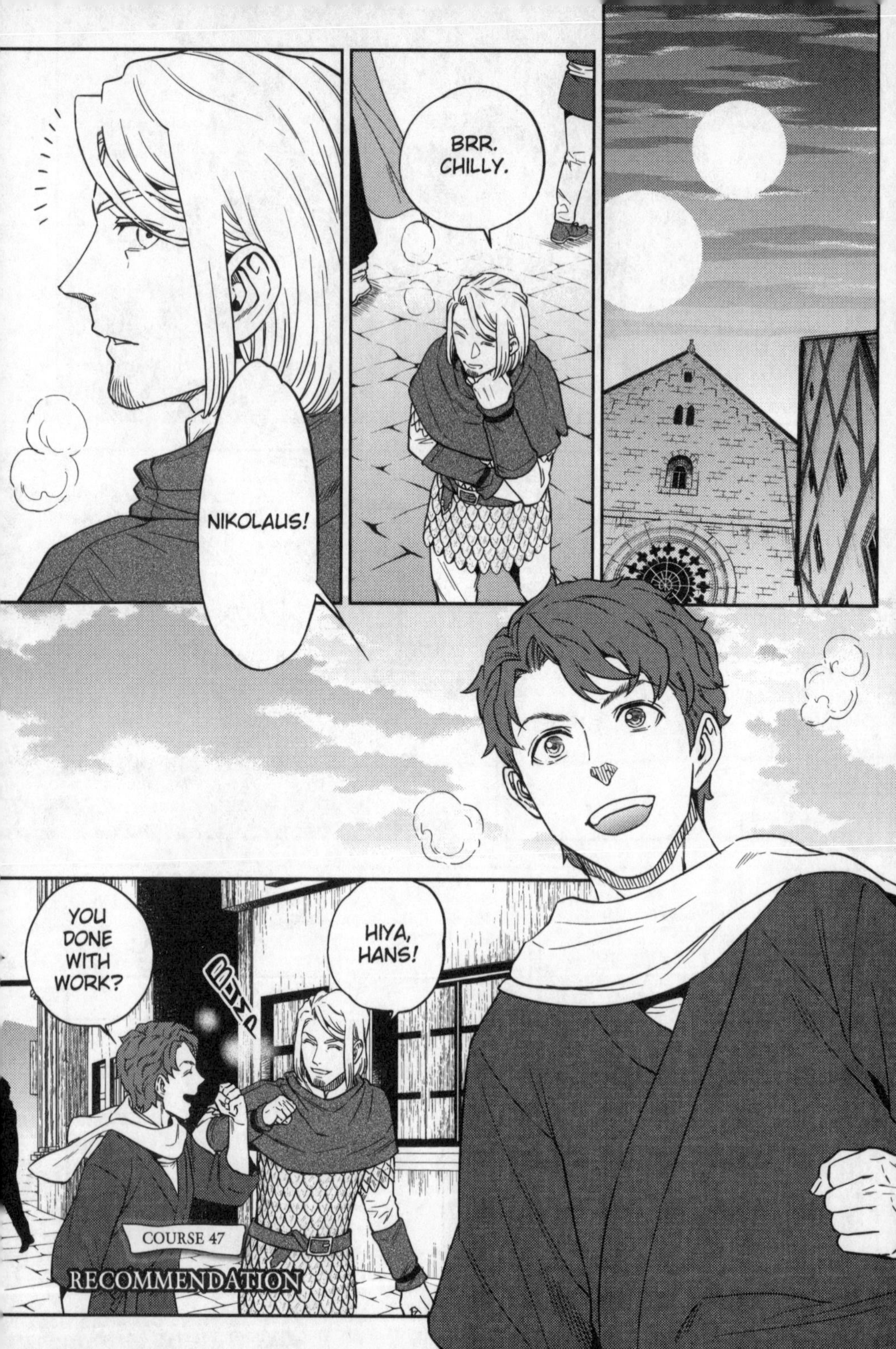

BRR. CHILLY.
NIKOLAUS!
HIYA, HANS!
YOU DONE WITH WORK?
COURSE 47
RECOMMENDATION

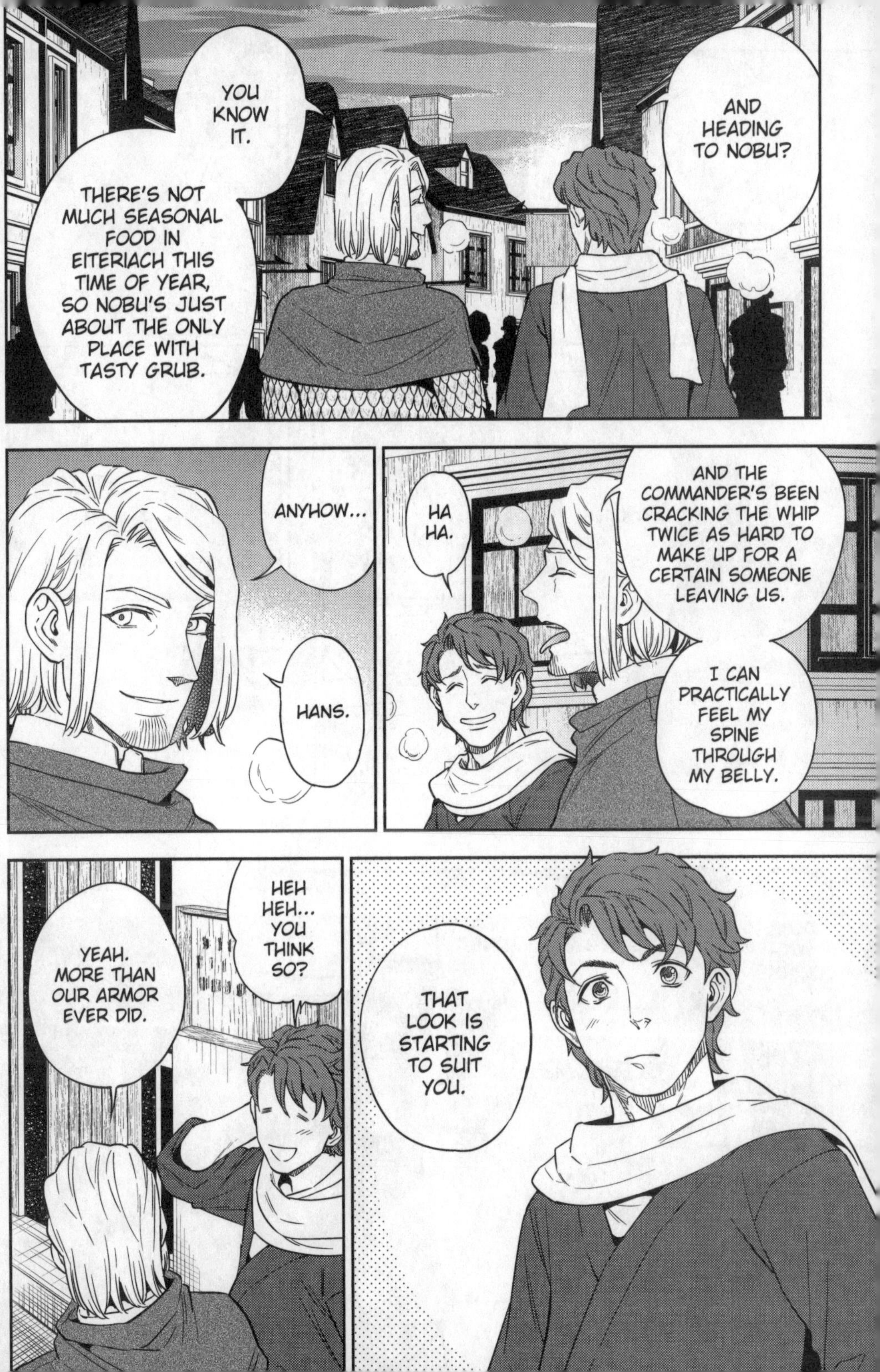
AND HEADING TO NOBU?
YOU KNOW IT.
THERE'S NOT MUCH SEASONAL FOOD IN EITERIACH THIS TIME OF YEAR, SO NOBU'S JUST ABOUT THE ONLY PLACE WITH TASTY GRUB.
AND THE COMMANDER'S BEEN CRACKING THE WHIP TWICE AS HARD TO MAKE UP FOR A CERTAIN SOMEONE LEAVING US.
I CAN PRACTICALLY FEEL MY SPINE THROUGH MY BELLY.
HA HA.
ANYHOW...
HANS.
THAT LOOK IS STARTING TO SUIT YOU.
HEH HEH... YOU THINK SO?
YEAH. MORE THAN OUR ARMOR EVER DID.

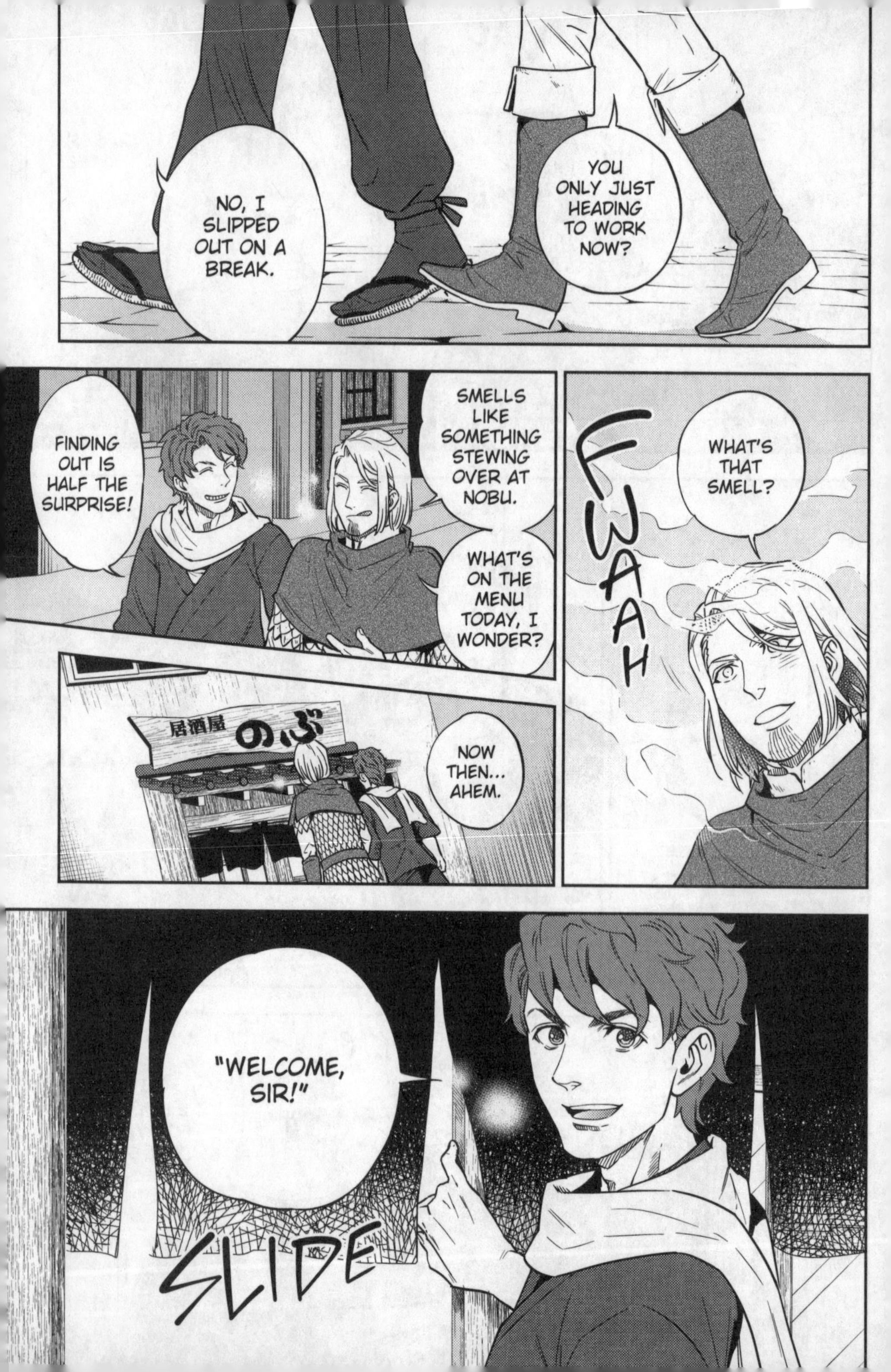
YOU ONLY JUST HEADING TO WORK NOW?
NO, I SLIPPED OUT ON A BREAK.
FWAAH
WHAT'S THAT SMELL?
SMELLS LIKE SOMETHING STEWING OVER AT NOBU.
WHAT'S ON THE MENU TODAY, I WONDER?
FINDING OUT IS HALF THE SURPRISE!
居酒屋 のぶ
NOW THEN... AHEM.
"WELCOME, SIR!"
SLIDE

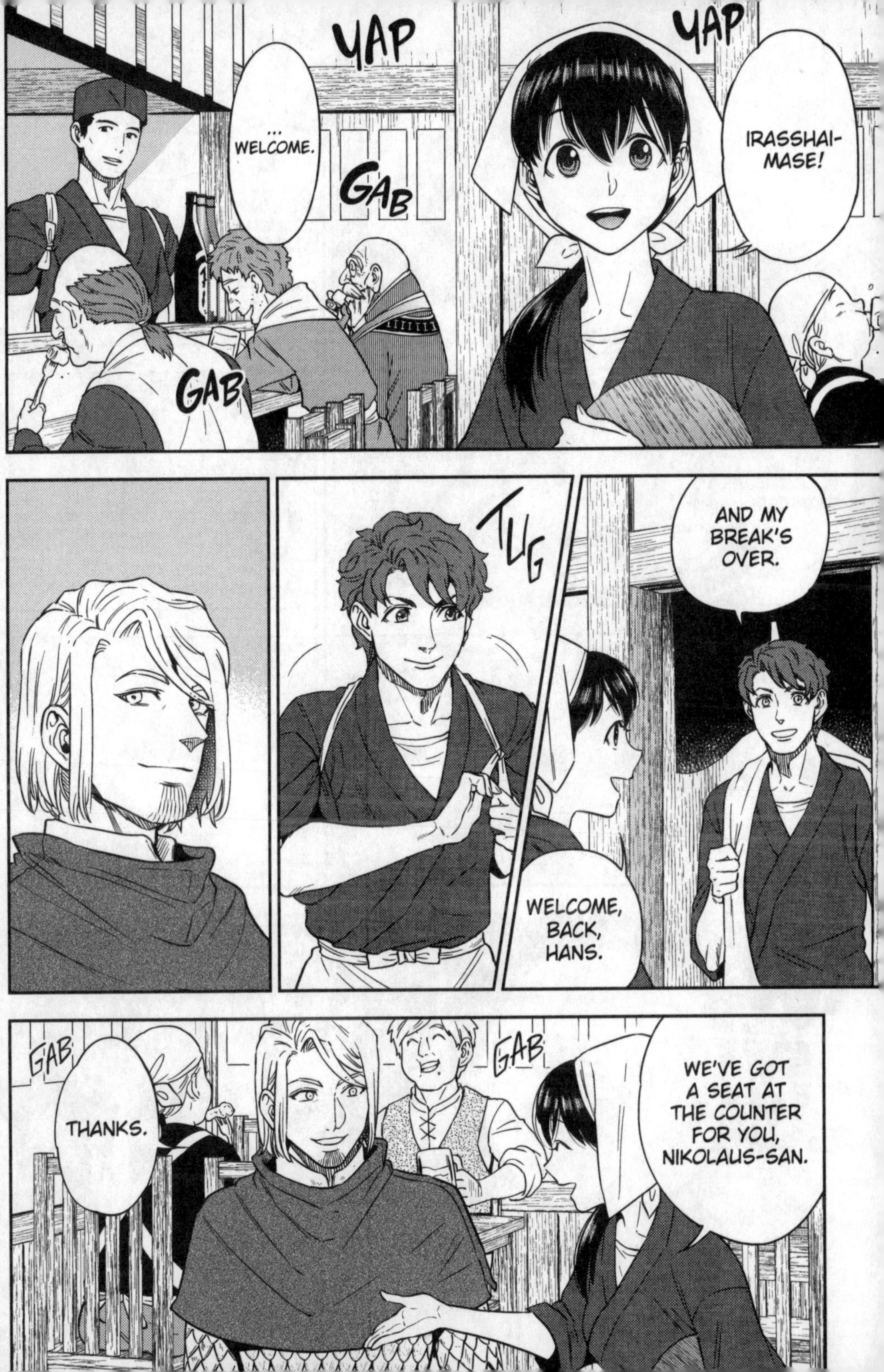
YAP
YAP
IRASSHAI-MASE!
... WELCOME.
GAB
GAB
AND MY BREAK'S OVER.
WELCOME, BACK, HANS.
TUG
WE'VE GOT A SEAT AT THE COUNTER FOR YOU, NIKOLAUS-SAN.
GAB
THANKS.
GAB

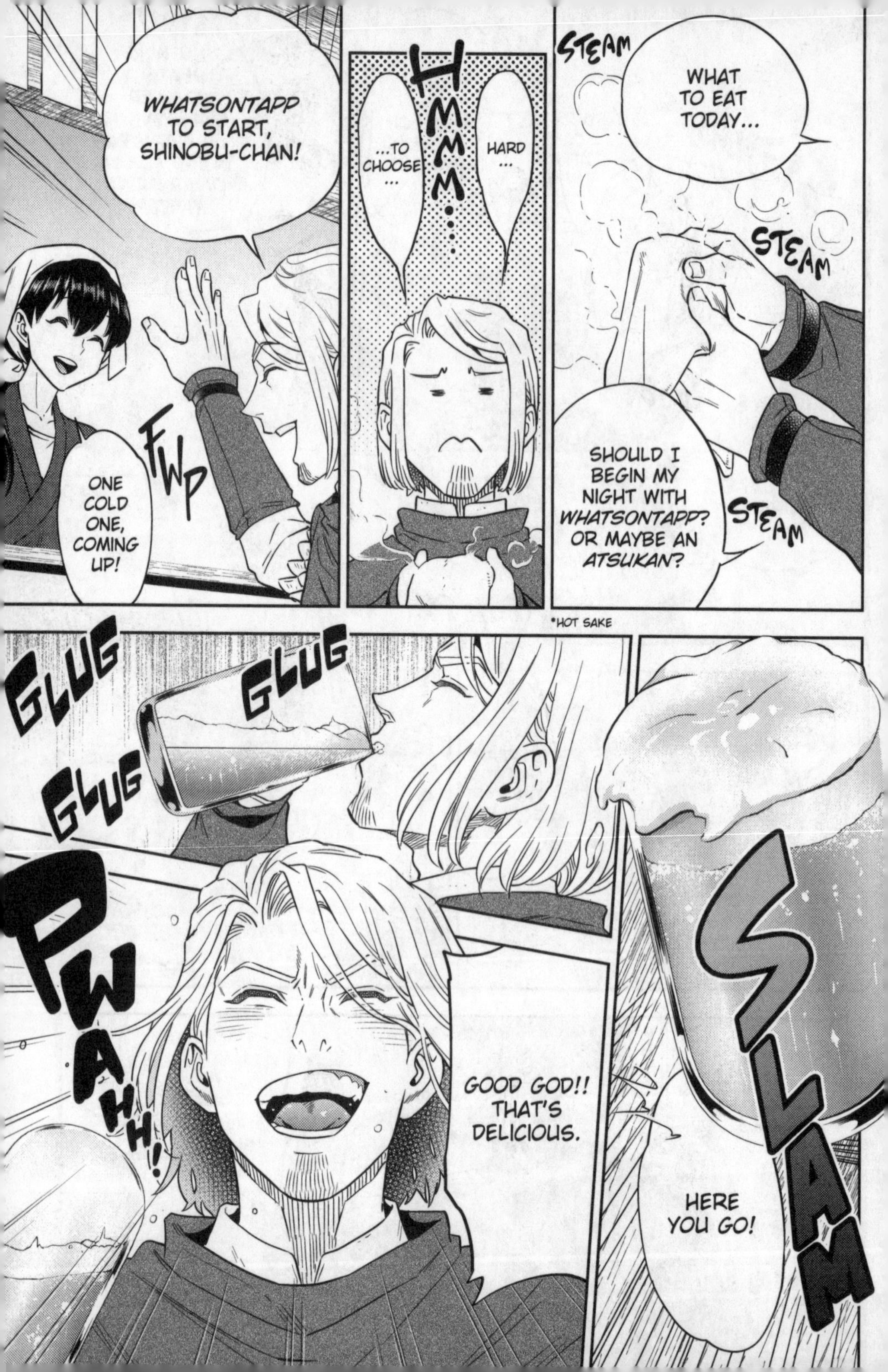
STEAM
WHAT TO EAT TODAY...
STEAM
SHOULD I BEGIN MY NIGHT WITH WHATSONTAPP? OR MAYBE AN ATSUKAN?
STEAM
*HOT SAKE
HMMM...
HARD...
...TO CHOOSE...
WHATSONTAPP TO START, SHINOBU-CHAN!
FWP
ONE COLD ONE, COMING UP!
SLAM
HERE YOU GO!
GLUG
GLUG
GLUG
PWAHH!!
GOOD GOD!! THAT'S DELICIOUS.

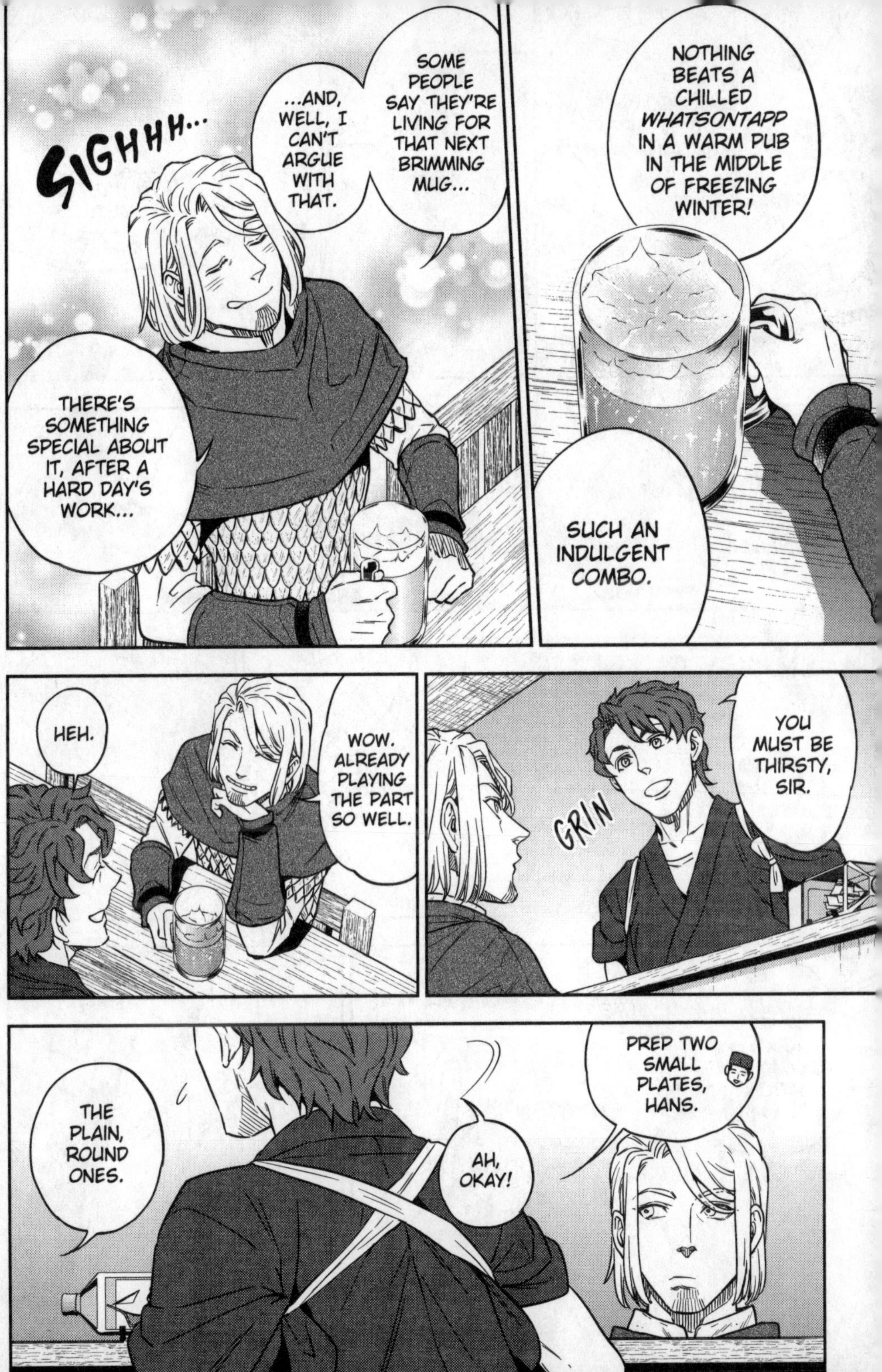

NOTHING BEATS A CHILLED *WHATSONTAPP* IN A WARM PUB IN THE MIDDLE OF FREEZING WINTER!
SUCH AN INDULGENT COMBO.
SOME PEOPLE SAY THEY'RE LIVING FOR THAT NEXT BRIMMING MUG...
...AND, WELL, I CAN'T ARGUE WITH THAT.
SIGHHH...
THERE'S SOMETHING SPECIAL ABOUT IT, AFTER A HARD DAY'S WORK...
YOU MUST BE THIRSTY, SIR.
GRIN
WOW. ALREADY PLAYING THE PART SO WELL.
HEH.
PREP TWO SMALL PLATES, HANS.
AH, OKAY!
THE PLAIN, ROUND ONES.

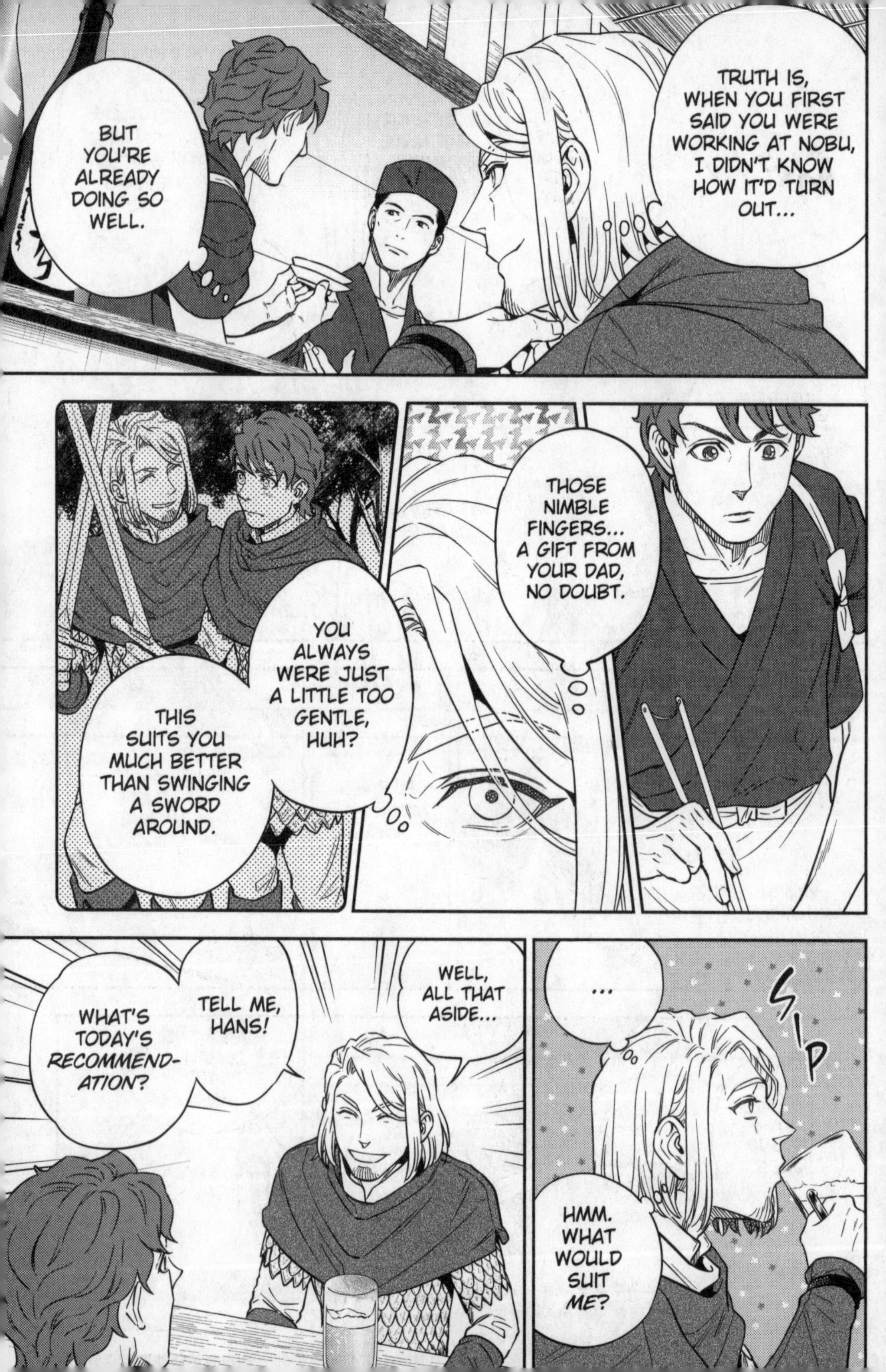
TRUTH IS, WHEN YOU FIRST SAID YOU WERE WORKING AT NOBU, I DIDN'T KNOW HOW IT'D TURN OUT...
BUT YOU'RE ALREADY DOING SO WELL.
THOSE NIMBLE FINGERS... A GIFT FROM YOUR DAD, NO DOUBT.
YOU ALWAYS WERE JUST A LITTLE TOO GENTLE, HUH?
THIS SUITS YOU MUCH BETTER THAN SWINGING A SWORD AROUND.
...
SIP
HMM. WHAT WOULD SUIT *ME*?
WELL, ALL THAT ASIDE...
TELL ME, HANS!
WHAT'S TODAY'S *RECOMMENDATION*?

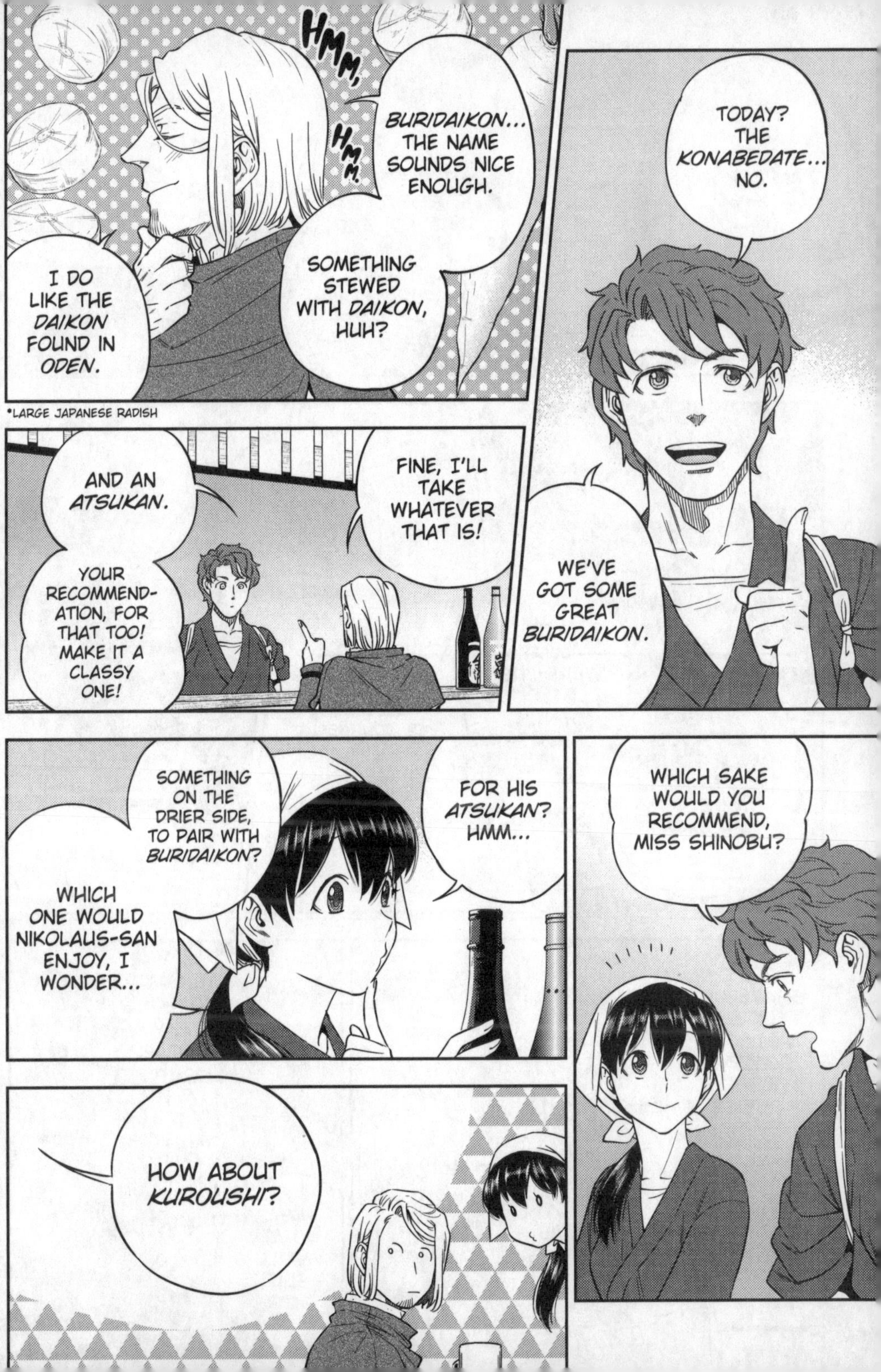
TODAY? THE *KONABEDATE*... NO.
WE'VE GOT SOME GREAT *BURIDAIKON*.
HMM, HMM.
BURIDAIKON... THE NAME SOUNDS NICE ENOUGH.
SOMETHING STEWED WITH *DAIKON*, HUH?
I DO LIKE THE *DAIKON* FOUND IN *ODEN*.
FINE, I'LL TAKE WHATEVER THAT IS!
AND AN *ATSUKAN*.
YOUR RECOMMENDATION, FOR THAT TOO! MAKE IT A CLASSY ONE!
WHICH SAKE WOULD YOU RECOMMEND, MISS SHINOBU?
FOR HIS *ATSUKAN*? HMM...
SOMETHING ON THE DRIER SIDE, TO PAIR WITH *BURIDAIKON*?
WHICH ONE WOULD NIKOLAUS-SAN ENJOY, I WONDER...
HOW ABOUT *KUROUSHI*?

*LARGE JAPANESE RADISH

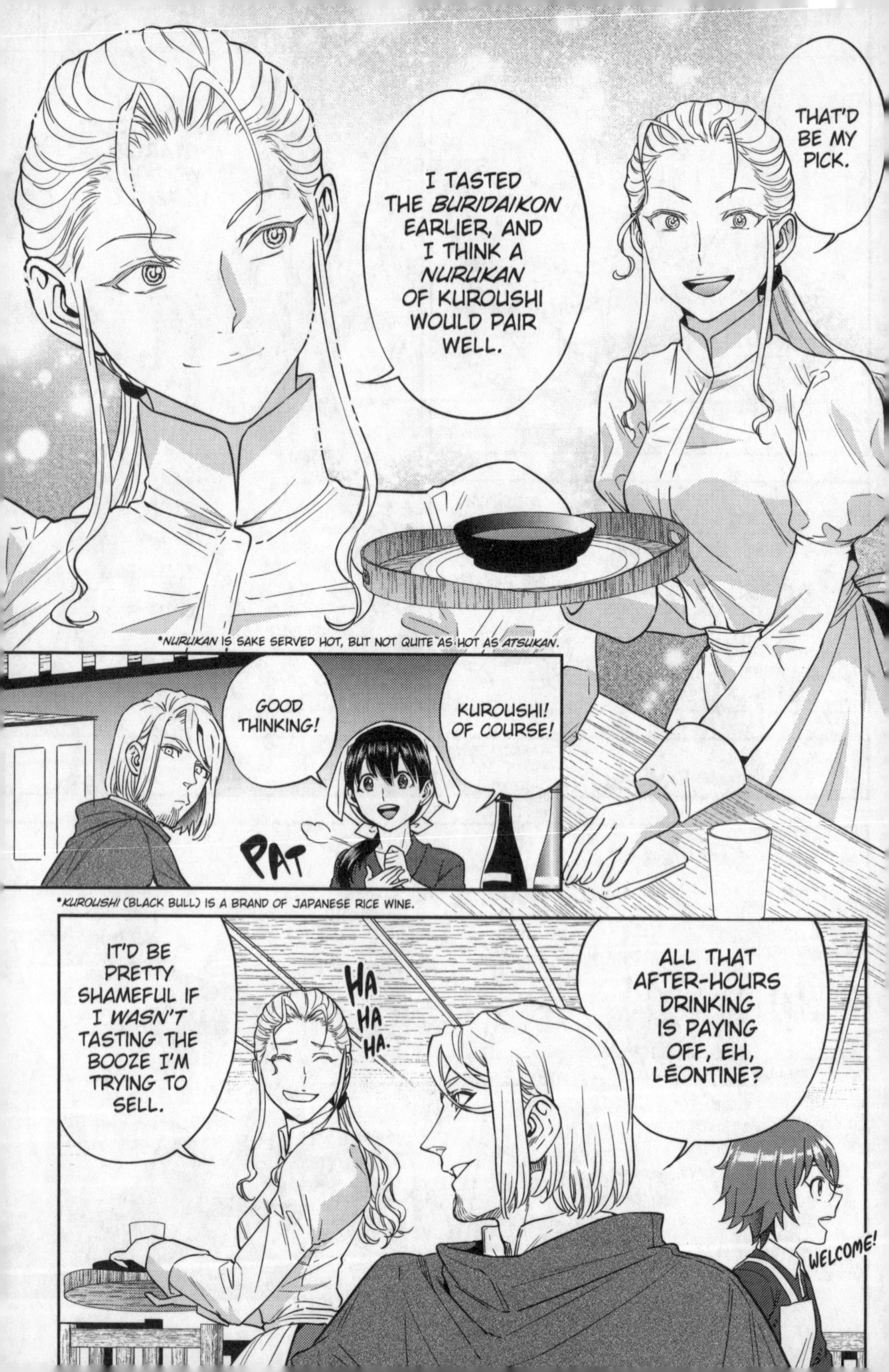
THAT'D BE MY PICK.
I TASTED THE BURIDAIKON EARLIER, AND I THINK A NURUKAN OF KUROUSHI WOULD PAIR WELL.
*NURUKAN IS SAKE SERVED HOT, BUT NOT QUITE AS HOT AS ATSUKAN.
KUROUSHI! OF COURSE!
GOOD THINKING!
PAT
*KUROUSHI (BLACK BULL) IS A BRAND OF JAPANESE RICE WINE.
ALL THAT AFTER-HOURS DRINKING IS PAYING OFF, EH, LÉONTINE?
IT'D BE PRETTY SHAMEFUL IF I WASN'T TASTING THE BOOZE I'M TRYING TO SELL.
HA HA HA.
WELCOME!

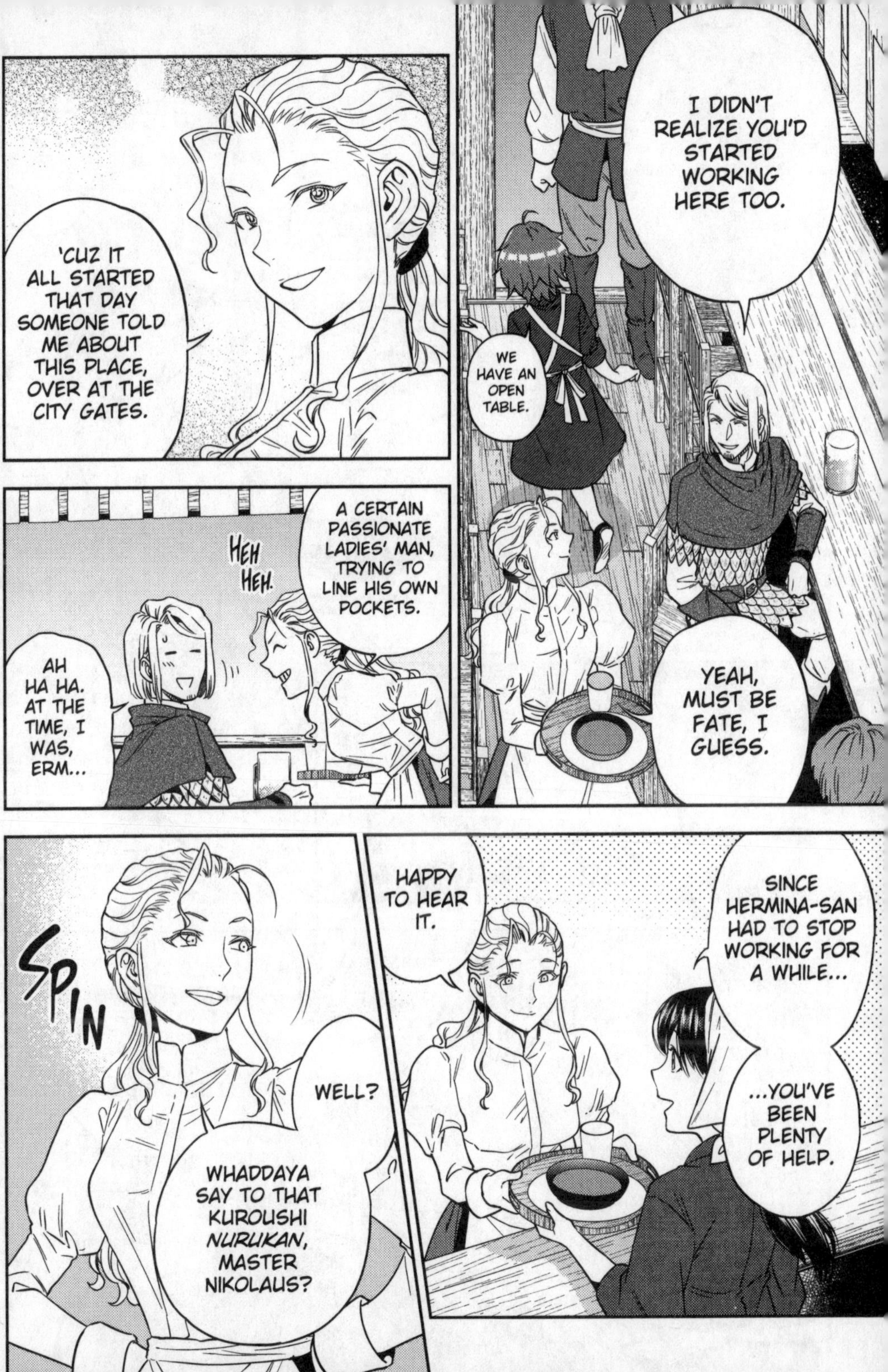
I DIDN'T REALIZE YOU'D STARTED WORKING HERE TOO.
WE HAVE AN OPEN TABLE.
YEAH, MUST BE FATE, I GUESS.
'CUZ IT ALL STARTED THAT DAY SOMEONE TOLD ME ABOUT THIS PLACE, OVER AT THE CITY GATES.
A CERTAIN PASSIONATE LADIES' MAN, TRYING TO LINE HIS OWN POCKETS.
HEH HEH.
AH HA HA. AT THE TIME, I WAS, ERM...
SINCE HERMINA-SAN HAD TO STOP WORKING FOR A WHILE...
...YOU'VE BEEN PLENTY OF HELP.
HAPPY TO HEAR IT.
SPIN
WELL?
WHADDAYA SAY TO THAT KUROUSHI *NURUKAN*, MASTER NIKOLAUS?

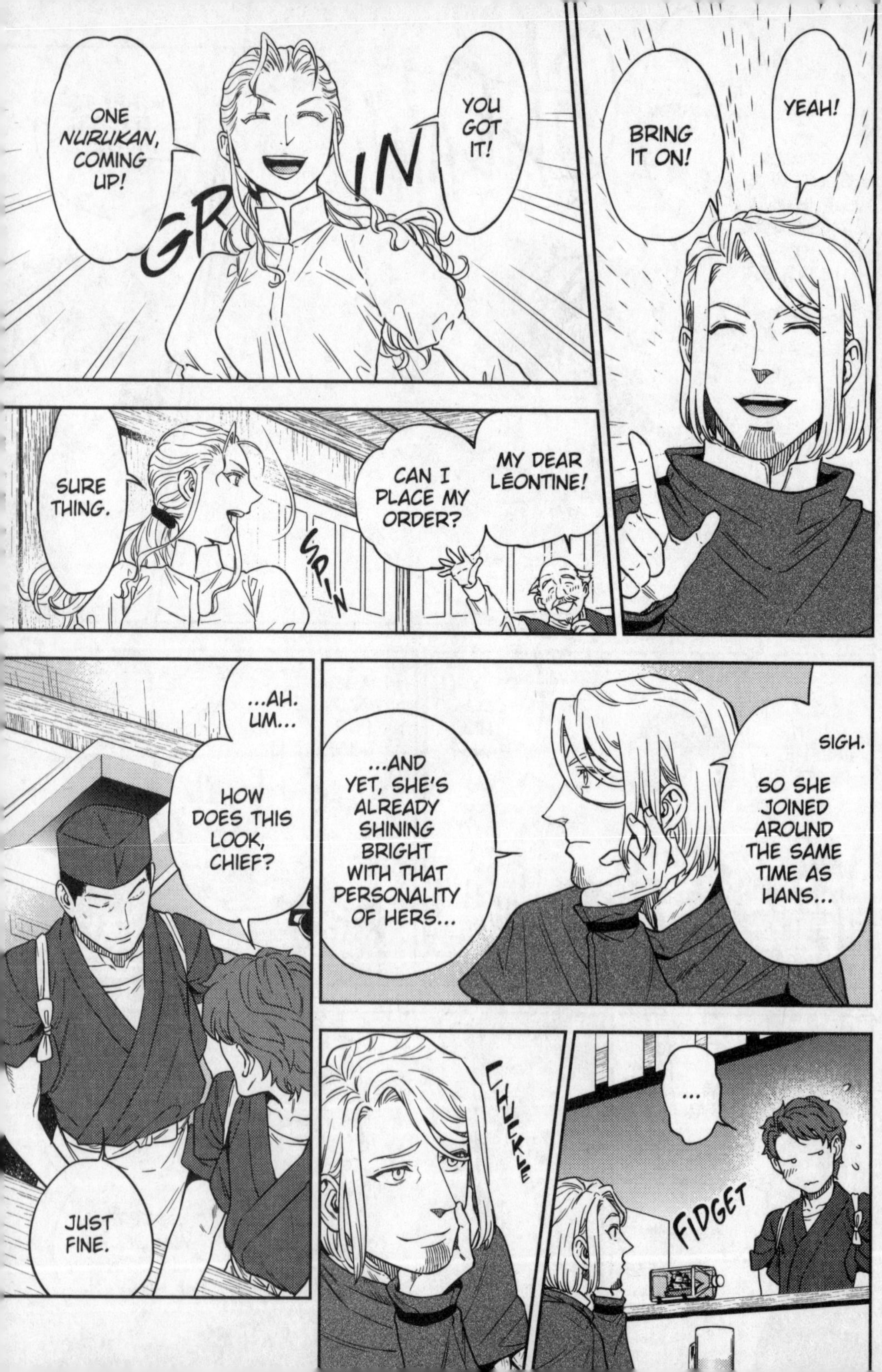
YEAH!
BRING IT ON!
YOU GOT IT!
ONE NURUKAN, COMING UP!
GRIN
MY DEAR LÉONTINE!
CAN I PLACE MY ORDER?
SPIN
SURE THING.
SIGH.
SO SHE JOINED AROUND THE SAME TIME AS HANS...
...AND YET, SHE'S ALREADY SHINING BRIGHT WITH THAT PERSONALITY OF HERS...
...
FIDGET
CHUCKLE
...AH. UM...
HOW DOES THIS LOOK, CHIEF?
JUST FINE.

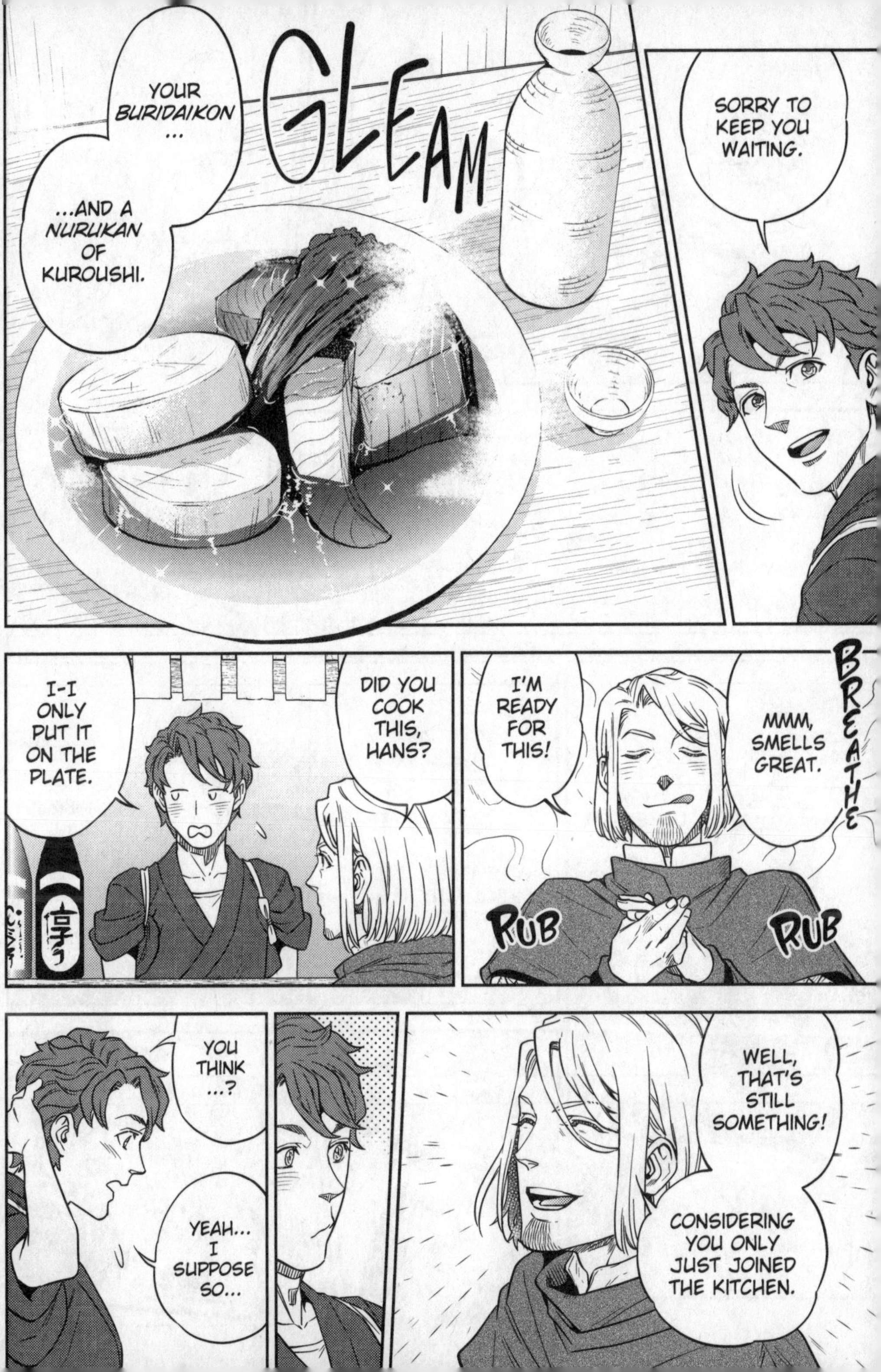
SORRY TO KEEP YOU WAITING.
GLEAM
YOUR *BURIDAIKON* ...
...AND A *NURUKAN* OF KUROUSHI.
BREATHE
MMM, SMELLS GREAT.
I'M READY FOR THIS!
RUB
RUB
DID YOU COOK THIS, HANS?
I-I ONLY PUT IT ON THE PLATE.
WELL, THAT'S STILL SOMETHING!
CONSIDERING YOU ONLY JUST JOINED THE KITCHEN.
YOU THINK ...?
YEAH... I SUPPOSE SO...

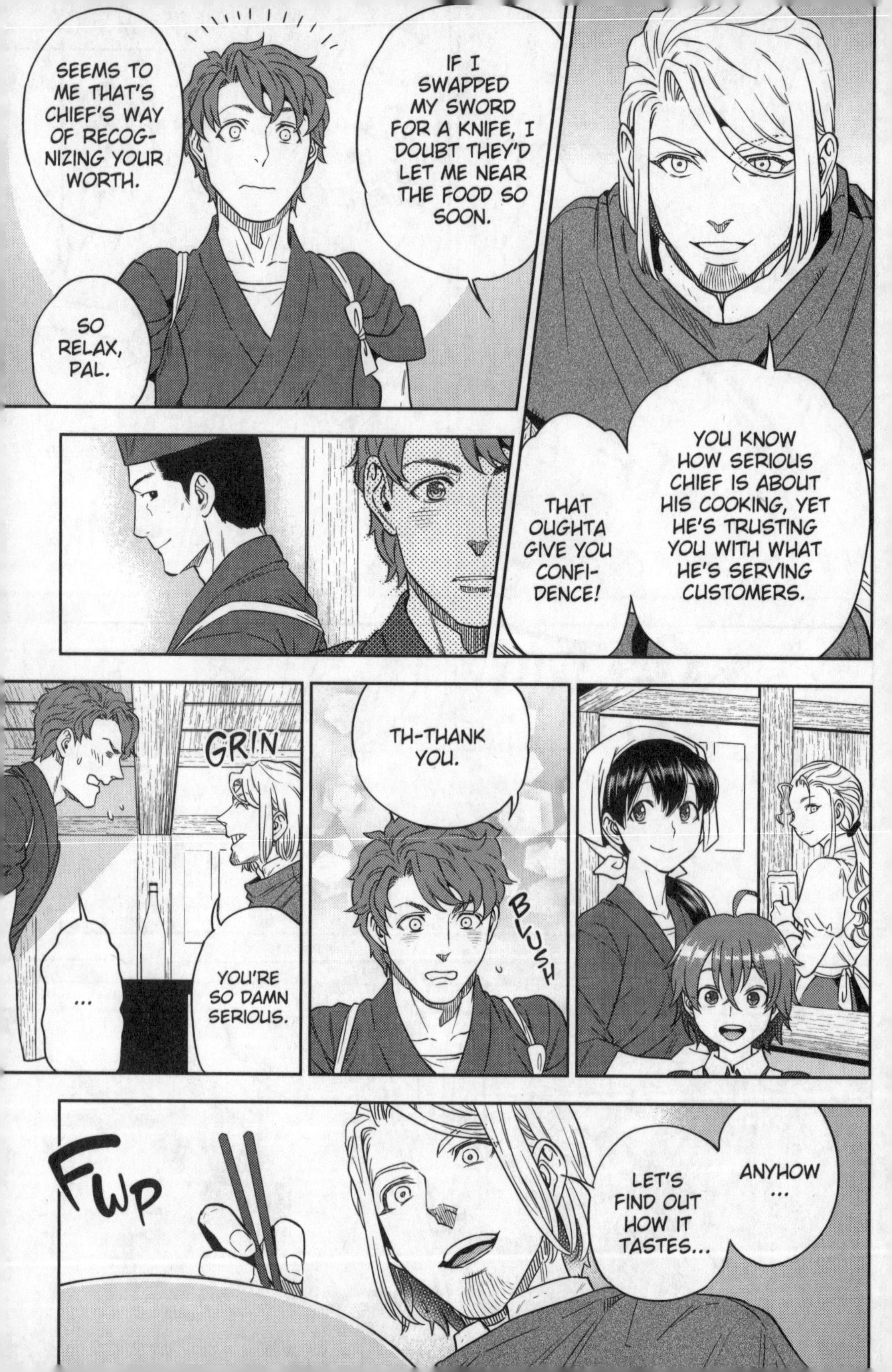
YOU KNOW HOW SERIOUS CHIEF IS ABOUT HIS COOKING, YET HE'S TRUSTING YOU WITH WHAT HE'S SERVING CUSTOMERS.
THAT OUGHTA GIVE YOU CONFI-DENCE!
IF I SWAPPED MY SWORD FOR A KNIFE, I DOUBT THEY'D LET ME NEAR THE FOOD SO SOON.
SEEMS TO ME THAT'S CHIEF'S WAY OF RECOG-NIZING YOUR WORTH.
SO RELAX, PAL.
TH-THANK YOU.
BLUSH
GRIN
YOU'RE SO DAMN SERIOUS.
...
ANYHOW...
LET'S FIND OUT HOW IT TASTES...
FWP

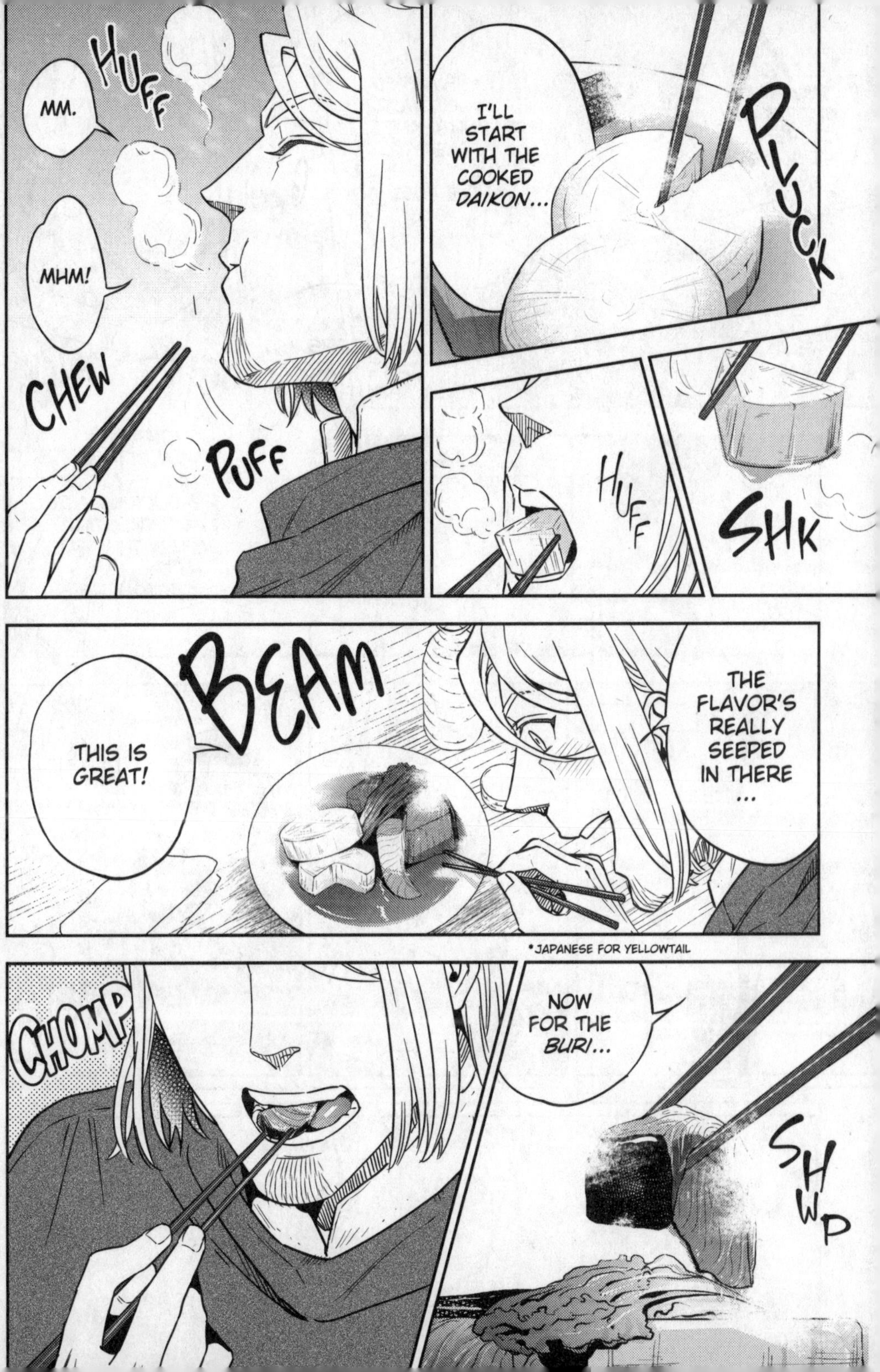
I'LL START WITH THE COOKED *DAIKON*...
PLUCK
SHK
HUFF
MM.
HUFF
MHM!
CHEW
PUFF
THE FLAVOR'S REALLY SEEPED IN THERE ...
BEAM
THIS IS GREAT!
*JAPANESE FOR YELLOWTAIL
NOW FOR THE *BURI*...
SHWP
CHOMP

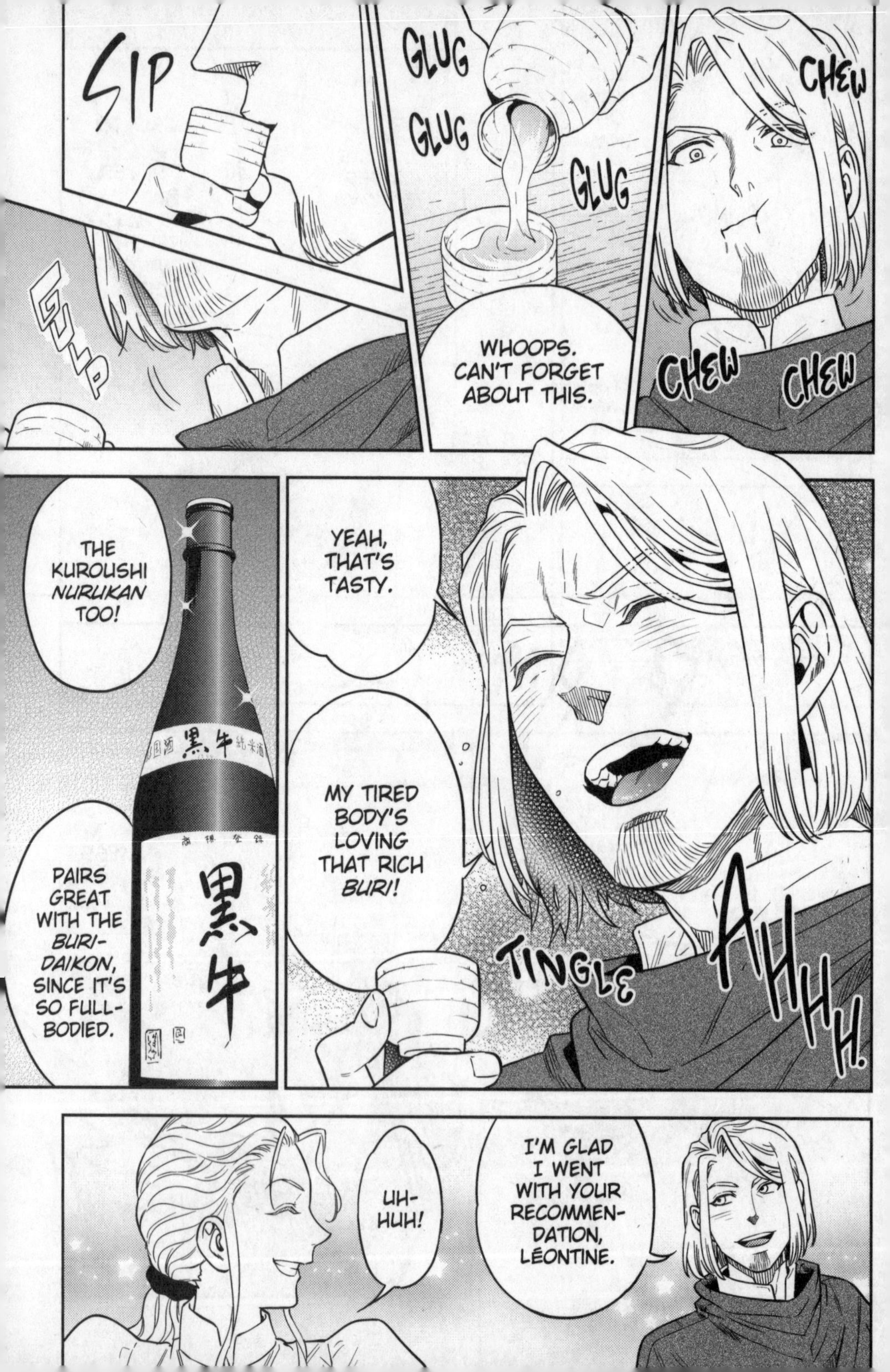
CHEW
CHEW
CHEW
GLUG
GLUG
GLUG
WHOOPS. CAN'T FORGET ABOUT THIS.
SIP
GULP
YEAH, THAT'S TASTY.
MY TIRED BODY'S LOVING THAT RICH *BURI*!
TINGLE
AHHHH.
THE KUROUSHI *NURUKAN* TOO!
黒牛 純米酒
商標登録
黒牛
PAIRS GREAT WITH THE *BURI-DAIKON*, SINCE IT'S SO FULL-BODIED.
I'M GLAD I WENT WITH YOUR RECOMMENDATION, LÉONTINE.
UH-HUH!

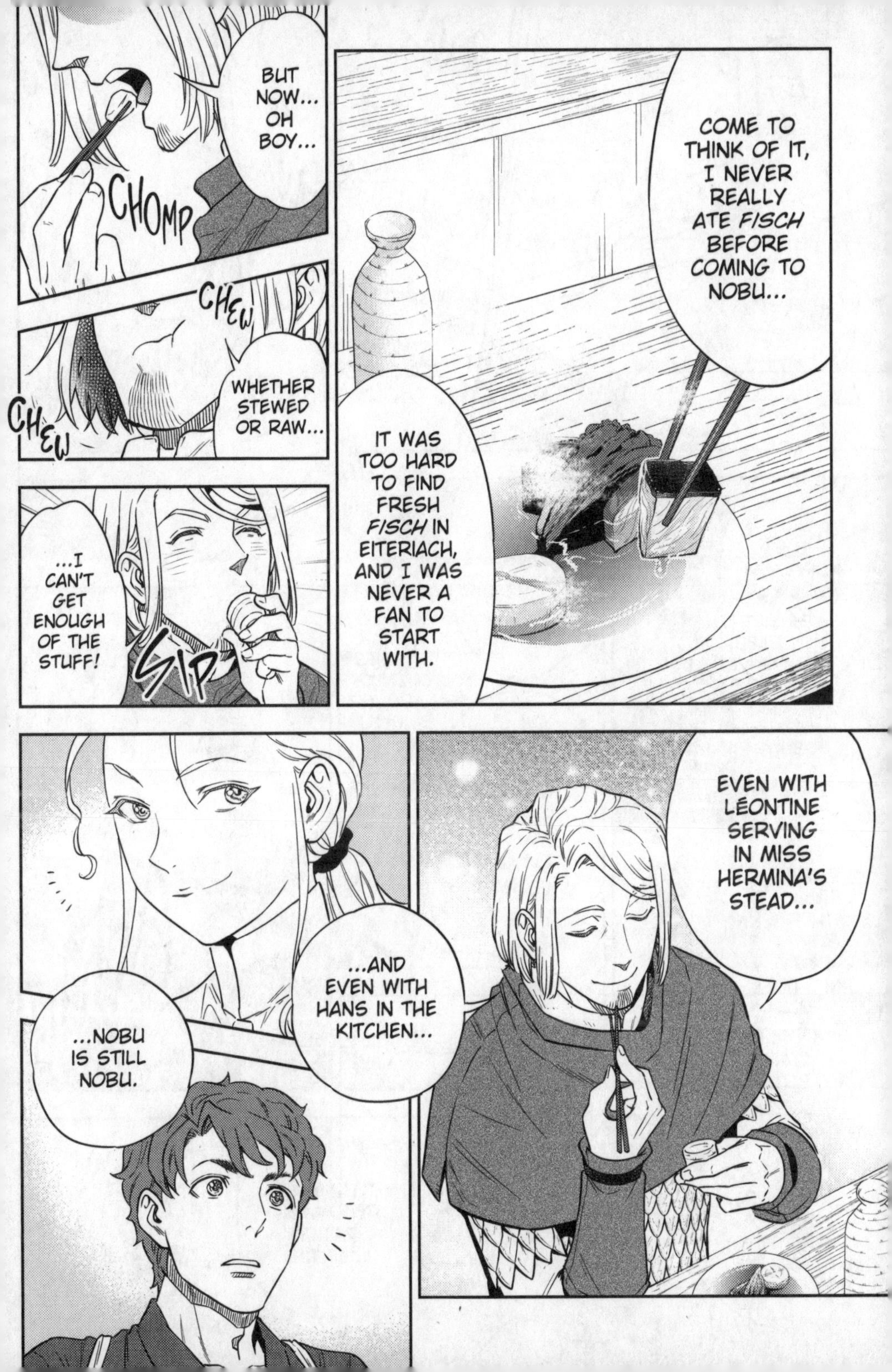
COME TO THINK OF IT, I NEVER REALLY ATE *FISCH* BEFORE COMING TO NOBU...
IT WAS TOO HARD TO FIND FRESH *FISCH* IN EITERIACH, AND I WAS NEVER A FAN TO START WITH.
BUT NOW... OH BOY...
CHOMP
CHEW
CHEW
WHETHER STEWED OR RAW...
...I CAN'T GET ENOUGH OF THE STUFF!
SIP
EVEN WITH LÉONTINE SERVING IN MISS HERMINA'S STEAD...
...AND EVEN WITH HANS IN THE KITCHEN...
...NOBU IS STILL NOBU.

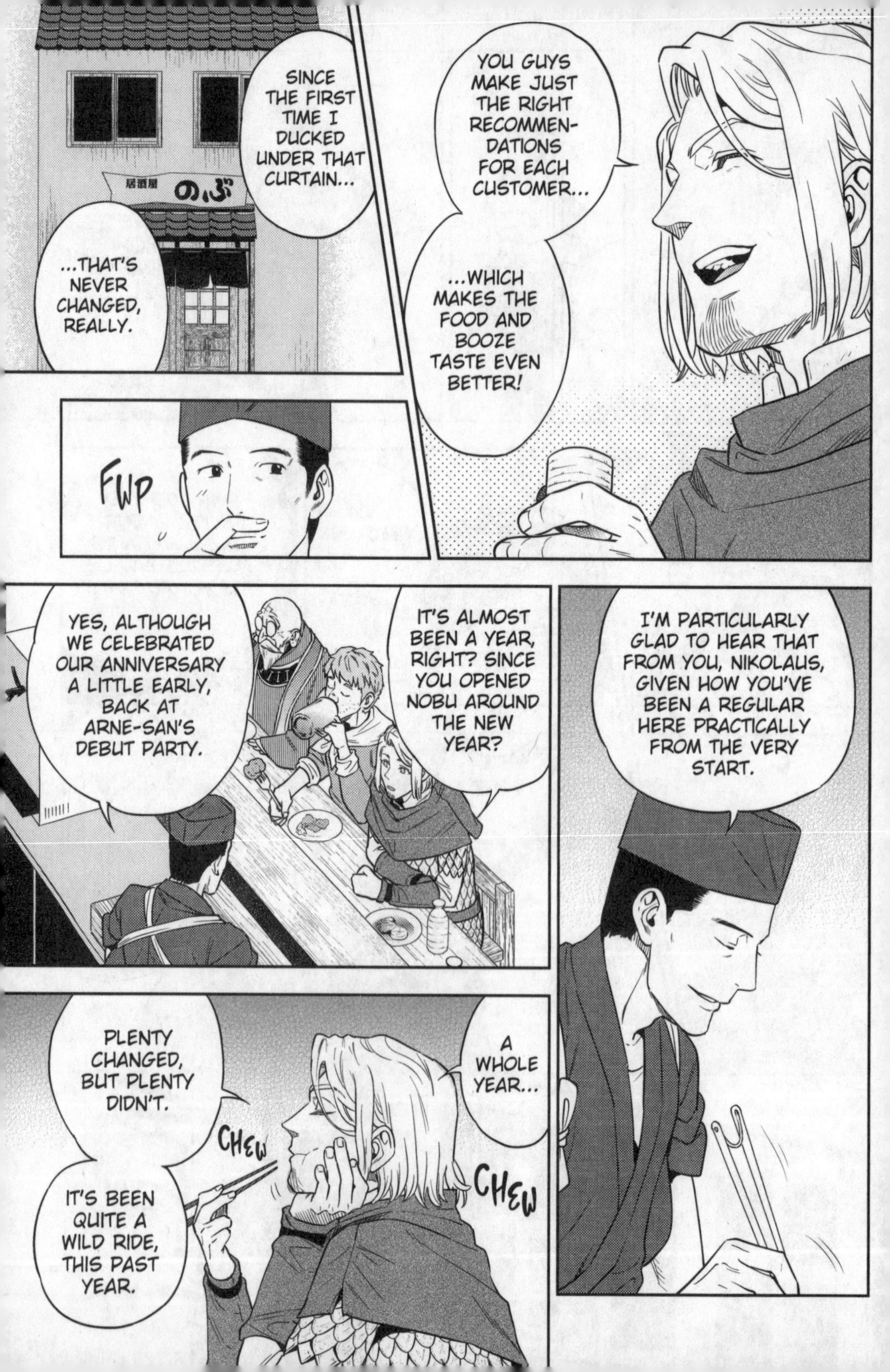
YOU GUYS MAKE JUST THE RIGHT RECOMMEN-DATIONS FOR EACH CUSTOMER...
...WHICH MAKES THE FOOD AND BOOZE TASTE EVEN BETTER!
SINCE THE FIRST TIME I DUCKED UNDER THAT CURTAIN...
居酒屋 のぶ
...THAT'S NEVER CHANGED, REALLY.
FWP
I'M PARTICULARLY GLAD TO HEAR THAT FROM YOU, NIKOLAUS, GIVEN HOW YOU'VE BEEN A REGULAR HERE PRACTICALLY FROM THE VERY START.
IT'S ALMOST BEEN A YEAR, RIGHT? SINCE YOU OPENED NOBU AROUND THE NEW YEAR?
YES, ALTHOUGH WE CELEBRATED OUR ANNIVERSARY A LITTLE EARLY, BACK AT ARNE-SAN'S DEBUT PARTY.
A WHOLE YEAR...
PLENTY CHANGED, BUT PLENTY DIDN'T.
CHEW
CHEW
IT'S BEEN QUITE A WILD RIDE, THIS PAST YEAR.

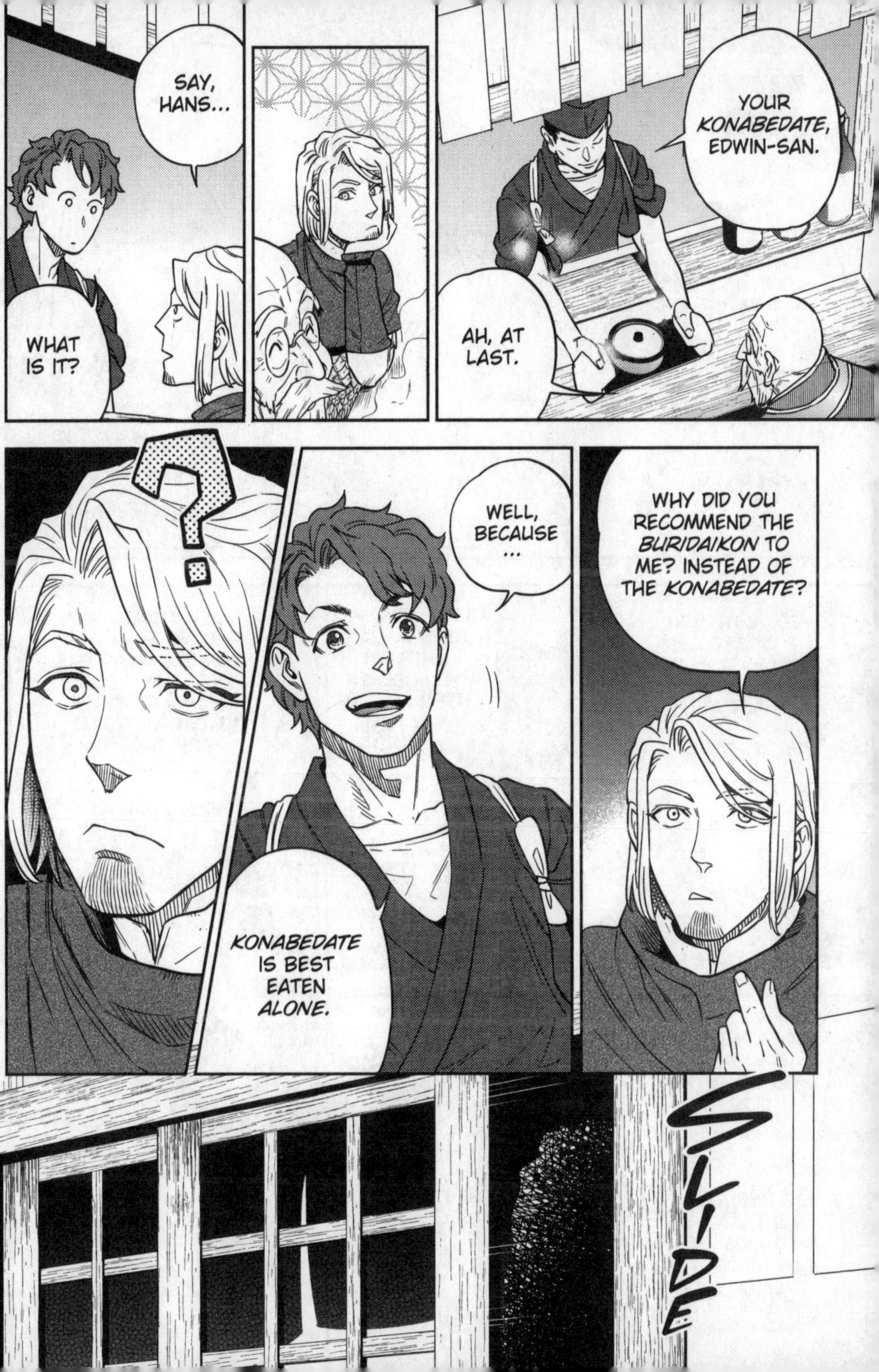
YOUR *KONABEDATE*, EDWIN-SAN.
AH, AT LAST.
SAY, HANS...
WHAT IS IT?
WHY DID YOU RECOMMEND THE *BURIDAIKON* TO ME? INSTEAD OF THE *KONABEDATE*?
WELL, BECAUSE ...
KONABEDATE IS BEST EATEN *ALONE*.
?
SLIDE

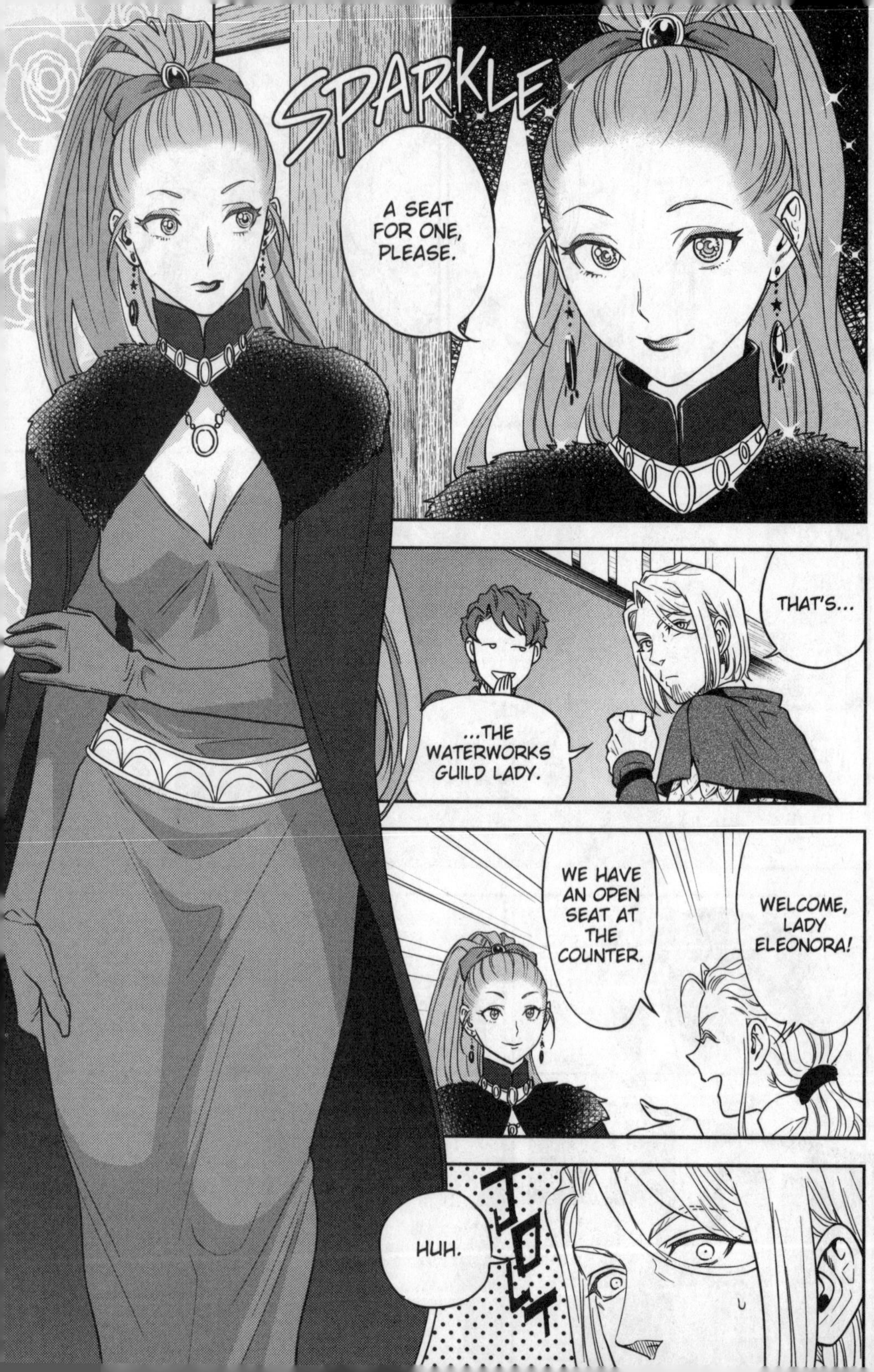
SPARKLE
A SEAT FOR ONE, PLEASE.
THAT'S...
...THE WATERWORKS GUILD LADY.
WELCOME, LADY ELEONORA!
WE HAVE AN OPEN SEAT AT THE COUNTER.
JOLT
HUH.

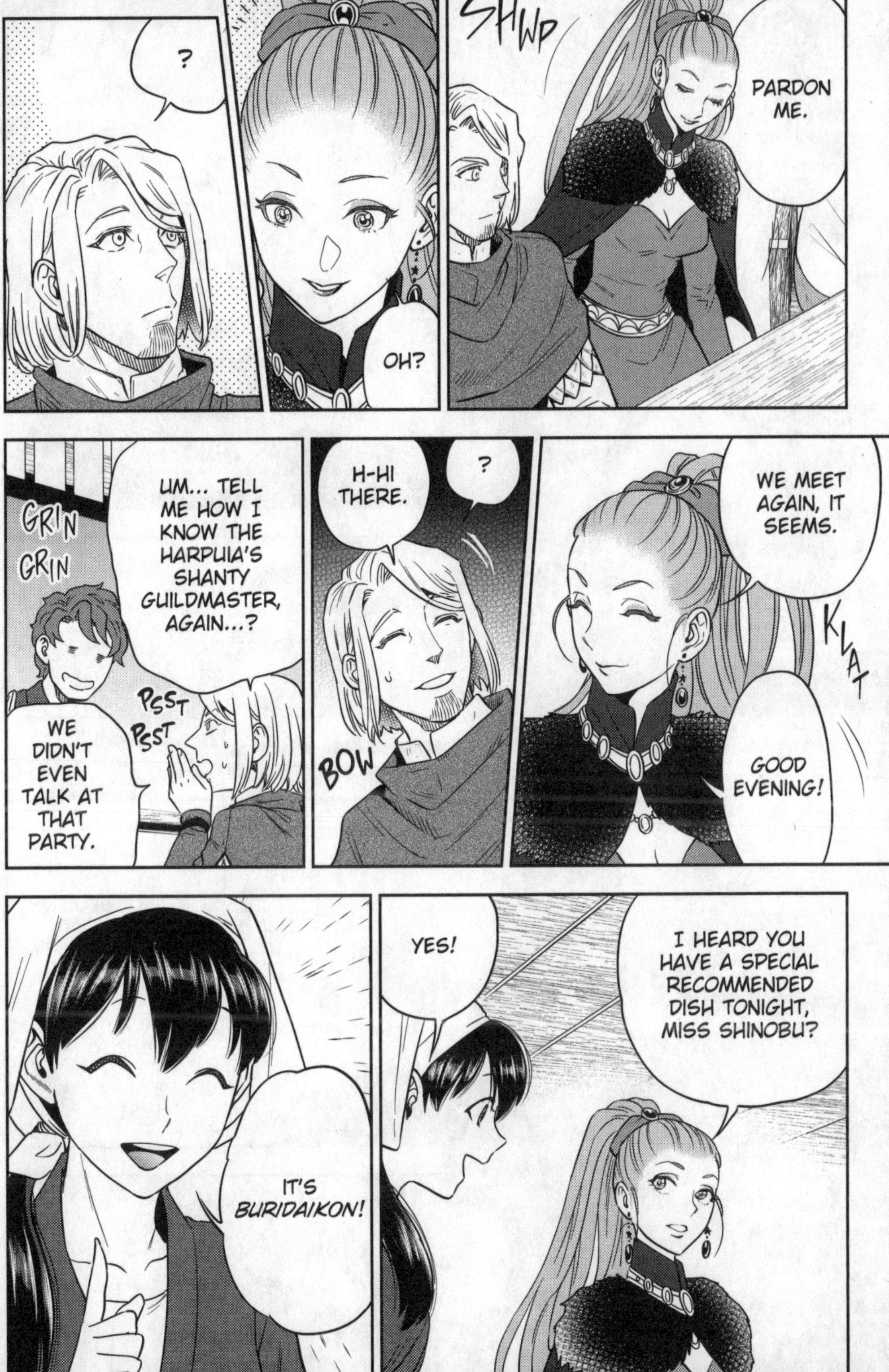
SHWP
PARDON ME.
OH?
?
WE MEET AGAIN, IT SEEMS.
KLAT
GOOD EVENING!
H-HI THERE.
?
BOW
UM... TELL ME HOW I KNOW THE HARPUIA'S SHANTY GUILDMASTER, AGAIN...?
GRIN GRIN
PSST PSST
WE DIDN'T EVEN TALK AT THAT PARTY.
I HEARD YOU HAVE A SPECIAL RECOMMENDED DISH TONIGHT, MISS SHINOBU?
YES!
IT'S *BURIDAIKON*!

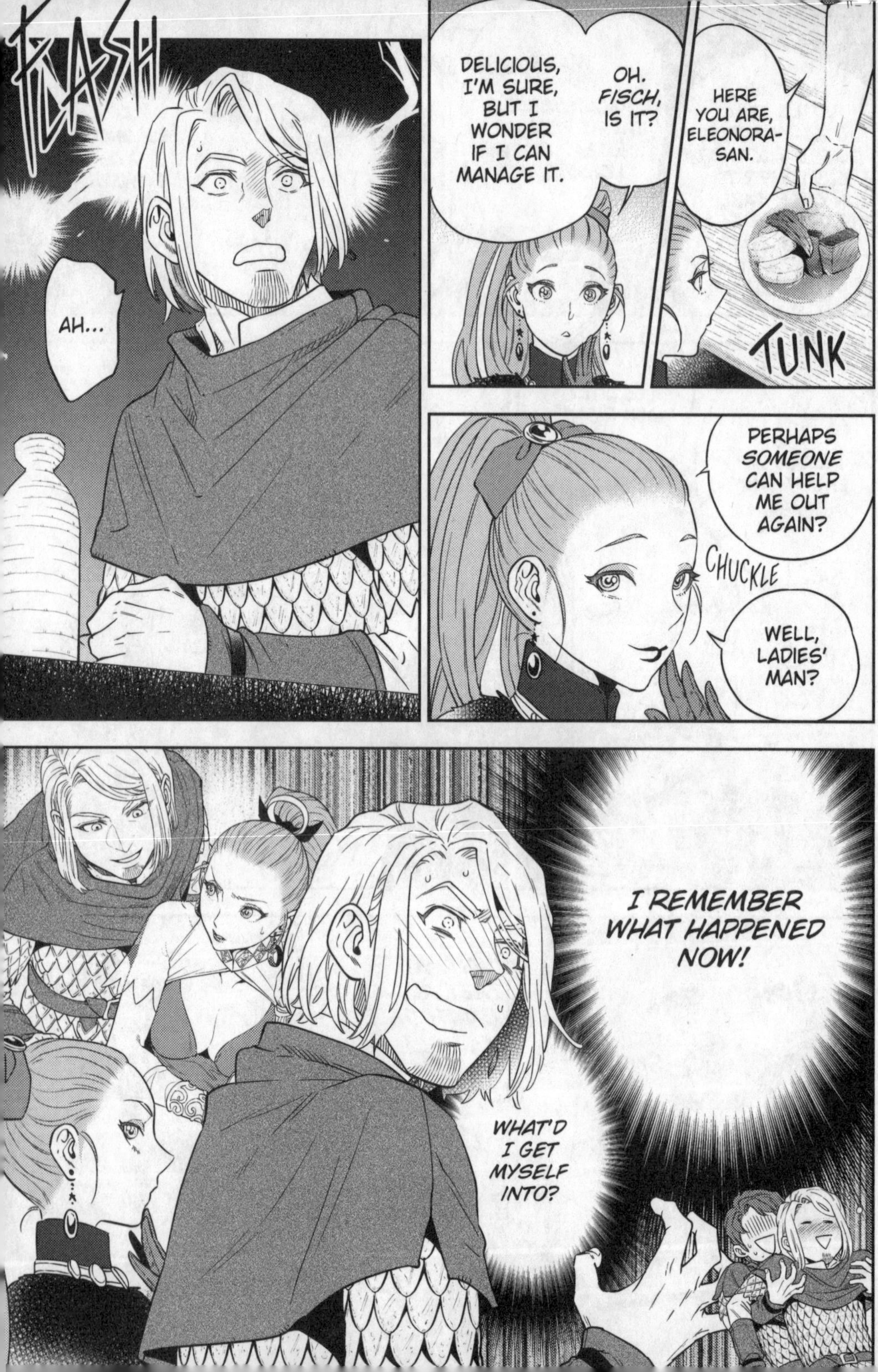
HERE YOU ARE, ELEONORA-SAN.
TUNK
OH. FISCH, IS IT?
DELICIOUS, I'M SURE, BUT I WONDER IF I CAN MANAGE IT.
PERHAPS SOMEONE CAN HELP ME OUT AGAIN?
CHUCKLE
WELL, LADIES' MAN?
FLASH
AH...
I REMEMBER WHAT HAPPENED NOW!
WHAT'D I GET MYSELF INTO?

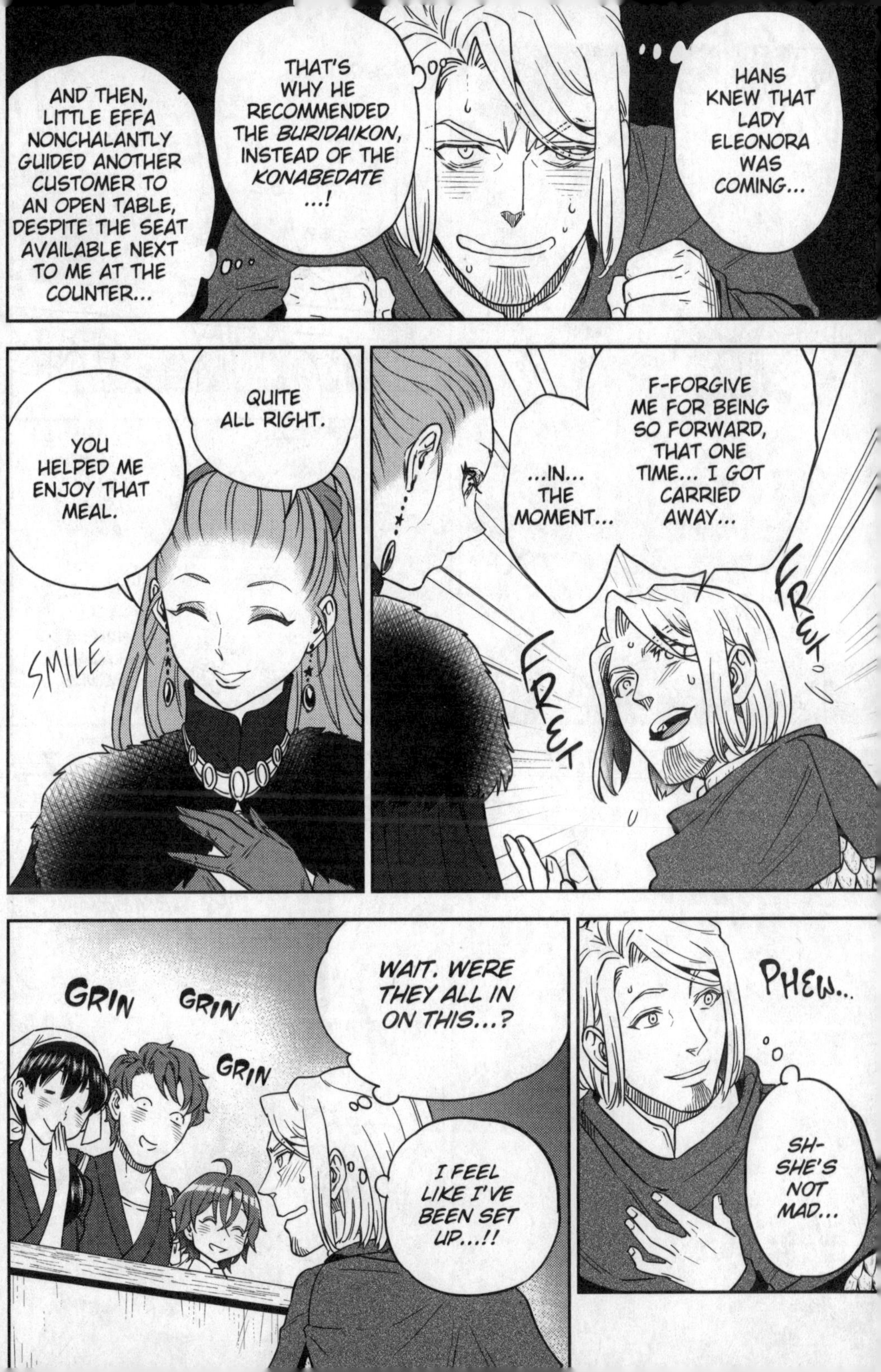
...!
HANS KNEW THAT LADY ELEONORA WAS COMING...
THAT'S WHY HE RECOMMENDED THE *BURIDAIKON*, INSTEAD OF THE *KONABEDATE* ...!
AND THEN, LITTLE EFFA NONCHALANTLY GUIDED ANOTHER CUSTOMER TO AN OPEN TABLE, DESPITE THE SEAT AVAILABLE NEXT TO ME AT THE COUNTER...
F-FORGIVE ME FOR BEING SO FORWARD, THAT ONE TIME... I GOT CARRIED AWAY...
...IN... THE MOMENT...
FREAK
FREAK
QUITE ALL RIGHT.
YOU HELPED ME ENJOY THAT MEAL.
SMILE
PHEW...
SH-SHE'S NOT MAD...
WAIT. WERE THEY ALL IN ON THIS...?
I FEEL LIKE I'VE BEEN SET UP...!!
GRIN
GRIN
GRIN

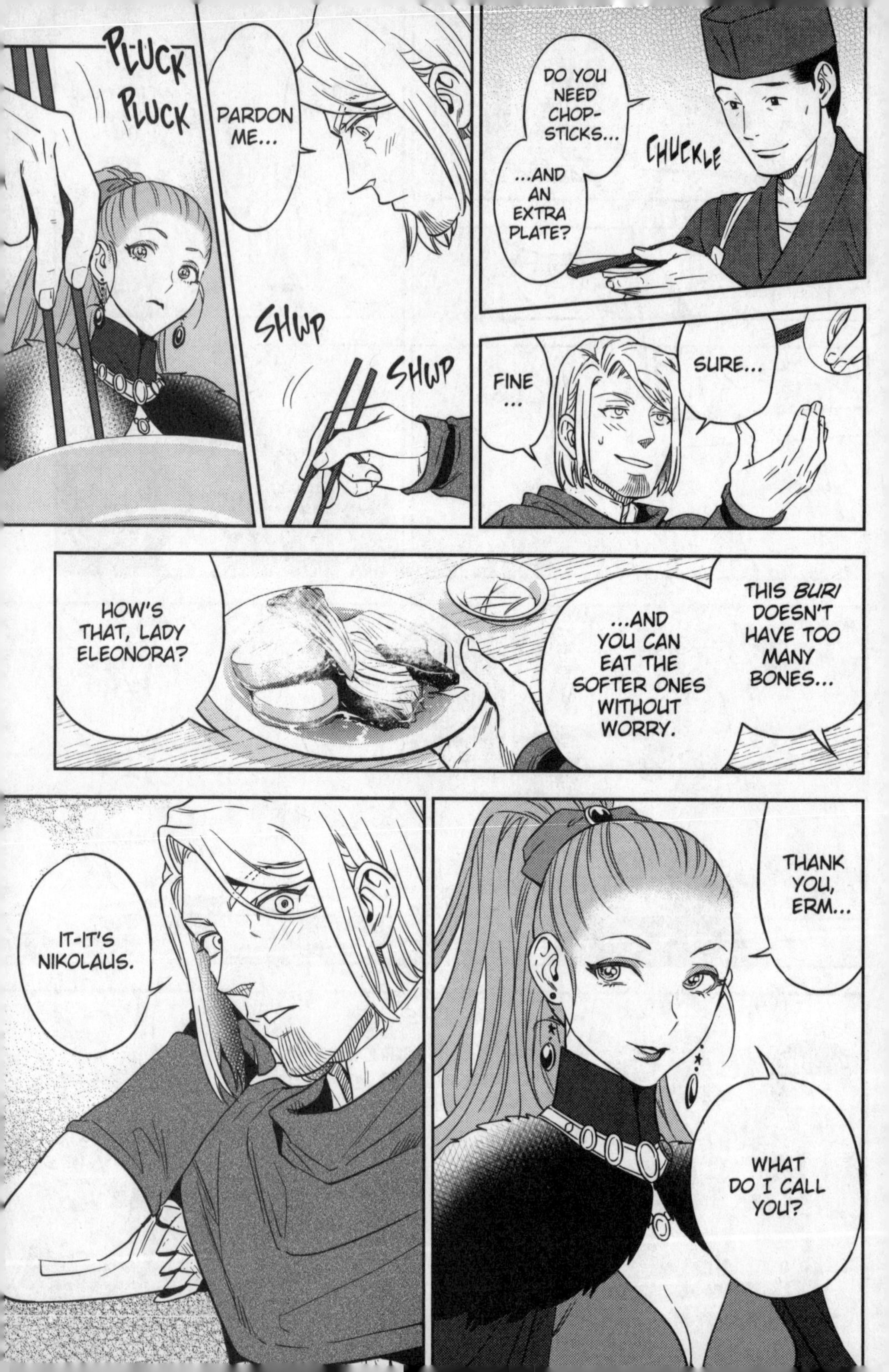
DO YOU NEED CHOP-STICKS...
...AND AN EXTRA PLATE?
CHUCKLE
SURE...
FINE ...
PARDON ME...
SHWP
SHWP
PLUCK
PLUCK
THIS *BURI* DOESN'T HAVE TOO MANY BONES...
...AND YOU CAN EAT THE SOFTER ONES WITHOUT WORRY.
HOW'S THAT, LADY ELEONORA?
THANK YOU, ERM...
WHAT DO I CALL YOU?
IT-IT'S NIKOLAUS.

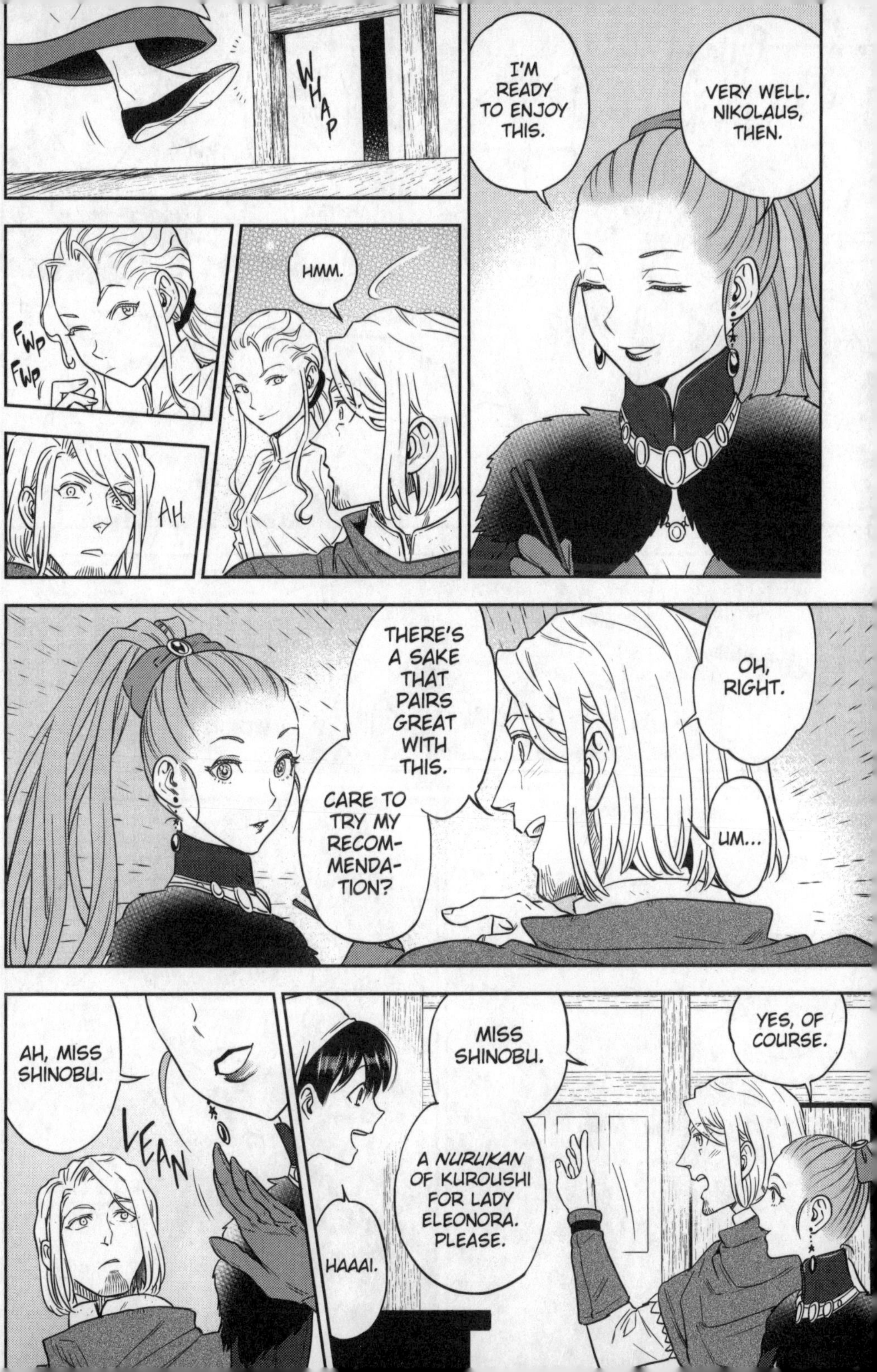
VERY WELL. NIKOLAUS, THEN.
I'M READY TO ENJOY THIS.
WHAP
HMM.
FWP FWP
AH.
OH, RIGHT.
THERE'S A SAKE THAT PAIRS GREAT WITH THIS.
UM...
CARE TO TRY MY RECOMMENDATION?
YES, OF COURSE.
MISS SHINOBU.
A *NURUKAN* OF KUROUSHI FOR LADY ELEONORA. PLEASE.
HAAAI.
AH, MISS SHINOBU.
LEAN

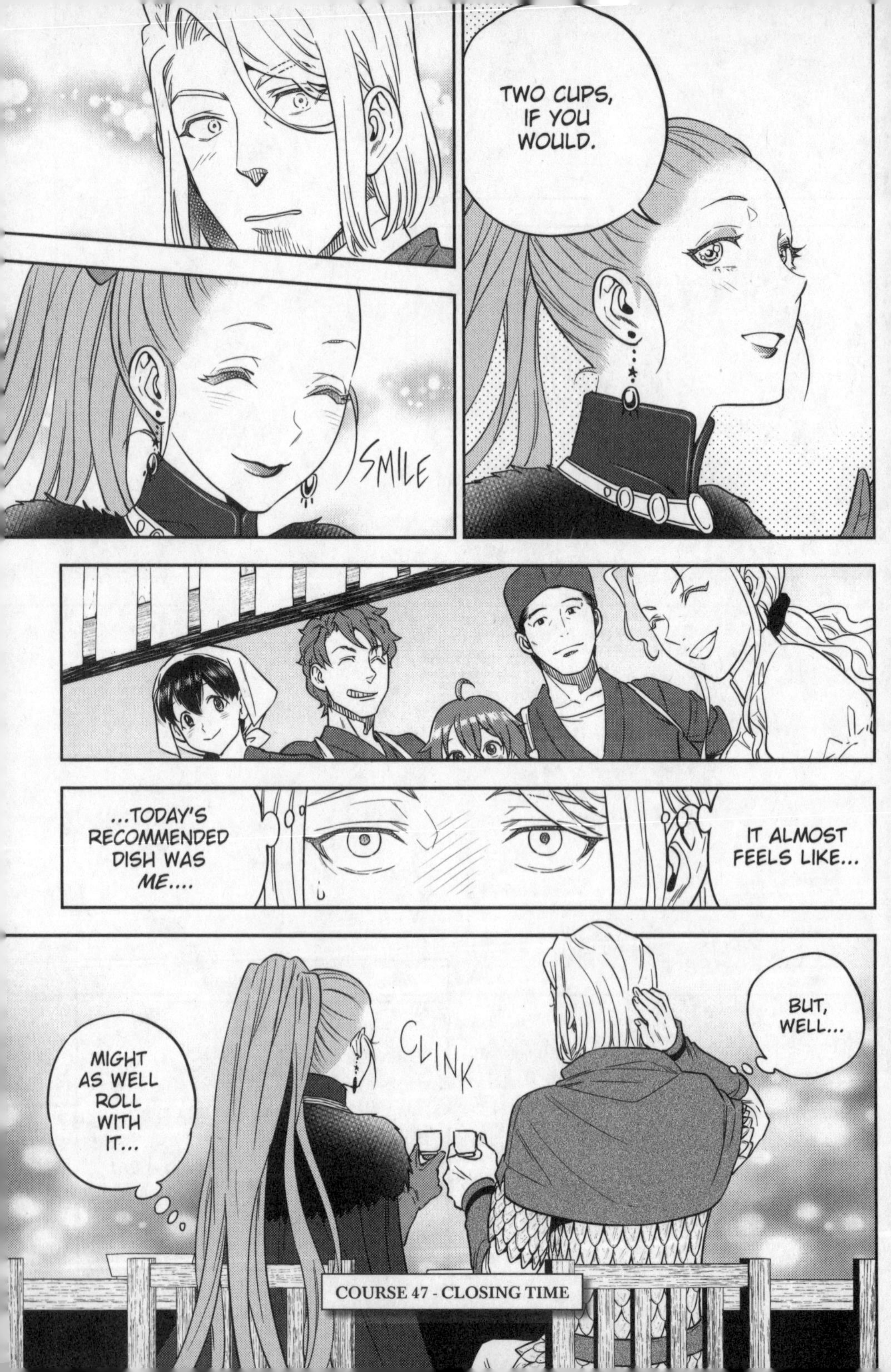
TWO CUPS, IF YOU WOULD.
SMILE
IT ALMOST FEELS LIKE...
...TODAY'S RECOMMENDED DISH WAS ME....
BUT, WELL...
CLINK
MIGHT AS WELL ROLL WITH IT...
COURSE 47 - CLOSING TIME

Buridaikon

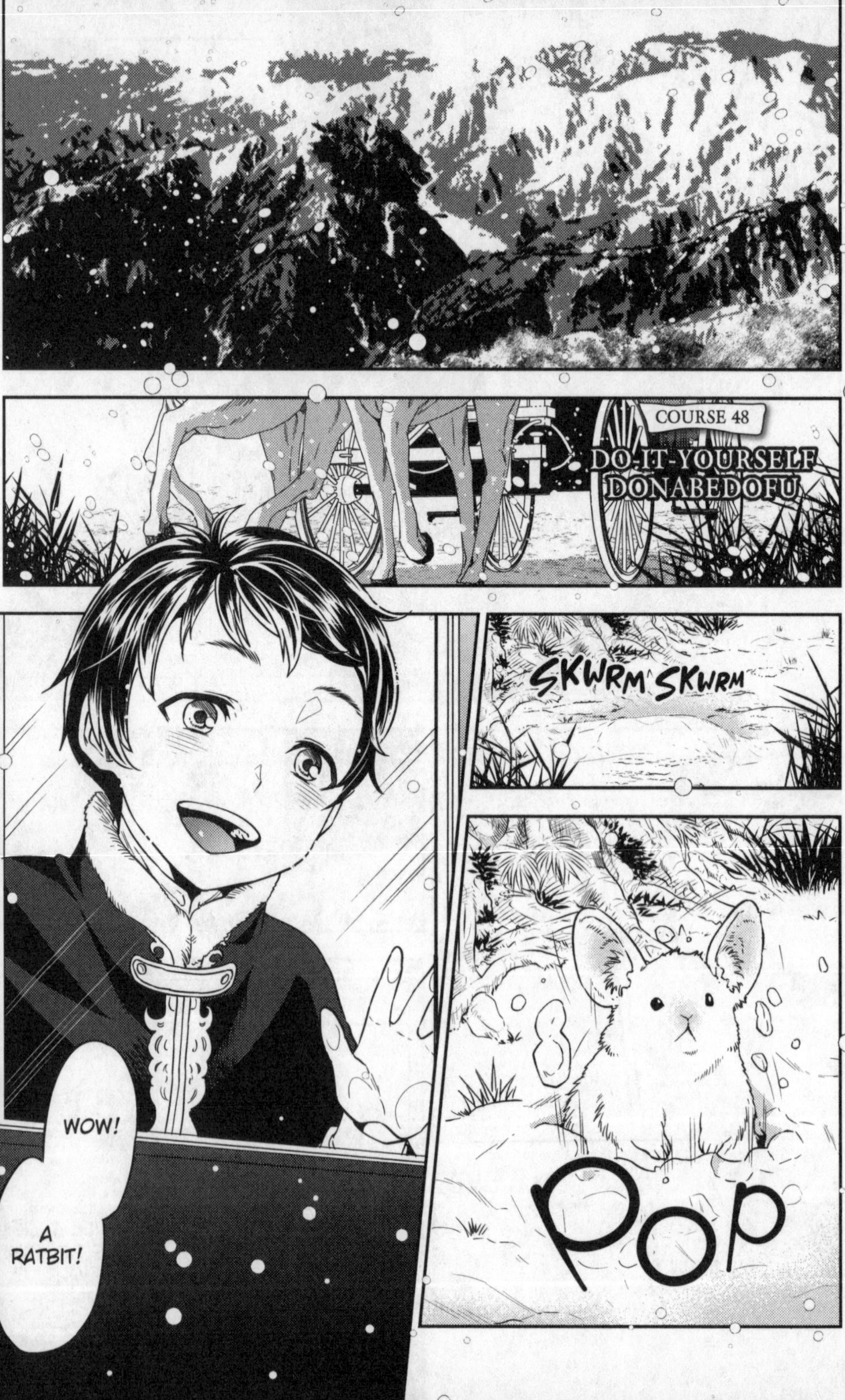
COURSE 48
DO-IT-YOURSELF DONABEDOFU
SKWRM SKWRM
Pop
WOW!
A RATBIT!

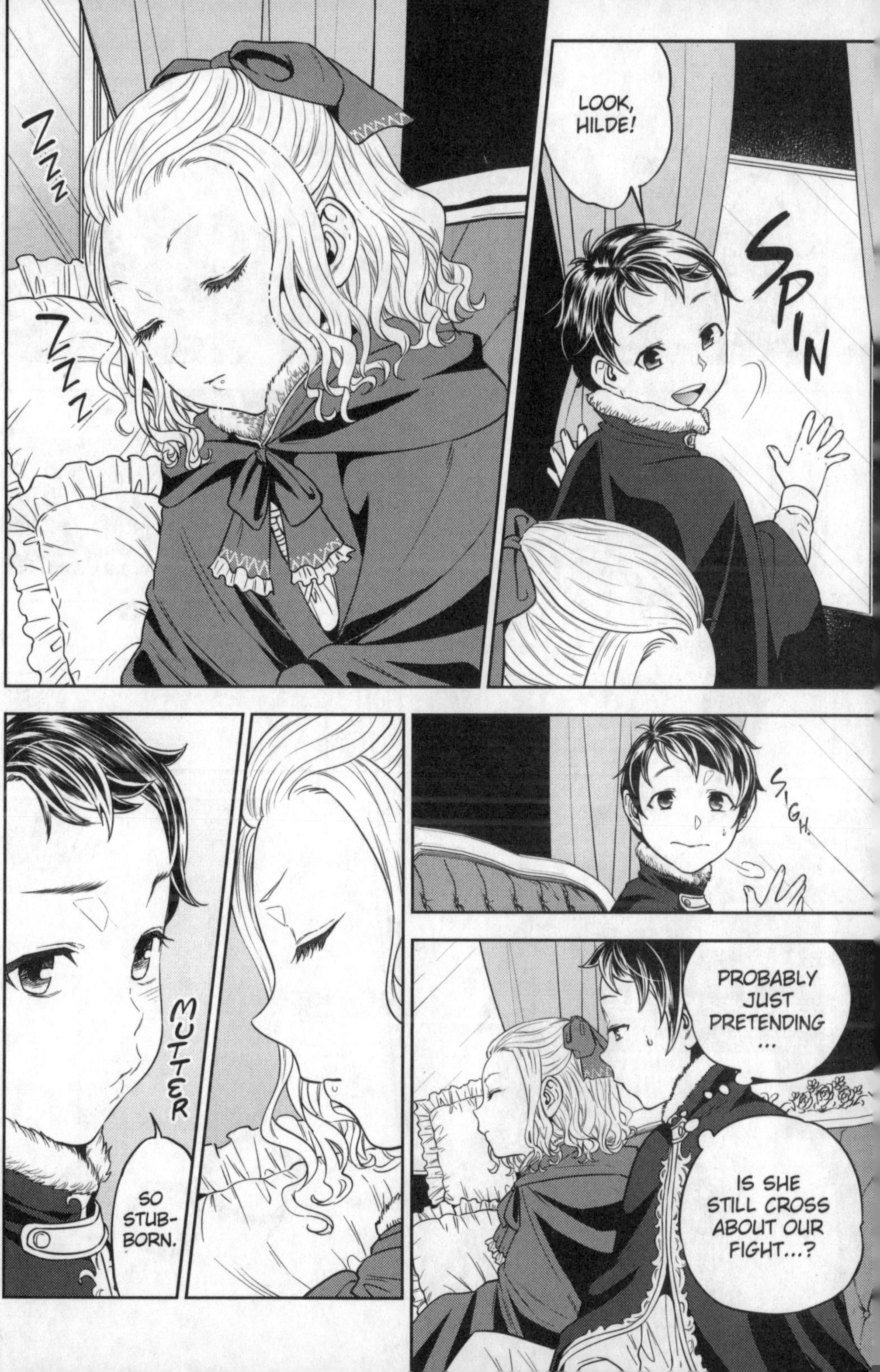
LOOK, HILDE!
SPIN
ZZZ
ZZZ
SIGH.
PROBABLY JUST PRETENDING...
IS SHE STILL CROSS ABOUT OUR FIGHT...?
MUTTER
SO STUB-BORN.

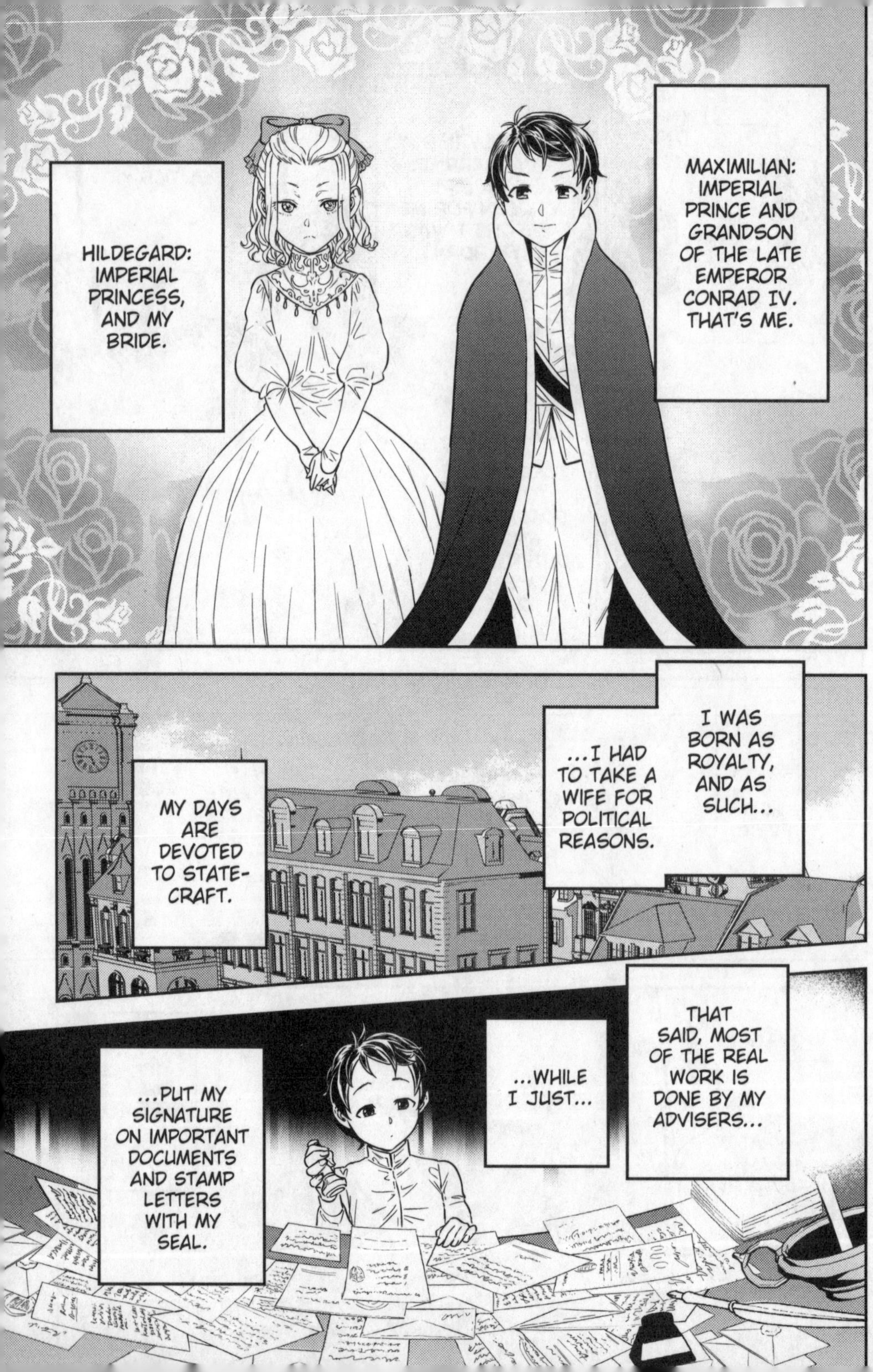
MAXIMILIAN: IMPERIAL PRINCE AND GRANDSON OF THE LATE EMPEROR CONRAD IV. THAT'S ME.
HILDEGARD: IMPERIAL PRINCESS, AND MY BRIDE.
I WAS BORN AS ROYALTY, AND AS SUCH...
...I HAD TO TAKE A WIFE FOR POLITICAL REASONS.
MY DAYS ARE DEVOTED TO STATE-CRAFT.
THAT SAID, MOST OF THE REAL WORK IS DONE BY MY ADVISERS...
...WHILE I JUST...
...PUT MY SIGNATURE ON IMPORTANT DOCUMENTS AND STAMP LETTERS WITH MY SEAL.

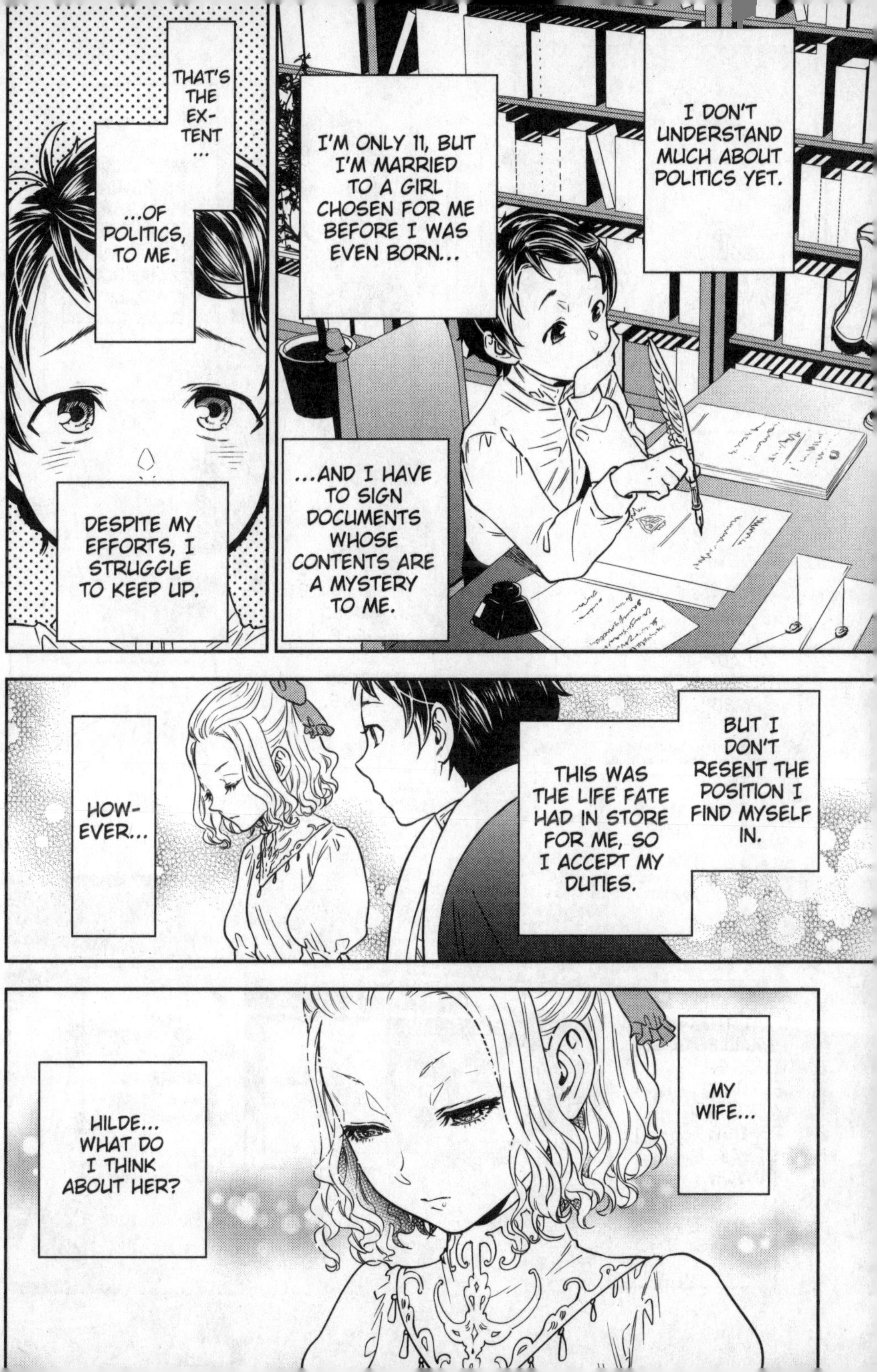
I DON'T UNDERSTAND MUCH ABOUT POLITICS YET.
I'M ONLY 11, BUT I'M MARRIED TO A GIRL CHOSEN FOR ME BEFORE I WAS EVEN BORN...
...AND I HAVE TO SIGN DOCUMENTS WHOSE CONTENTS ARE A MYSTERY TO ME.
THAT'S THE EX-TENT...
...OF POLITICS, TO ME.
DESPITE MY EFFORTS, I STRUGGLE TO KEEP UP.
BUT I DON'T RESENT THE POSITION I FIND MYSELF IN.
THIS WAS THE LIFE FATE HAD IN STORE FOR ME, SO I ACCEPT MY DUTIES.
HOW-EVER...
MY WIFE...
HILDE... WHAT DO I THINK ABOUT HER?

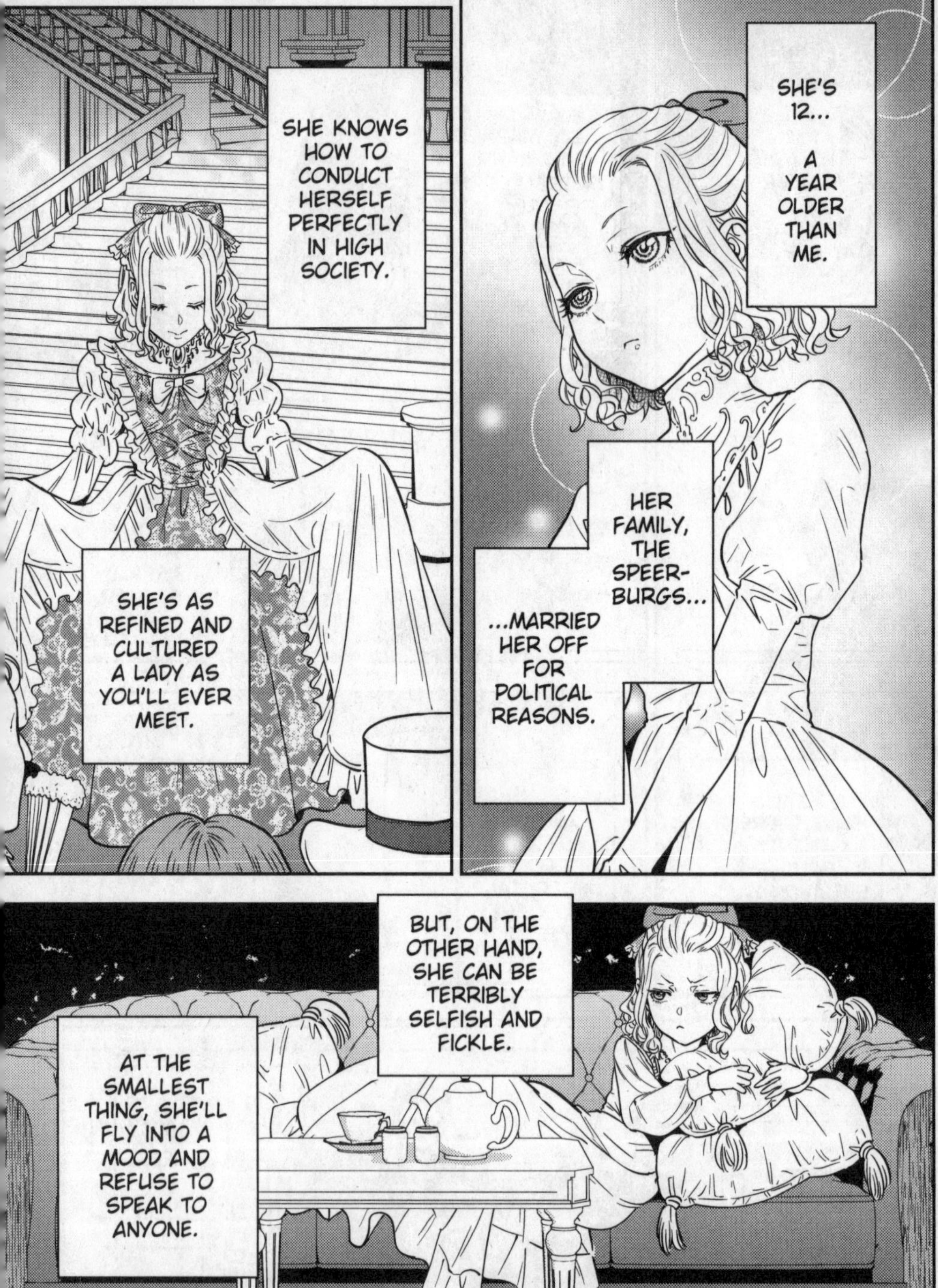
SHE'S 12... A YEAR OLDER THAN ME.
HER FAMILY, THE SPEER-BURGS...
...MARRIED HER OFF FOR POLITICAL REASONS.
SHE KNOWS HOW TO CONDUCT HERSELF PERFECTLY IN HIGH SOCIETY.
SHE'S AS REFINED AND CULTURED A LADY AS YOU'LL EVER MEET.
BUT, ON THE OTHER HAND, SHE CAN BE TERRIBLY SELFISH AND FICKLE.
AT THE SMALLEST THING, SHE'LL FLY INTO A MOOD AND REFUSE TO SPEAK TO ANYONE.

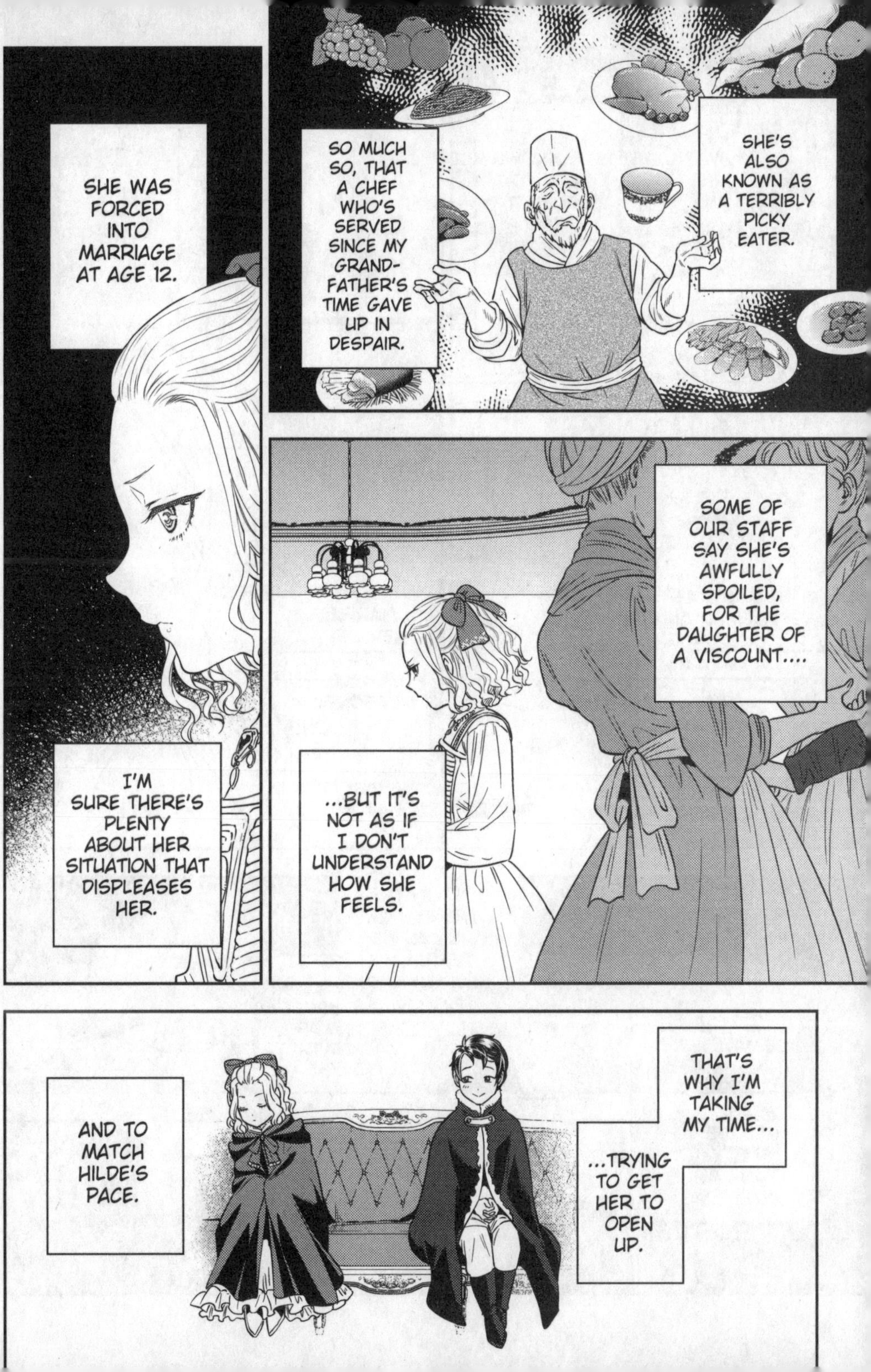
SHE'S ALSO KNOWN AS A TERRIBLY PICKY EATER.
SO MUCH SO, THAT A CHEF WHO'S SERVED SINCE MY GRAND-FATHER'S TIME GAVE UP IN DESPAIR.
SOME OF OUR STAFF SAY SHE'S AWFULLY SPOILED, FOR THE DAUGHTER OF A VISCOUNT....
...BUT IT'S NOT AS IF I DON'T UNDERSTAND HOW SHE FEELS.
SHE WAS FORCED INTO MARRIAGE AT AGE 12.
I'M SURE THERE'S PLENTY ABOUT HER SITUATION THAT DISPLEASES HER.
THAT'S WHY I'M TAKING MY TIME...
...TRYING TO GET HER TO OPEN UP.
AND TO MATCH HILDE'S PACE.

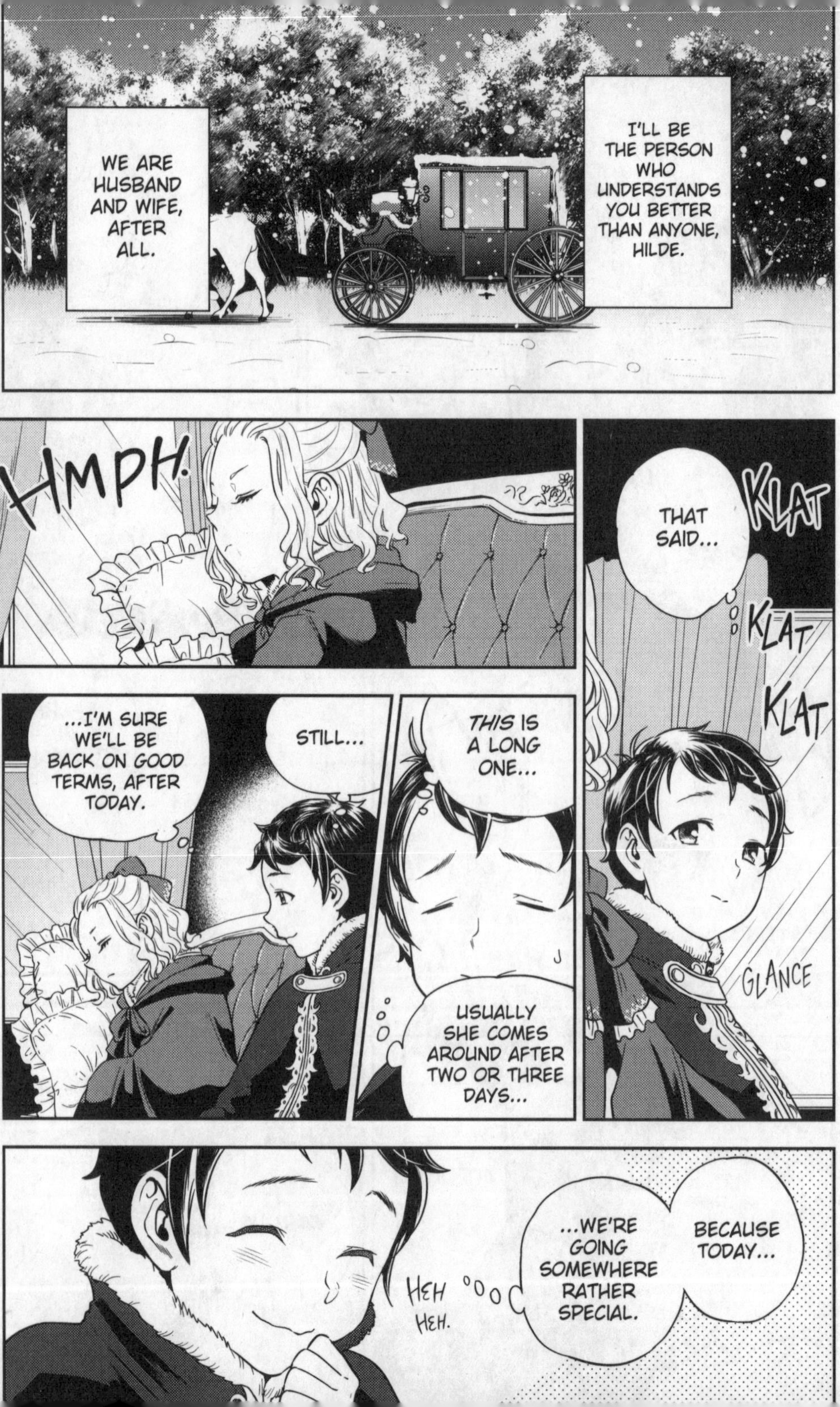
I'LL BE THE PERSON WHO UNDERSTANDS YOU BETTER THAN ANYONE, HILDE.
WE ARE HUSBAND AND WIFE, AFTER ALL.
THAT SAID...
KLAT
KLAT
KLAT
GLANCE
HMPH.
THIS IS A LONG ONE...
USUALLY SHE COMES AROUND AFTER TWO OR THREE DAYS...
STILL...
...I'M SURE WE'LL BE BACK ON GOOD TERMS, AFTER TODAY.
BECAUSE TODAY...
...WE'RE GOING SOMEWHERE RATHER SPECIAL.
HEH HEH.

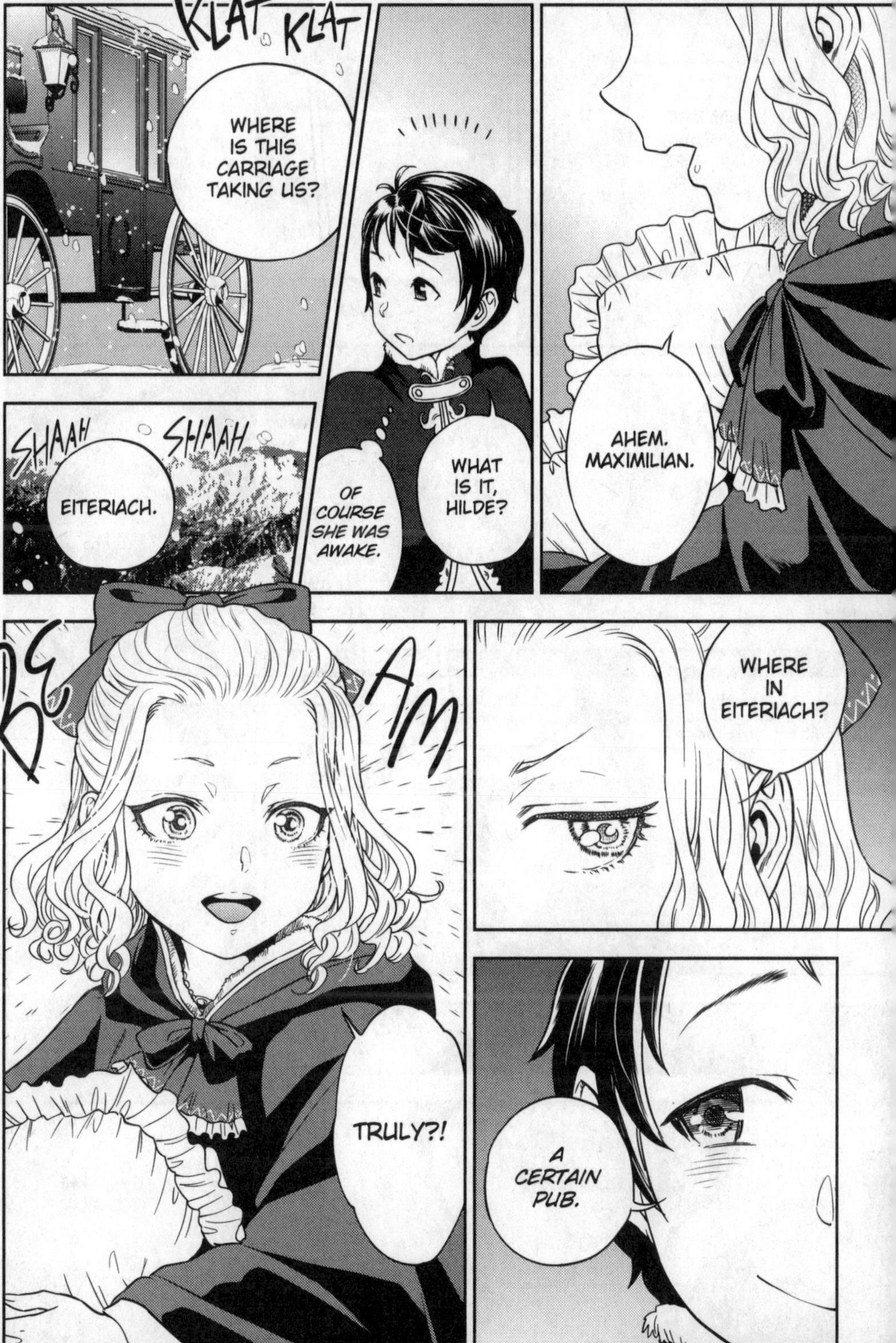
AHEM. MAXIMILIAN.
WHAT IS IT, HILDE?
OF COURSE SHE WAS AWAKE.
KLAT KLAT
WHERE IS THIS CARRIAGE TAKING US?
SHAAH SHAAH
EITERIACH.
WHERE IN EITERIACH?
A CERTAIN PUB.
BEAM
TRULY?!

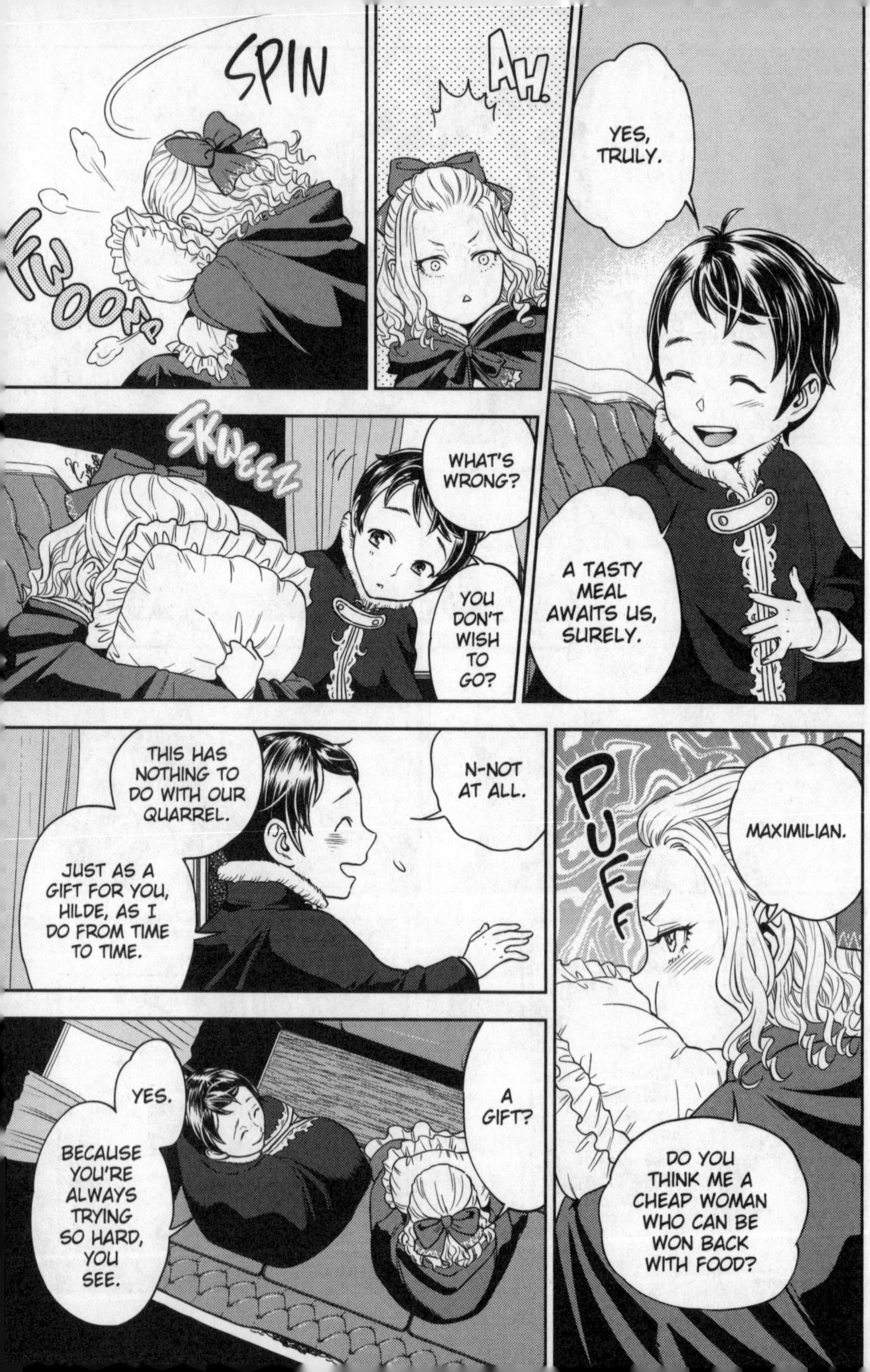
YES, TRULY.
A TASTY MEAL AWAITS US, SURELY.
AH.
SPIN
FWOOMP
SKWEEN
WHAT'S WRONG?
YOU DON'T WISH TO GO?
PUFF
MAXIMILIAN.
DO YOU THINK ME A CHEAP WOMAN WHO CAN BE WON BACK WITH FOOD?
N-NOT AT ALL.
THIS HAS NOTHING TO DO WITH OUR QUARREL.
JUST AS A GIFT FOR YOU, HILDE, AS I DO FROM TIME TO TIME.
A GIFT?
YES.
BECAUSE YOU'RE ALWAYS TRYING SO HARD, YOU SEE.

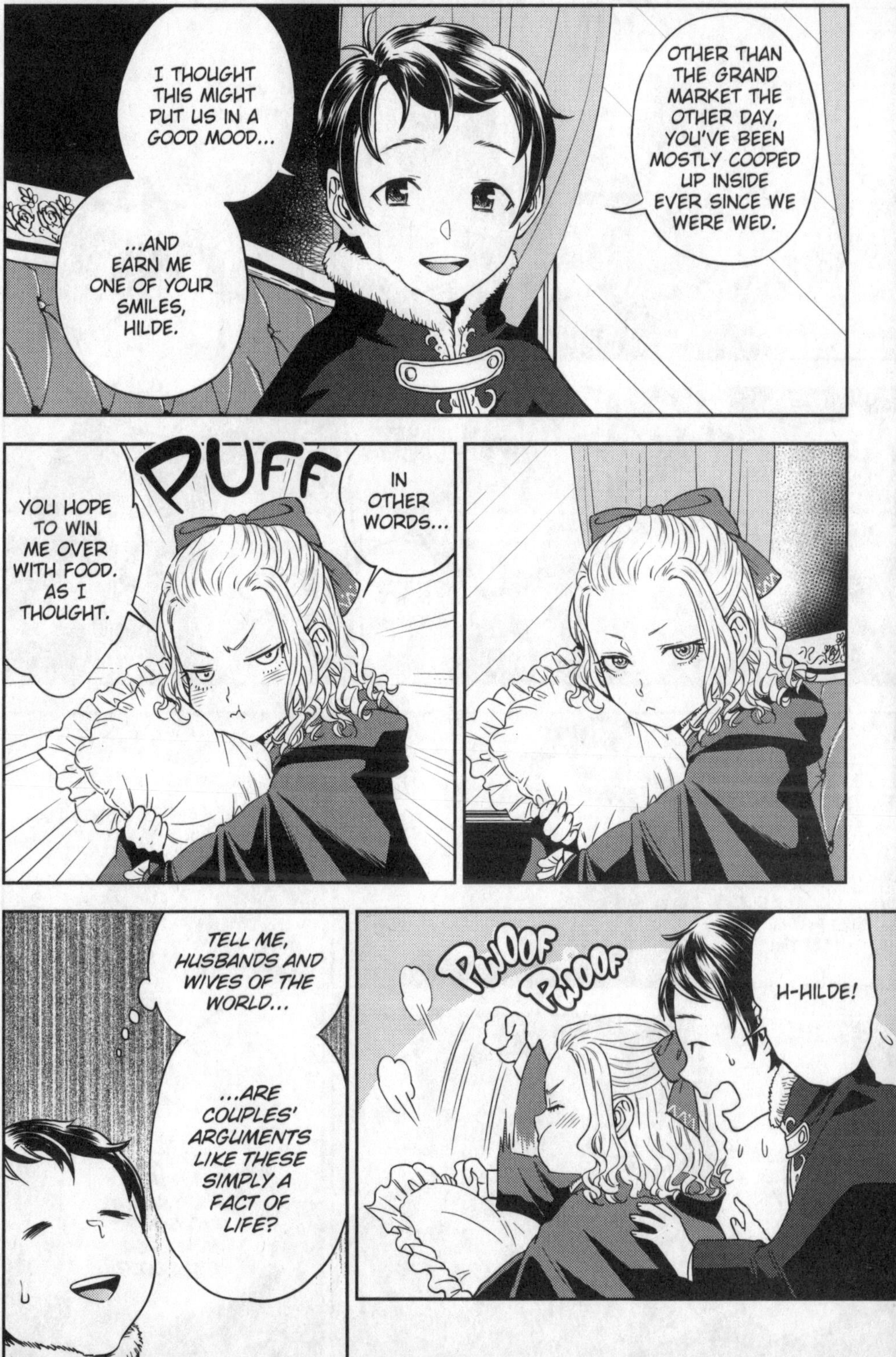
OTHER THAN THE GRAND MARKET THE OTHER DAY, YOU'VE BEEN MOSTLY COOPED UP INSIDE EVER SINCE WE WERE WED.
I THOUGHT THIS MIGHT PUT US IN A GOOD MOOD...
...AND EARN ME ONE OF YOUR SMILES, HILDE.
IN OTHER WORDS...
PUFF
YOU HOPE TO WIN ME OVER WITH FOOD. AS I THOUGHT.
H-HILDE!
PWOOF PWOOF
TELL ME, HUSBANDS AND WIVES OF THE WORLD...
...ARE COUPLES' ARGUMENTS LIKE THESE SIMPLY A FACT OF LIFE?

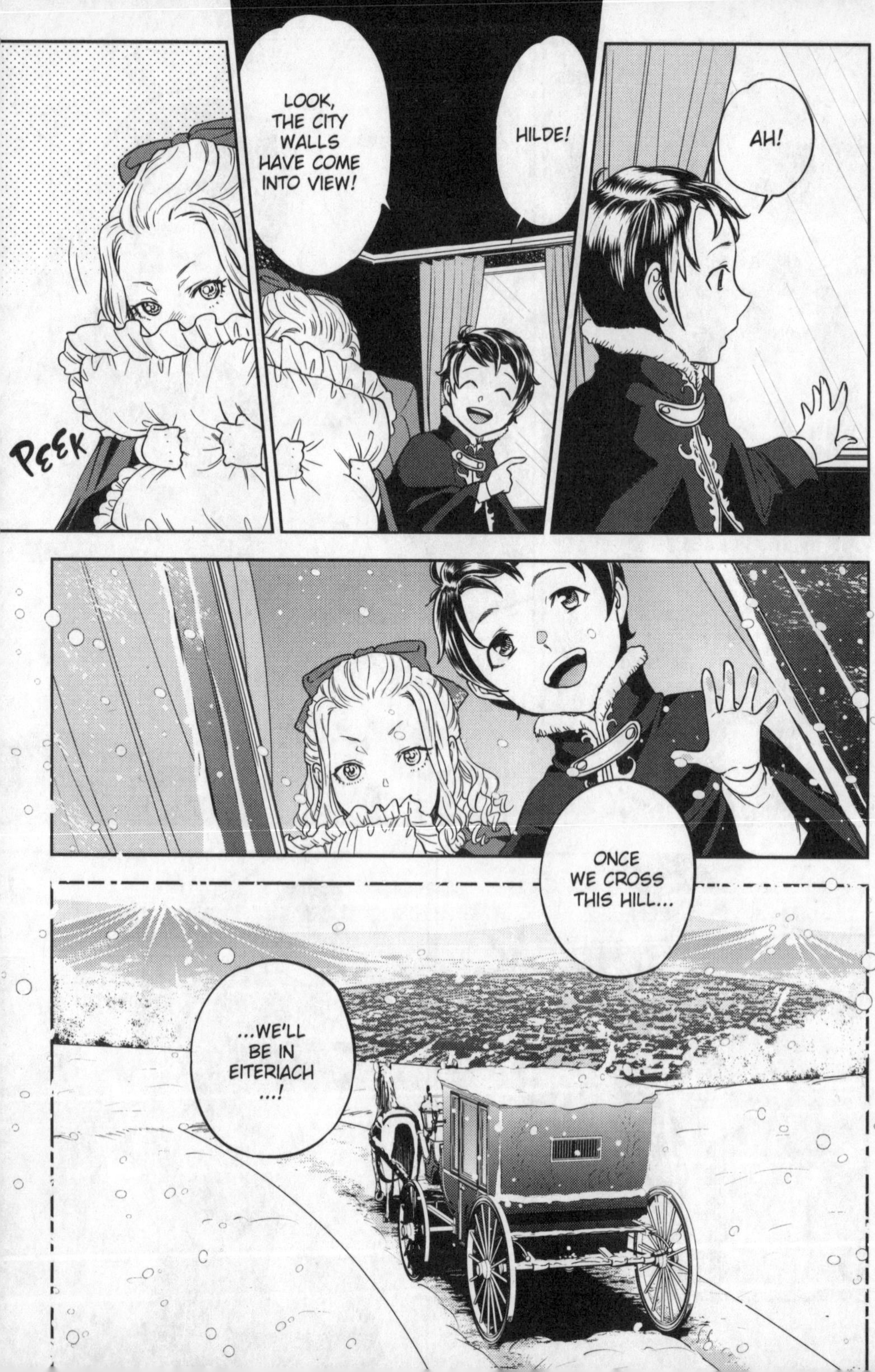
AH!
HILDE!
LOOK, THE CITY WALLS HAVE COME INTO VIEW!
PEEK
ONCE WE CROSS THIS HILL...
...WE'LL BE IN EITERIACH ...!

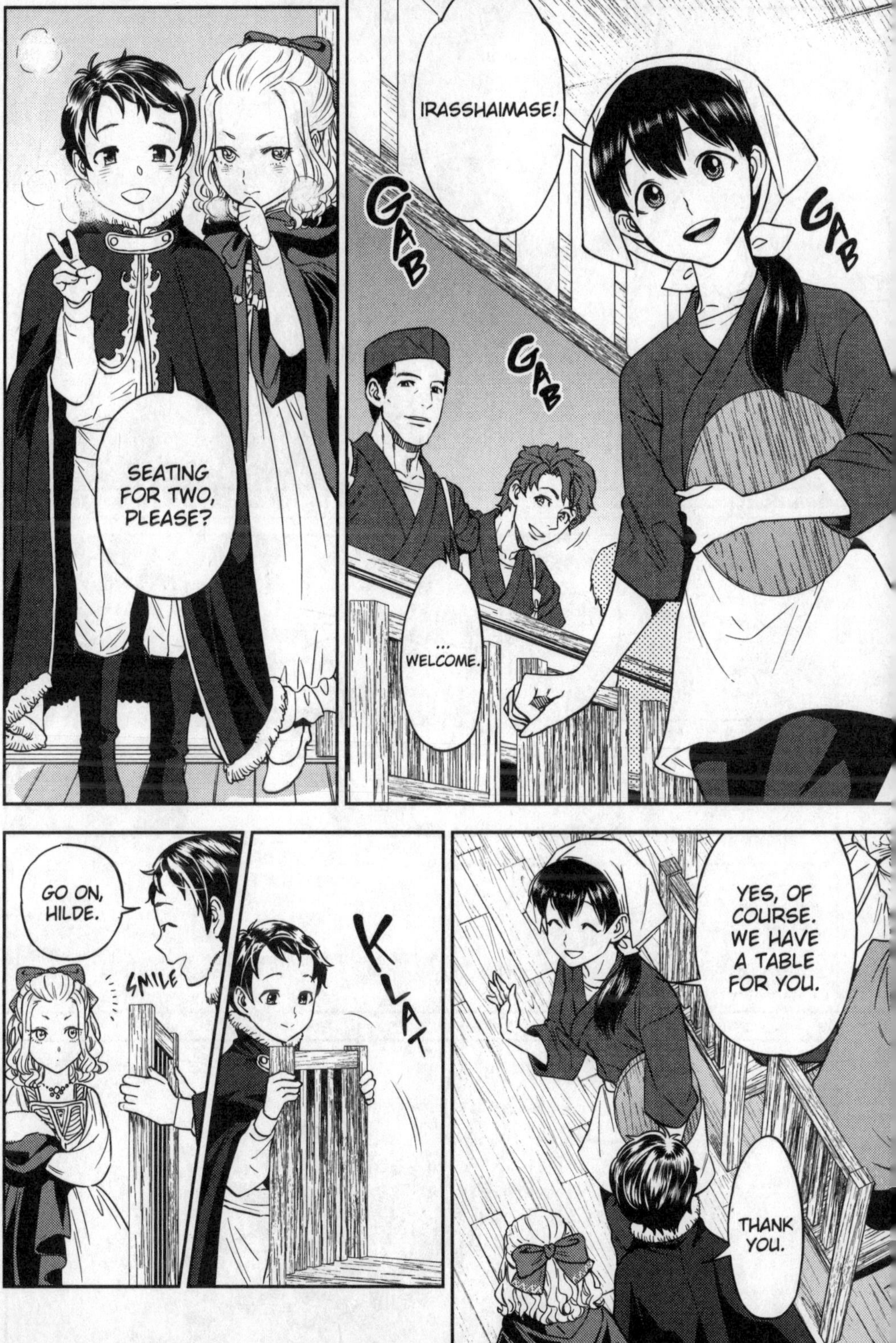
IRASSHAIMASE!
GAB
GAB
GAB
... WELCOME.
SEATING FOR TWO, PLEASE?
YES, OF COURSE. WE HAVE A TABLE FOR YOU.
THANK YOU.
KLAT
GO ON, HILDE.
SMILE

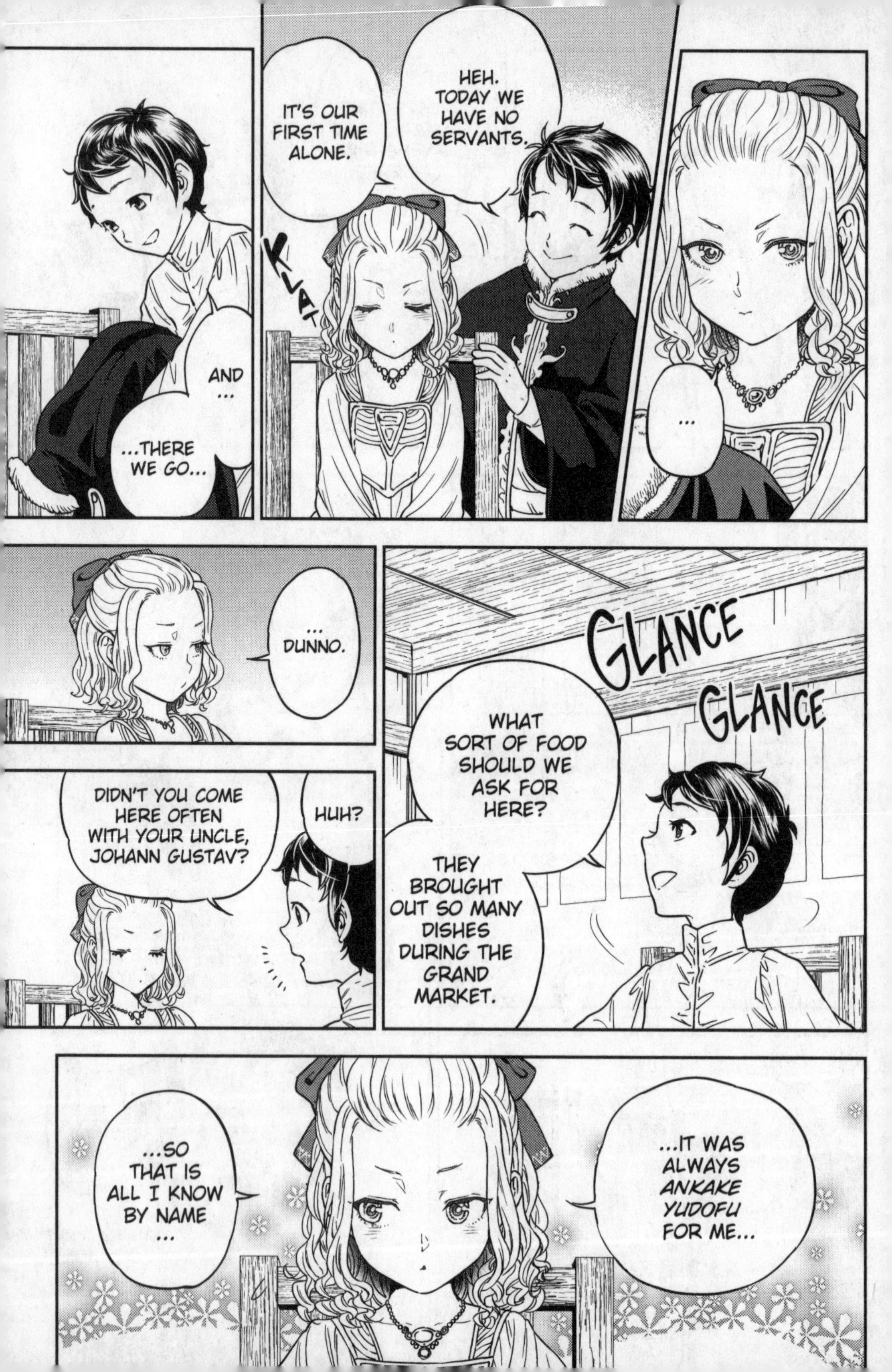
...
HEH. TODAY WE HAVE NO SERVANTS.
IT'S OUR FIRST TIME ALONE.
KLAT
AND ...
...THERE WE GO...
GLANCE
GLANCE
WHAT SORT OF FOOD SHOULD WE ASK FOR HERE?
THEY BROUGHT OUT SO MANY DISHES DURING THE GRAND MARKET.
... DUNNO.
HUH?
DIDN'T YOU COME HERE OFTEN WITH YOUR UNCLE, JOHANN GUSTAV?
...IT WAS ALWAYS ANKAKE YUDOFU FOR ME...
...SO THAT IS ALL I KNOW BY NAME ...

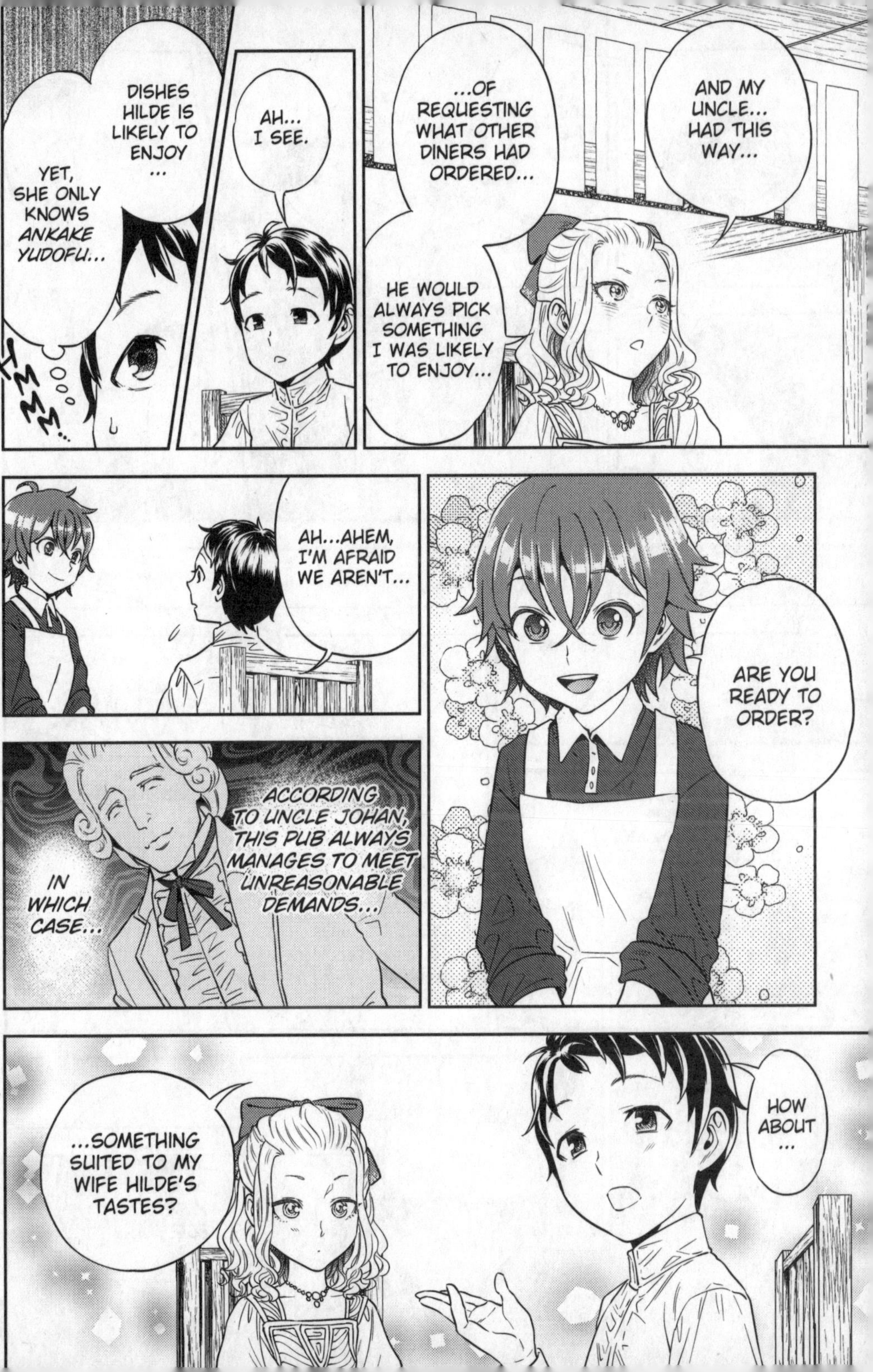
AND MY UNCLE... HAD THIS WAY...
...OF REQUESTING WHAT OTHER DINERS HAD ORDERED...
HE WOULD ALWAYS PICK SOMETHING I WAS LIKELY TO ENJOY...
AH... I SEE.
DISHES HILDE IS LIKELY TO ENJOY ...
YET, SHE ONLY KNOWS ANKAKE YUDOFU...
HMMM...
ARE YOU READY TO ORDER?
AH...AHEM, I'M AFRAID WE AREN'T...
ACCORDING TO UNCLE JOHAN, THIS PUB ALWAYS MANAGES TO MEET UNREASONABLE DEMANDS...
IN WHICH CASE...
HOW ABOUT ...
...SOMETHING SUITED TO MY WIFE HILDE'S TASTES?

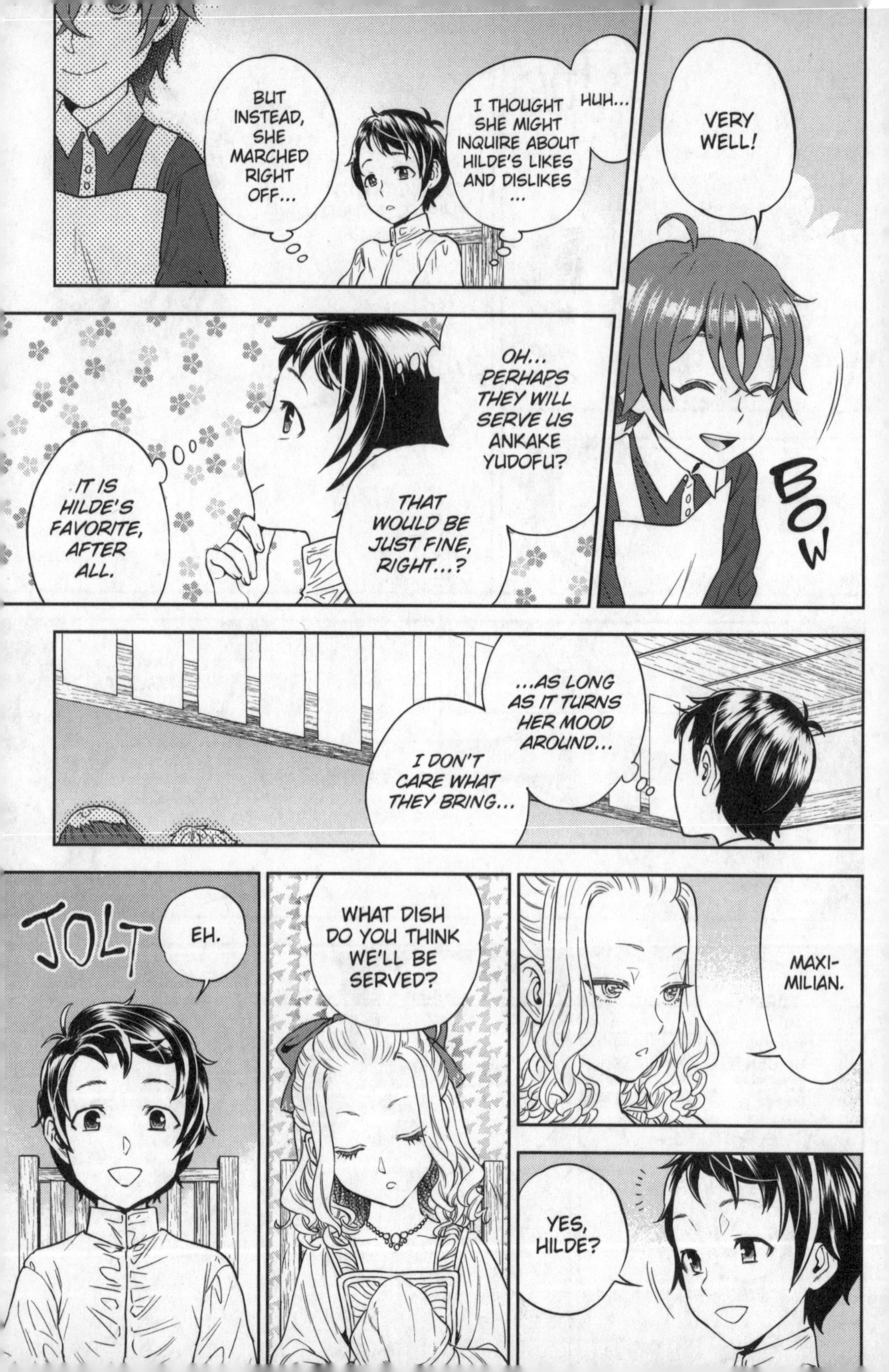
VERY WELL!
BOW
HUH...
I THOUGHT SHE MIGHT INQUIRE ABOUT HILDE'S LIKES AND DISLIKES ...
BUT INSTEAD, SHE MARCHED RIGHT OFF...
OH... PERHAPS THEY WILL SERVE US ANKAKE YUDOFU?
THAT WOULD BE JUST FINE, RIGHT...?
IT IS HILDE'S FAVORITE, AFTER ALL.
...AS LONG AS IT TURNS HER MOOD AROUND...
I DON'T CARE WHAT THEY BRING...
MAXI-MILIAN.
YES, HILDE?
WHAT DISH DO YOU THINK WE'LL BE SERVED?
JOLT
EH.

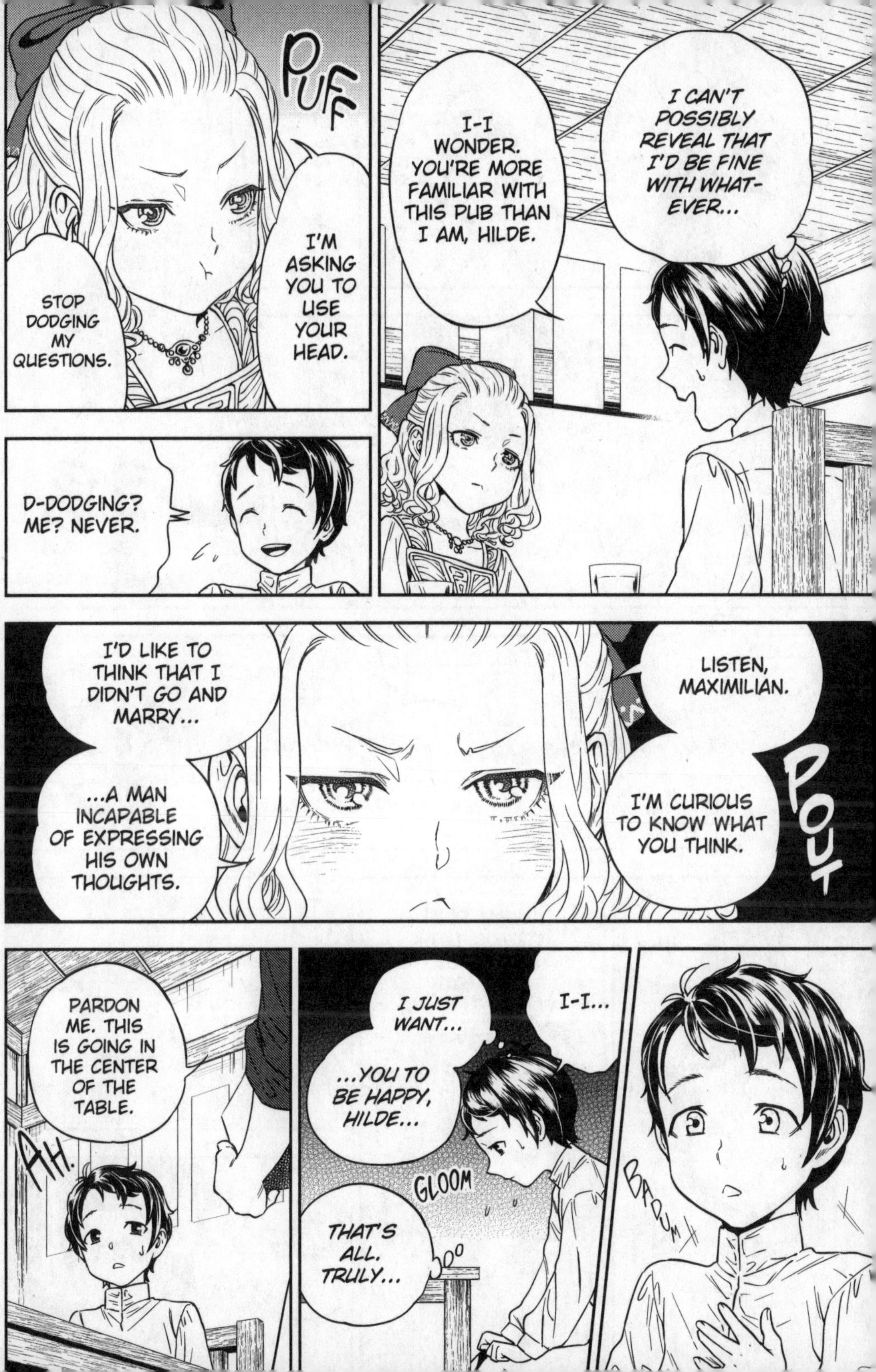
I CAN'T POSSIBLY REVEAL THAT I'D BE FINE WITH WHATEVER...
I-I WONDER. YOU'RE MORE FAMILIAR WITH THIS PUB THAN I AM, HILDE.
PUFF
I'M ASKING YOU TO USE YOUR HEAD.
STOP DODGING MY QUESTIONS.
D-DODGING? ME? NEVER.
LISTEN, MAXIMILIAN.
I'M CURIOUS TO KNOW WHAT YOU THINK.
POUT
I'D LIKE TO THINK THAT I DIDN'T GO AND MARRY...
...A MAN INCAPABLE OF EXPRESSING HIS OWN THOUGHTS.
I-I...
BADUM
I JUST WANT...
...YOU TO BE HAPPY, HILDE...
GLOOM
THAT'S ALL. TRULY...
PARDON ME. THIS IS GOING IN THE CENTER OF THE TABLE.
AH.

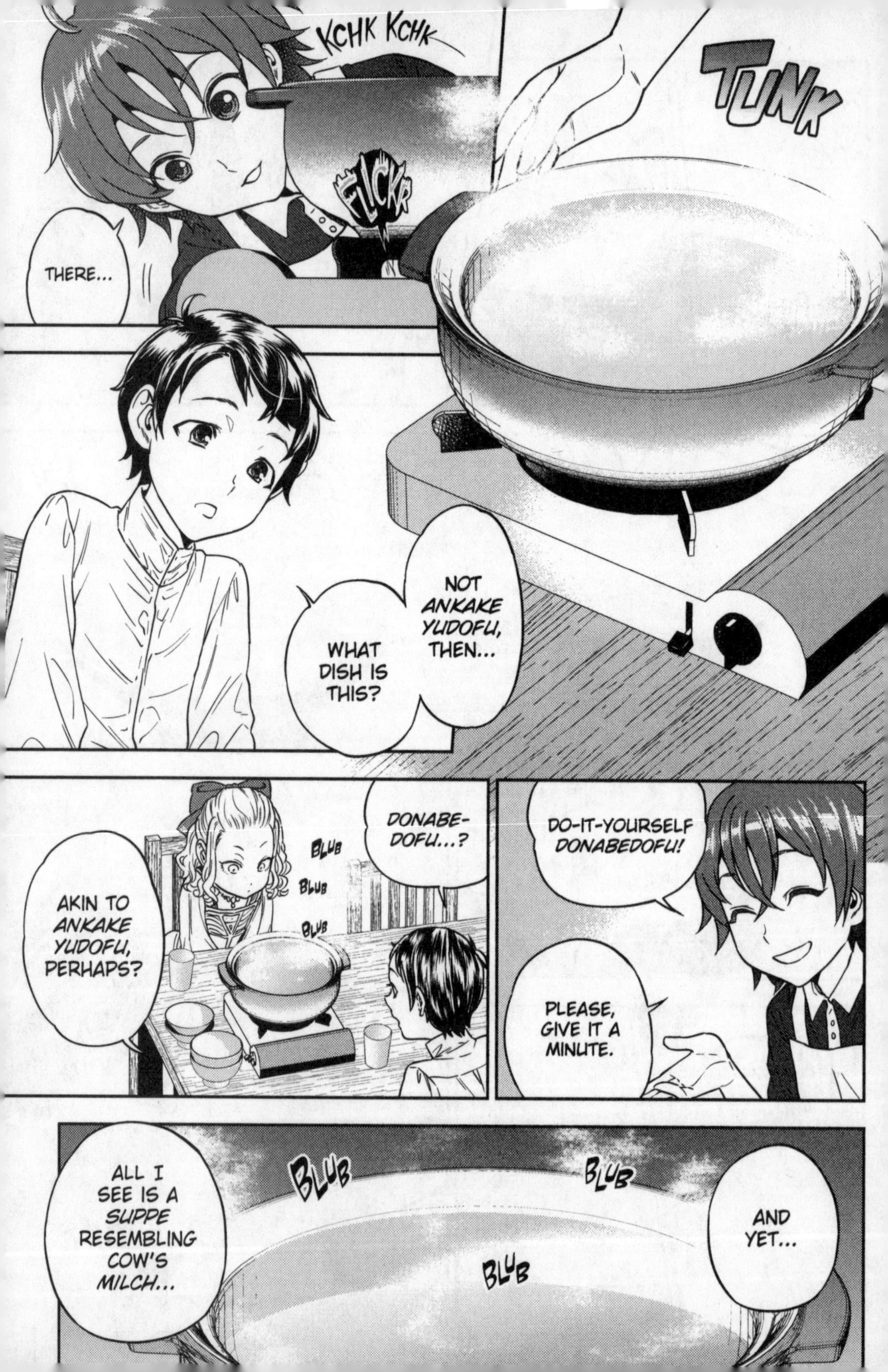
TUNK
KCHK KCHK
FLICKR
THERE...
NOT ANKAKE YUDOFU, THEN...
WHAT DISH IS THIS?
DO-IT-YOURSELF DONABEDOFU!
PLEASE, GIVE IT A MINUTE.
DONABE-DOFU...?
BLUB
BLUB
BLUB
AKIN TO ANKAKE YUDOFU, PERHAPS?
BLUB
AND YET...
BLUB
BLUB
ALL I SEE IS A SUPPE RESEMBLING COW'S MILCH...

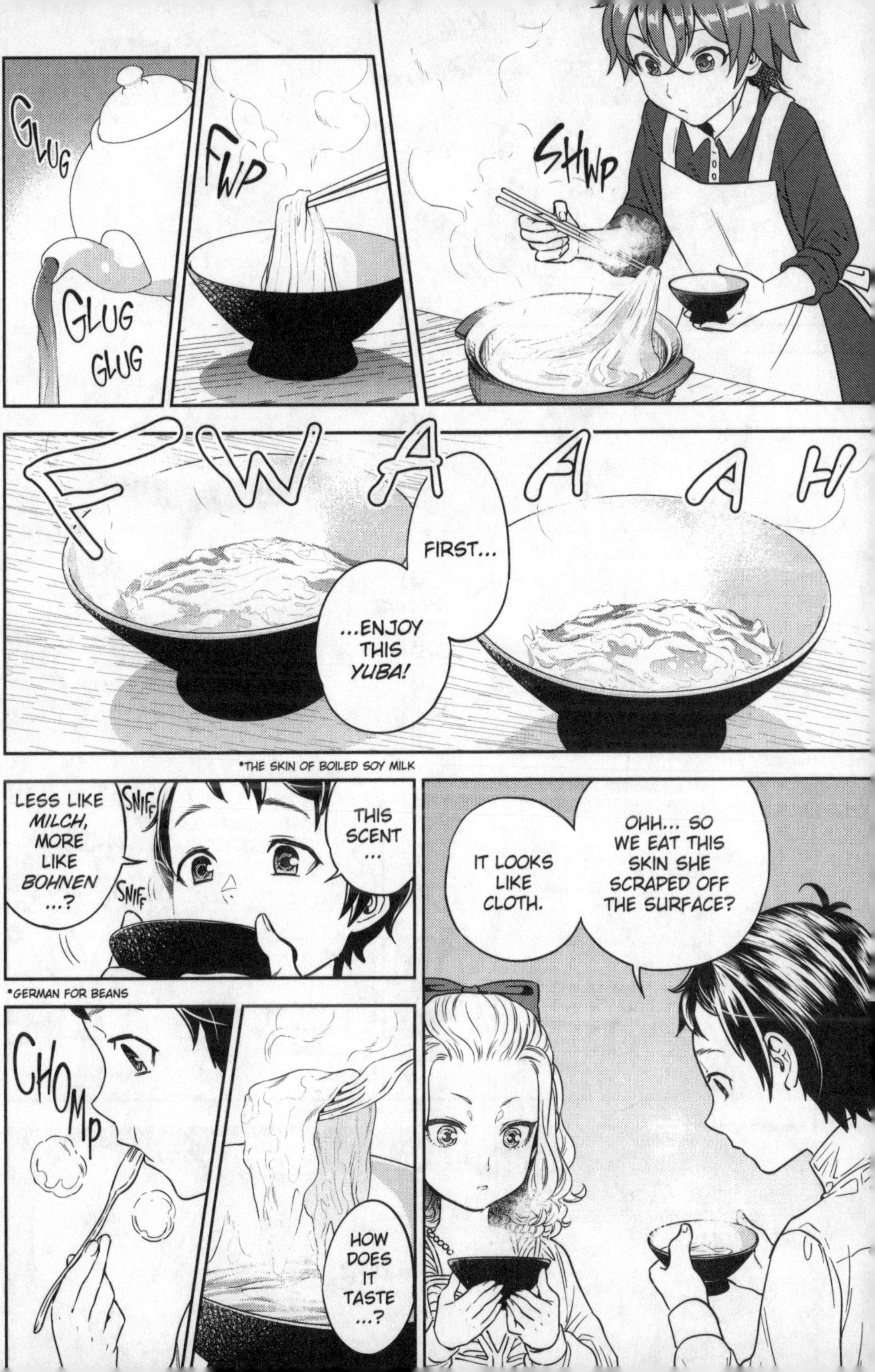
SHWP
FWP
GLUG
GLUG
GLUG
GLUG
FWAAAH
FIRST...
...ENJOY THIS YUBA!
*THE SKIN OF BOILED SOY MILK
OHH... SO WE EAT THIS SKIN SHE SCRAPED OFF THE SURFACE?
IT LOOKS LIKE CLOTH.
THIS SCENT...
SNIFF
SNIFF
LESS LIKE MILCH, MORE LIKE BOHNEN...?
*GERMAN FOR BEANS
HOW DOES IT TASTE...?
CHOMP

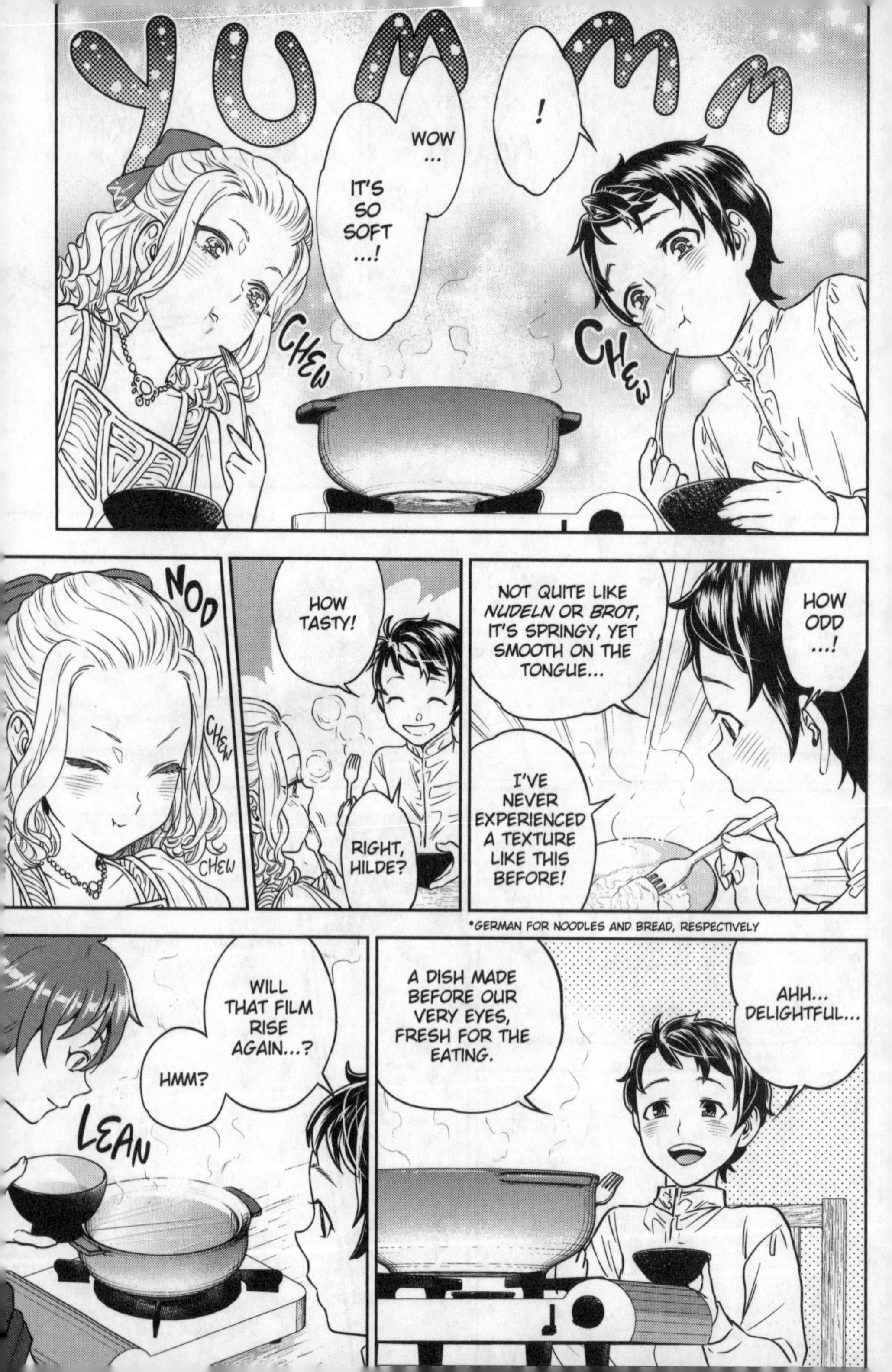
YUMMM
!
WOW ... IT'S SO SOFT ...!
CHEW
CHEW
HOW ODD ...!
NOT QUITE LIKE *NUDELN* OR *BROT*, IT'S SPRINGY, YET SMOOTH ON THE TONGUE...
I'VE NEVER EXPERIENCED A TEXTURE LIKE THIS BEFORE!
HOW TASTY!
RIGHT, HILDE?
NOD
CHEW
CHEW
*GERMAN FOR NOODLES AND BREAD, RESPECTIVELY
AHH... DELIGHTFUL...
A DISH MADE BEFORE OUR VERY EYES, FRESH FOR THE EATING.
WILL THAT FILM RISE AGAIN...?
HMM?
LEAN

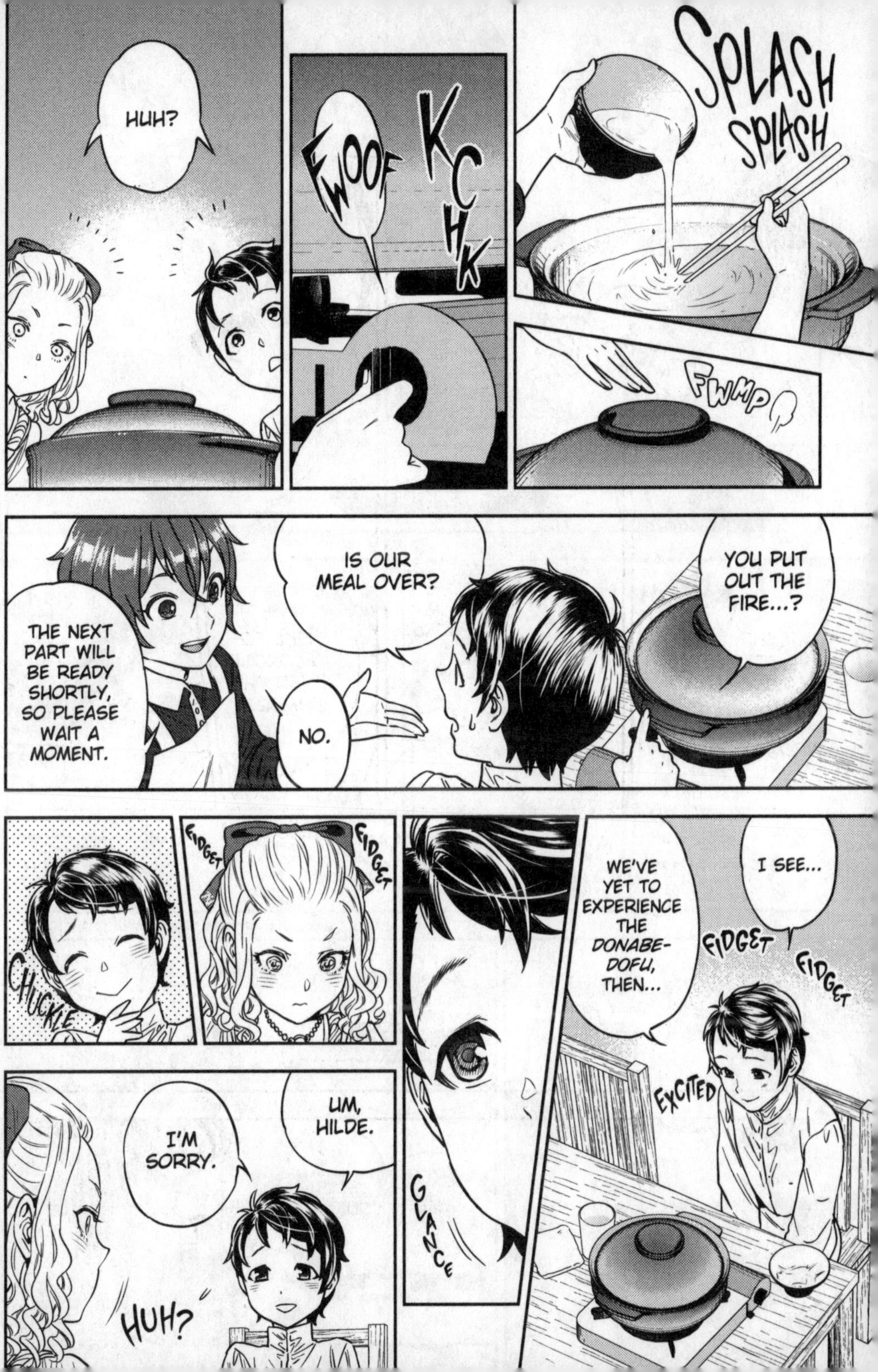
SPLASH
SPLASH
FWMP
KCHK
FWOOF
HUH?
YOU PUT OUT THE FIRE...?
IS OUR MEAL OVER?
NO.
THE NEXT PART WILL BE READY SHORTLY, SO PLEASE WAIT A MOMENT.
I SEE...
WE'VE YET TO EXPERIENCE THE *DONABE-DOFU*, THEN...
FIDGET
FIDGET
EXCITED
GLANCE
FIDGET
FIDGET
CHUCKLE
UM, HILDE.
I'M SORRY.
HUH?

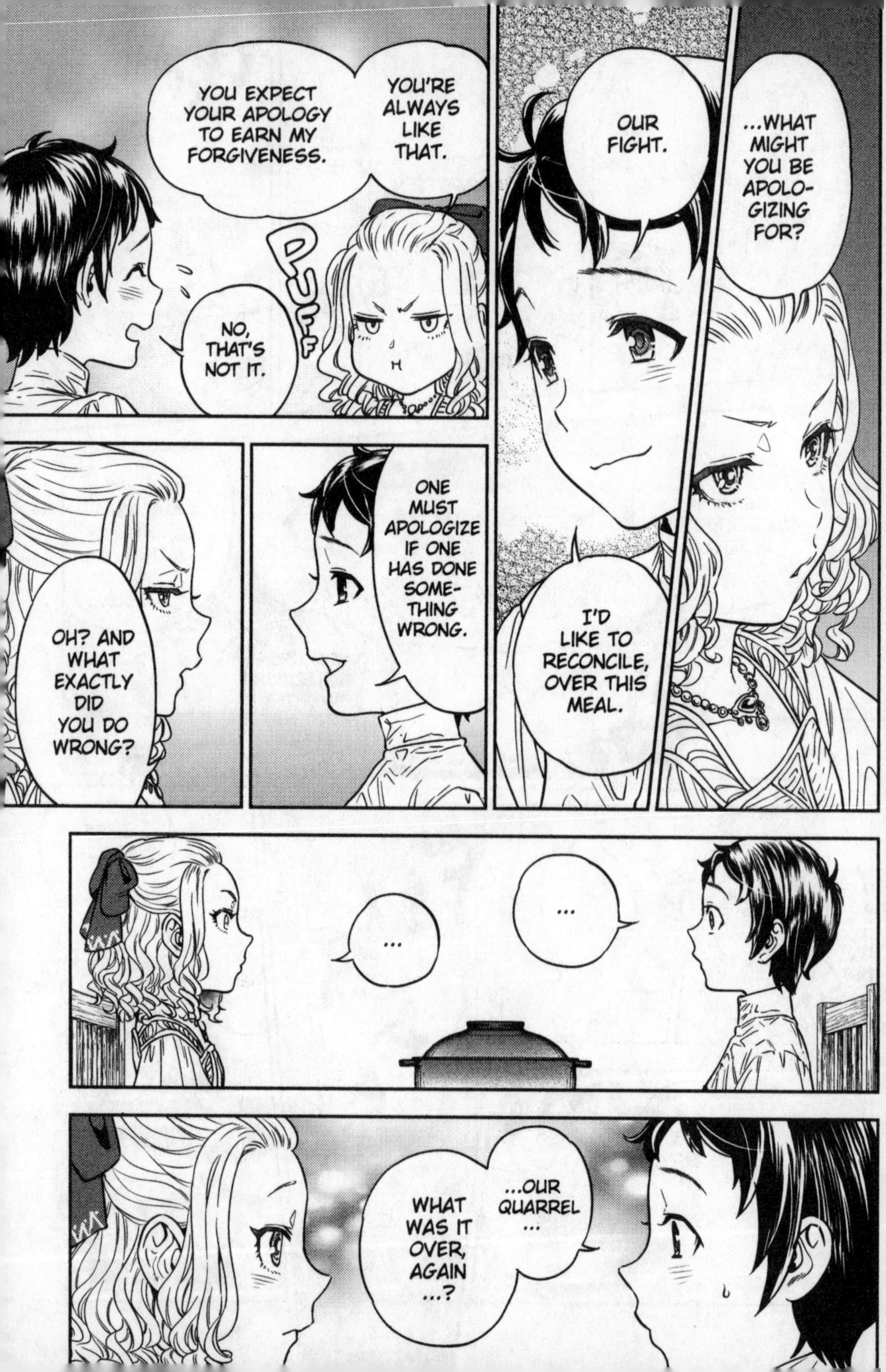
...WHAT MIGHT YOU BE APOLOGIZING FOR?
OUR FIGHT.
I'D LIKE TO RECONCILE, OVER THIS MEAL.
YOU'RE ALWAYS LIKE THAT.
YOU EXPECT YOUR APOLOGY TO EARN MY FORGIVENESS.
PUFF
NO, THAT'S NOT IT.
ONE MUST APOLOGIZE IF ONE HAS DONE SOMETHING WRONG.
OH? AND WHAT EXACTLY DID YOU DO WRONG?
...
...
...OUR QUARREL ...
WHAT WAS IT OVER, AGAIN ...?

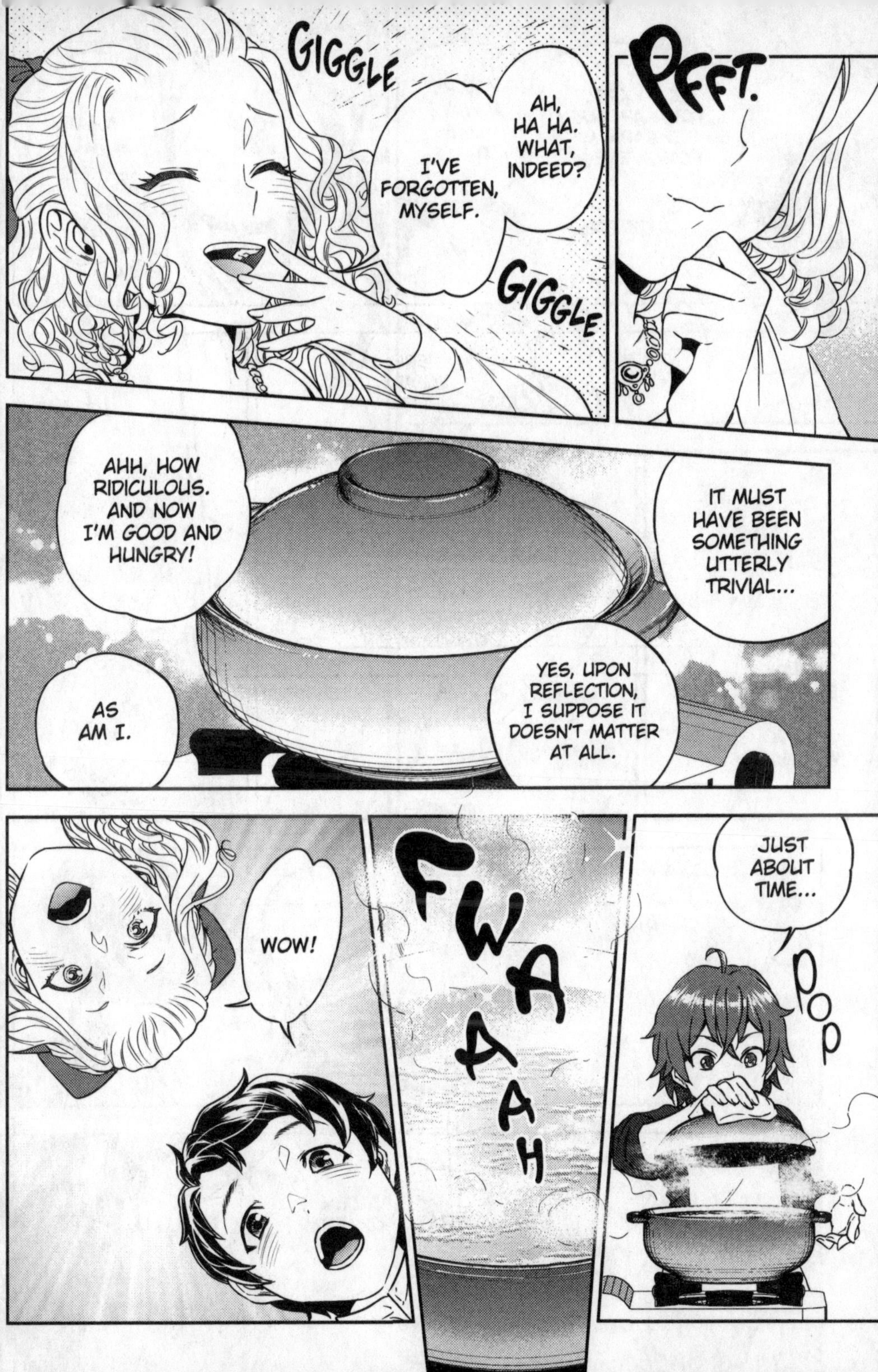
PFFT.
AH, HA HA. WHAT, INDEED?
GIGGLE
I'VE FORGOTTEN, MYSELF.
GIGGLE
IT MUST HAVE BEEN SOMETHING UTTERLY TRIVIAL...
AHH, HOW RIDICULOUS. AND NOW I'M GOOD AND HUNGRY!
YES, UPON REFLECTION, I SUPPOSE IT DOESN'T MATTER AT ALL.
AS AM I.
JUST ABOUT TIME...
POP
FWAAAH
WOW!

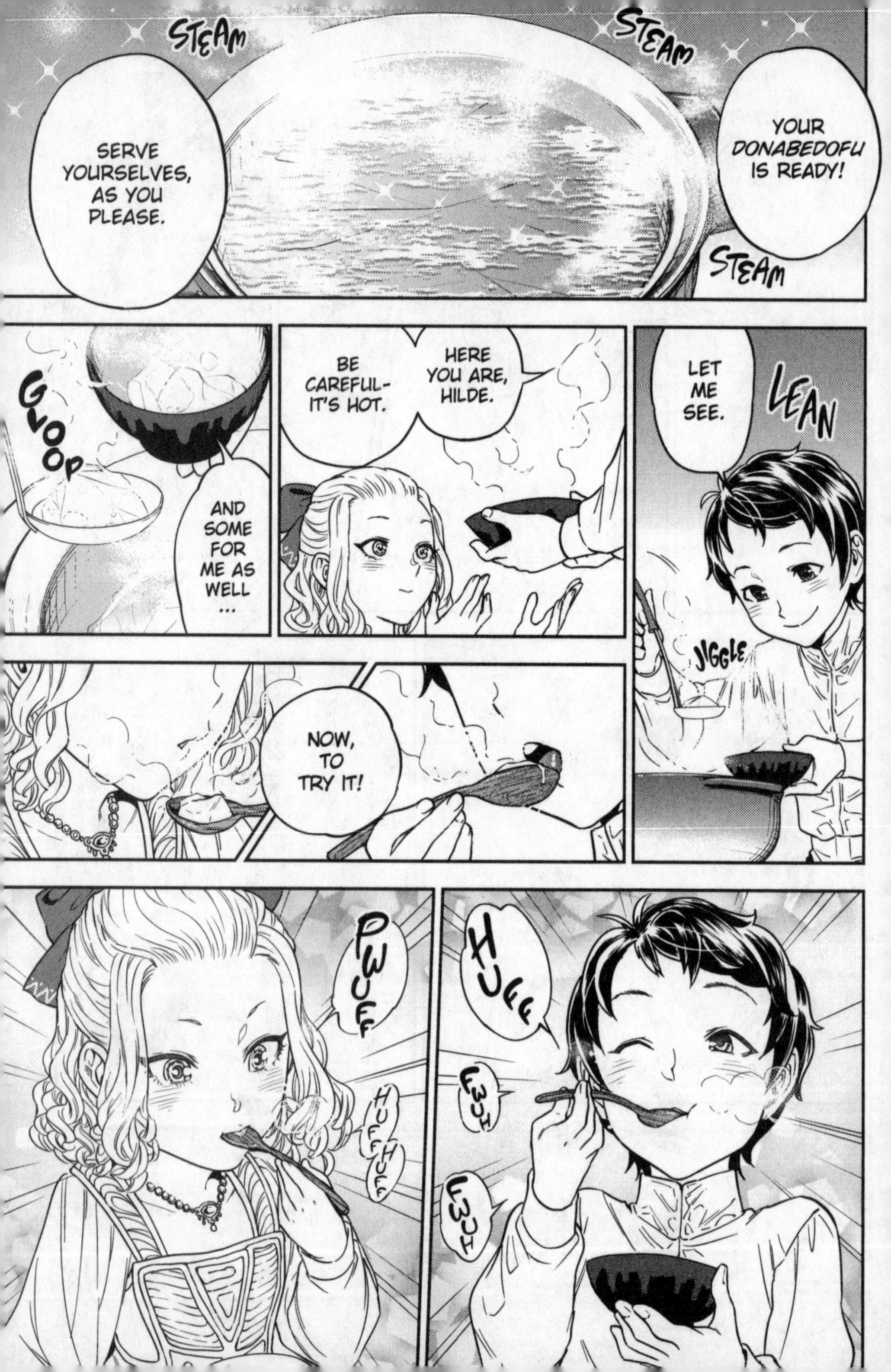
STEAM
YOUR DONABEDOFU IS READY!
STEAM
STEAM
SERVE YOURSELVES, AS YOU PLEASE.
LET ME SEE.
LEAN
JIGGLE
HERE YOU ARE, HILDE.
BE CAREFUL- IT'S HOT.
AND SOME FOR ME AS WELL ...
GLOOP
NOW, TO TRY IT!
HUFF
FWUH
FWUH
PWUFF
HUFF HUFF HUFF

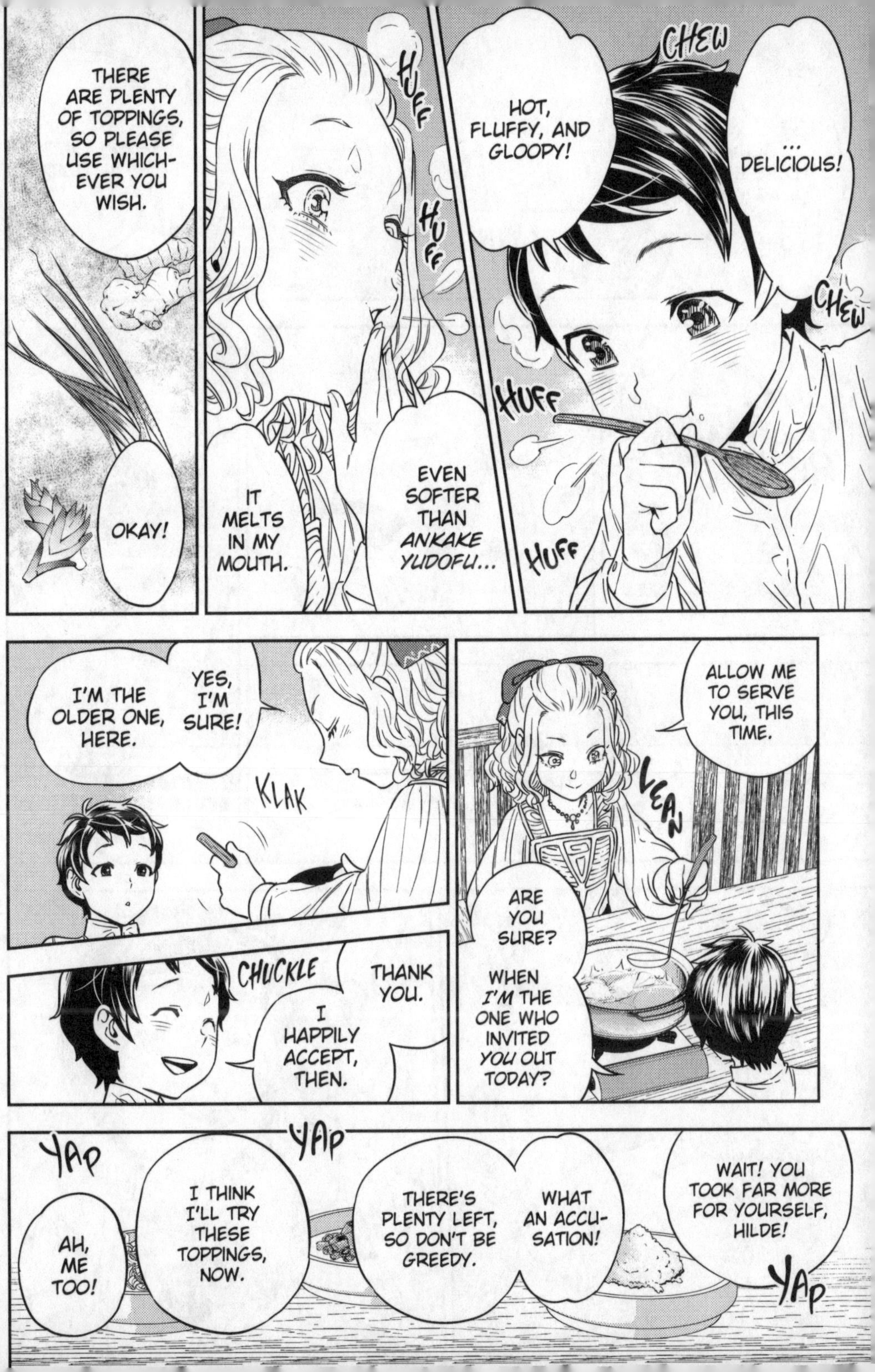
CHEW
... DELICIOUS!
HOT, FLUFFY, AND GLOOPY!
CHEW
HUFF
HUFF
HUFF
HUFF HUFF
EVEN SOFTER THAN *ANKAKE YUDOFU*...
IT MELTS IN MY MOUTH.
THERE ARE PLENTY OF TOPPINGS, SO PLEASE USE WHICH-EVER YOU WISH.
OKAY!
ALLOW ME TO SERVE YOU, THIS TIME.
LEAN
ARE YOU SURE?
WHEN *I'M* THE ONE WHO INVITED *YOU* OUT TODAY?
YES, I'M SURE!
I'M THE OLDER ONE, HERE.
KLAK
THANK YOU.
I HAPPILY ACCEPT, THEN.
CHUCKLE
WAIT! YOU TOOK FAR MORE FOR YOURSELF, HILDE!
YAP
WHAT AN ACCU-SATION!
THERE'S PLENTY LEFT, SO DON'T BE GREEDY.
YAP
I THINK I'LL TRY THESE TOPPINGS, NOW.
AH, ME TOO!
YAP

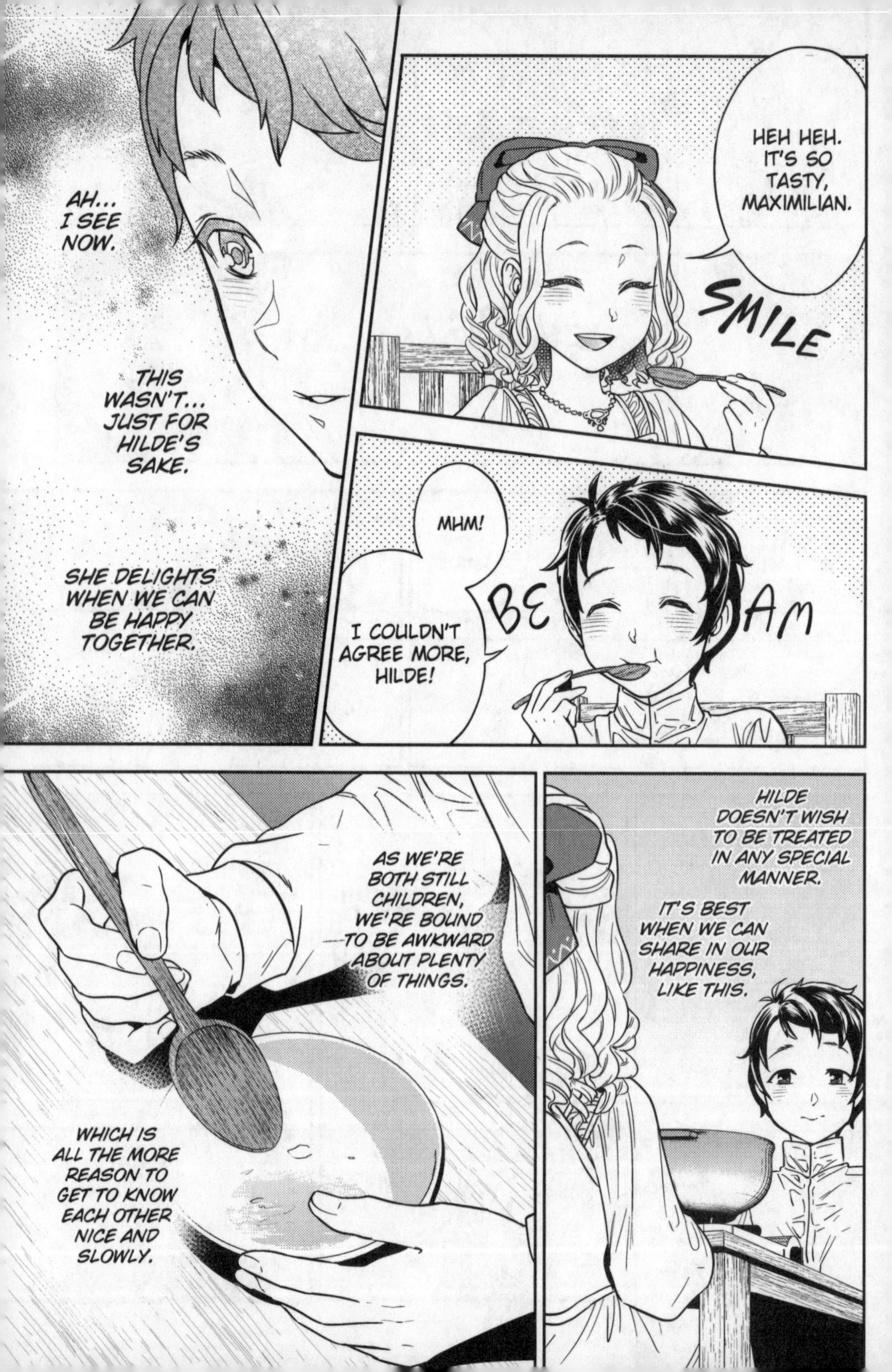
HEH HEH. IT'S SO TASTY, MAXIMILIAN.
SMILE
MHM!
I COULDN'T AGREE MORE, HILDE!
BEAM
AH... I SEE NOW.
THIS WASN'T... JUST FOR HILDE'S SAKE.
SHE DELIGHTS WHEN WE CAN BE HAPPY TOGETHER.
HILDE DOESN'T WISH TO BE TREATED IN ANY SPECIAL MANNER.
IT'S BEST WHEN WE CAN SHARE IN OUR HAPPINESS, LIKE THIS.
AS WE'RE BOTH STILL CHILDREN, WE'RE BOUND TO BE AWKWARD ABOUT PLENTY OF THINGS.
WHICH IS ALL THE MORE REASON TO GET TO KNOW EACH OTHER NICE AND SLOWLY.

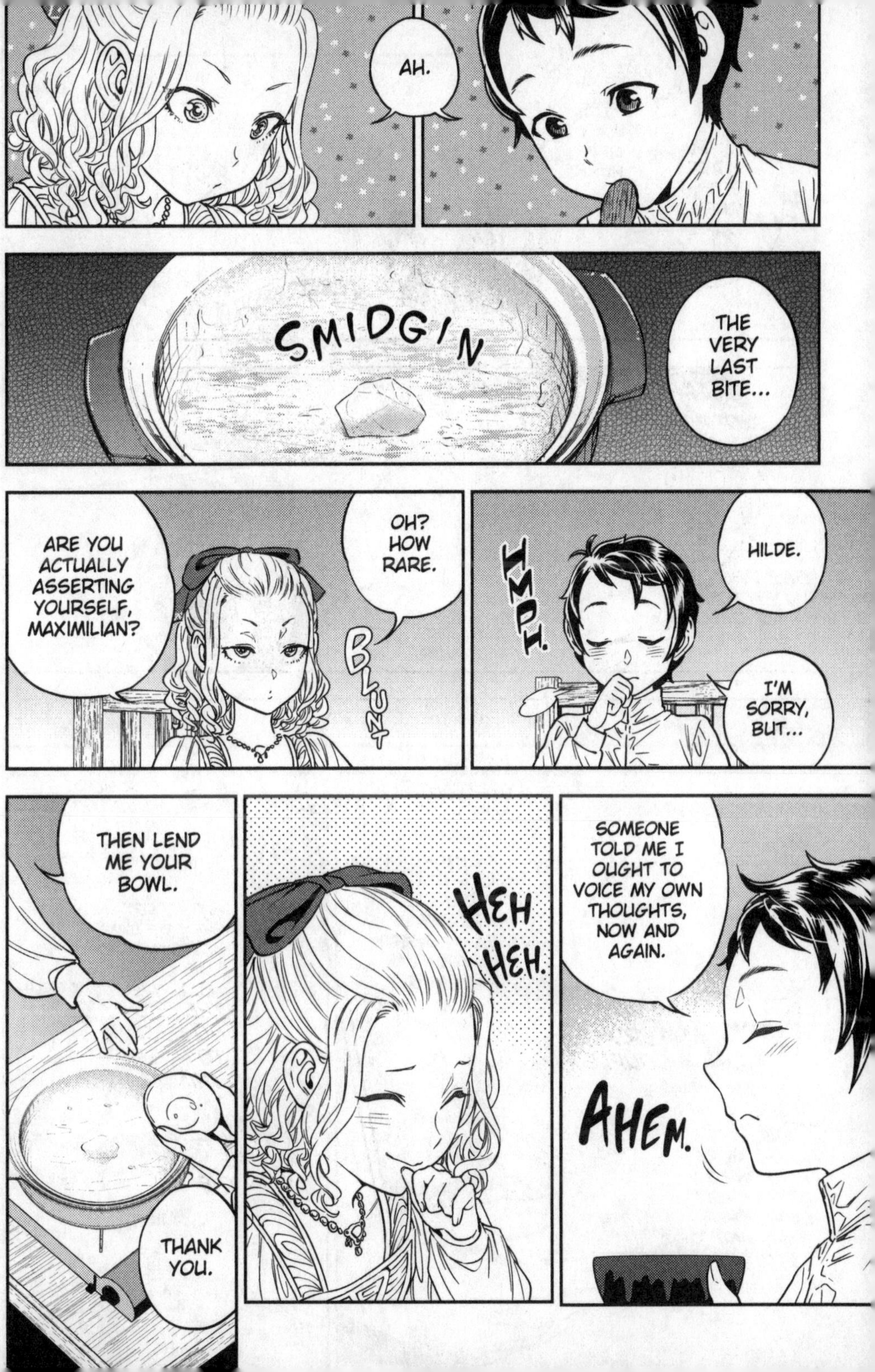
AH.
THE VERY LAST BITE...
SMIDGIN
HILDE.
HMPH.
I'M SORRY, BUT...
OH? HOW RARE.
ARE YOU ACTUALLY ASSERTING YOURSELF, MAXIMILIAN?
BLUNT
SOMEONE TOLD ME I OUGHT TO VOICE MY OWN THOUGHTS, NOW AND AGAIN.
AHEM.
HEH HEH.
THEN LEND ME YOUR BOWL.
THANK YOU.

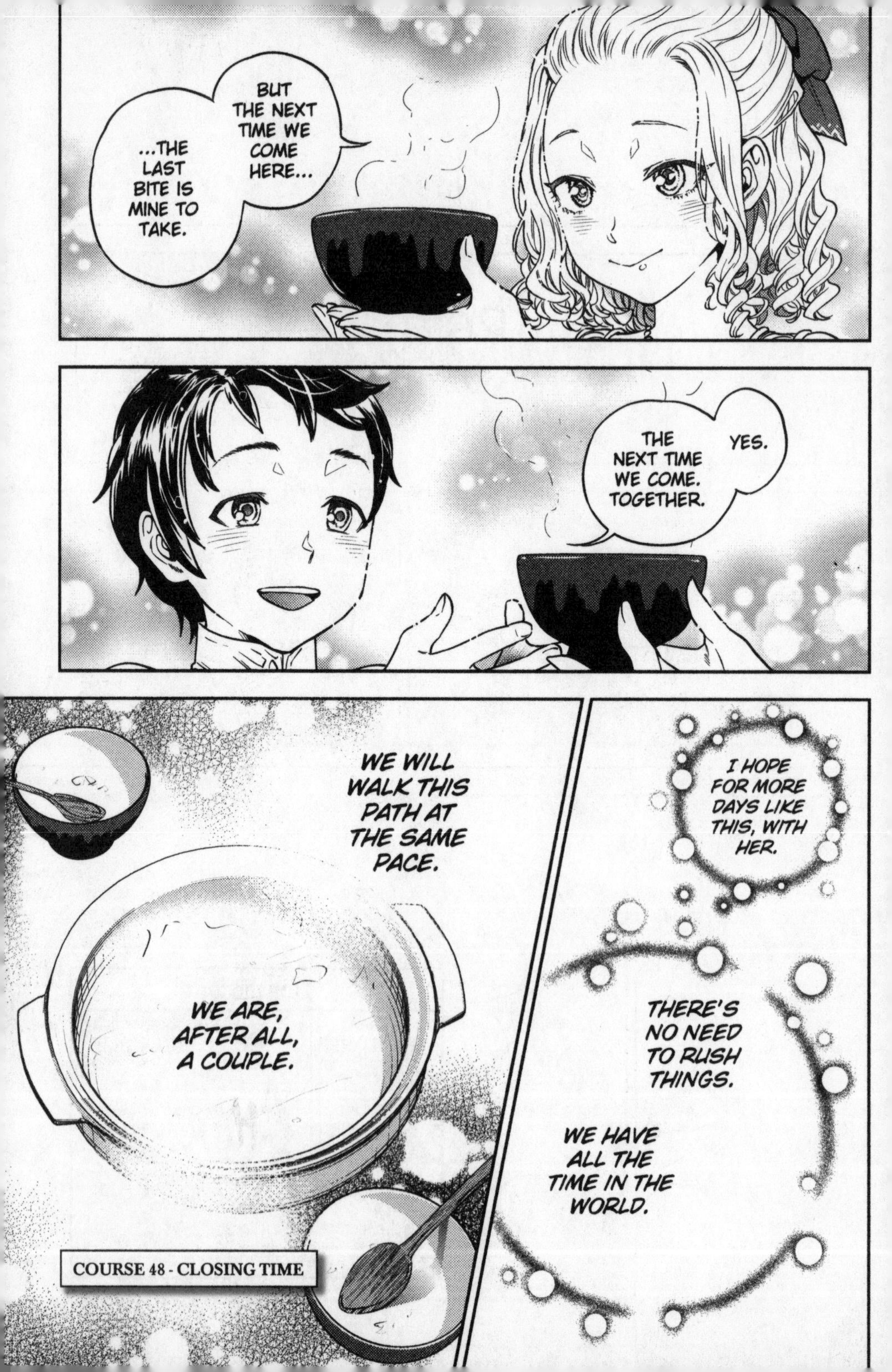
BUT THE NEXT TIME WE COME HERE...
...THE LAST BITE IS MINE TO TAKE.
YES.
THE NEXT TIME WE COME. TOGETHER.
I HOPE FOR MORE DAYS LIKE THIS, WITH HER.
THERE'S NO NEED TO RUSH THINGS.
WE HAVE ALL THE TIME IN THE WORLD.
WE WILL WALK THIS PATH AT THE SAME PACE.
WE ARE, AFTER ALL, A COUPLE.
COURSE 48 - CLOSING TIME

Donabedofu

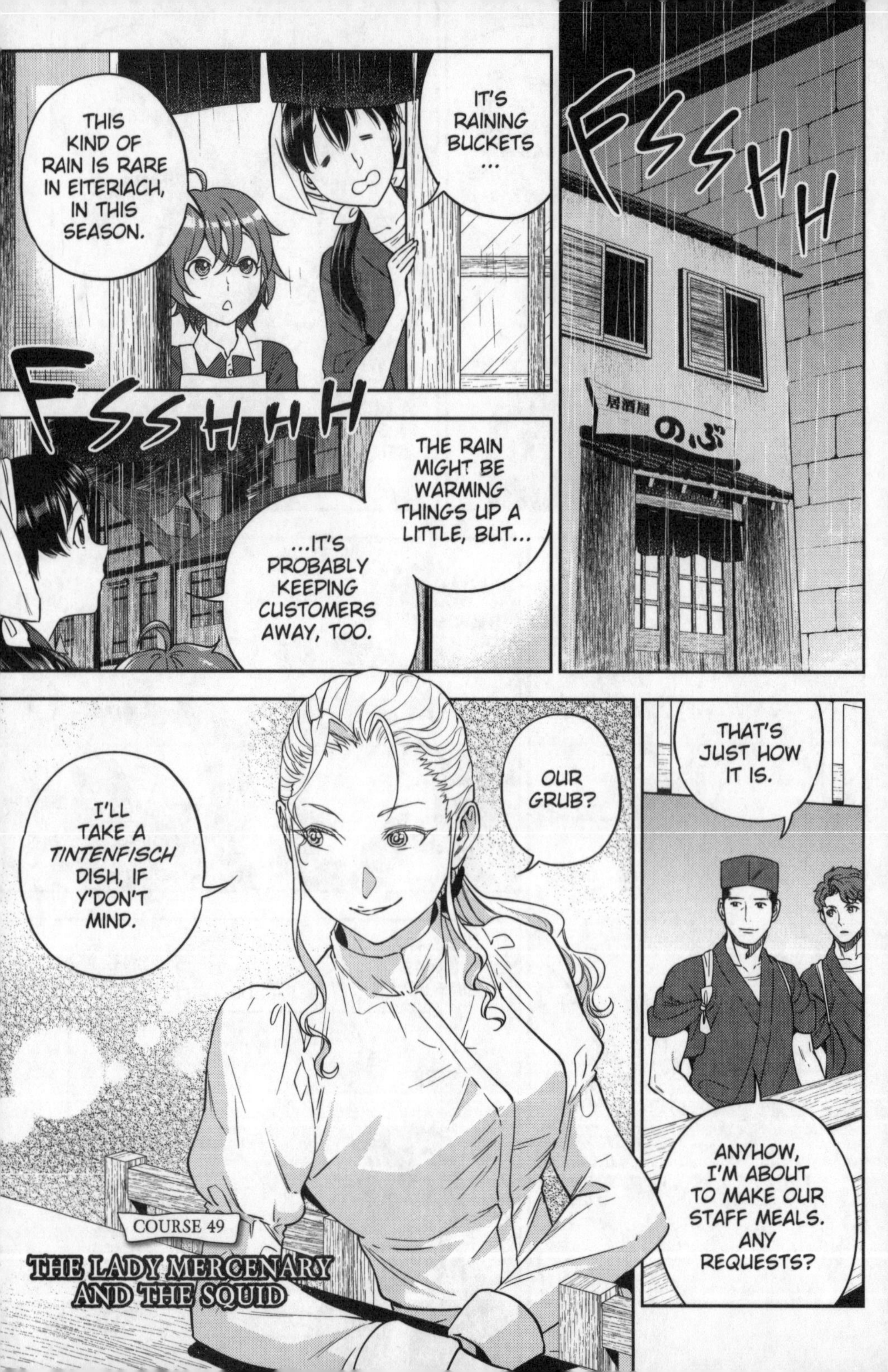
FSSHH
居酒屋
のぶ
IT'S RAINING BUCKETS ...
THIS KIND OF RAIN IS RARE IN EITERIACH, IN THIS SEASON.
FSSHHH
THE RAIN MIGHT BE WARMING THINGS UP A LITTLE, BUT...
...IT'S PROBABLY KEEPING CUSTOMERS AWAY, TOO.
THAT'S JUST HOW IT IS.
ANYHOW, I'M ABOUT TO MAKE OUR STAFF MEALS. ANY REQUESTS?
OUR GRUB?
I'LL TAKE A *TINTENFISCH* DISH, IF Y'DON'T MIND.
COURSE 49
THE LADY MERCENARY AND THE SQUID

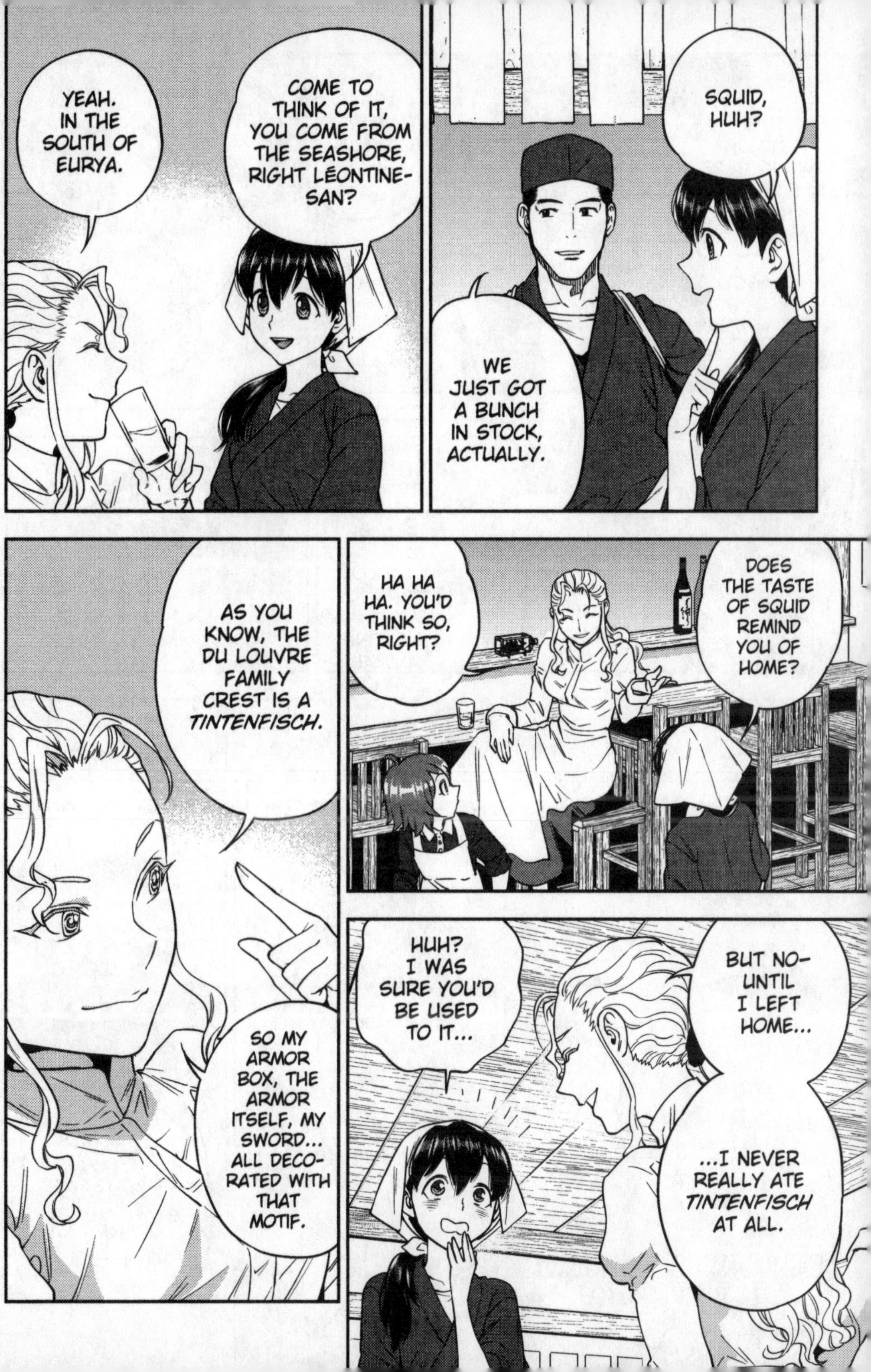
SQUID, HUH?
WE JUST GOT A BUNCH IN STOCK, ACTUALLY.
COME TO THINK OF IT, YOU COME FROM THE SEASHORE, RIGHT LÉONTINE-SAN?
YEAH. IN THE SOUTH OF EURYA.
DOES THE TASTE OF SQUID REMIND YOU OF HOME?
HA HA HA. YOU'D THINK SO, RIGHT?
BUT NO- UNTIL I LEFT HOME...
...I NEVER REALLY ATE *TINTENFISCH* AT ALL.
HUH? I WAS SURE YOU'D BE USED TO IT...
AS YOU KNOW, THE DU LOUVRE FAMILY CREST IS A *TINTENFISCH*.
SO MY ARMOR BOX, THE ARMOR ITSELF, MY SWORD... ALL DECO-RATED WITH THAT MOTIF.

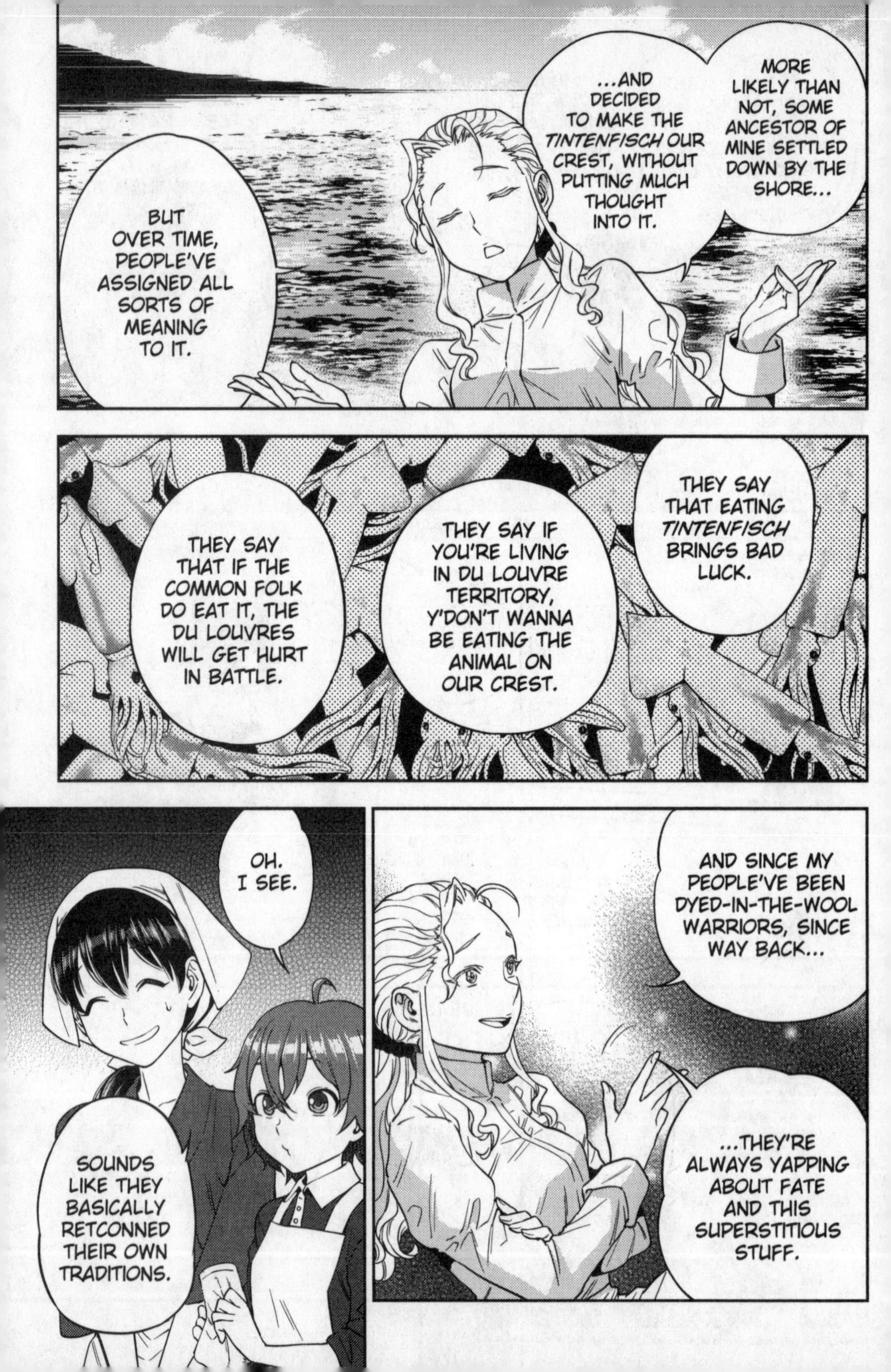
MORE LIKELY THAN NOT, SOME ANCESTOR OF MINE SETTLED DOWN BY THE SHORE...
...AND DECIDED TO MAKE THE *TINTENFISCH* OUR CREST, WITHOUT PUTTING MUCH THOUGHT INTO IT.
BUT OVER TIME, PEOPLE'VE ASSIGNED ALL SORTS OF MEANING TO IT.
THEY SAY THAT EATING *TINTENFISCH* BRINGS BAD LUCK.
THEY SAY IF YOU'RE LIVING IN DU LOUVRE TERRITORY, Y'DON'T WANNA BE EATING THE ANIMAL ON OUR CREST.
THEY SAY THAT IF THE COMMON FOLK DO EAT IT, THE DU LOUVRES WILL GET HURT IN BATTLE.
AND SINCE MY PEOPLE'VE BEEN DYED-IN-THE-WOOL WARRIORS, SINCE WAY BACK...
...THEY'RE ALWAYS YAPPING ABOUT FATE AND THIS SUPERSTITIOUS STUFF.
OH. I SEE.
SOUNDS LIKE THEY BASICALLY RETCONNED THEIR OWN TRADITIONS.

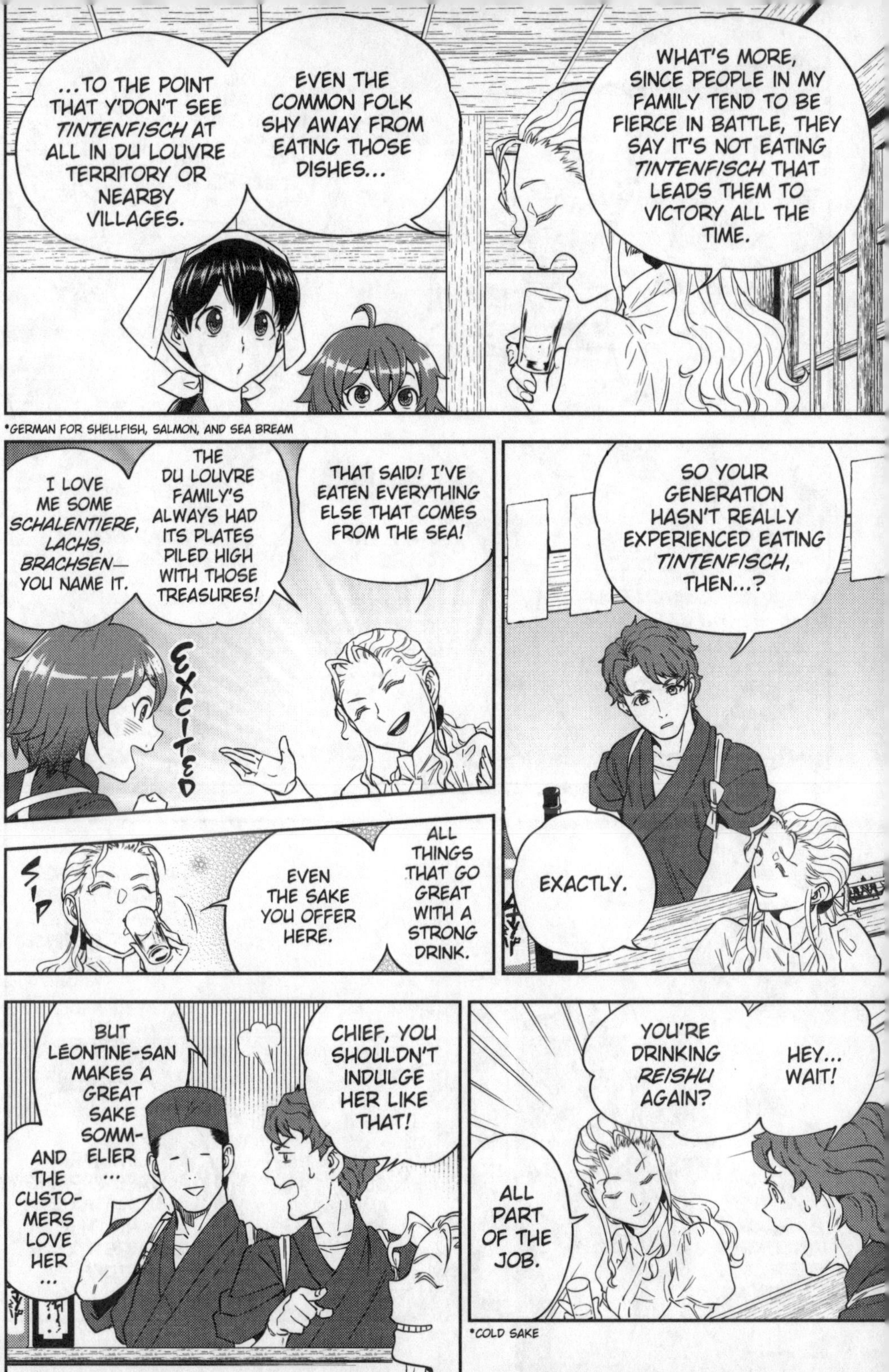
WHAT'S MORE, SINCE PEOPLE IN MY FAMILY TEND TO BE FIERCE IN BATTLE, THEY SAY IT'S NOT EATING TINTENFISCH THAT LEADS THEM TO VICTORY ALL THE TIME.
EVEN THE COMMON FOLK SHY AWAY FROM EATING THOSE DISHES...
...TO THE POINT THAT Y'DON'T SEE TINTENFISCH AT ALL IN DU LOUVRE TERRITORY OR NEARBY VILLAGES.
*GERMAN FOR SHELLFISH, SALMON, AND SEA BREAM
SO YOUR GENERATION HASN'T REALLY EXPERIENCED EATING TINTENFISCH, THEN...?
EXACTLY.
THAT SAID! I'VE EATEN EVERYTHING ELSE THAT COMES FROM THE SEA!
THE DU LOUVRE FAMILY'S ALWAYS HAD ITS PLATES PILED HIGH WITH THOSE TREASURES!
I LOVE ME SOME SCHALENTIERE, LACHS, BRACHSEN—YOU NAME IT.
EXCITED
ALL THINGS THAT GO GREAT WITH A STRONG DRINK.
EVEN THE SAKE YOU OFFER HERE.
SIP
HEY... WAIT!
YOU'RE DRINKING REISHU AGAIN?
ALL PART OF THE JOB.
*COLD SAKE
CHIEF, YOU SHOULDN'T INDULGE HER LIKE THAT!
BUT LÉONTINE-SAN MAKES A GREAT SAKE SOMM-ELIER...
AND THE CUSTO-MERS LOVE HER...

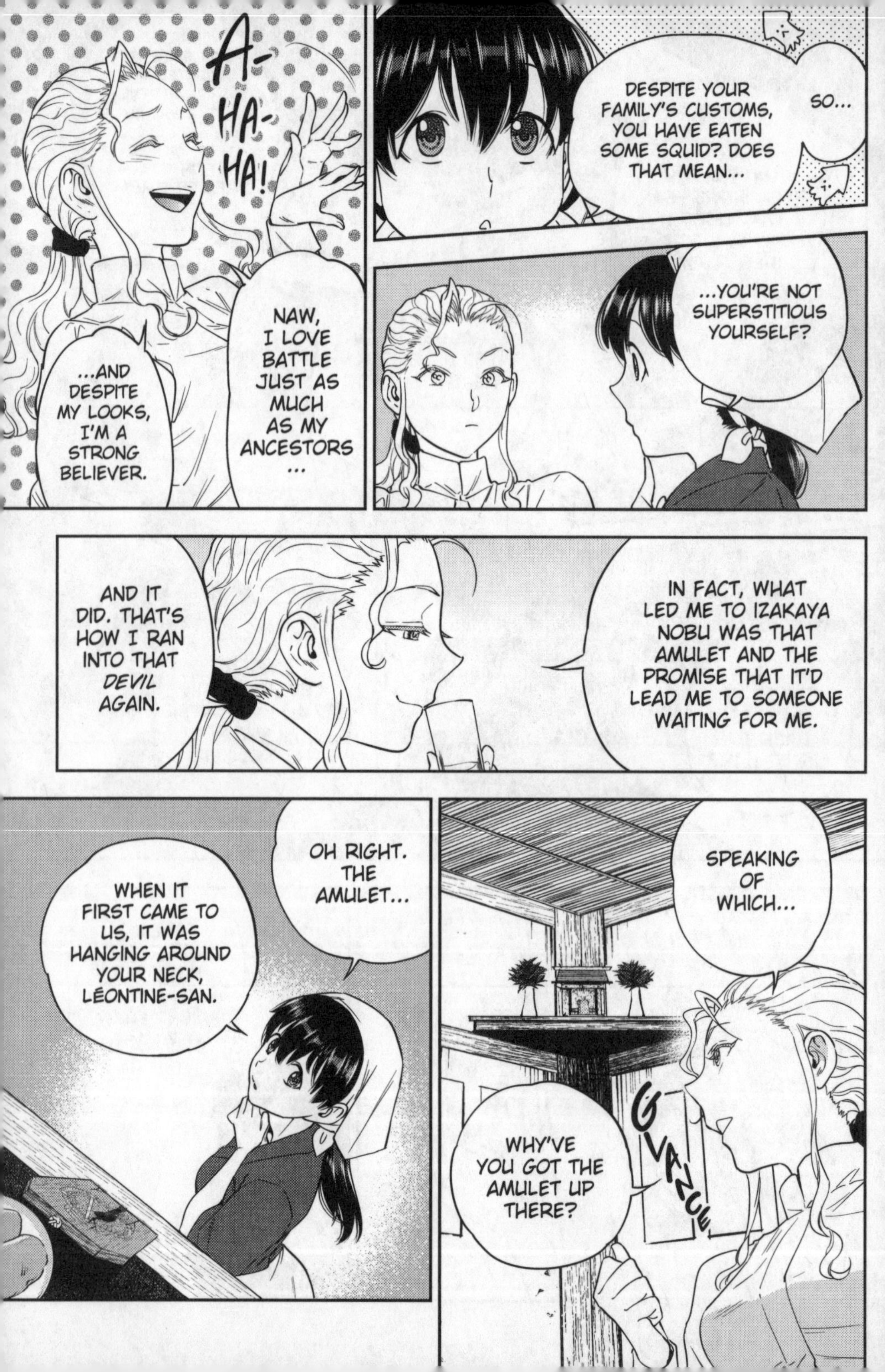
SO...
DESPITE YOUR FAMILY'S CUSTOMS, YOU HAVE EATEN SOME SQUID? DOES THAT MEAN...
...YOU'RE NOT SUPERSTITIOUS YOURSELF?
A-HA-HA!
NAW, I LOVE BATTLE JUST AS MUCH AS MY ANCESTORS...
...AND DESPITE MY LOOKS, I'M A STRONG BELIEVER.
IN FACT, WHAT LED ME TO IZAKAYA NOBU WAS THAT AMULET AND THE PROMISE THAT IT'D LEAD ME TO SOMEONE WAITING FOR ME.
AND IT DID. THAT'S HOW I RAN INTO THAT *DEVIL* AGAIN.
SPEAKING OF WHICH...
GLANCE
WHY'VE YOU GOT THE AMULET UP THERE?
OH RIGHT. THE AMULET...
WHEN IT FIRST CAME TO US, IT WAS HANGING AROUND YOUR NECK, LÉONTINE-SAN.

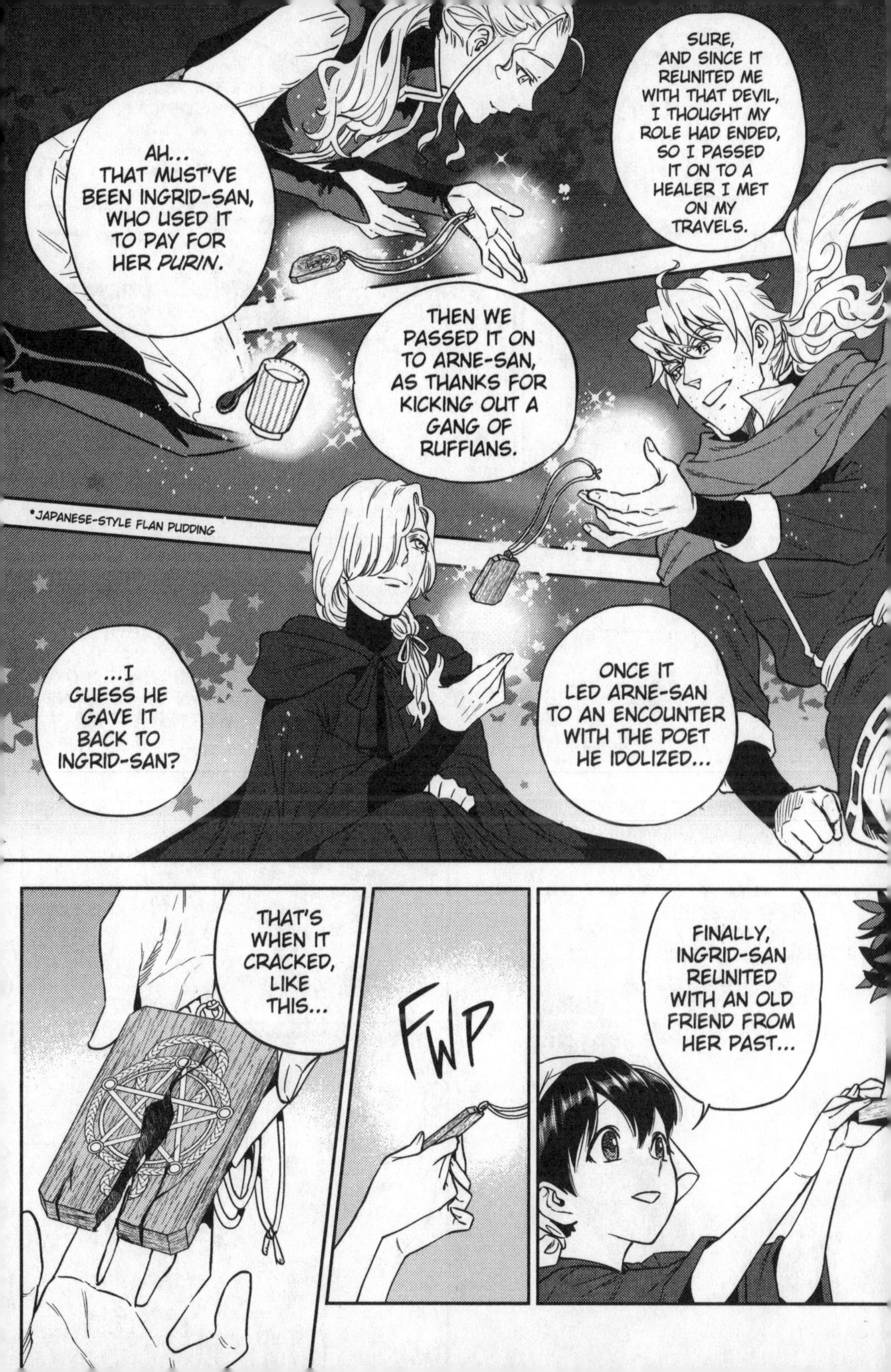
SURE, AND SINCE IT REUNITED ME WITH THAT DEVIL, I THOUGHT MY ROLE HAD ENDED, SO I PASSED IT ON TO A HEALER I MET ON MY TRAVELS.
AH... THAT MUST'VE BEEN INGRID-SAN, WHO USED IT TO PAY FOR HER *PURIN*.
THEN WE PASSED IT ON TO ARNE-SAN, AS THANKS FOR KICKING OUT A GANG OF RUFFIANS.
•JAPANESE-STYLE FLAN PUDDING
ONCE IT LED ARNE-SAN TO AN ENCOUNTER WITH THE POET HE IDOLIZED...
...I GUESS HE GAVE IT BACK TO INGRID-SAN?
FINALLY, INGRID-SAN REUNITED WITH AN OLD FRIEND FROM HER PAST...
FWP
THAT'S WHEN IT CRACKED, LIKE THIS...

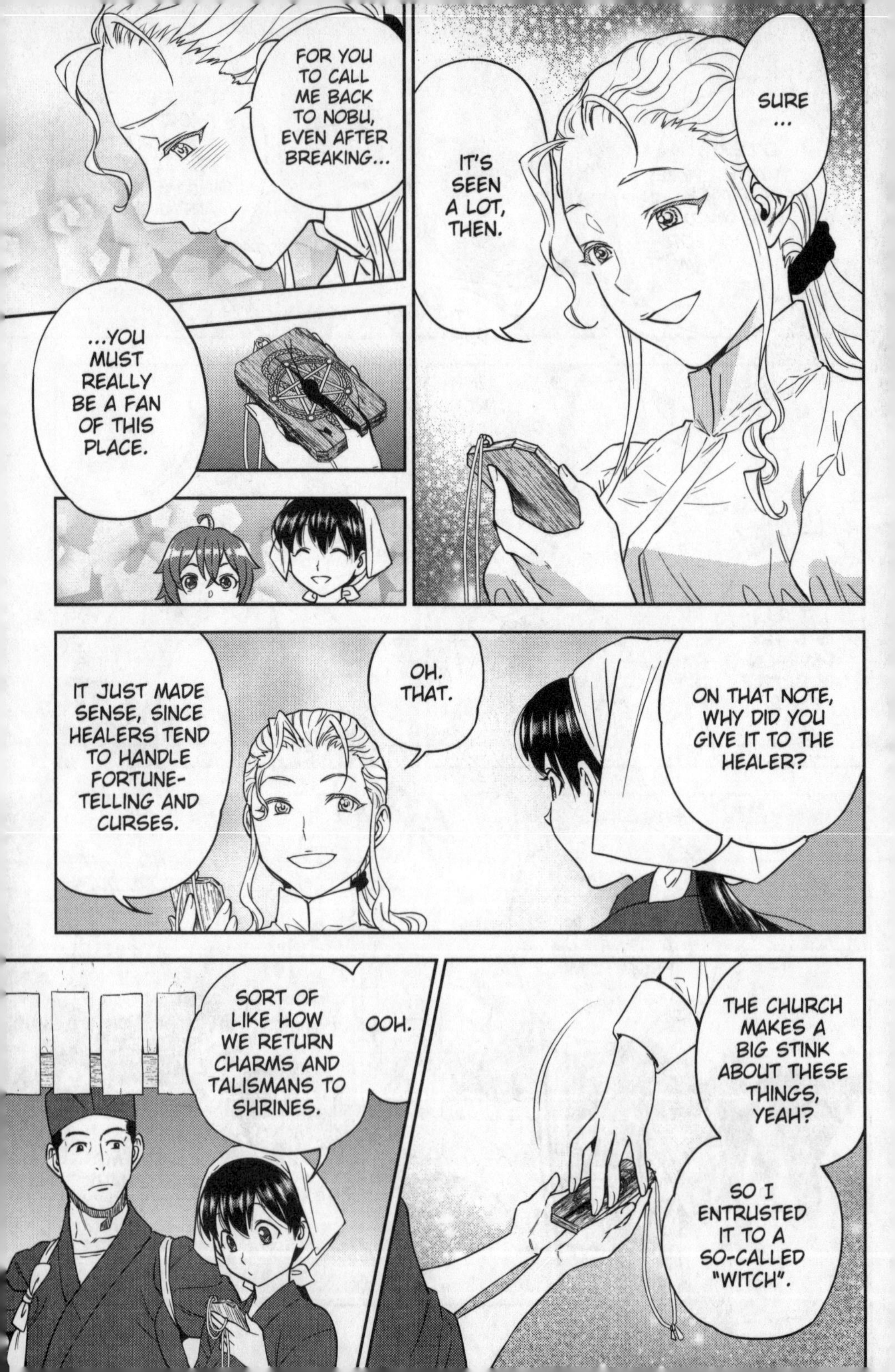
SURE ...
IT'S SEEN A LOT, THEN.
FOR YOU TO CALL ME BACK TO NOBU, EVEN AFTER BREAKING...
...YOU MUST REALLY BE A FAN OF THIS PLACE.
ON THAT NOTE, WHY DID YOU GIVE IT TO THE HEALER?
OH. THAT.
IT JUST MADE SENSE, SINCE HEALERS TEND TO HANDLE FORTUNE-TELLING AND CURSES.
THE CHURCH MAKES A BIG STINK ABOUT THESE THINGS, YEAH?
SO I ENTRUSTED IT TO A SO-CALLED "WITCH".
SORT OF LIKE HOW WE RETURN CHARMS AND TALISMANS TO SHRINES.
OOH.

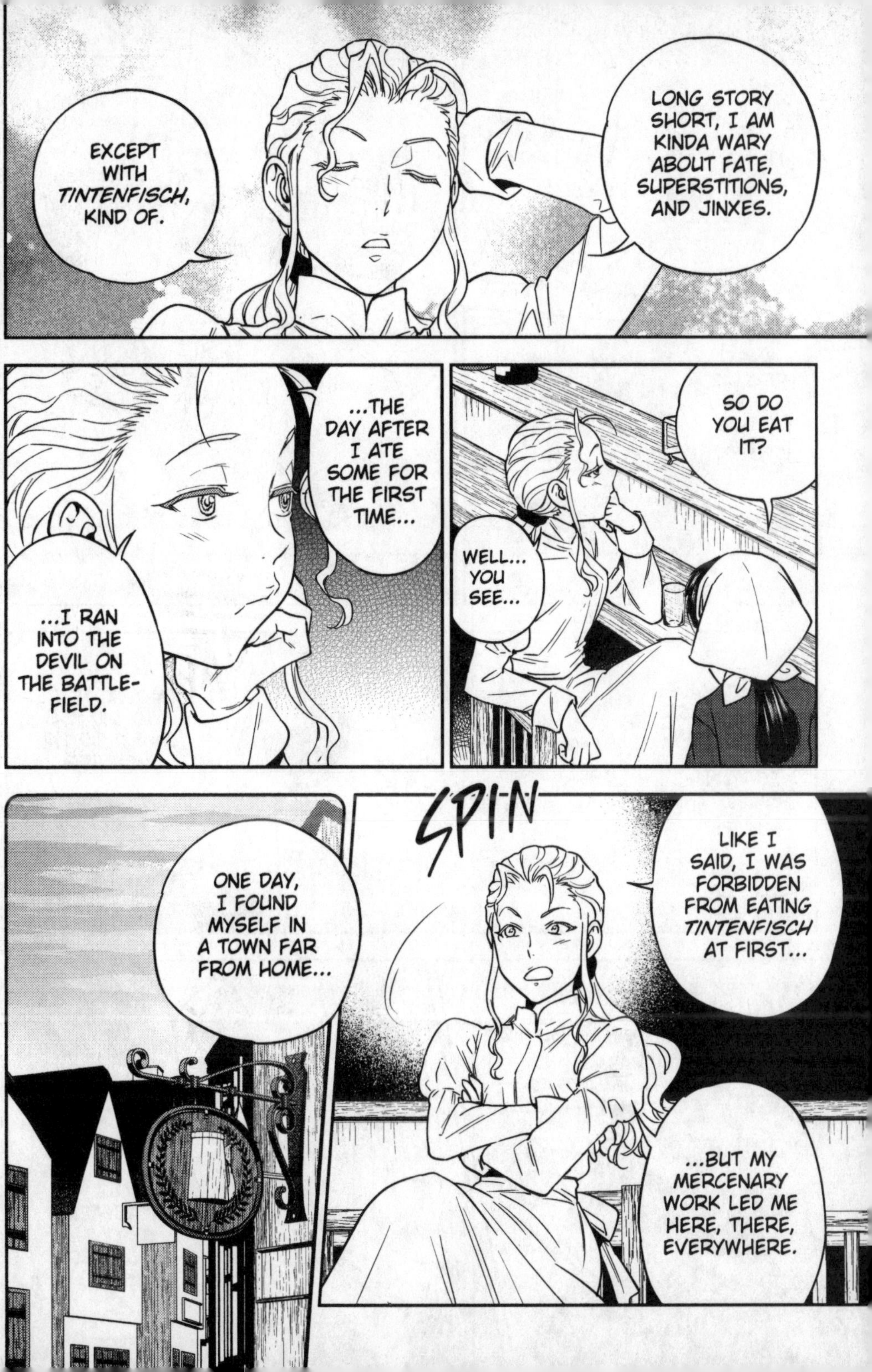
LONG STORY SHORT, I AM KINDA WARY ABOUT FATE, SUPERSTITIONS, AND JINXES.
EXCEPT WITH *TINTENFISCH*, KIND OF.
SO DO YOU EAT IT?
WELL... YOU SEE...
...THE DAY AFTER I ATE SOME FOR THE FIRST TIME...
...I RAN INTO THE DEVIL ON THE BATTLE-FIELD.
SPIN
LIKE I SAID, I WAS FORBIDDEN FROM EATING *TINTENFISCH* AT FIRST...
...BUT MY MERCENARY WORK LED ME HERE, THERE, EVERYWHERE.
ONE DAY, I FOUND MYSELF IN A TOWN FAR FROM HOME...

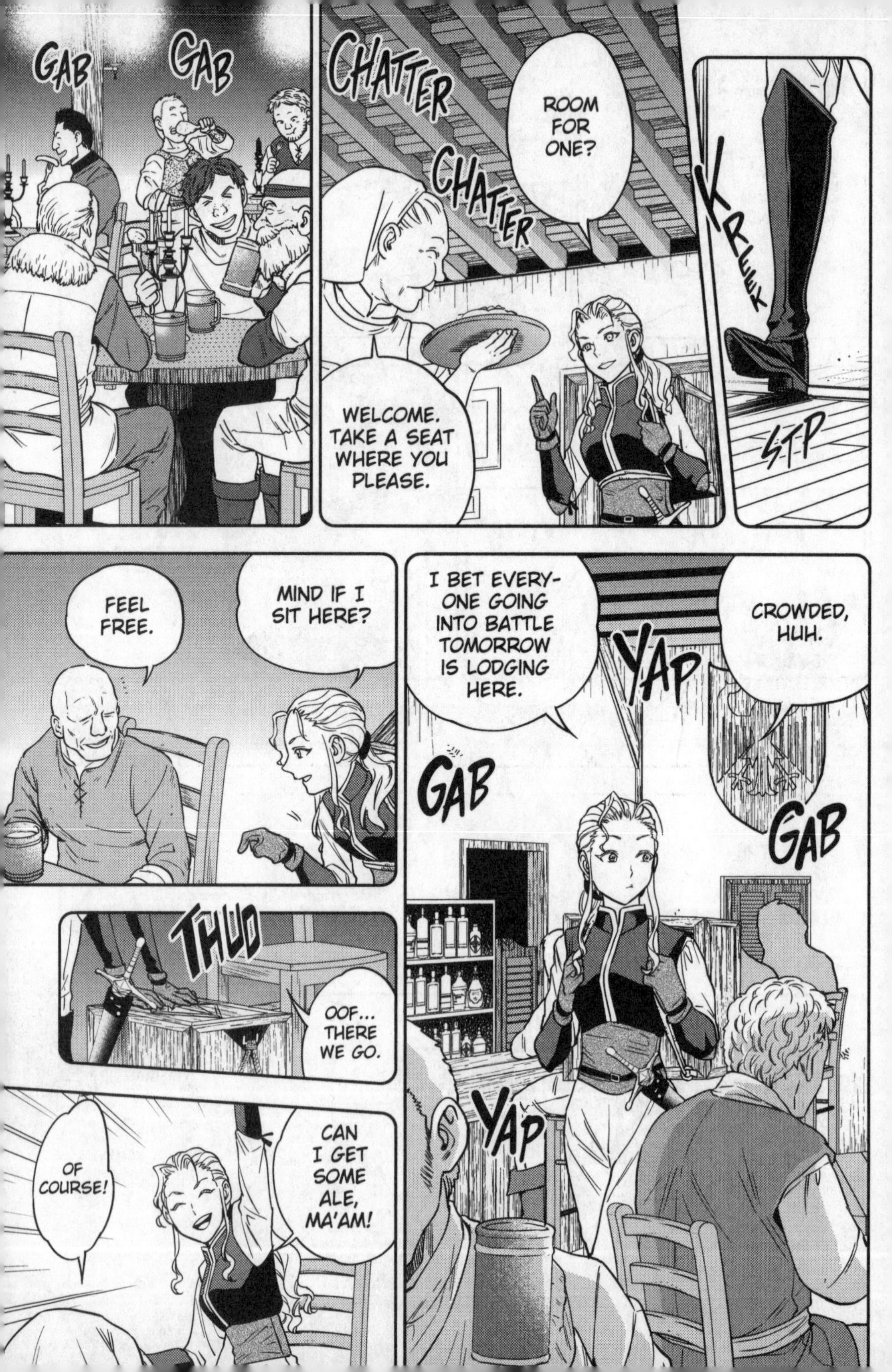
KREEK
STP
ROOM FOR ONE?
CHATTER
CHATTER
WELCOME. TAKE A SEAT WHERE YOU PLEASE.
GAB
GAB
CROWDED, HUH.
I BET EVERY-ONE GOING INTO BATTLE TOMORROW IS LODGING HERE.
YAP
GAB
GAB
YAP
MIND IF I SIT HERE?
FEEL FREE.
THUD
OOF... THERE WE GO.
CAN I GET SOME ALE, MA'AM!
OF COURSE!

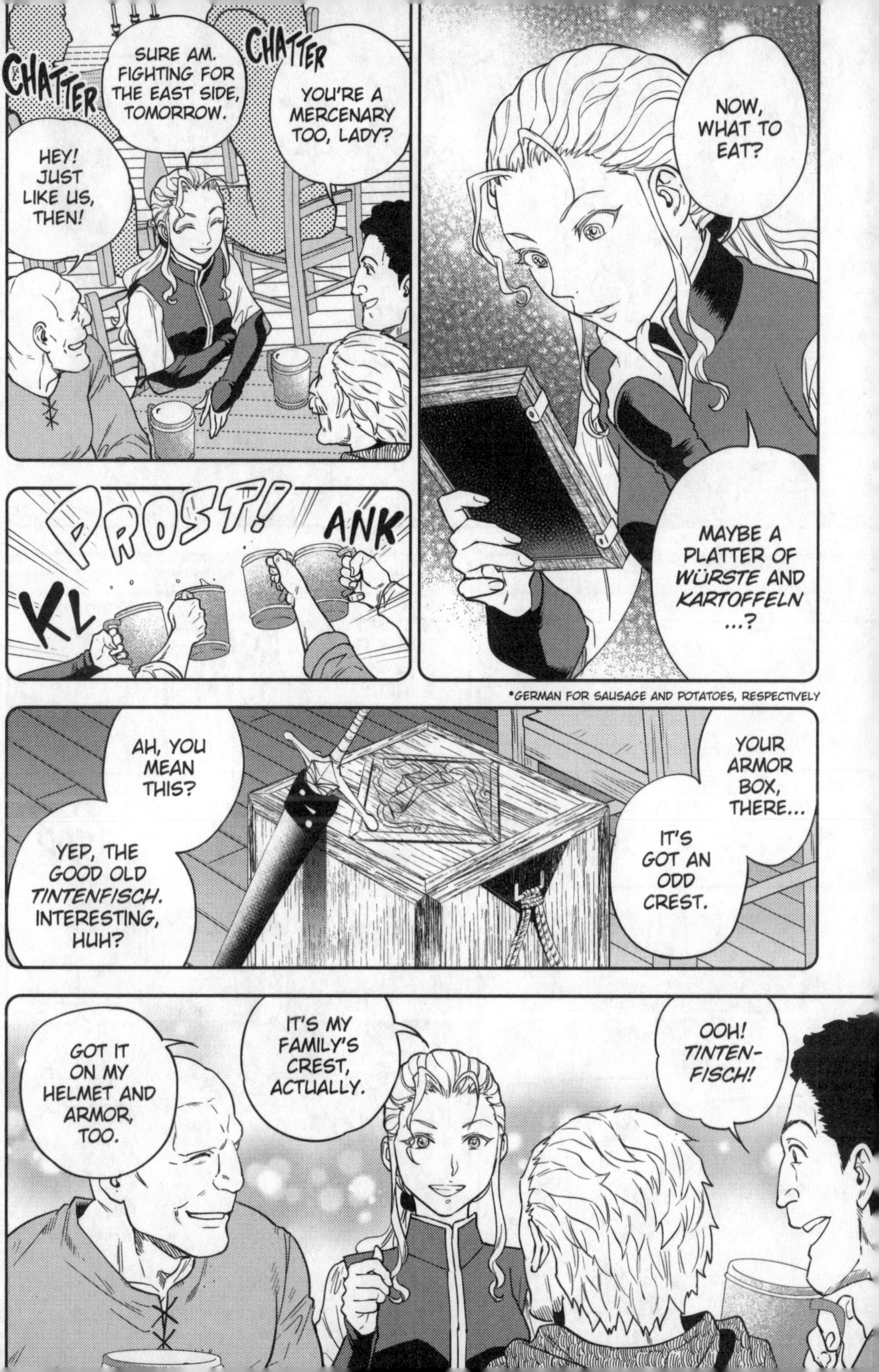
NOW, WHAT TO EAT?
MAYBE A PLATTER OF *WÜRSTE* AND *KARTOFFELN* ...?
CHATTER
YOU'RE A MERCENARY TOO, LADY?
SURE AM. FIGHTING FOR THE EAST SIDE, TOMORROW.
CHATTER
HEY! JUST LIKE US, THEN!
PROST!
ANK
KL
YOUR ARMOR BOX, THERE...
IT'S GOT AN ODD CREST.
AH, YOU MEAN THIS?
YEP, THE GOOD OLD *TINTENFISCH*. INTERESTING, HUH?
OOH! *TINTEN-FISCH*!
IT'S MY FAMILY'S CREST, ACTUALLY.
GOT IT ON MY HELMET AND ARMOR, TOO.

*GERMAN FOR SAUSAGE AND POTATOES, RESPECTIVELY

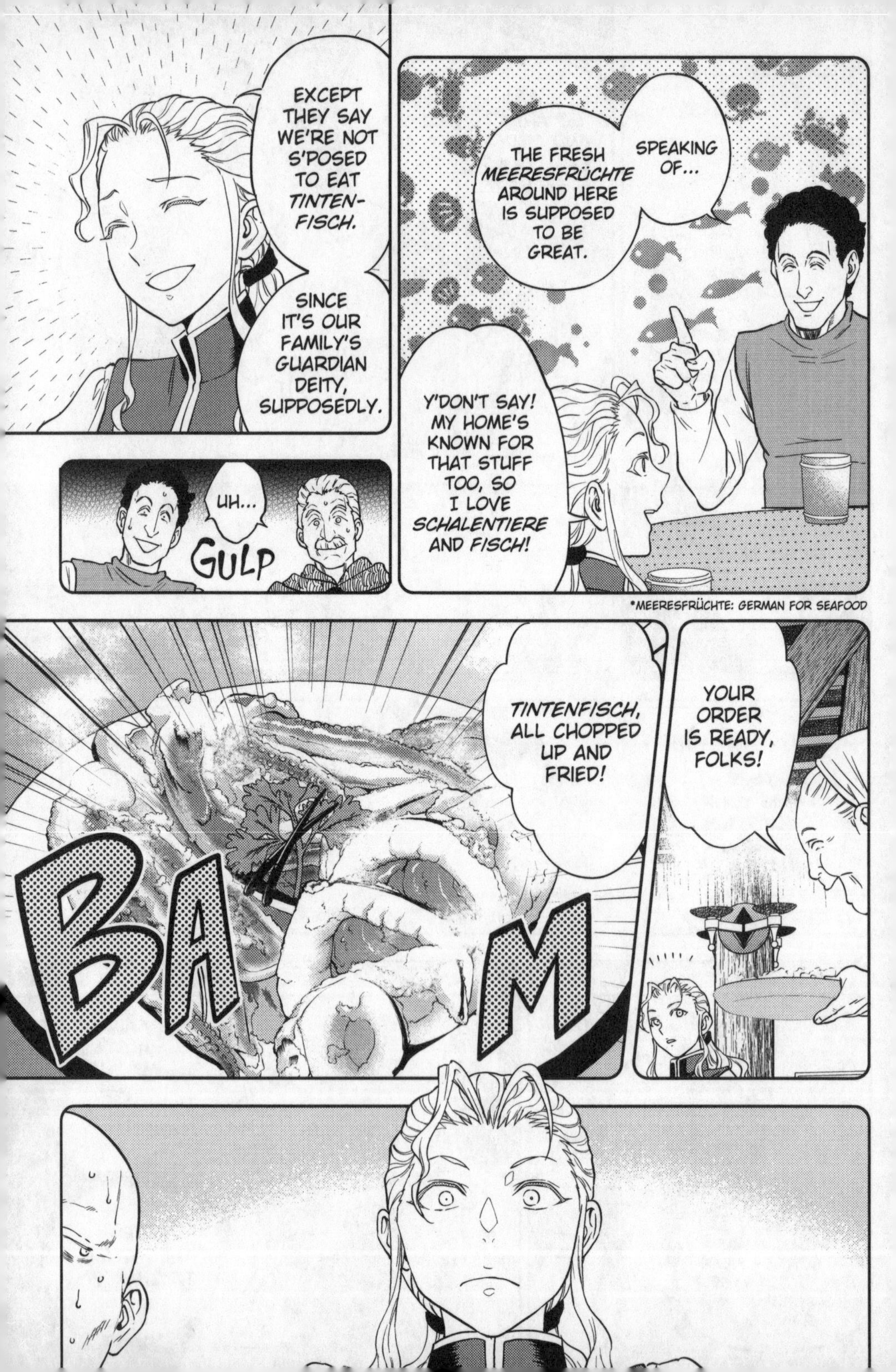
SPEAKING OF...
THE FRESH MEERESFRÜCHTE AROUND HERE IS SUPPOSED TO BE GREAT.
Y'DON'T SAY! MY HOME'S KNOWN FOR THAT STUFF TOO, SO I LOVE SCHALENTIERE AND FISCH!
EXCEPT THEY SAY WE'RE NOT S'POSED TO EAT TINTEN-FISCH.
SINCE IT'S OUR FAMILY'S GUARDIAN DEITY, SUPPOSEDLY.
UH...
GULP
YOUR ORDER IS READY, FOLKS!
TINTENFISCH, ALL CHOPPED UP AND FRIED!
BAM

*MEERESFRÜCHTE: GERMAN FOR SEAFOOD

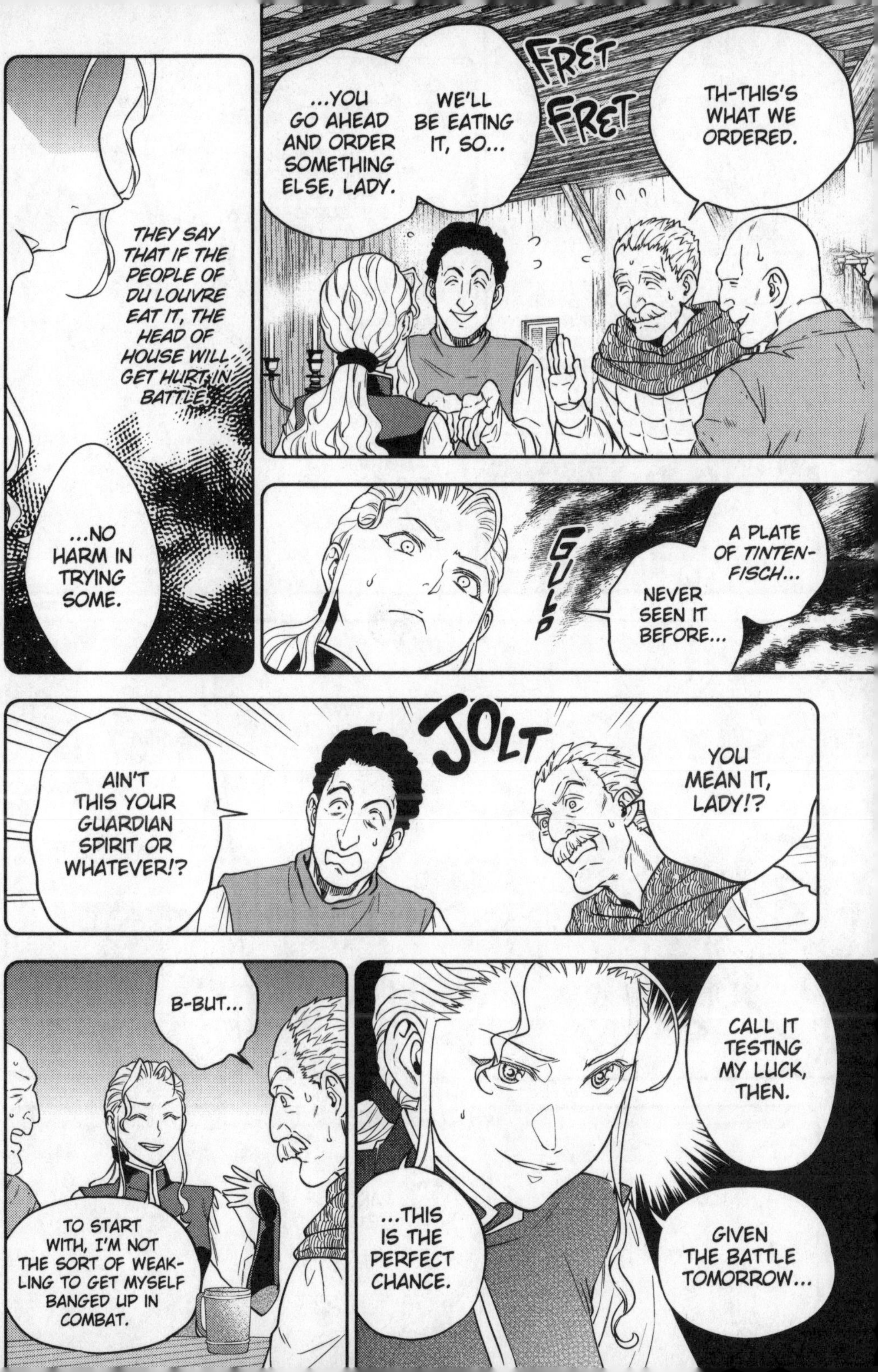
TH-THIS'S WHAT WE ORDERED.
FRET FRET
WE'LL BE EATING IT, SO...
...YOU GO AHEAD AND ORDER SOMETHING ELSE, LADY.
A PLATE OF *TINTEN-FISCH*...
NEVER SEEN IT BEFORE...
GULP
THEY SAY THAT IF THE PEOPLE OF DU LOUVRE EAT IT, THE HEAD OF HOUSE WILL GET HURT IN BATTLE.
...NO HARM IN TRYING SOME.
YOU MEAN IT, LADY!?
JOLT
AIN'T THIS YOUR GUARDIAN SPIRIT OR WHATEVER!?
CALL IT TESTING MY LUCK, THEN.
GIVEN THE BATTLE TOMORROW...
...THIS IS THE PERFECT CHANCE.
B-BUT...
TO START WITH, I'M NOT THE SORT OF WEAK-LING TO GET MYSELF BANGED UP IN COMBAT.

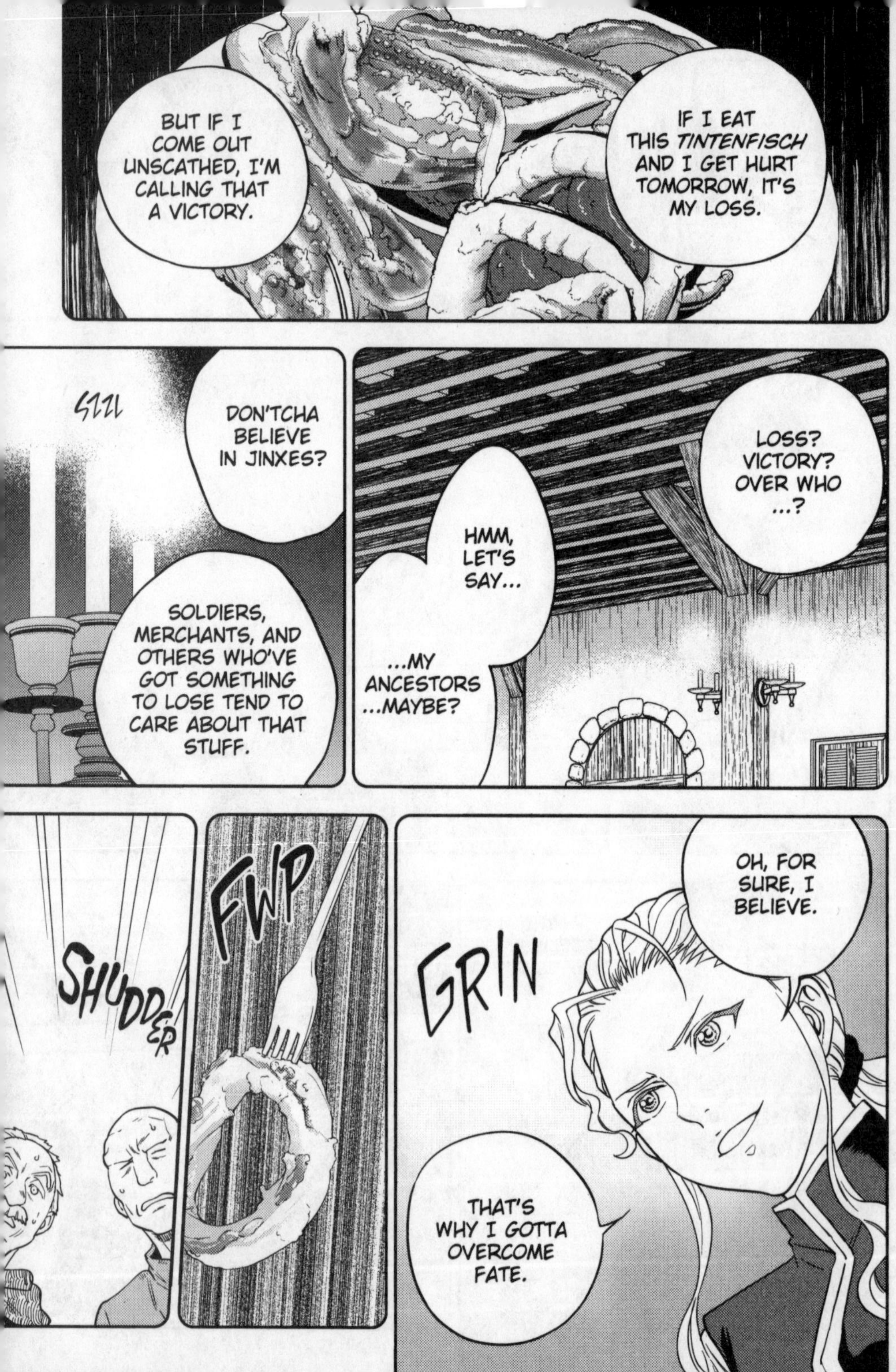
IF I EAT THIS *TINTENFISCH* AND I GET HURT TOMORROW, IT'S MY LOSS.
BUT IF I COME OUT UNSCATHED, I'M CALLING THAT A VICTORY.
LOSS? VICTORY? OVER WHO ...?
HMM, LET'S SAY...
...MY ANCESTORS ...MAYBE?
DON'TCHA BELIEVE IN JINXES?
SOLDIERS, MERCHANTS, AND OTHERS WHO'VE GOT SOMETHING TO LOSE TEND TO CARE ABOUT THAT STUFF.
OH, FOR SURE, I BELIEVE.
GRIN
THAT'S WHY I GOTTA OVERCOME FATE.
FWP
SHUDDER

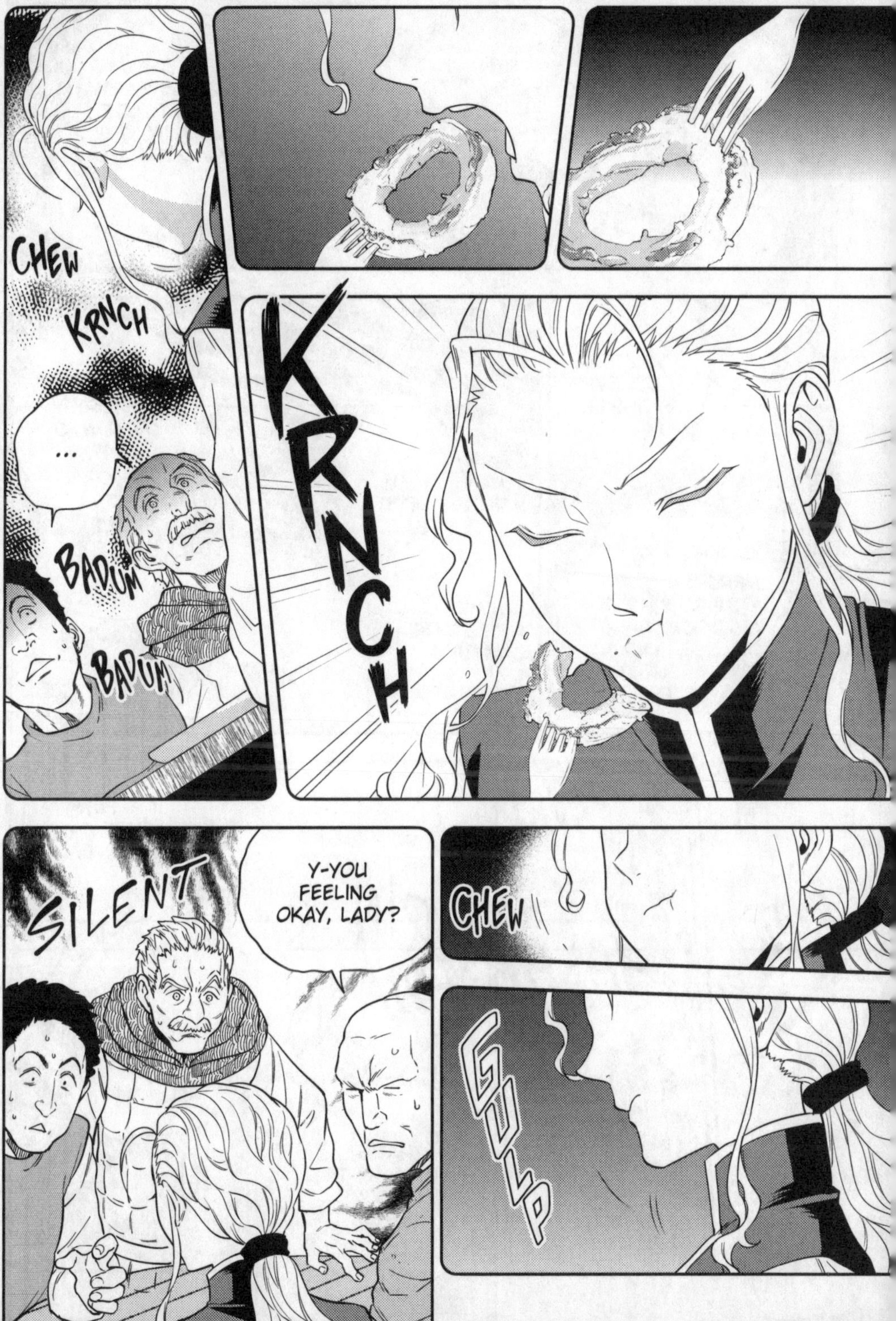
KRNCH
CHEW
KRNCH
...
BADUM
BADUM
CHEW
GULP
SILENT
Y-YOU FEELING OKAY, LADY?

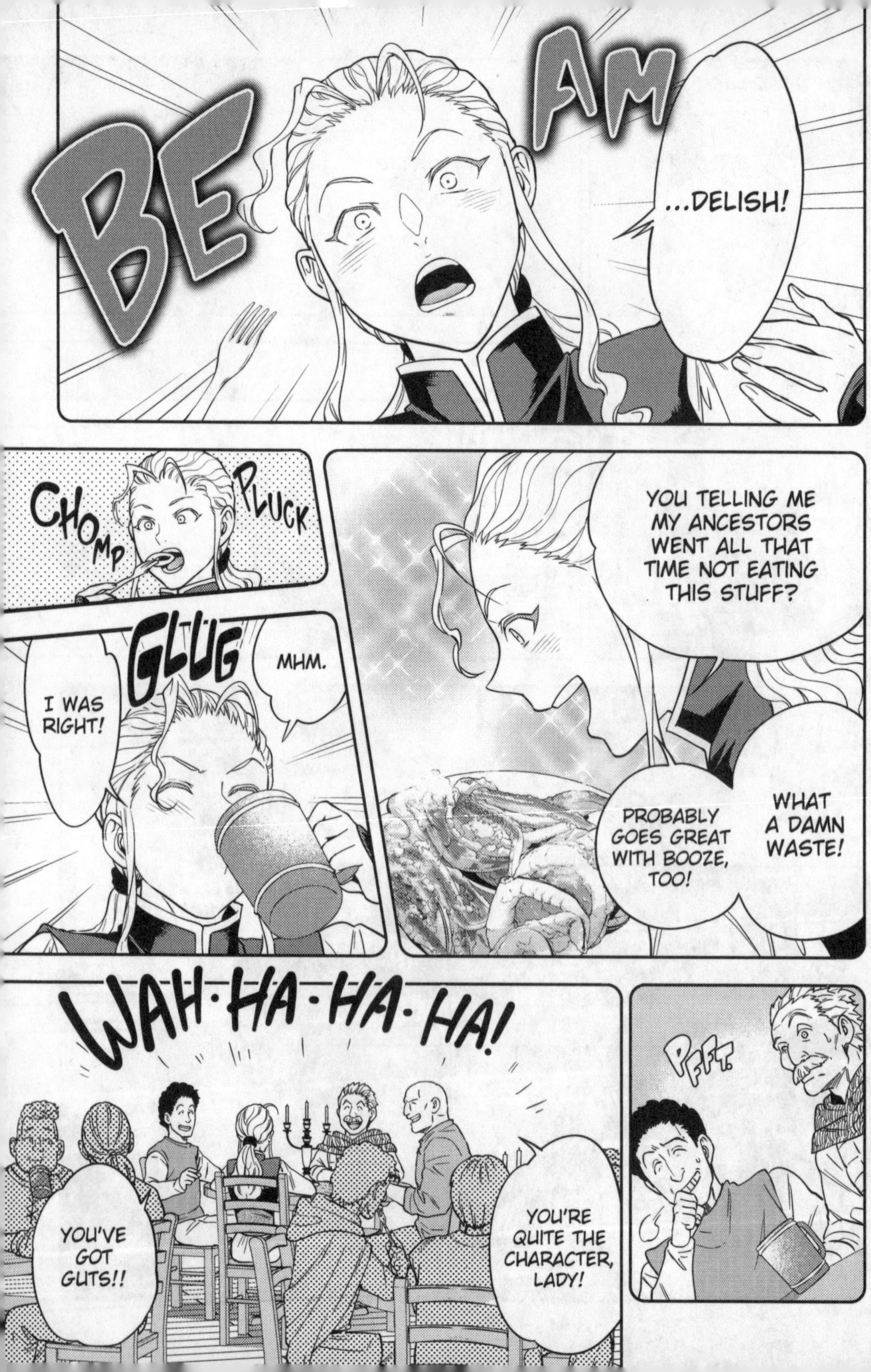
BEAM
...DELISH!
YOU TELLING ME MY ANCESTORS WENT ALL THAT TIME NOT EATING THIS STUFF?
WHAT A DAMN WASTE!
PROBABLY GOES GREAT WITH BOOZE, TOO!
CHOMP
PLUCK
GLUG
MHM.
I WAS RIGHT!
PFFT.
WAH·HA·HA·HA!
YOU'RE QUITE THE CHARACTER, LADY!
YOU'VE GOT GUTS!!

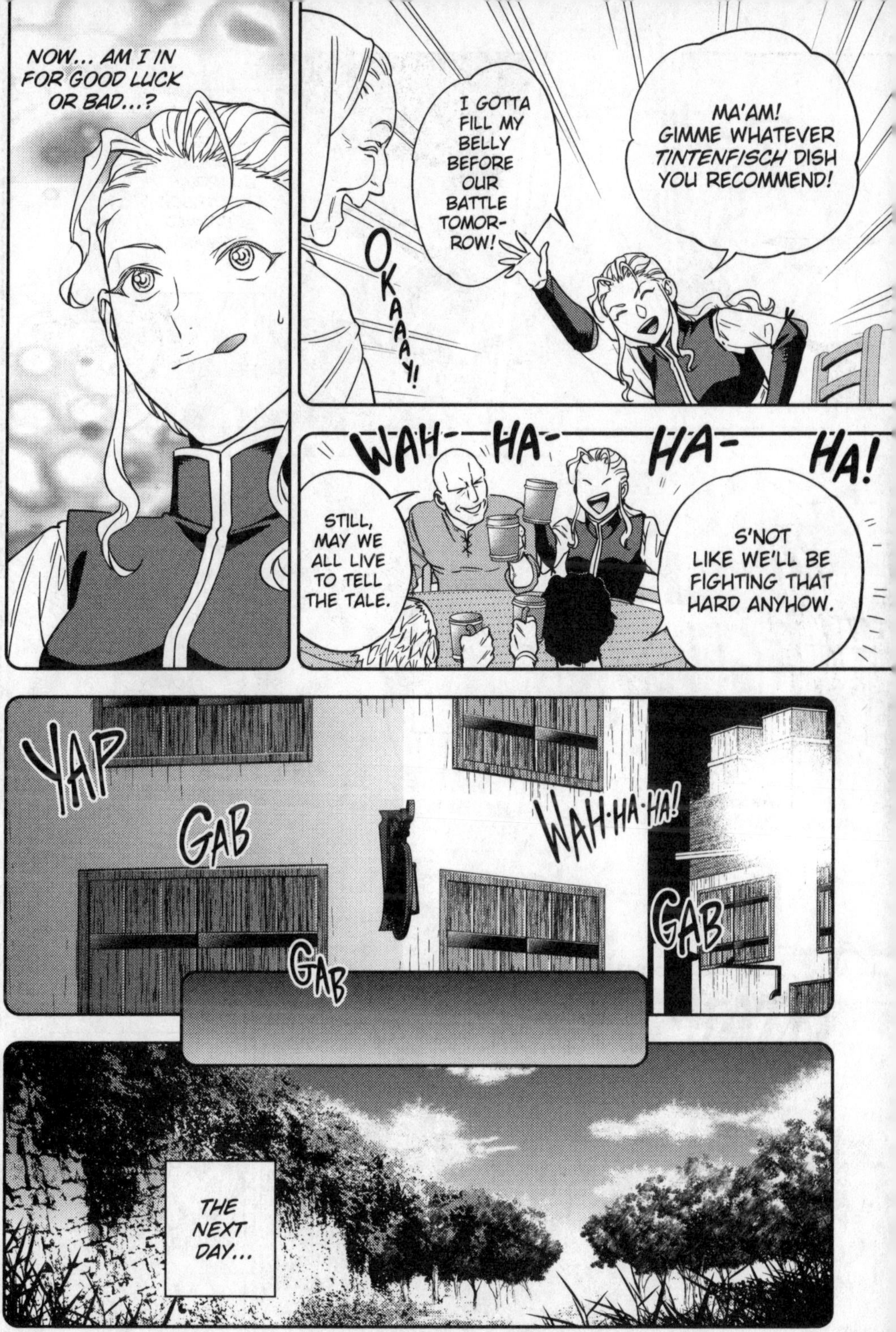
MA'AM! GIMME WHATEVER *TINTENFISCH* DISH YOU RECOMMEND!
I GOTTA FILL MY BELLY BEFORE OUR BATTLE TOMOR-ROW!
OKAAAY!
WAH-HA-HA-HA!
S'NOT LIKE WE'LL BE FIGHTING THAT HARD ANYHOW.
STILL, MAY WE ALL LIVE TO TELL THE TALE.
NOW... AM I IN FOR GOOD LUCK OR BAD...?
GAB
WAH-HA-HA!
GAB
YAP
GAB
THE NEXT DAY...

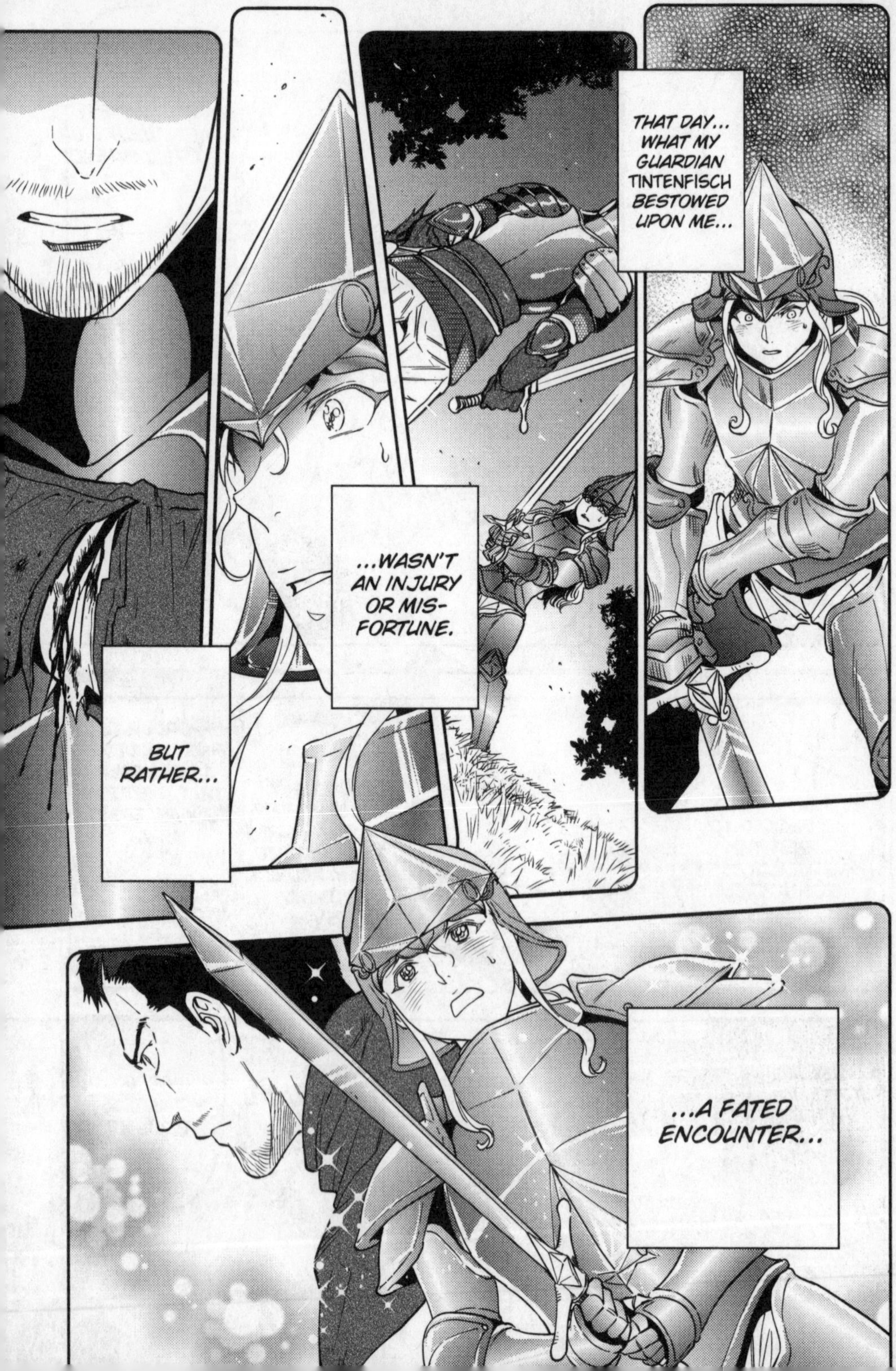
THAT DAY... WHAT MY GUARDIAN TINTENFISCH BESTOWED UPON ME...
...WASN'T AN INJURY OR MIS-FORTUNE.
BUT RATHER...
...A FATED ENCOUNTER...

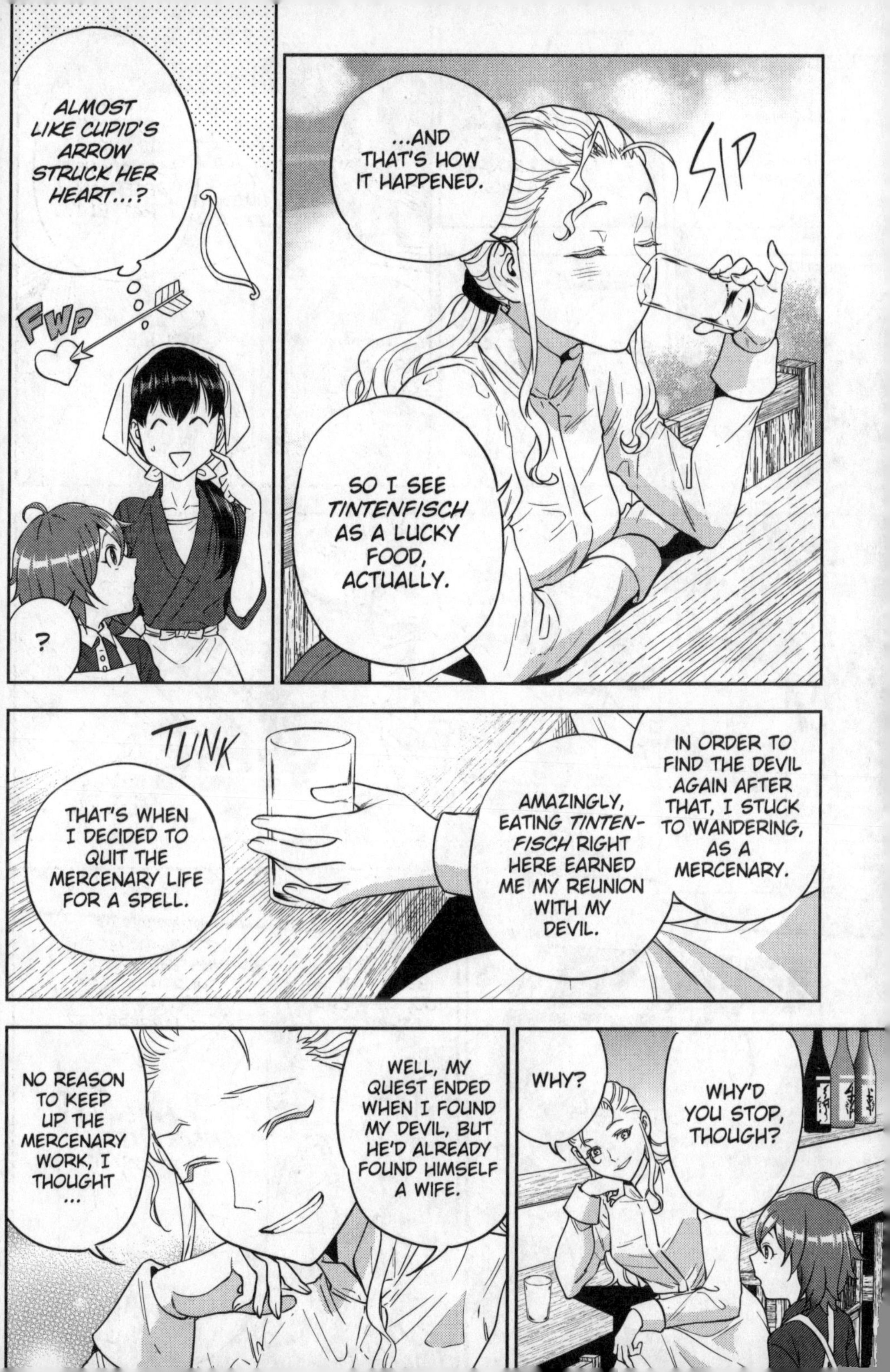
...AND THAT'S HOW IT HAPPENED.
SIP
SO I SEE *TINTENFISCH* AS A LUCKY FOOD, ACTUALLY.
ALMOST LIKE CUPID'S ARROW STRUCK HER HEART...?
FWP
?
IN ORDER TO FIND THE DEVIL AGAIN AFTER THAT, I STUCK TO WANDERING, AS A MERCENARY.
AMAZINGLY, EATING *TINTENFISCH* RIGHT HERE EARNED ME MY REUNION WITH MY DEVIL.
TUNK
THAT'S WHEN I DECIDED TO QUIT THE MERCENARY LIFE FOR A SPELL.
WHY'D YOU STOP, THOUGH?
WHY?
WELL, MY QUEST ENDED WHEN I FOUND MY DEVIL, BUT HE'D ALREADY FOUND HIMSELF A WIFE.
NO REASON TO KEEP UP THE MERCENARY WORK, I THOUGHT ...

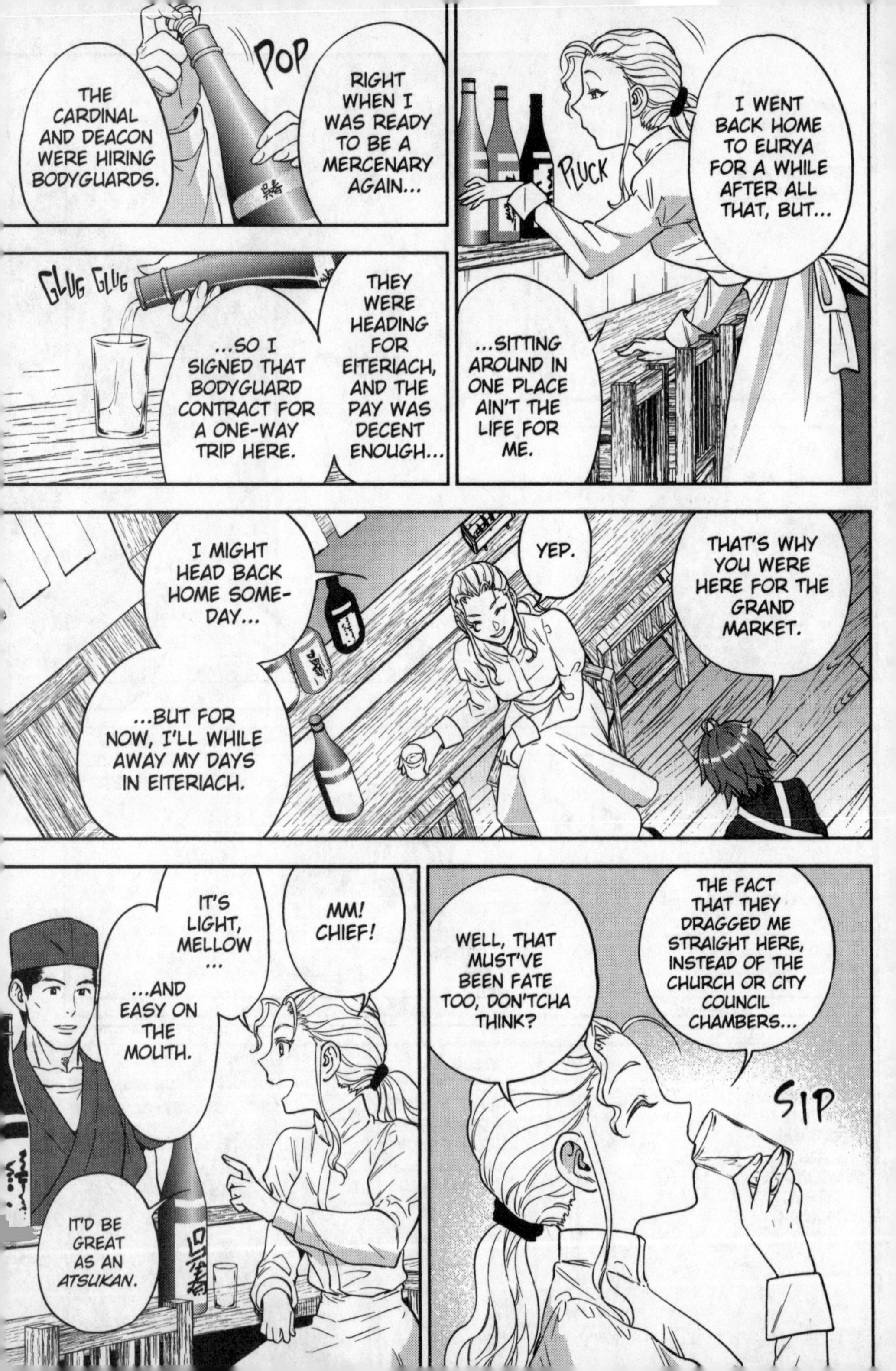
PLUCK
I WENT BACK HOME TO EURYA FOR A WHILE AFTER ALL THAT, BUT...
...SITTING AROUND IN ONE PLACE AIN'T THE LIFE FOR ME.
POP
RIGHT WHEN I WAS READY TO BE A MERCENARY AGAIN...
THE CARDINAL AND DEACON WERE HIRING BODYGUARDS.
THEY WERE HEADING FOR EITERIACH, AND THE PAY WAS DECENT ENOUGH...
...SO I SIGNED THAT BODYGUARD CONTRACT FOR A ONE-WAY TRIP HERE.
GLUG GLUG
THAT'S WHY YOU WERE HERE FOR THE GRAND MARKET.
YEP.
I MIGHT HEAD BACK HOME SOME-DAY...
...BUT FOR NOW, I'LL WHILE AWAY MY DAYS IN EITERIACH.
THE FACT THAT THEY DRAGGED ME STRAIGHT HERE, INSTEAD OF THE CHURCH OR CITY COUNCIL CHAMBERS...
WELL, THAT MUST'VE BEEN FATE TOO, DON'TCHA THINK?
SIP
MM! CHIEF!
IT'S LIGHT, MELLOW ...
...AND EASY ON THE MOUTH.
IT'D BE GREAT AS AN ATSUKAN.

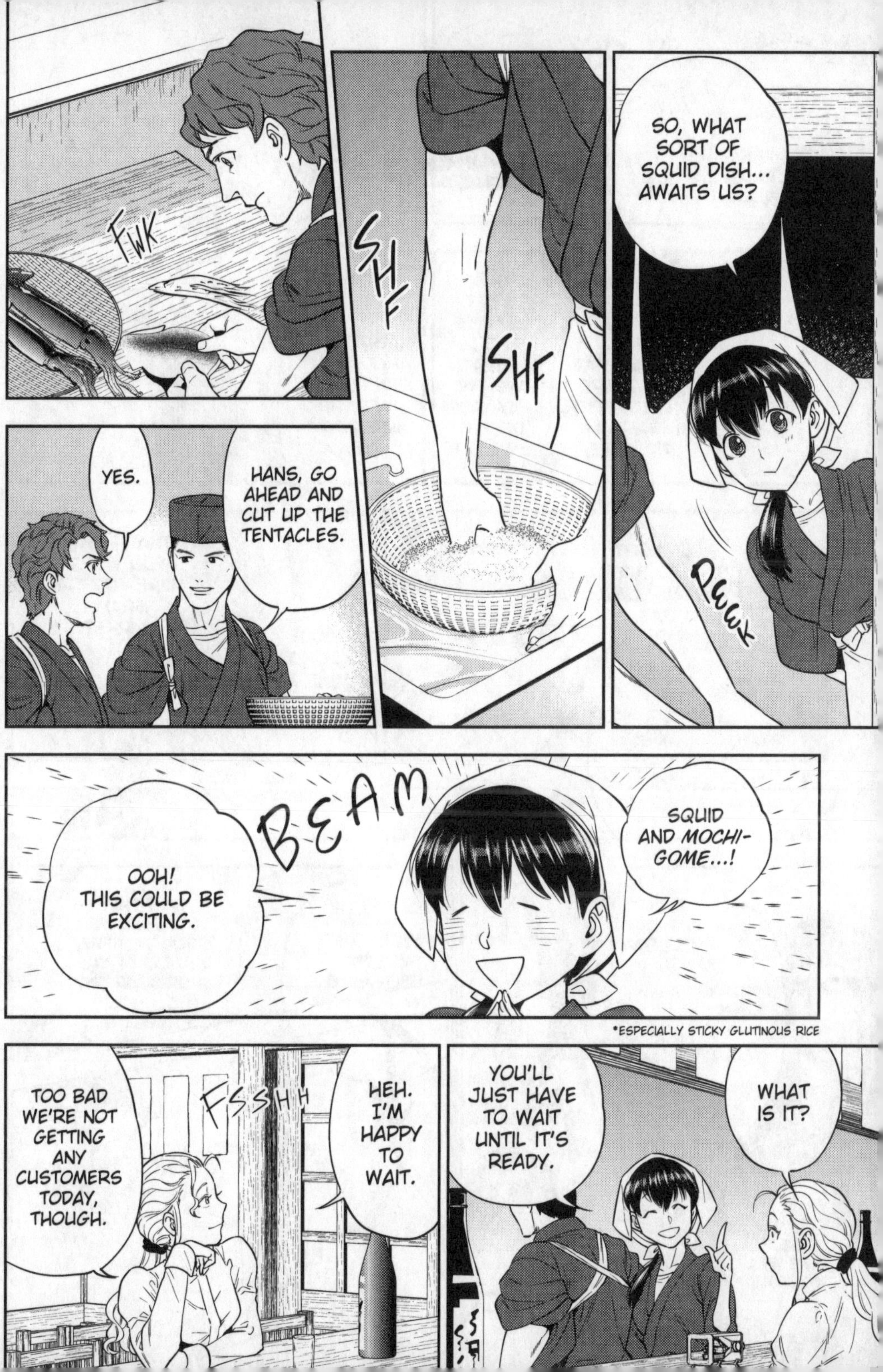
SO, WHAT SORT OF SQUID DISH... AWAITS US?
PEEK
SHF
SHF
FWK
HANS, GO AHEAD AND CUT UP THE TENTACLES.
YES.
SQUID AND MOCHI-GOME...!
BEAM
OOH! THIS COULD BE EXCITING.
WHAT IS IT?
YOU'LL JUST HAVE TO WAIT UNTIL IT'S READY.
HEH. I'M HAPPY TO WAIT.
FSSHH
TOO BAD WE'RE NOT GETTING ANY CUSTOMERS TODAY, THOUGH.

*ESPECIALLY STICKY GLUTINOUS RICE

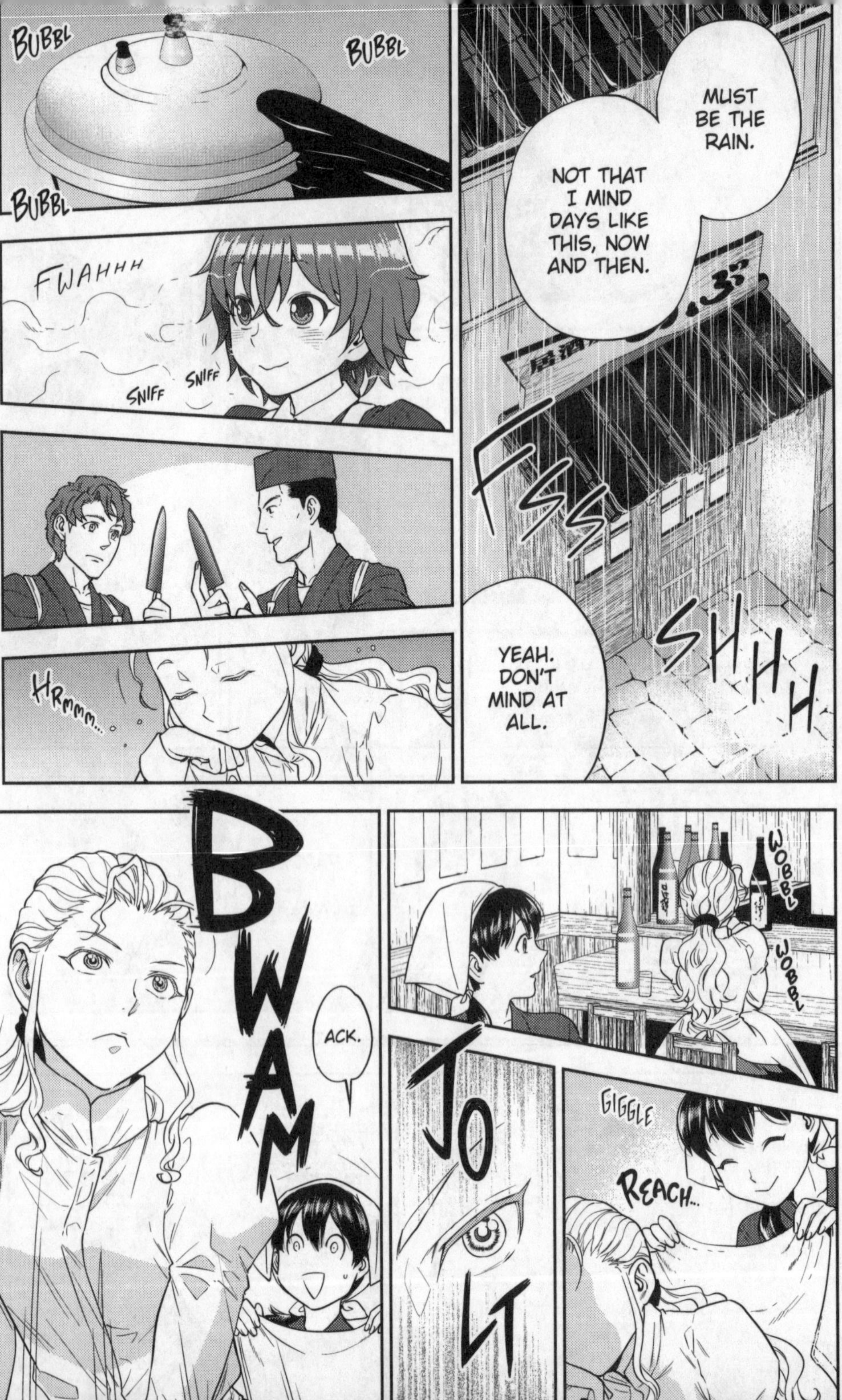

MUST BE THE RAIN.
NOT THAT I MIND DAYS LIKE THIS, NOW AND THEN.
FSSS
SHHHH
YEAH. DON'T MIND AT ALL.
BUBBL
BUBBL
BUBBL
FWAHHH
SNIFF
SNIFF
HRMMM...
WOBBL
WOBBL
GIGGLE
REACH...
JOLT
BWAM
ACK.

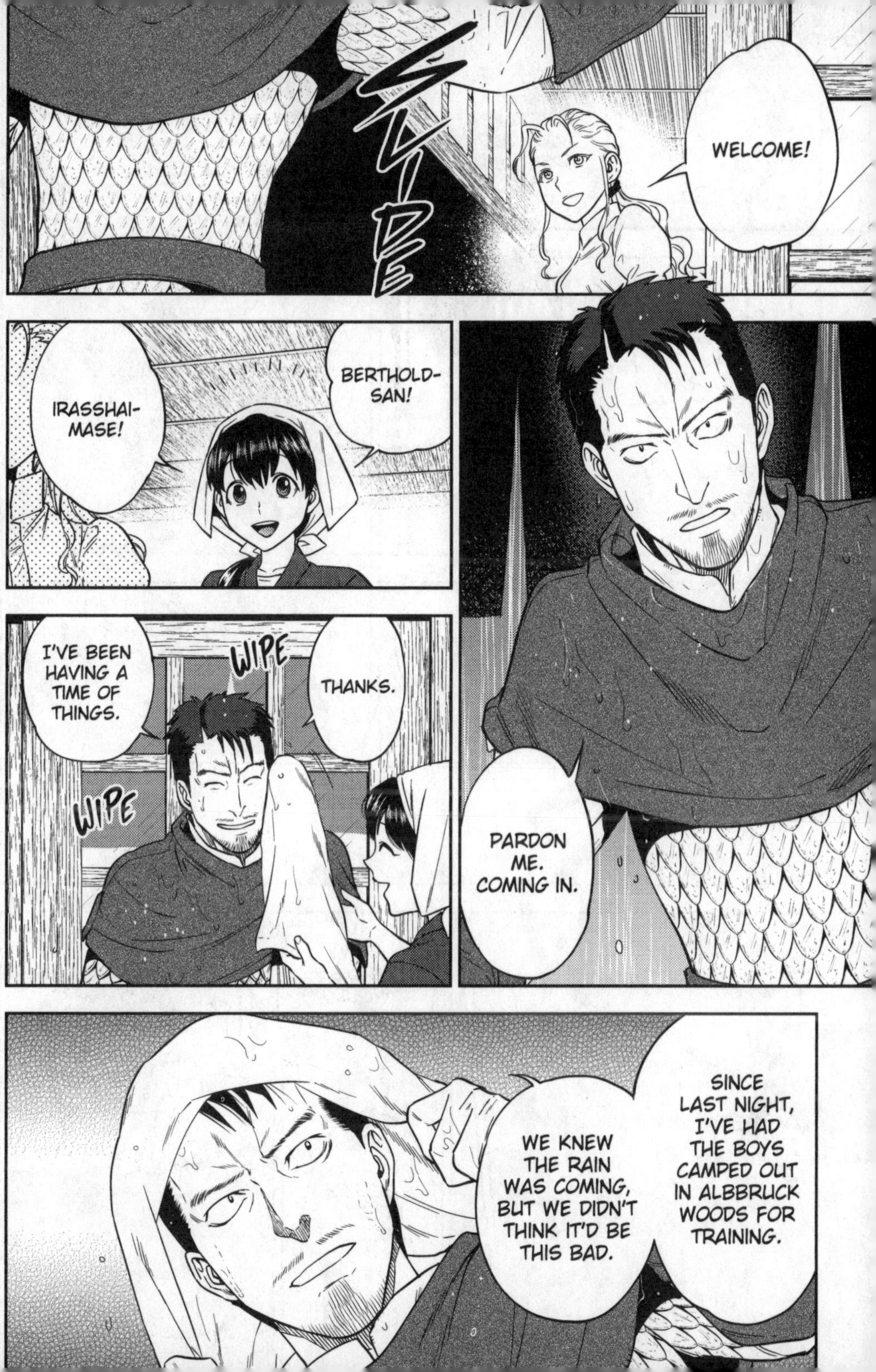
SLIDE
WELCOME!
PARDON ME. COMING IN.
BERTHOLD-SAN!
IRASSHAI-MASE!
THANKS.
WIPE
I'VE BEEN HAVING A TIME OF THINGS.
WIPE
SINCE LAST NIGHT, I'VE HAD THE BOYS CAMPED OUT IN ALBBRUCK WOODS FOR TRAINING.
WE KNEW THE RAIN WAS COMING, BUT WE DIDN'T THINK IT'D BE THIS BAD.

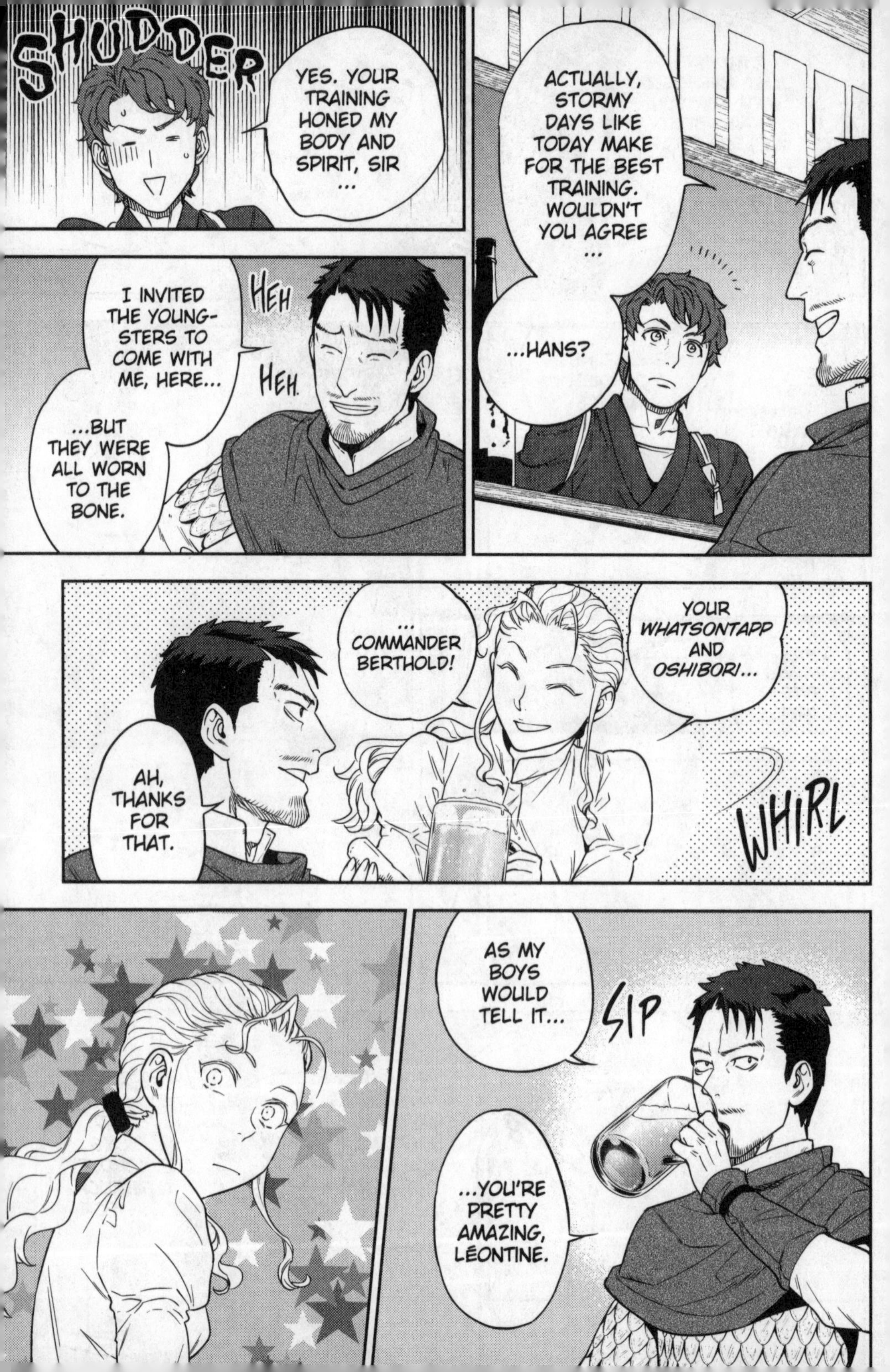
ACTUALLY, STORMY DAYS LIKE TODAY MAKE FOR THE BEST TRAINING. WOULDN'T YOU AGREE ...
...HANS?
SHUDDER
YES. YOUR TRAINING HONED MY BODY AND SPIRIT, SIR ...
HEH HEH.
I INVITED THE YOUNG-STERS TO COME WITH ME, HERE...
...BUT THEY WERE ALL WORN TO THE BONE.
YOUR WHATSONTAPP AND OSHIBORI...
... COMMANDER BERTHOLD!
WHIRL
AH, THANKS FOR THAT.
AS MY BOYS WOULD TELL IT...
SIP
...YOU'RE PRETTY AMAZING, LÉONTINE.

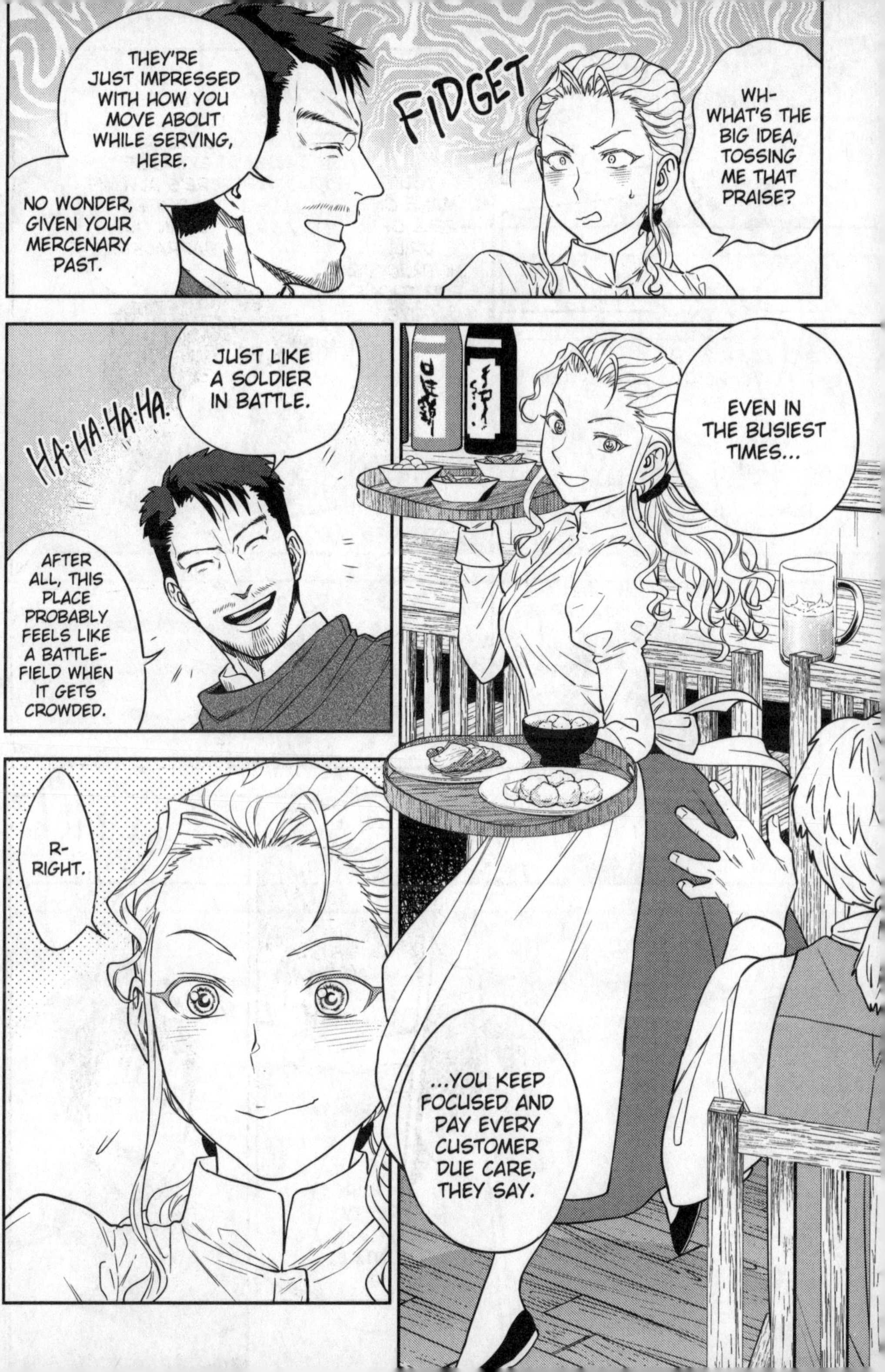
WH- WHAT'S THE BIG IDEA, TOSSING ME THAT PRAISE?
FIDGET
THEY'RE JUST IMPRESSED WITH HOW YOU MOVE ABOUT WHILE SERVING, HERE.
NO WONDER, GIVEN YOUR MERCENARY PAST.
EVEN IN THE BUSIEST TIMES...
...YOU KEEP FOCUSED AND PAY EVERY CUSTOMER DUE CARE, THEY SAY.
JUST LIKE A SOLDIER IN BATTLE.
HA-HA-HA-HA.
AFTER ALL, THIS PLACE PROBABLY FEELS LIKE A BATTLE-FIELD WHEN IT GETS CROWDED.
R- RIGHT.

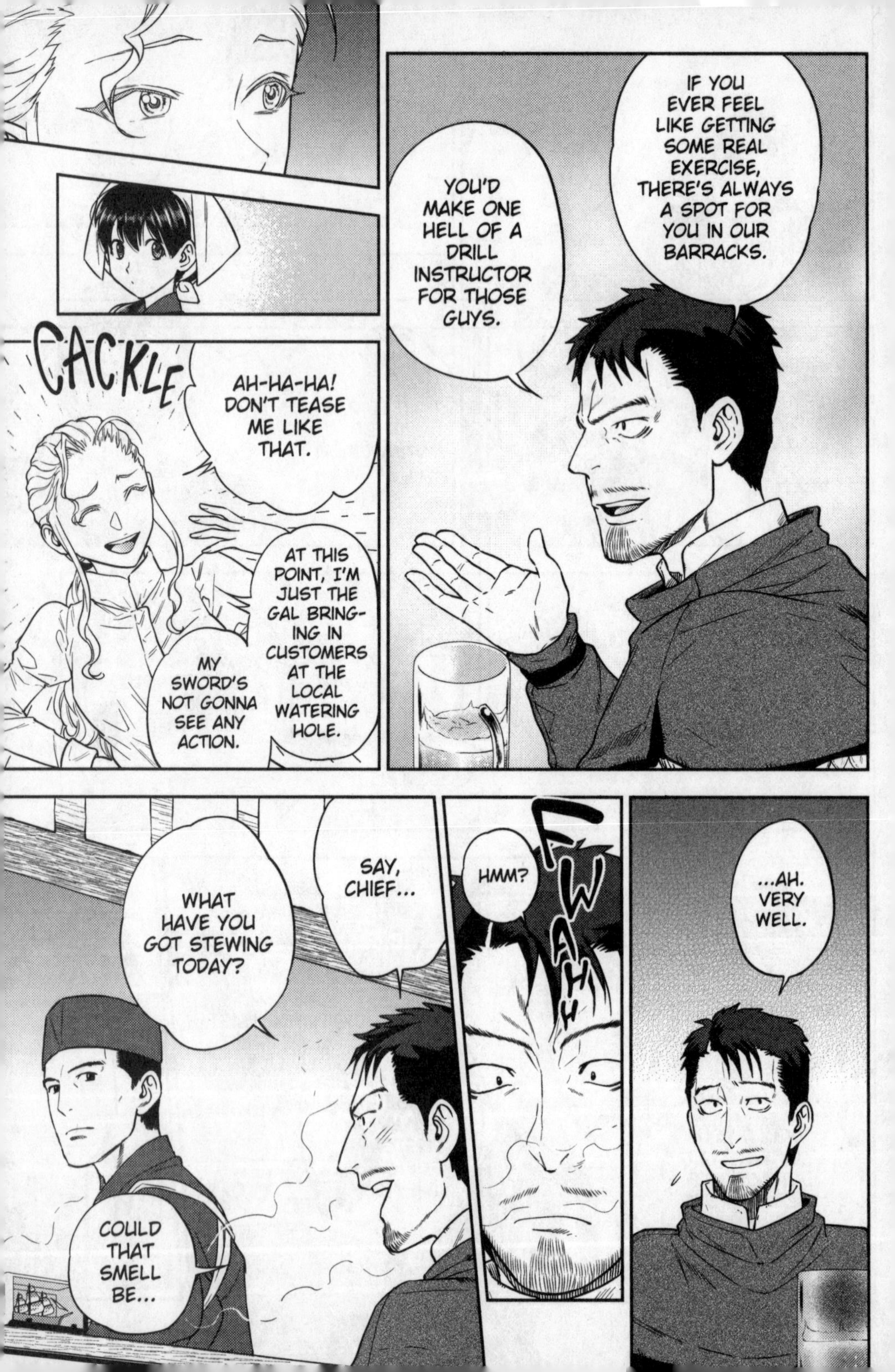
IF YOU EVER FEEL LIKE GETTING SOME REAL EXERCISE, THERE'S ALWAYS A SPOT FOR YOU IN OUR BARRACKS.
YOU'D MAKE ONE HELL OF A DRILL INSTRUCTOR FOR THOSE GUYS.
CACKLE
AH-HA-HA! DON'T TEASE ME LIKE THAT.
AT THIS POINT, I'M JUST THE GAL BRING-ING IN CUSTOMERS AT THE LOCAL WATERING HOLE.
MY SWORD'S NOT GONNA SEE ANY ACTION.
...AH. VERY WELL.
FWAHH
HMM?
SAY, CHIEF...
WHAT HAVE YOU GOT STEWING TODAY?
COULD THAT SMELL BE...

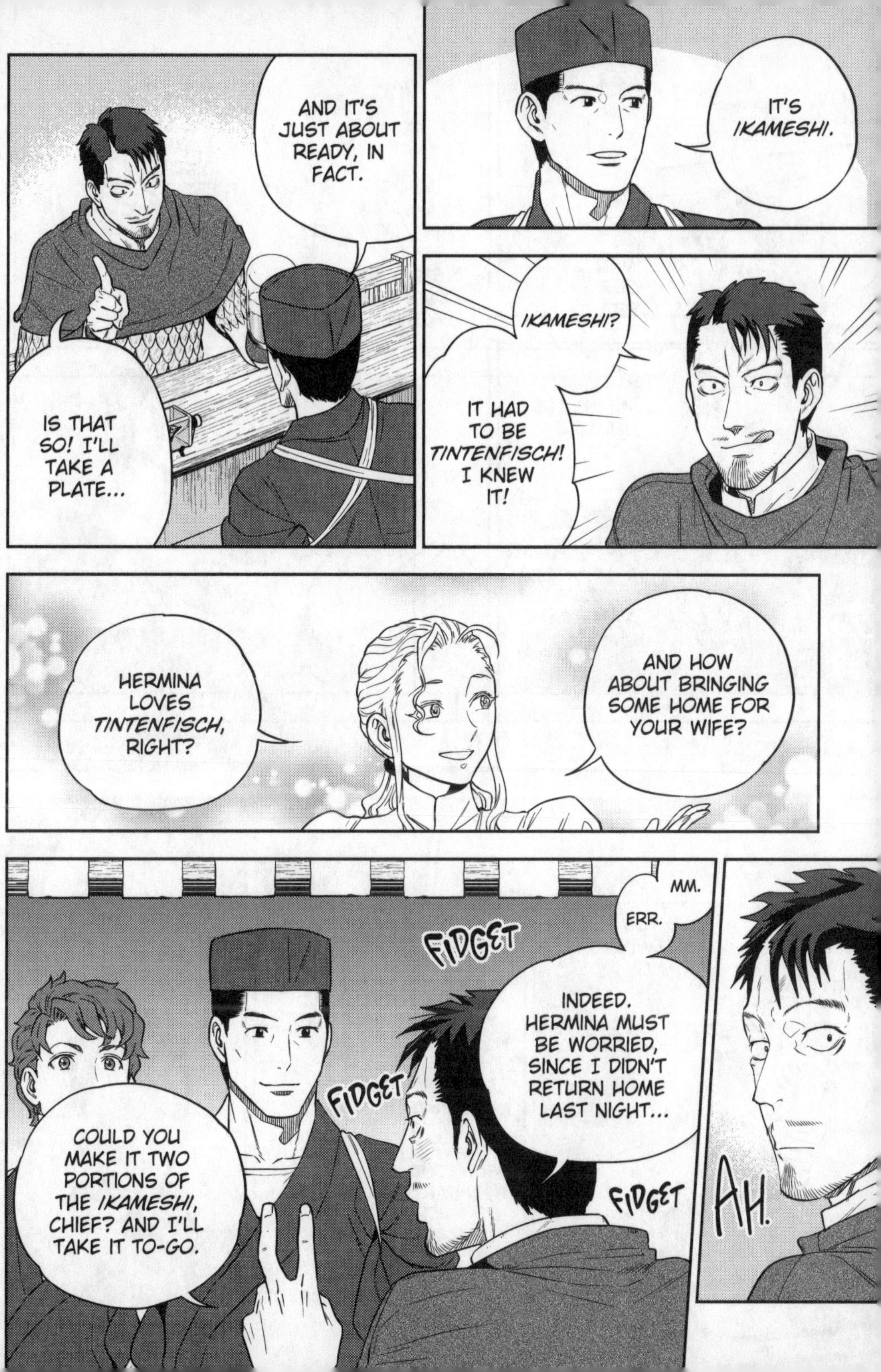
IT'S IKAMESHI.
IKAMESHI?
IT HAD TO BE TINTENFISCH! I KNEW IT!
AND IT'S JUST ABOUT READY, IN FACT.
IS THAT SO! I'LL TAKE A PLATE...
AND HOW ABOUT BRINGING SOME HOME FOR YOUR WIFE?
HERMINA LOVES TINTENFISCH, RIGHT?
AH.
MM.
ERR.
FIDGET
INDEED. HERMINA MUST BE WORRIED, SINCE I DIDN'T RETURN HOME LAST NIGHT...
FIDGET
FIDGET
COULD YOU MAKE IT TWO PORTIONS OF THE IKAMESHI, CHIEF? AND I'LL TAKE IT TO-GO.

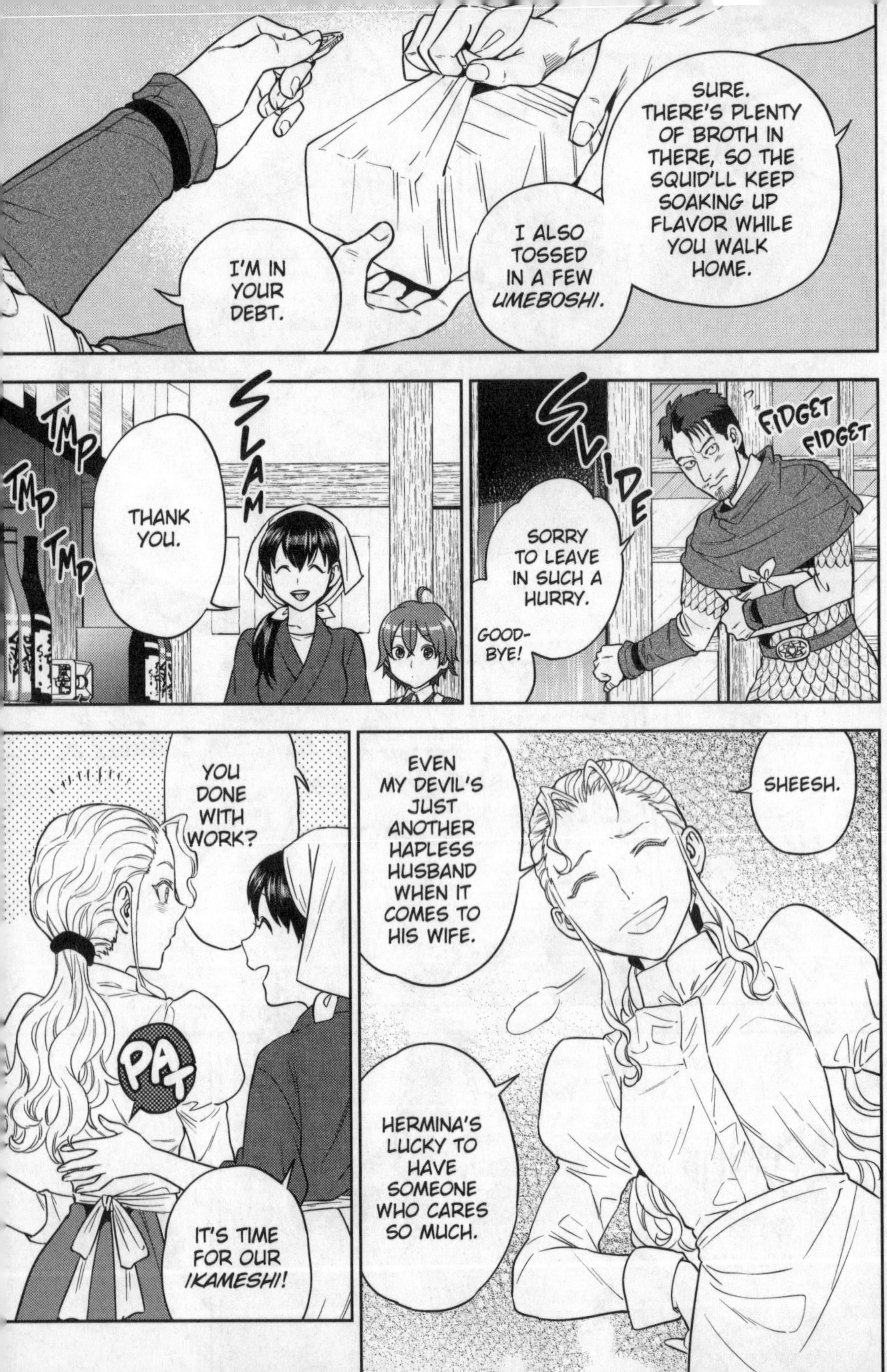
SURE. THERE'S PLENTY OF BROTH IN THERE, SO THE SQUID'LL KEEP SOAKING UP FLAVOR WHILE YOU WALK HOME.
I ALSO TOSSED IN A FEW *UMEBOSHI*.
I'M IN YOUR DEBT.
FIDGET FIDGET
SLIDE
SORRY TO LEAVE IN SUCH A HURRY.
GOOD-BYE!
SLAM
TMP TMP TMP
THANK YOU.
SHEESH.
EVEN MY DEVIL'S JUST ANOTHER HAPLESS HUSBAND WHEN IT COMES TO HIS WIFE.
HERMINA'S LUCKY TO HAVE SOMEONE WHO CARES SO MUCH.
YOU DONE WITH WORK?
PAT
IT'S TIME FOR OUR *IKAMESHI*!

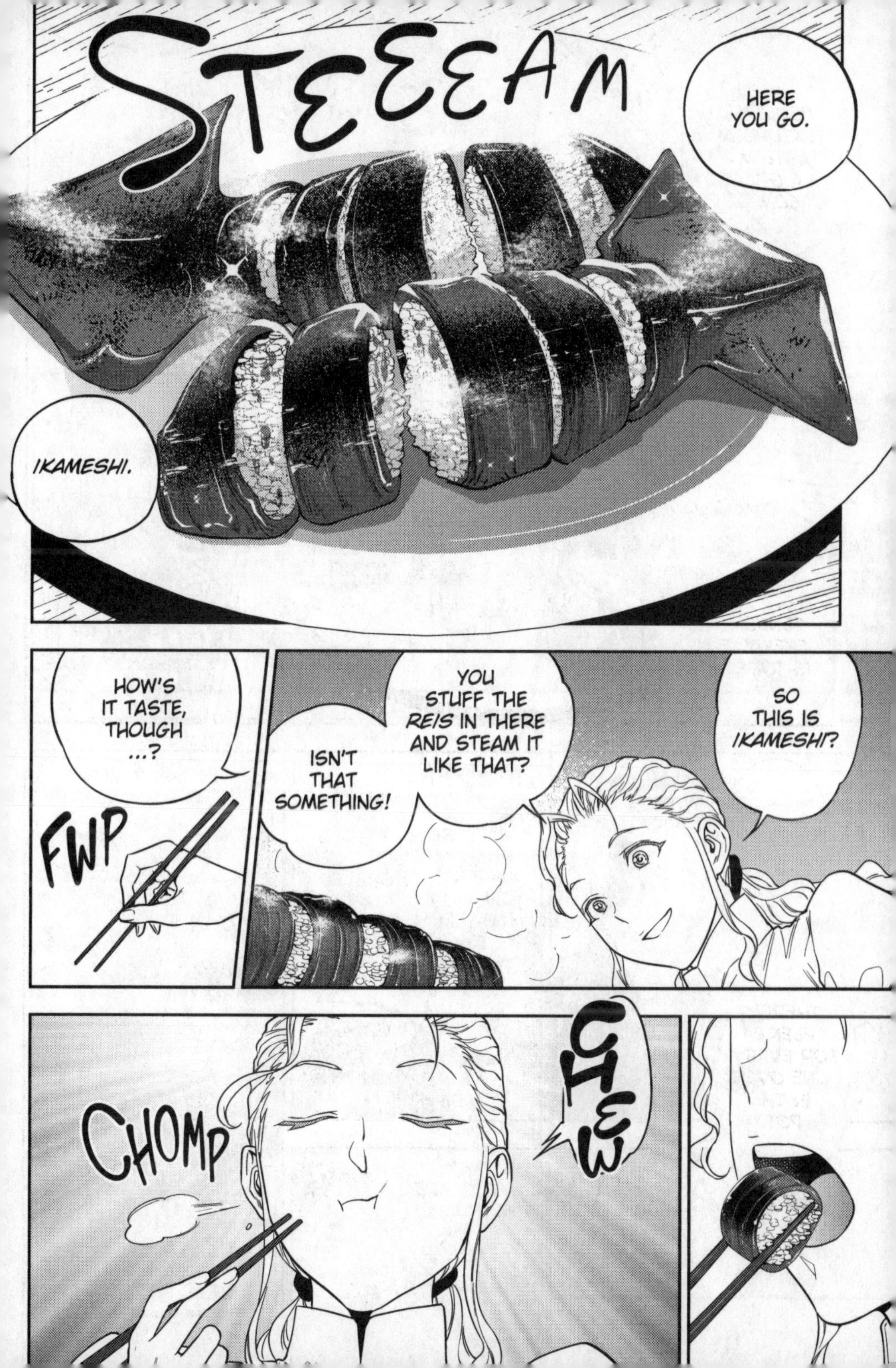
STEEEAM
HERE YOU GO.
IKAMESHI.
SO THIS IS IKAMESHI?
YOU STUFF THE REIS IN THERE AND STEAM IT LIKE THAT?
ISN'T THAT SOMETHING!
HOW'S IT TASTE, THOUGH ...?
FWP
CHEW
CHOMP

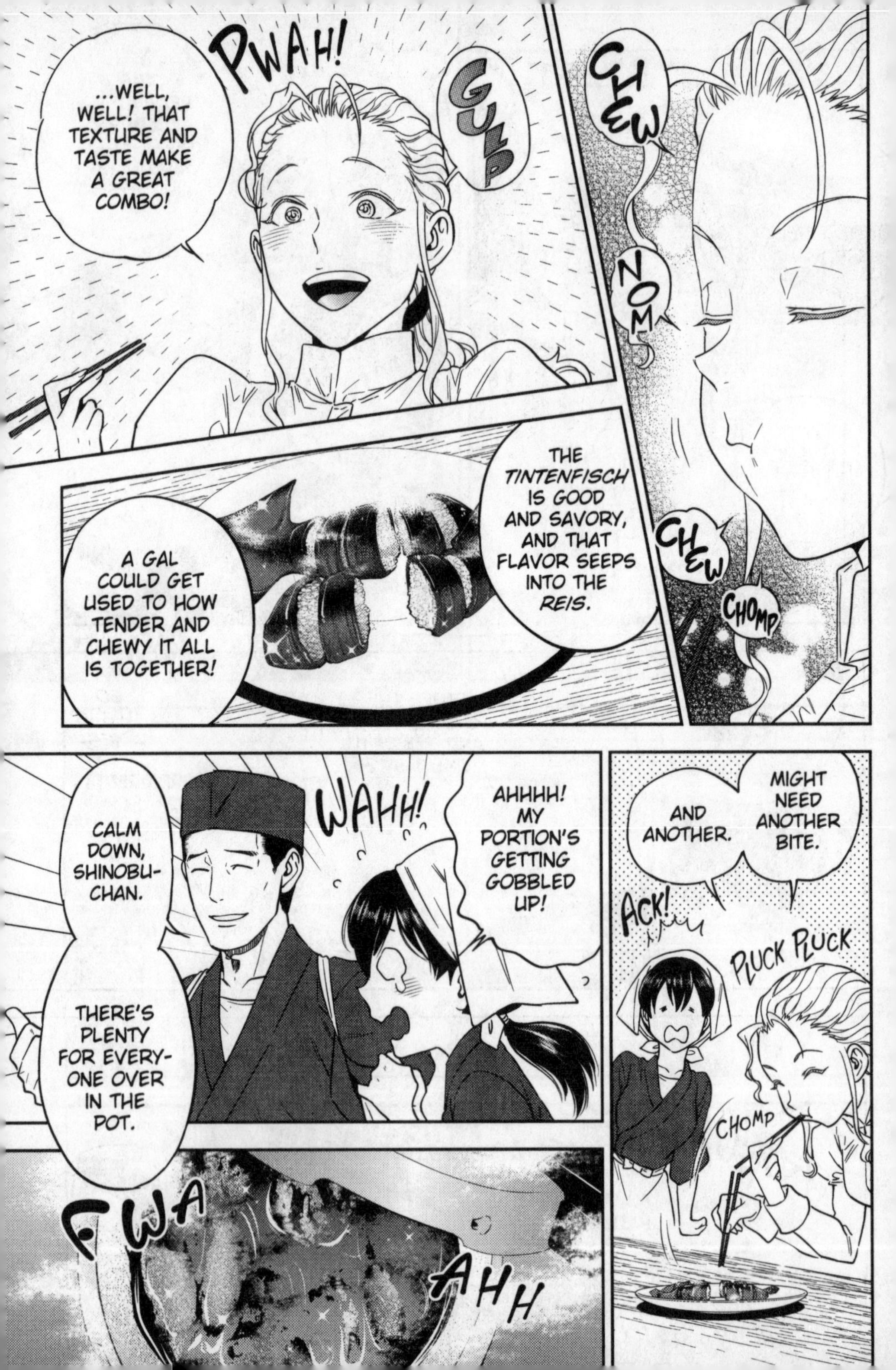
CHEW
NOM
CHEW
CHOMP
GULP
PWAH!
...WELL, WELL! THAT TEXTURE AND TASTE MAKE A GREAT COMBO!
THE *TINTENFISCH* IS GOOD AND SAVORY, AND THAT FLAVOR SEEPS INTO THE *REIS*.
A GAL COULD GET USED TO HOW TENDER AND CHEWY IT ALL IS TOGETHER!
MIGHT NEED ANOTHER BITE.
AND ANOTHER.
ACK!
PLUCK PLUCK
CHOMP
AHHHH! MY PORTION'S GETTING GOBBLED UP!
WAHH!
CALM DOWN, SHINOBU-CHAN.
THERE'S PLENTY FOR EVERY-ONE OVER IN THE POT.
FWA
AHH

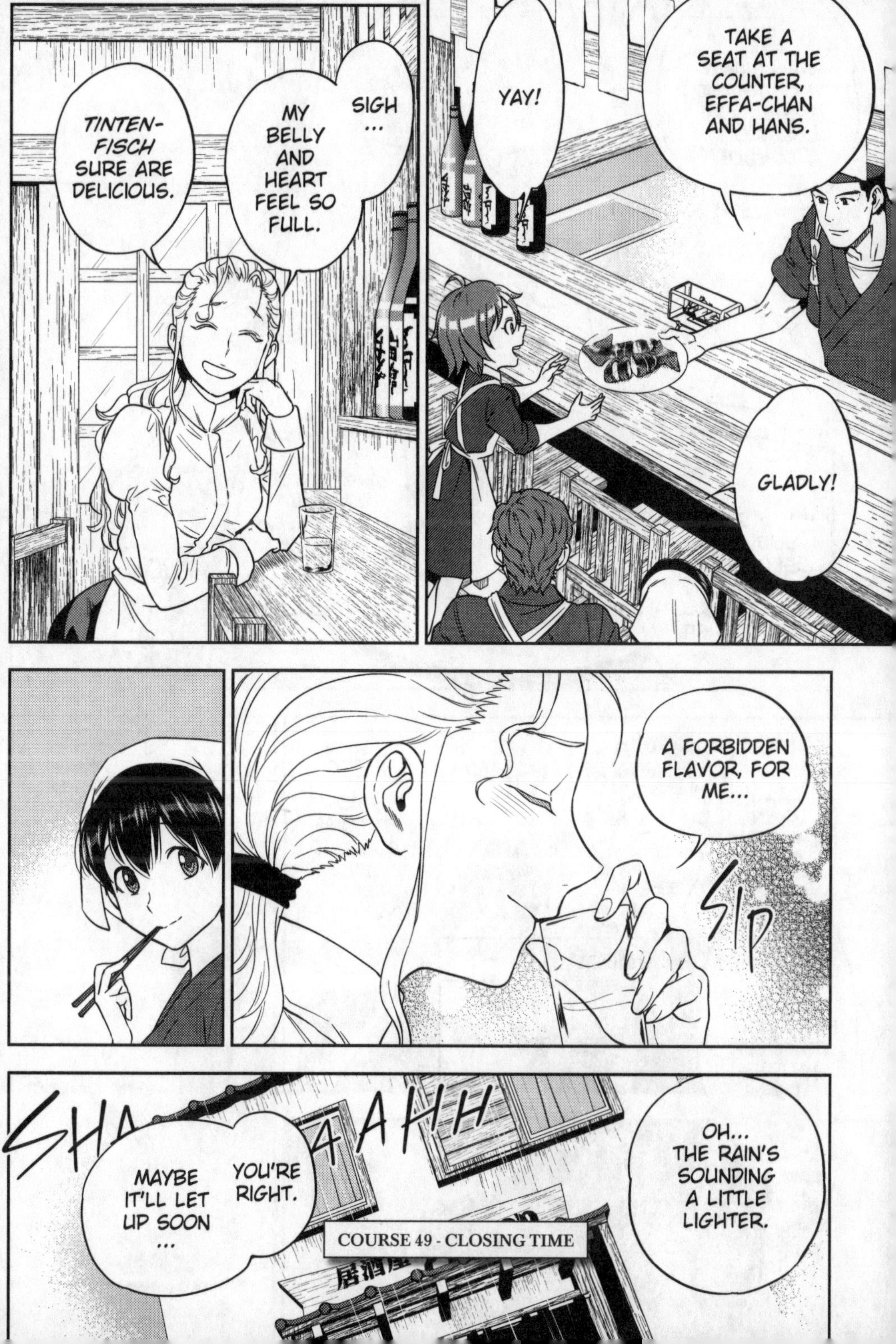
TAKE A SEAT AT THE COUNTER, EFFA-CHAN AND HANS.
YAY!
GLADLY!
SIGH ...
MY BELLY AND HEART FEEL SO FULL.
TINTEN-FISCH SURE ARE DELICIOUS.
A FORBIDDEN FLAVOR, FOR ME...
SIP
OH... THE RAIN'S SOUNDING A LITTLE LIGHTER.
SHA AAHH
YOU'RE RIGHT.
MAYBE IT'LL LET UP SOON ...
COURSE 49 - CLOSING TIME
居酒屋

Ikameshi

OTHERWORLDLY IZAKAYA

NOBU

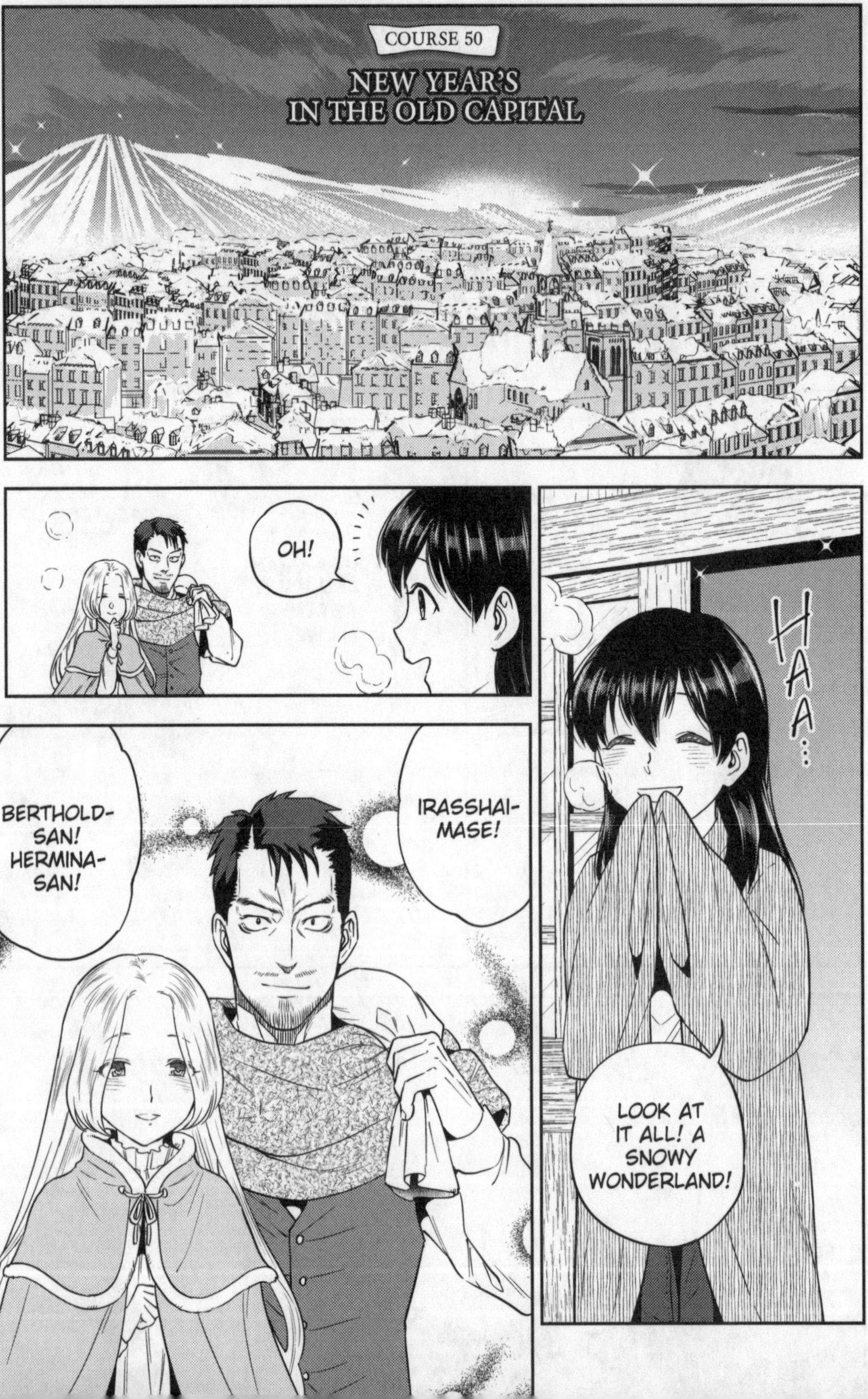
COURSE 50
NEW YEAR'S IN THE OLD CAPITAL
HAA...
LOOK AT IT ALL! A SNOWY WONDERLAND!
OH!
IRASSHAI-MASE!
BERTHOLD-SAN! HERMINA-SAN!

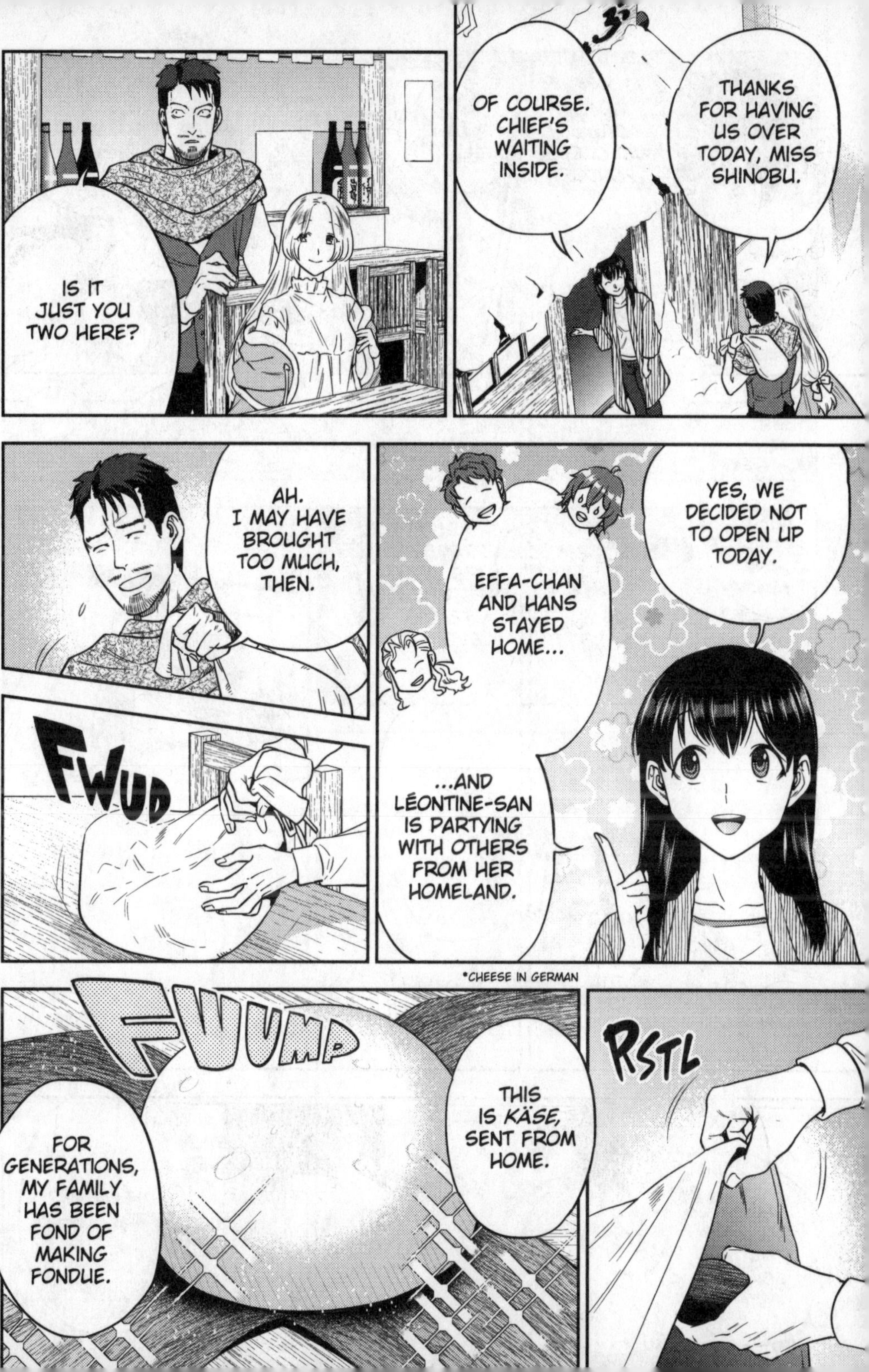
THANKS FOR HAVING US OVER TODAY, MISS SHINOBU.
OF COURSE. CHIEF'S WAITING INSIDE.
IS IT JUST YOU TWO HERE?
YES, WE DECIDED NOT TO OPEN UP TODAY.
EFFA-CHAN AND HANS STAYED HOME...
...AND LÉONTINE-SAN IS PARTYING WITH OTHERS FROM HER HOMELAND.
AH. I MAY HAVE BROUGHT TOO MUCH, THEN.
FWUD
RSTL
FWUMP
THIS IS KÄSE, SENT FROM HOME.
FOR GENERATIONS, MY FAMILY HAS BEEN FOND OF MAKING FONDUE.

*CHEESE IN GERMAN

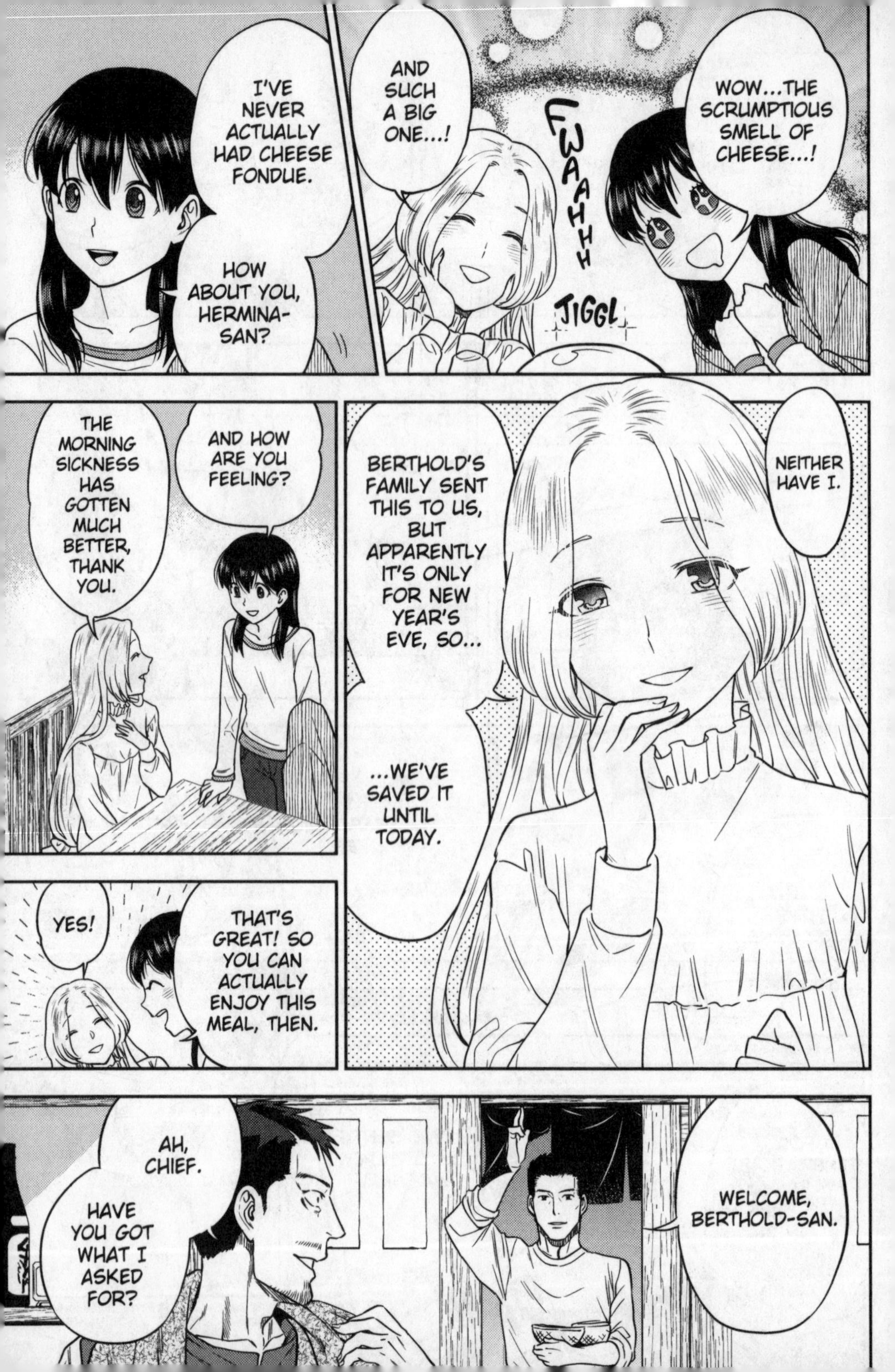
WOW...THE SCRUMPTIOUS SMELL OF CHEESE...!
FWAAHHH
JIGGL
AND SUCH A BIG ONE...!
I'VE NEVER ACTUALLY HAD CHEESE FONDUE.
HOW ABOUT YOU, HERMINA-SAN?
NEITHER HAVE I.
BERTHOLD'S FAMILY SENT THIS TO US, BUT APPARENTLY IT'S ONLY FOR NEW YEAR'S EVE, SO...
...WE'VE SAVED IT UNTIL TODAY.
AND HOW ARE YOU FEELING?
THE MORNING SICKNESS HAS GOTTEN MUCH BETTER, THANK YOU.
THAT'S GREAT! SO YOU CAN ACTUALLY ENJOY THIS MEAL, THEN.
YES!
WELCOME, BERTHOLD-SAN.
AH, CHIEF.
HAVE YOU GOT WHAT I ASKED FOR?

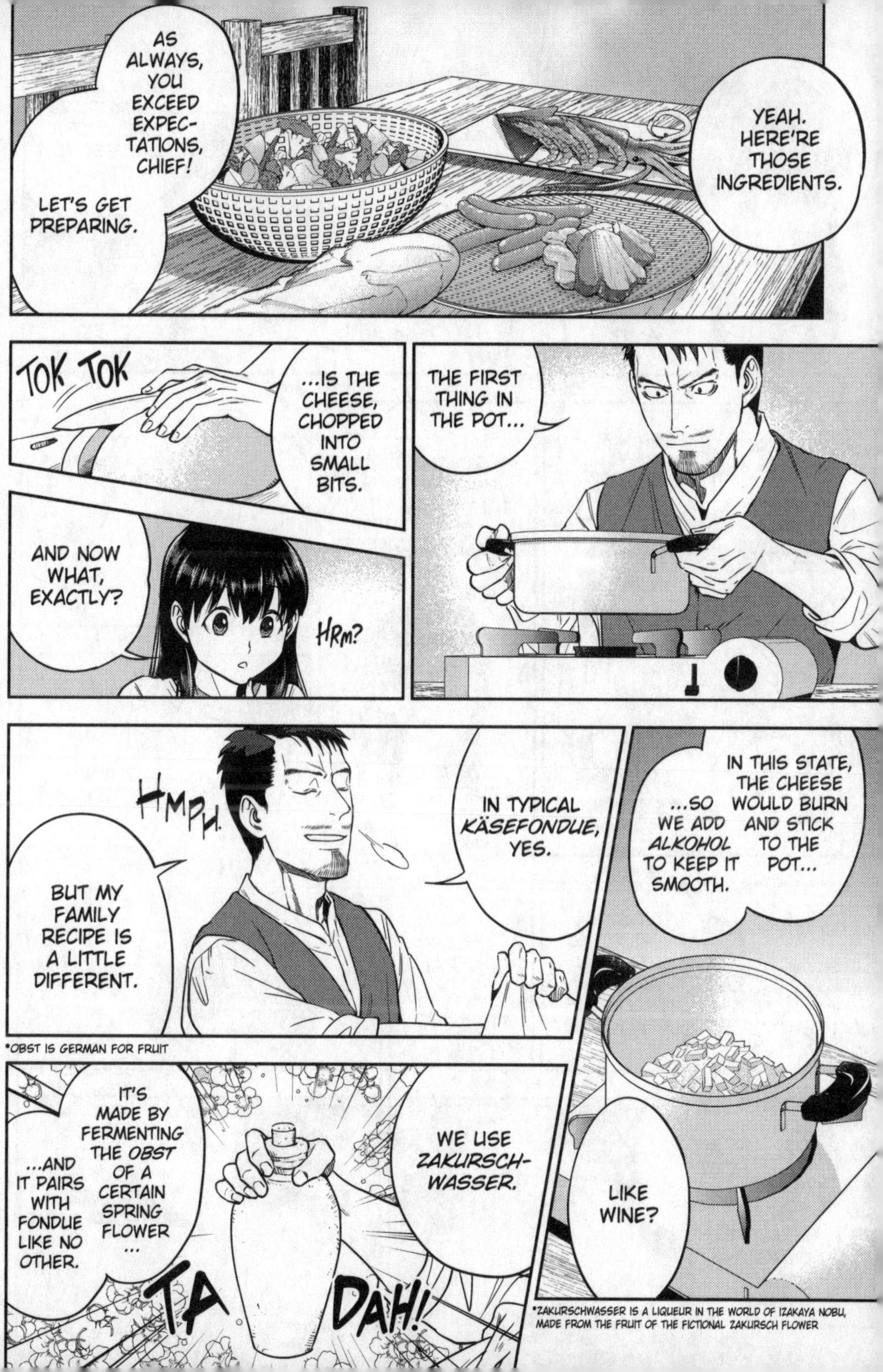
YEAH. HERE'RE THOSE INGREDIENTS.
AS ALWAYS, YOU EXCEED EXPECTATIONS, CHIEF!
LET'S GET PREPARING.
THE FIRST THING IN THE POT...
...IS THE CHEESE, CHOPPED INTO SMALL BITS.
TOK TOK
HRM?
AND NOW WHAT, EXACTLY?
IN THIS STATE, THE CHEESE WOULD BURN AND STICK TO THE POT...
...SO WE ADD *ALCOHOL* TO KEEP IT SMOOTH.
LIKE WINE?
IN TYPICAL *KÄSEFONDUE*, YES.
HMPH.
BUT MY FAMILY RECIPE IS A LITTLE DIFFERENT.
WE USE *ZAKURSCHWASSER.*
IT'S MADE BY FERMENTING THE *OBST* OF A CERTAIN SPRING FLOWER...
...AND IT PAIRS WITH FONDUE LIKE NO OTHER.
TA DAH!

*OBST IS GERMAN FOR FRUIT

*ZAKURSCHWASSER IS A LIQUEUR IN THE WORLD OF IZAKAYA NOBU, MADE FROM THE FRUIT OF THE FICTIONAL ZAKURSCH FLOWER

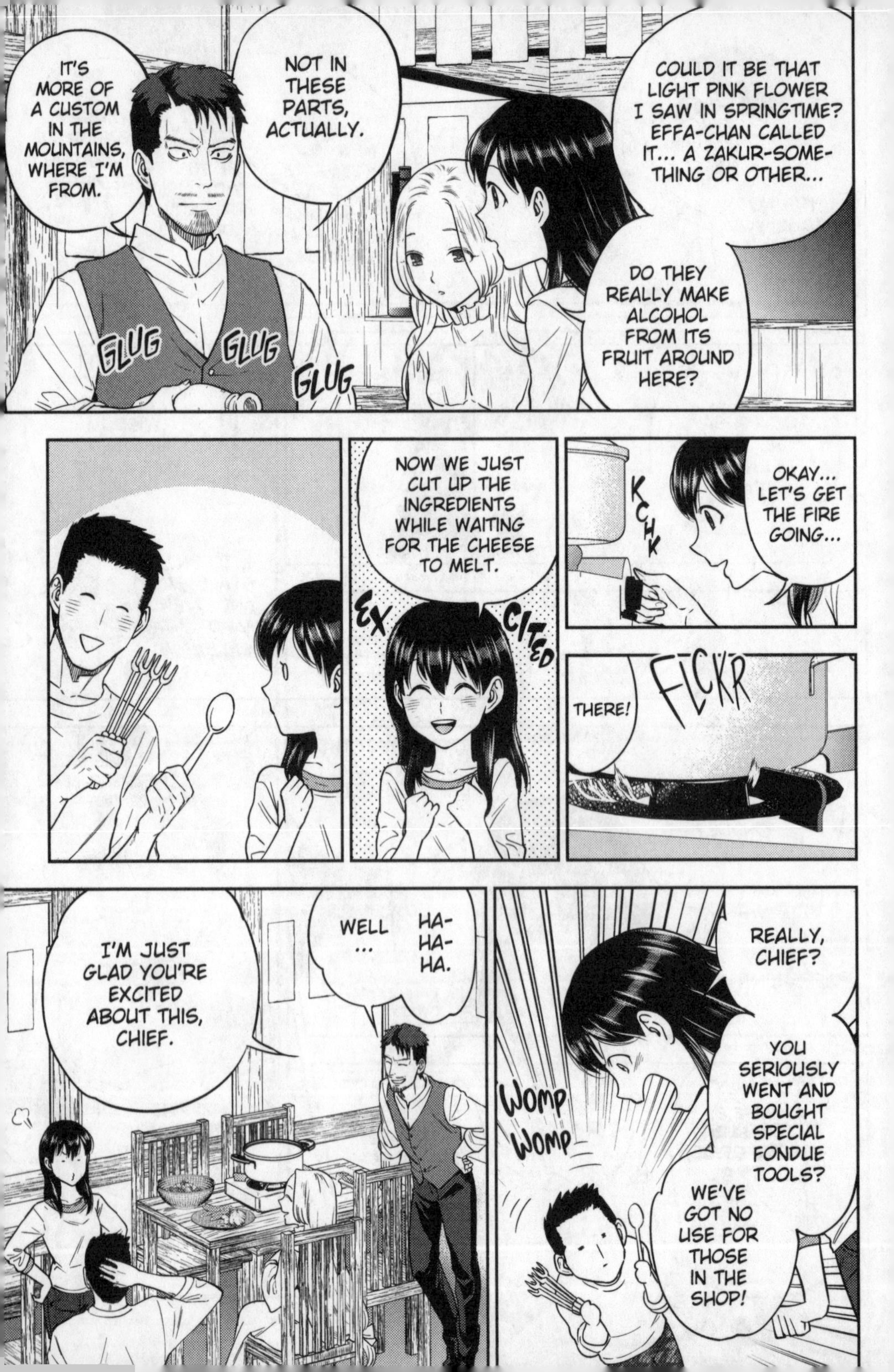
COULD IT BE THAT LIGHT PINK FLOWER I SAW IN SPRINGTIME? EFFA-CHAN CALLED IT... A ZAKUR-SOME-THING OR OTHER...
DO THEY REALLY MAKE ALCOHOL FROM ITS FRUIT AROUND HERE?
NOT IN THESE PARTS, ACTUALLY.
IT'S MORE OF A CUSTOM IN THE MOUNTAINS, WHERE I'M FROM.
GLUG GLUG GLUG
OKAY... LET'S GET THE FIRE GOING...
KCHK
FLCKR
THERE!
NOW WE JUST CUT UP THE INGREDIENTS WHILE WAITING FOR THE CHEESE TO MELT.
EX CITED
REALLY, CHIEF?
YOU SERIOUSLY WENT AND BOUGHT SPECIAL FONDUE TOOLS?
WE'VE GOT NO USE FOR THOSE IN THE SHOP!
WOMP WOMP
WELL ... HA-HA-HA.
I'M JUST GLAD YOU'RE EXCITED ABOUT THIS, CHIEF.

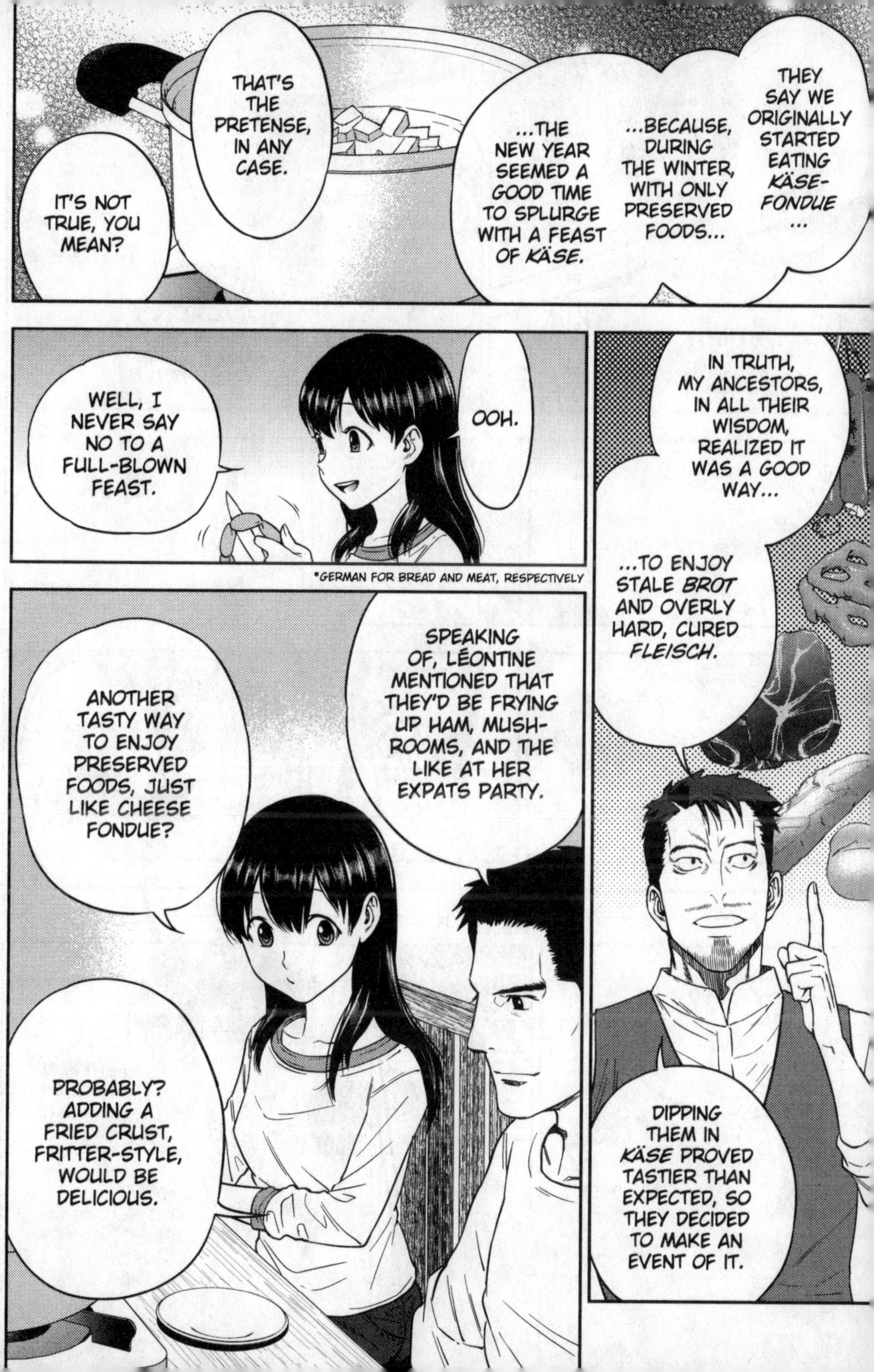
THEY SAY WE ORIGINALLY STARTED EATING KÄSE-FONDUE ...
...BECAUSE, DURING THE WINTER, WITH ONLY PRESERVED FOODS...
...THE NEW YEAR SEEMED A GOOD TIME TO SPLURGE WITH A FEAST OF KÄSE.
THAT'S THE PRETENSE, IN ANY CASE.
IT'S NOT TRUE, YOU MEAN?
IN TRUTH, MY ANCESTORS, IN ALL THEIR WISDOM, REALIZED IT WAS A GOOD WAY...
...TO ENJOY STALE BROT AND OVERLY HARD, CURED FLEISCH.
DIPPING THEM IN KÄSE PROVED TASTIER THAN EXPECTED, SO THEY DECIDED TO MAKE AN EVENT OF IT.
OOH.
WELL, I NEVER SAY NO TO A FULL-BLOWN FEAST.
SPEAKING OF, LÉONTINE MENTIONED THAT THEY'D BE FRYING UP HAM, MUSH-ROOMS, AND THE LIKE AT HER EXPATS PARTY.
ANOTHER TASTY WAY TO ENJOY PRESERVED FOODS, JUST LIKE CHEESE FONDUE?
PROBABLY? ADDING A FRIED CRUST, FRITTER-STYLE, WOULD BE DELICIOUS.
*GERMAN FOR BREAD AND MEAT, RESPECTIVELY

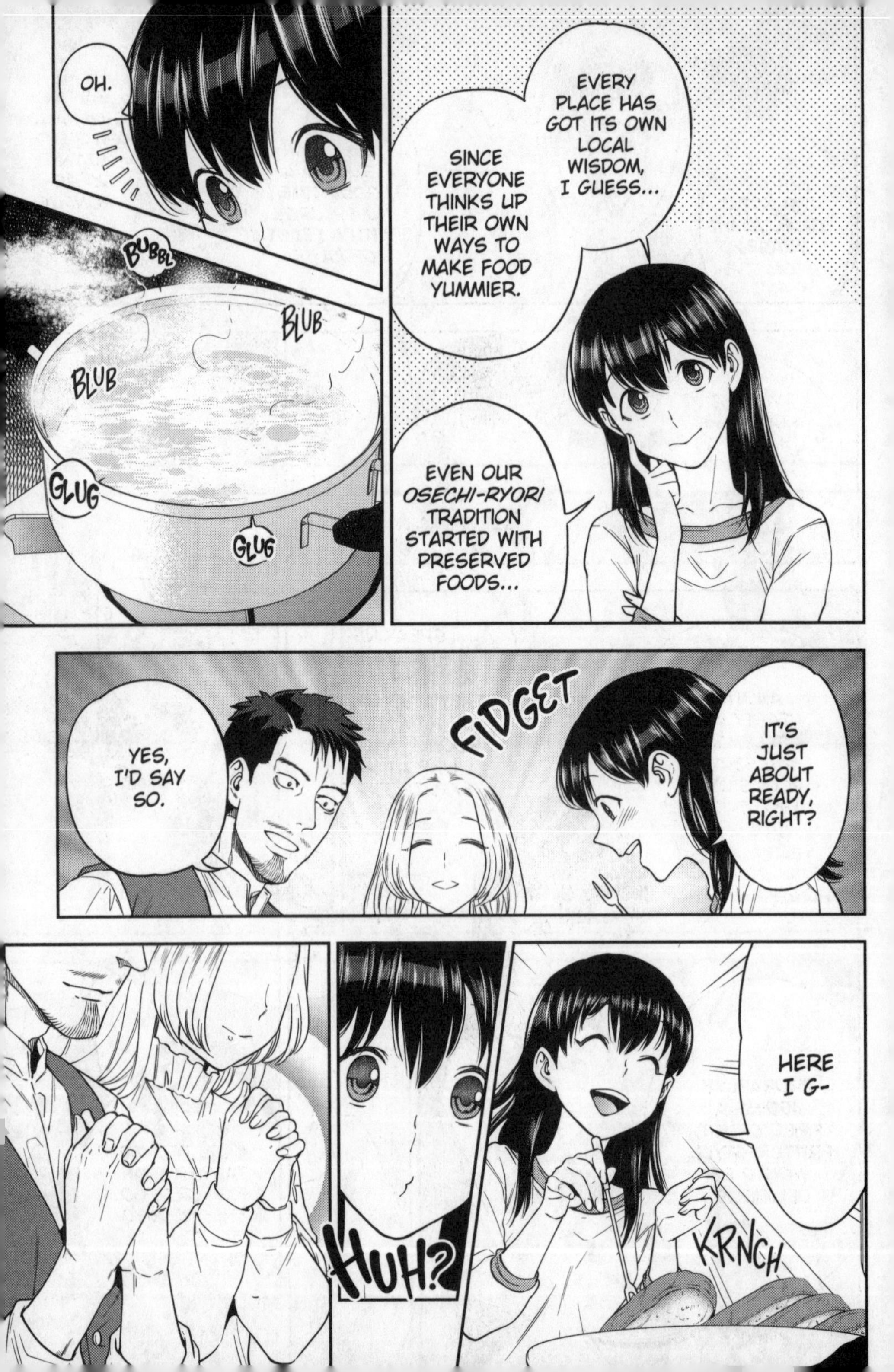
EVERY PLACE HAS GOT ITS OWN LOCAL WISDOM, I GUESS...
SINCE EVERYONE THINKS UP THEIR OWN WAYS TO MAKE FOOD YUMMIER.
EVEN OUR *OSECHI-RYORI* TRADITION STARTED WITH PRESERVED FOODS...
OH.
BUBBL
BLUB
BLUB
GLUG
GLUG
IT'S JUST ABOUT READY, RIGHT?
FIDGET
YES, I'D SAY SO.
HERE I G-
KRNCH
HUH?

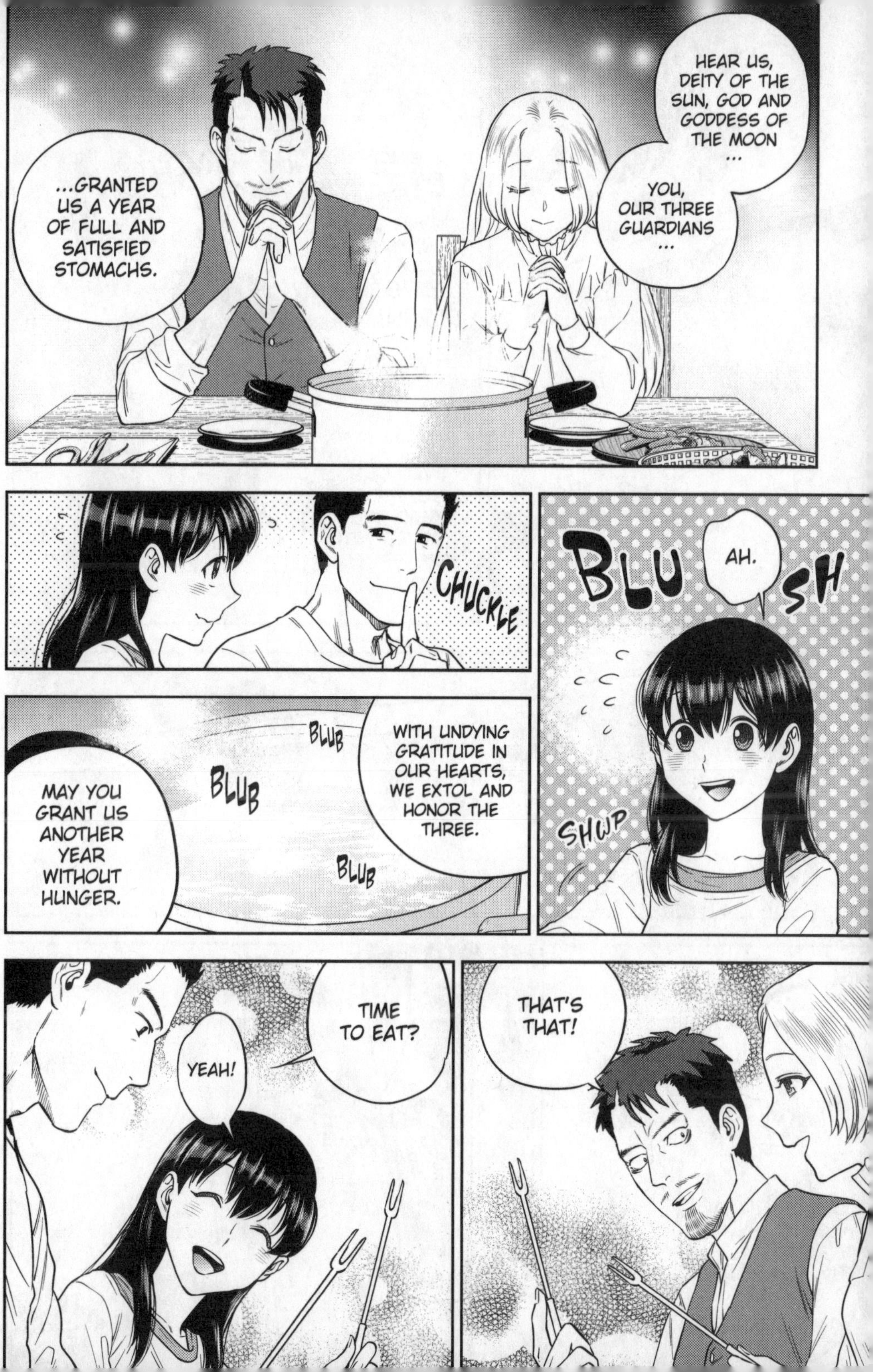
HEAR US, DEITY OF THE SUN, GOD AND GODDESS OF THE MOON ...
YOU, OUR THREE GUARDIANS ...
...GRANTED US A YEAR OF FULL AND SATISFIED STOMACHS.
BLU SH
AH.
SHWP
CHUCKLE
WITH UNDYING GRATITUDE IN OUR HEARTS, WE EXTOL AND HONOR THE THREE.
BLUB
BLUB
MAY YOU GRANT US ANOTHER YEAR WITHOUT HUNGER.
BLUB
THAT'S THAT!
TIME TO EAT?
YEAH!

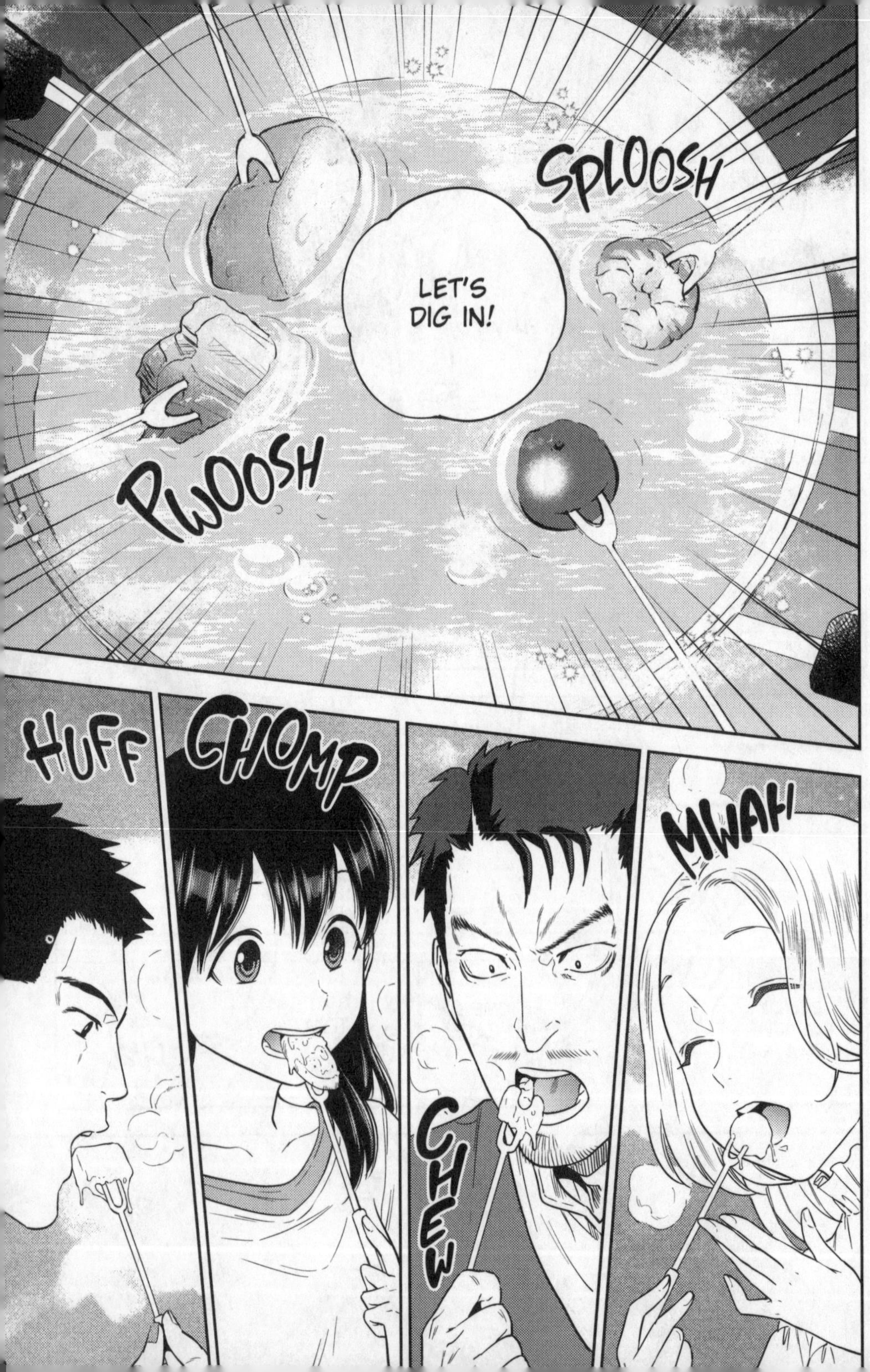
SPLOOSH
LET'S DIG IN!
PWOOSH
MWAH
CHEW
CHOMP
HUFF

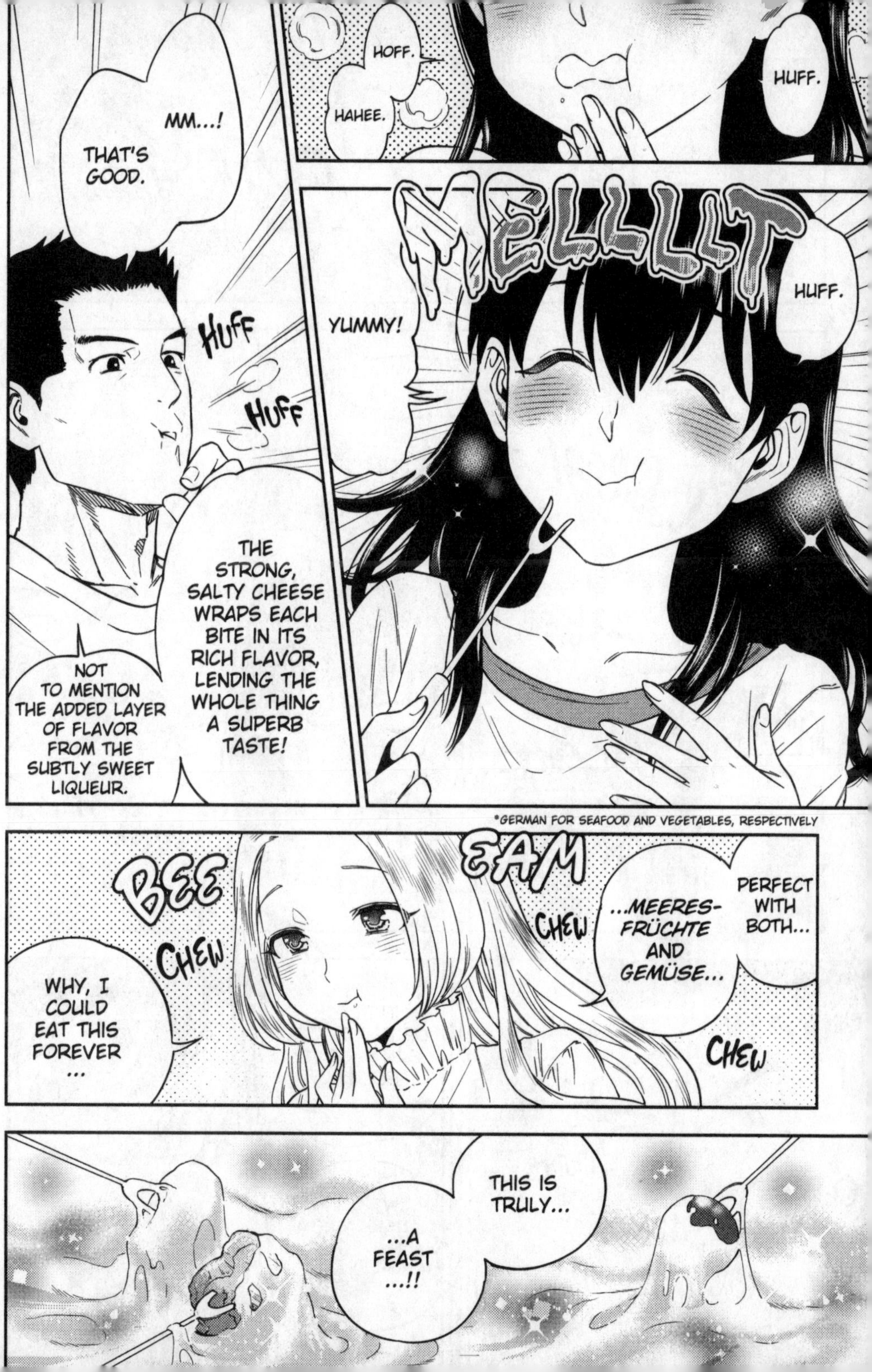
HUFF.
HOFF.
HAHEE.
MELLLIT
HUFF.
YUMMY!
MM...! THAT'S GOOD.
HUFF
HUFF
THE STRONG, SALTY CHEESE WRAPS EACH BITE IN ITS RICH FLAVOR, LENDING THE WHOLE THING A SUPERB TASTE!
NOT TO MENTION THE ADDED LAYER OF FLAVOR FROM THE SUBTLY SWEET LIQUEUR.
*GERMAN FOR SEAFOOD AND VEGETABLES, RESPECTIVELY
PERFECT WITH BOTH...
...MEERES-FRÜCHTE AND GEMÜSE...
CHEW
EAM
BEE
CHEW
WHY, I COULD EAT THIS FOREVER ...
CHEW
THIS IS TRULY...
...A FEAST ...!!

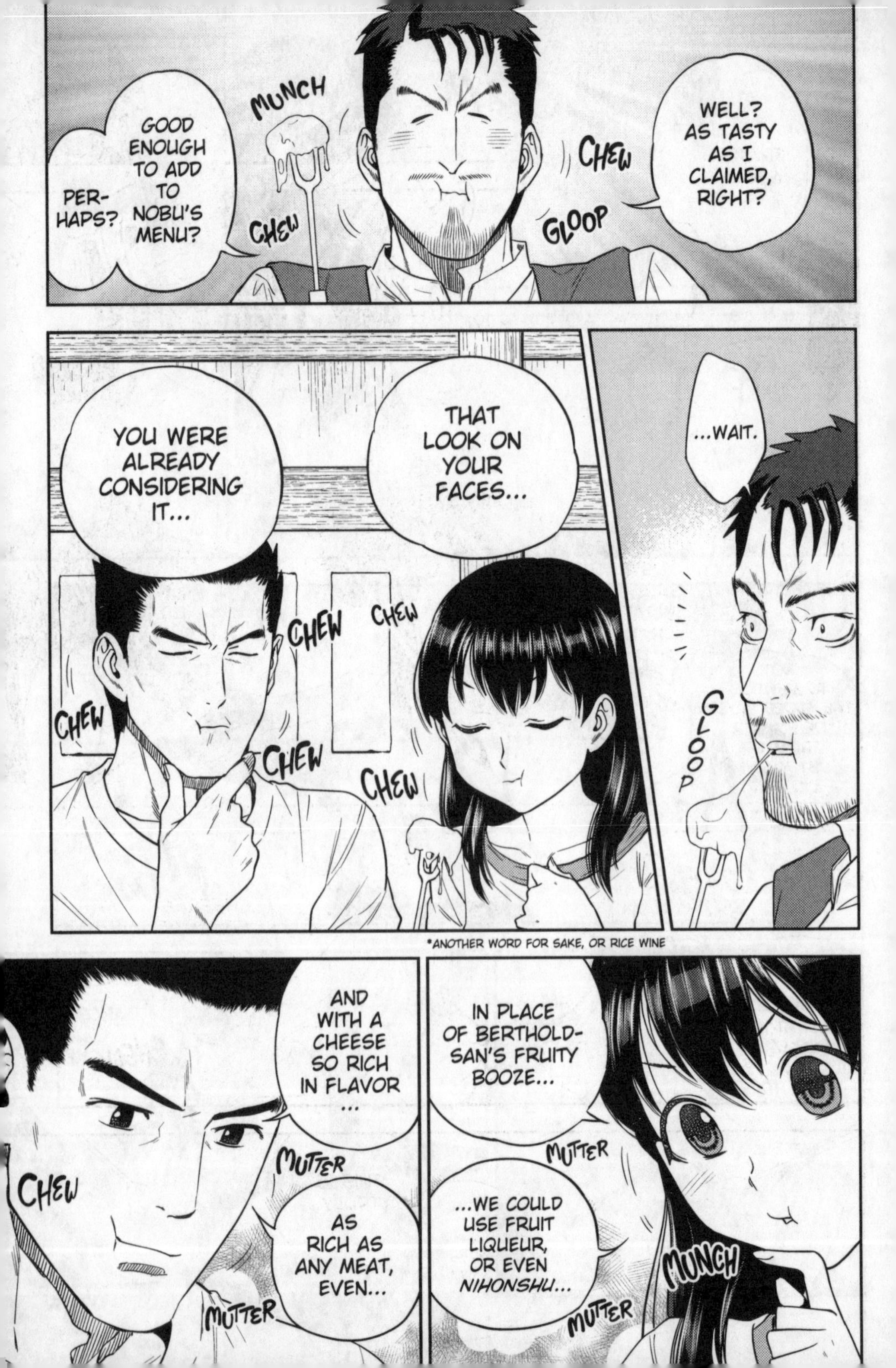
WELL? AS TASTY AS I CLAIMED, RIGHT?
CHEW
GLOOP
MUNCH
GOOD ENOUGH TO ADD TO NOBU'S MENU? PER-HAPS?
CHEW
...WAIT.
GLOOP
THAT LOOK ON YOUR FACES...
YOU WERE ALREADY CONSIDERING IT...
CHEW
CHEW
CHEW
CHEW
CHEW
IN PLACE OF BERTHOLD-SAN'S FRUITY BOOZE...
MUTTER
...WE COULD USE FRUIT LIQUEUR, OR EVEN *NIHONSHU*...
MUNCH
MUTTER
AND WITH A CHEESE SO RICH IN FLAVOR...
MUTTER
CHEW
AS RICH AS ANY MEAT, EVEN...
MUTTER

*ANOTHER WORD FOR SAKE, OR RICE WINE

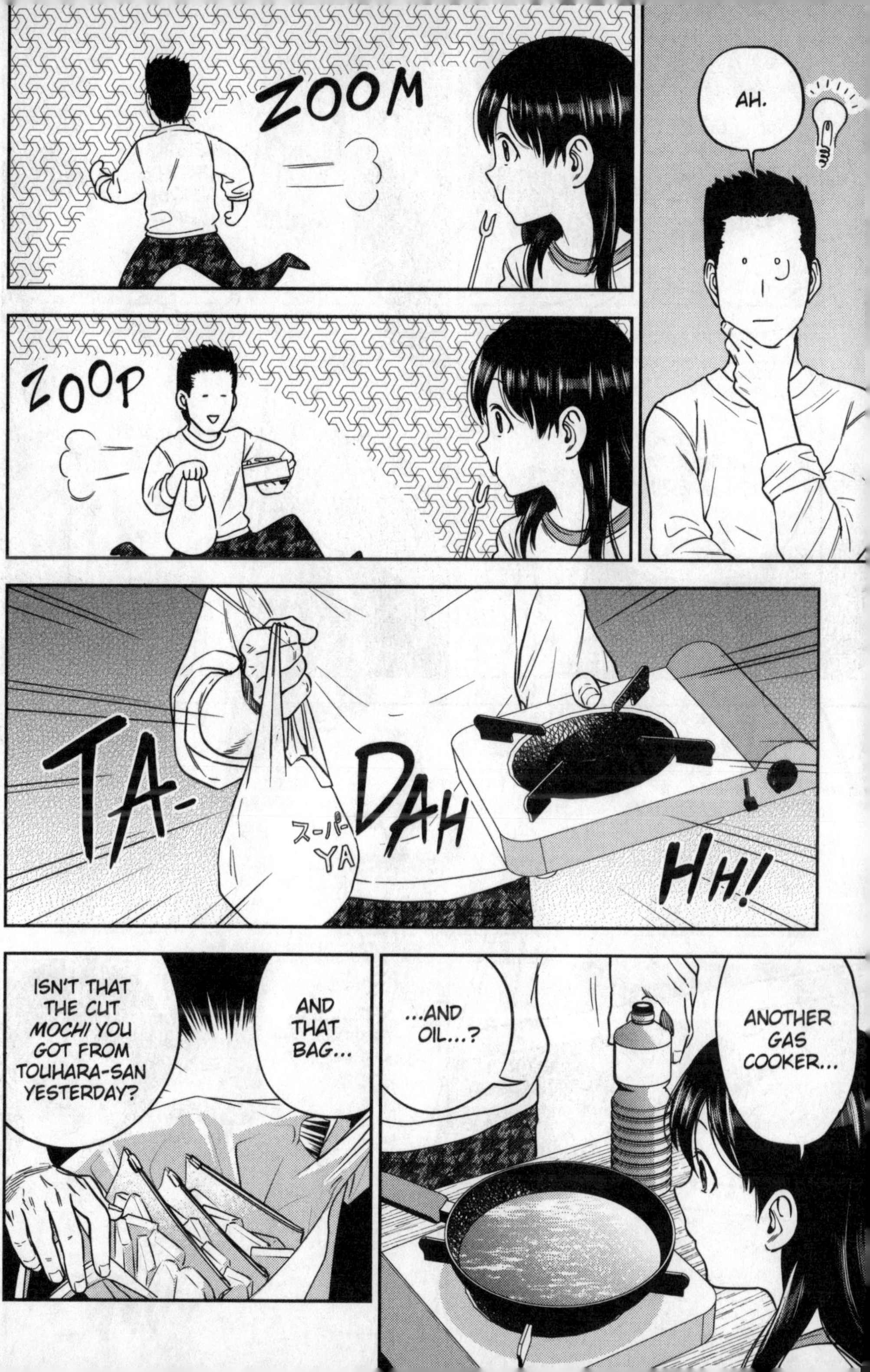
AH.
ZOOM
ZOOP
TA-DAHH!
スーパーYA
ANOTHER GAS COOKER...
...AND OIL...?
AND THAT BAG...
ISN'T THAT THE CUT *MOCHI* YOU GOT FROM TOUHARA-SAN YESTERDAY?

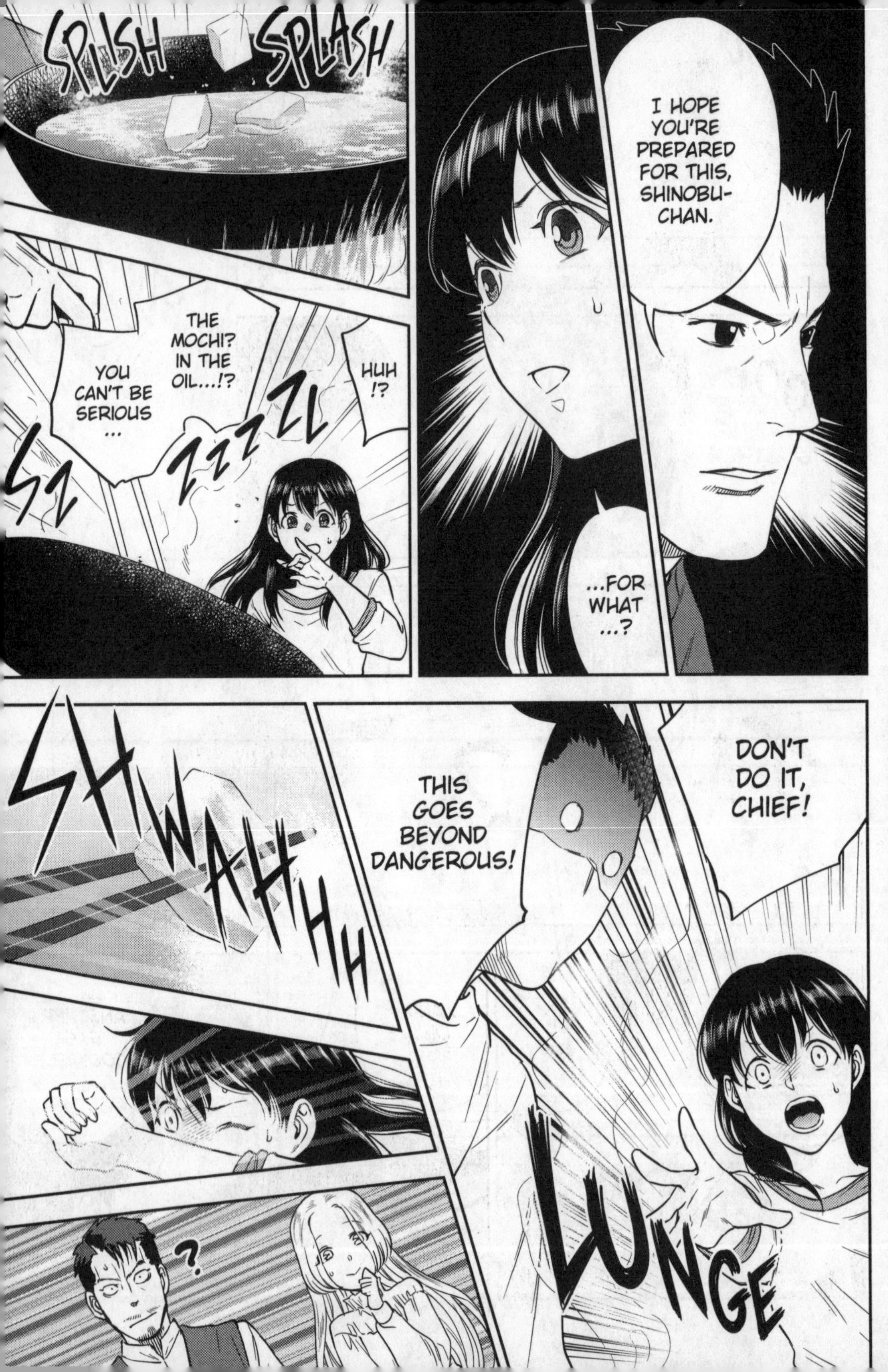
I HOPE YOU'RE PREPARED FOR THIS, SHINOBU-CHAN.
...FOR WHAT...?
SPLISH SPLASH
HUH!?
THE MOCHI? IN THE OIL...!?
YOU CAN'T BE SERIOUS...
SZZZZZZZL
DON'T DO IT, CHIEF!
THIS GOES BEYOND DANGEROUS!
LUNGE
SHWAHHHH
?

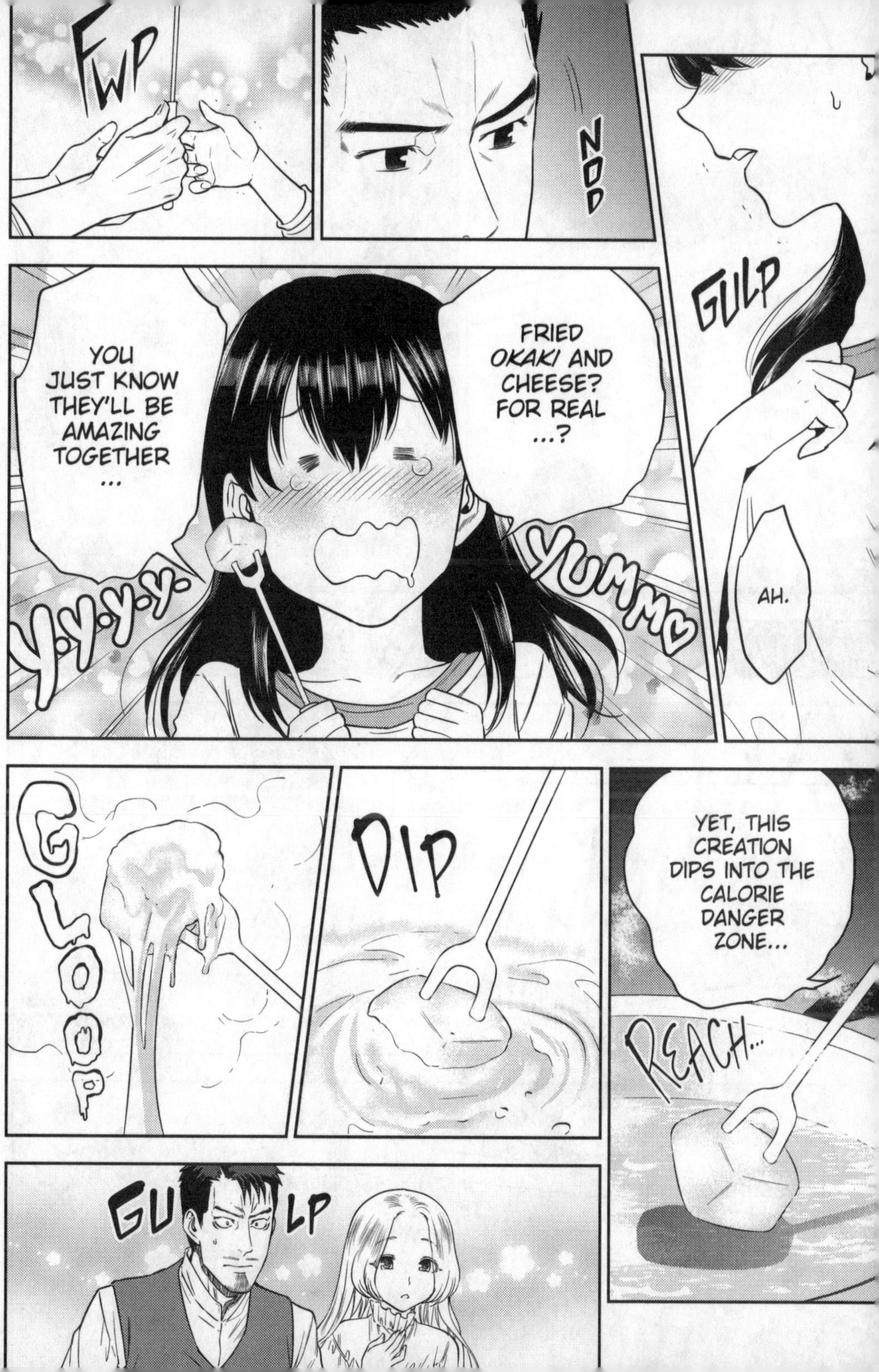
GULP
AH.
NOD
FWP
FRIED *OKAKI* AND CHEESE? FOR REAL ...?
YOU JUST KNOW THEY'LL BE AMAZING TOGETHER ...
Y-Y-Y-Y-
YUMM♡
YET, THIS CREATION DIPS INTO THE CALORIE DANGER ZONE...
REACH...
DIP
GLOOP
GU LP

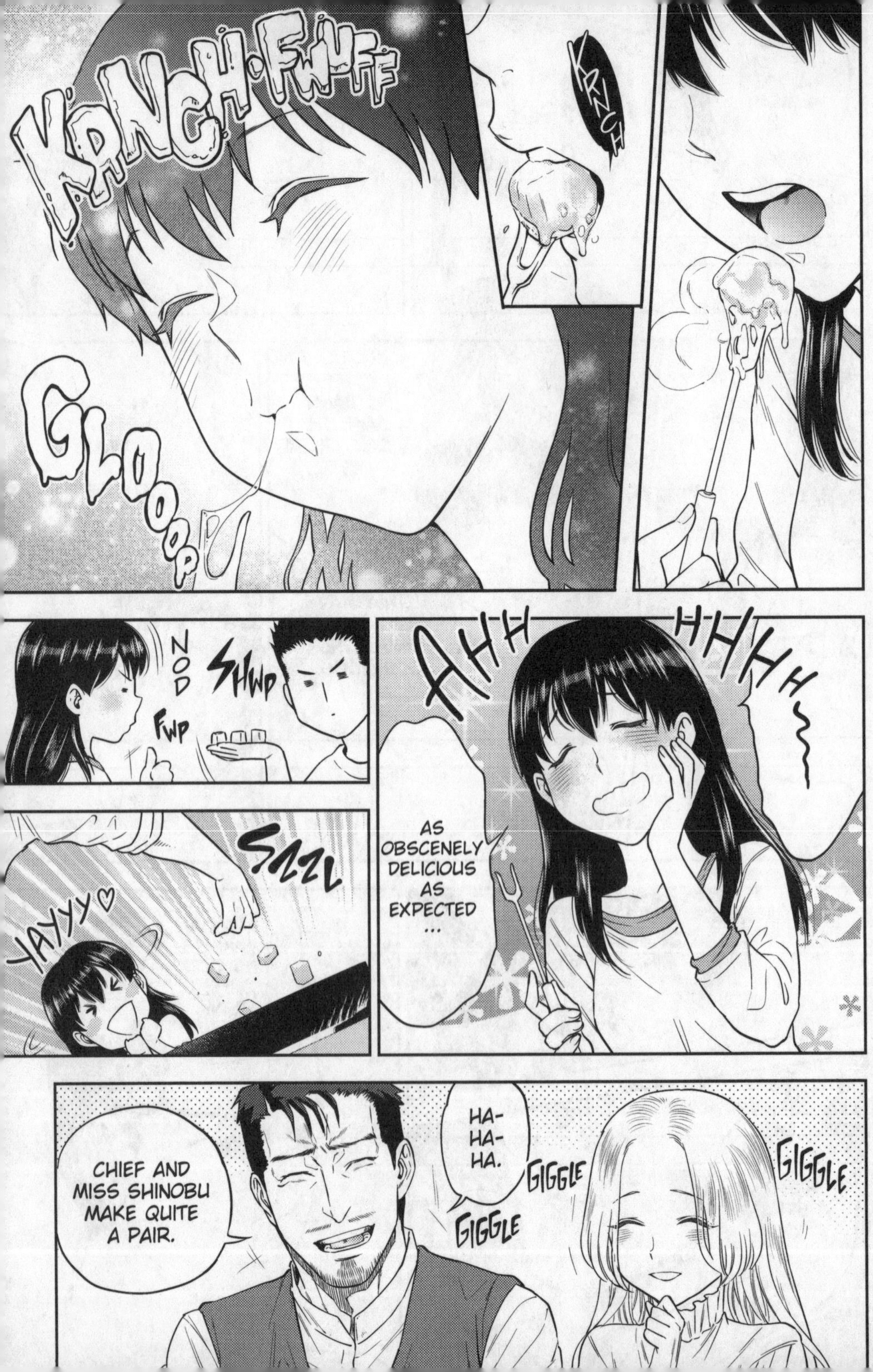
KRNCH
KRNCH FWUFF
GLOOOOP
AHHHHHHH~
AS OBSCENELY DELICIOUS AS EXPECTED...
NOD
SHWP
FWP
SZZZL
YAYYY♡
GIGGLE
HA-HA-HA.
GIGGLE
GIGGLE
CHIEF AND MISS SHINOBU MAKE QUITE A PAIR.

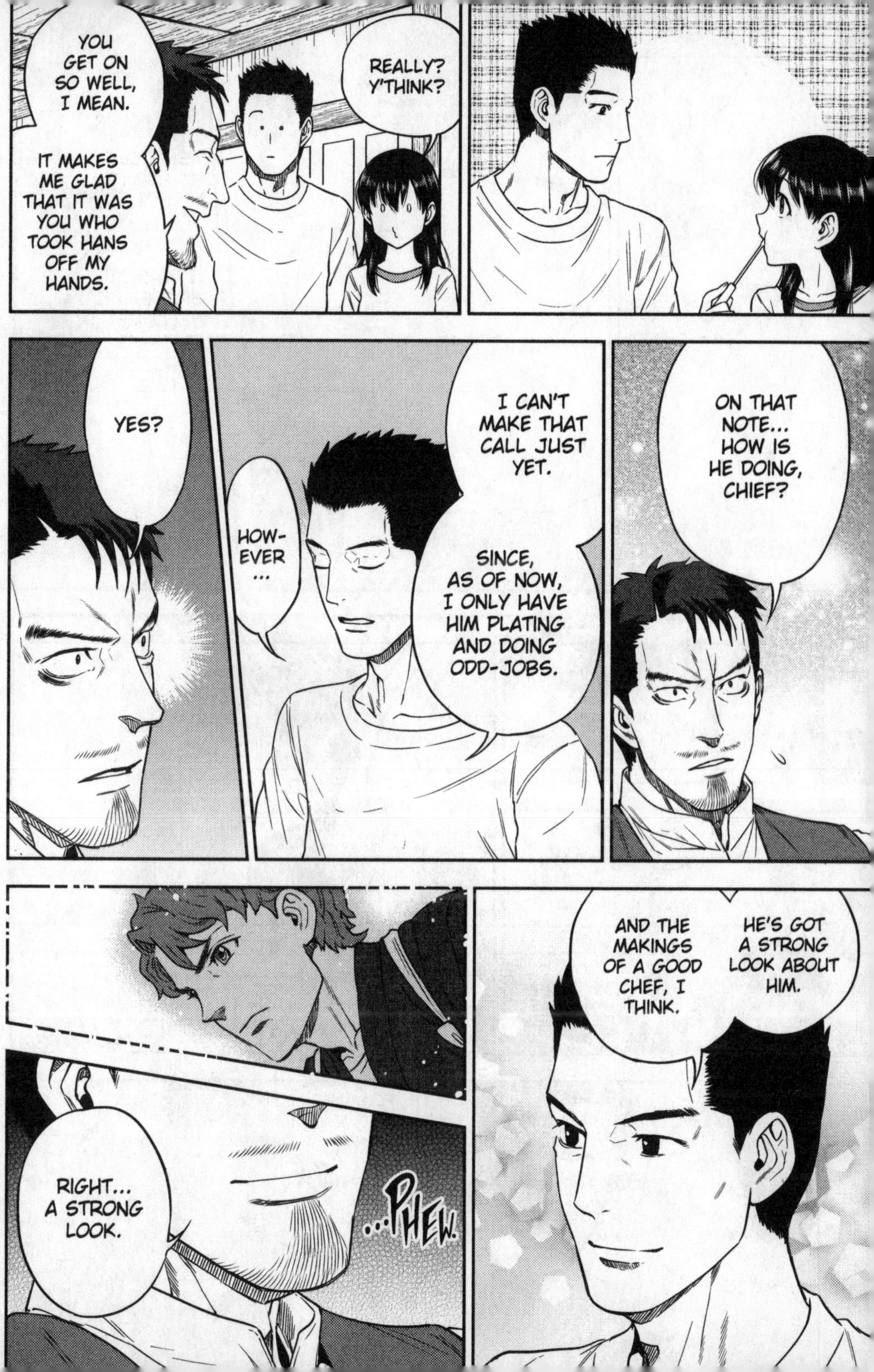
REALLY? Y'THINK?
YOU GET ON SO WELL, I MEAN.
IT MAKES ME GLAD THAT IT WAS YOU WHO TOOK HANS OFF MY HANDS.
ON THAT NOTE... HOW IS HE DOING, CHIEF?
I CAN'T MAKE THAT CALL JUST YET.
SINCE, AS OF NOW, I ONLY HAVE HIM PLATING AND DOING ODD-JOBS.
HOW-EVER...
YES?
HE'S GOT A STRONG LOOK ABOUT HIM.
AND THE MAKINGS OF A GOOD CHEF, I THINK.
RIGHT... A STRONG LOOK.
...PHEW.

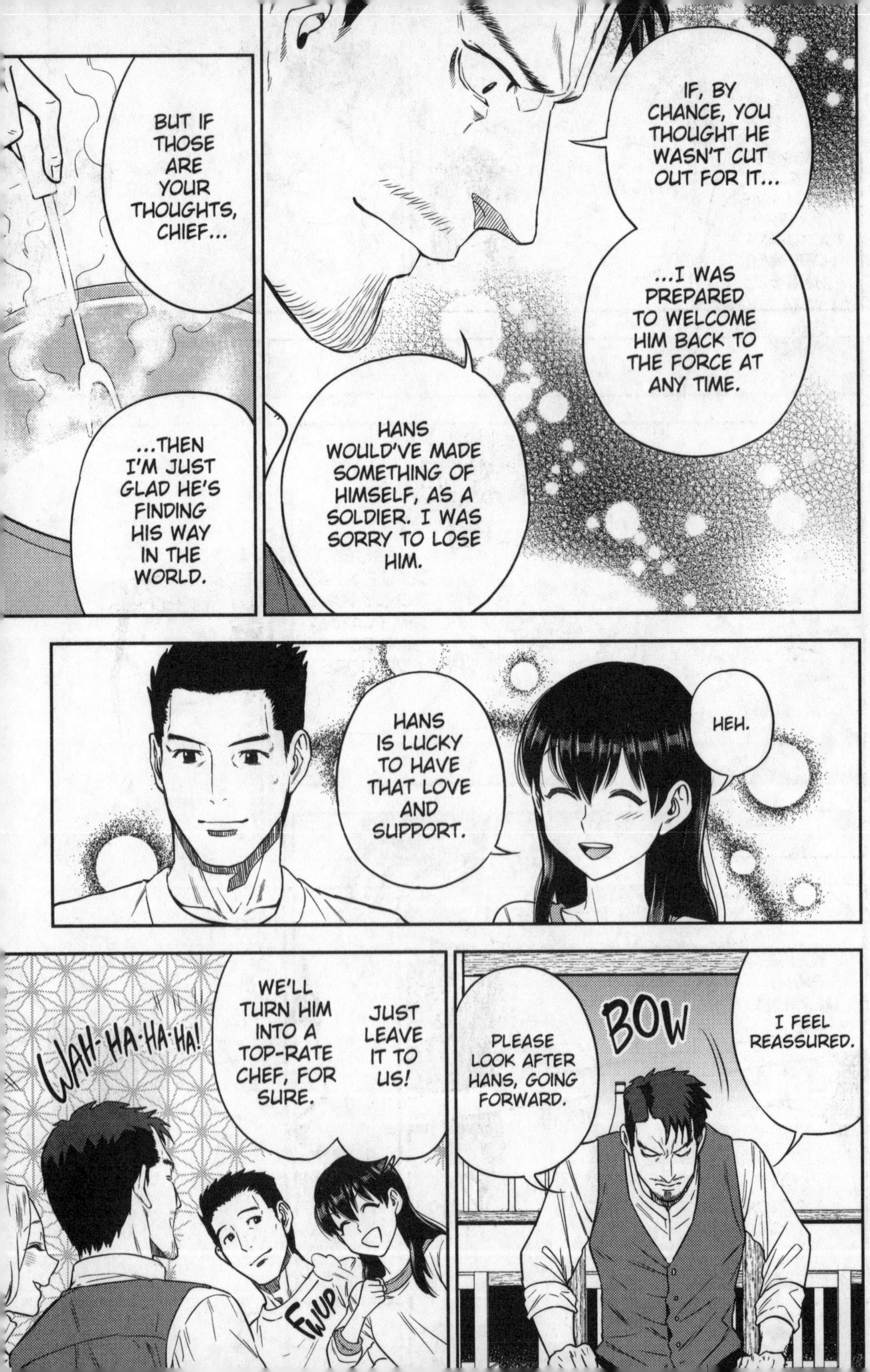
IF, BY CHANCE, YOU THOUGHT HE WASN'T CUT OUT FOR IT...
...I WAS PREPARED TO WELCOME HIM BACK TO THE FORCE AT ANY TIME.
HANS WOULD'VE MADE SOMETHING OF HIMSELF, AS A SOLDIER. I WAS SORRY TO LOSE HIM.
BUT IF THOSE ARE YOUR THOUGHTS, CHIEF...
...THEN I'M JUST GLAD HE'S FINDING HIS WAY IN THE WORLD.
HEH.
HANS IS LUCKY TO HAVE THAT LOVE AND SUPPORT.
I FEEL REASSURED.
BOW
PLEASE LOOK AFTER HANS, GOING FORWARD.
JUST LEAVE IT TO US!
WE'LL TURN HIM INTO A TOP-RATE CHEF, FOR SURE.
WAH-HA-HA-HA!
FWUP

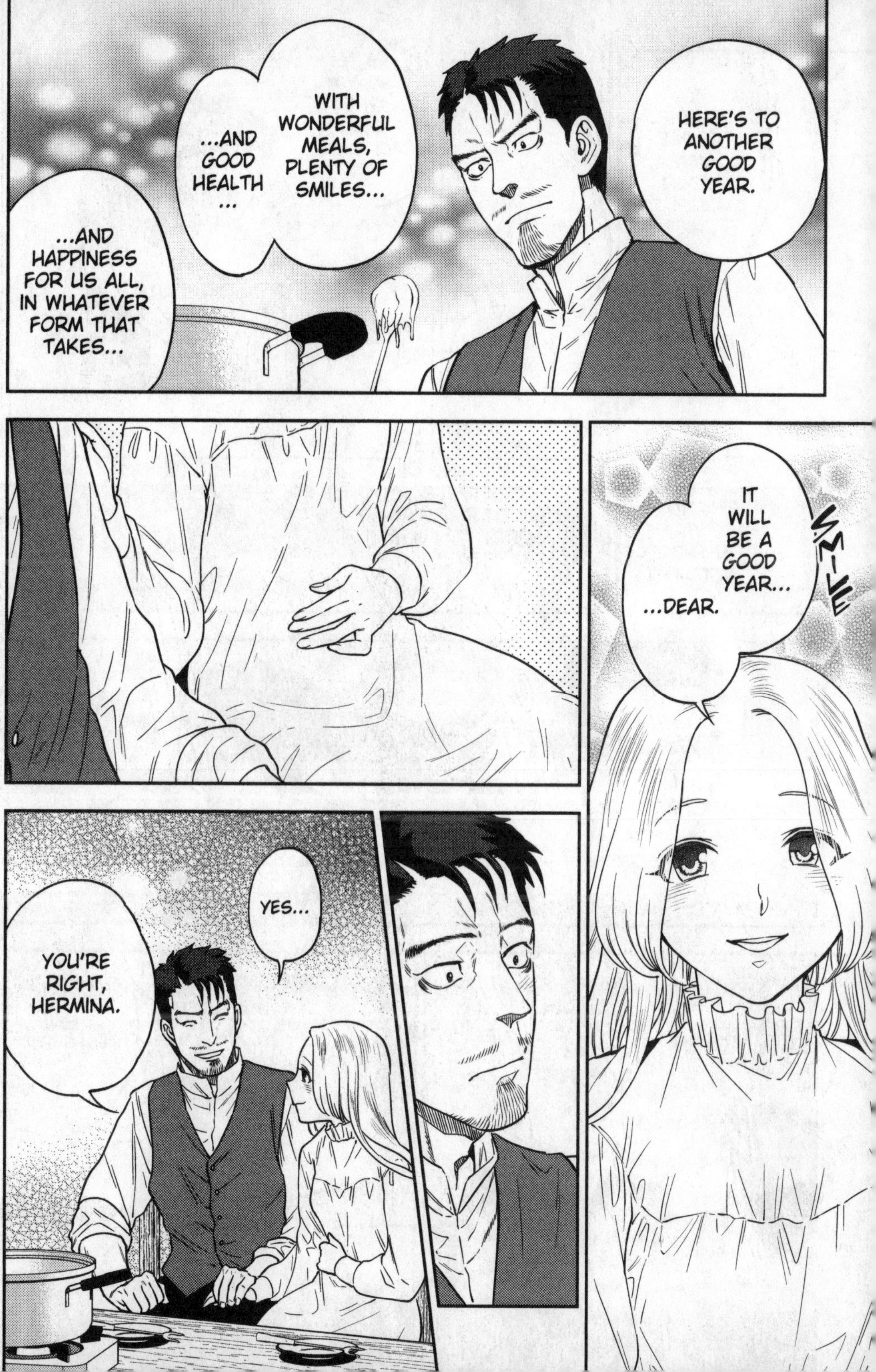
HERE'S TO ANOTHER GOOD YEAR.
WITH WONDERFUL MEALS, PLENTY OF SMILES...
...AND GOOD HEALTH ...
...AND HAPPINESS FOR US ALL, IN WHATEVER FORM THAT TAKES...
SMILE
IT WILL BE A GOOD YEAR... ...DEAR.
YES...
YOU'RE RIGHT, HERMINA.

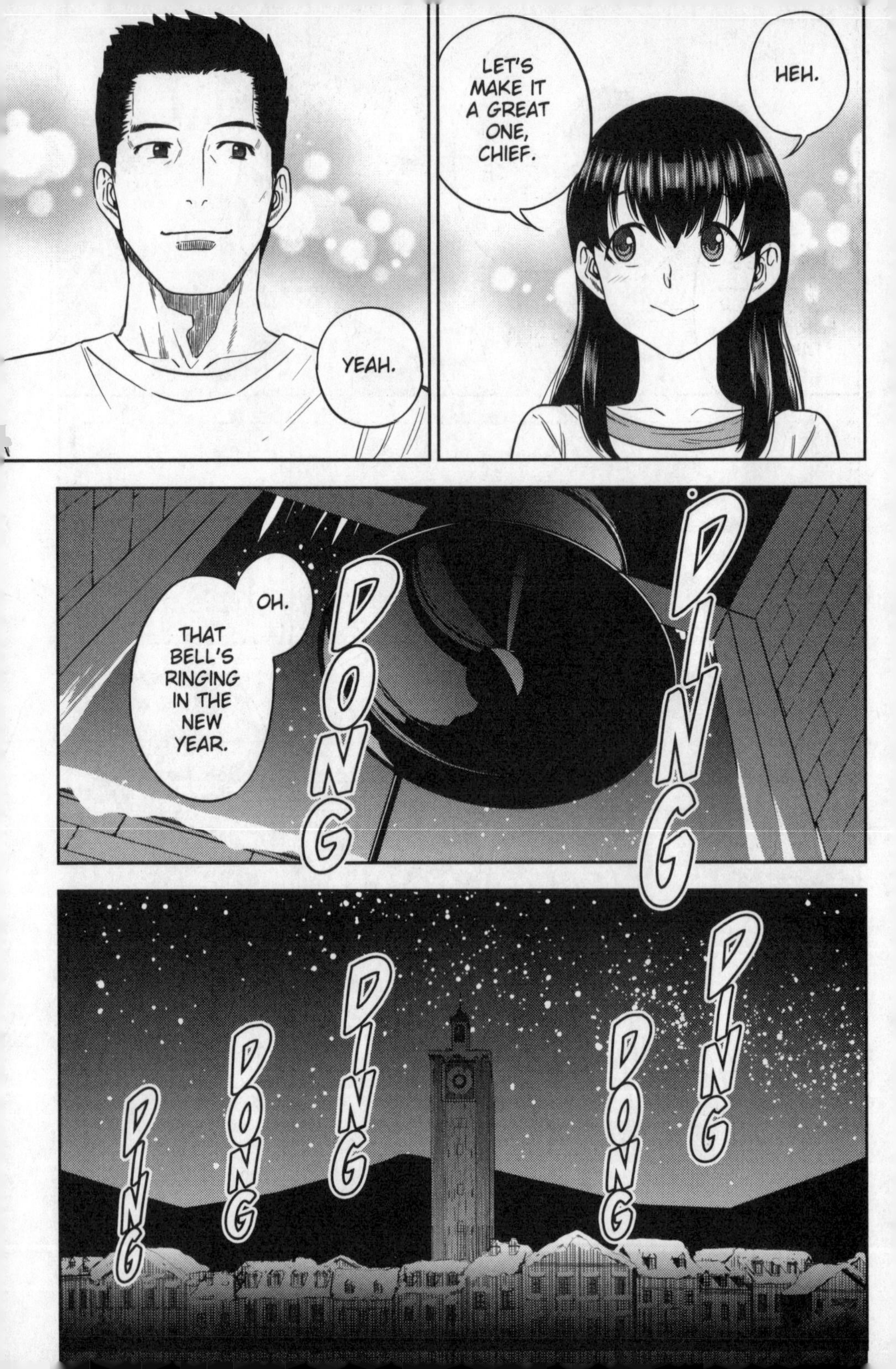
HEH.
LET'S MAKE IT A GREAT ONE, CHIEF.
YEAH.
DING
DONG
OH.
THAT BELL'S RINGING IN THE NEW YEAR.
DING
DONG
DING
DONG
DING

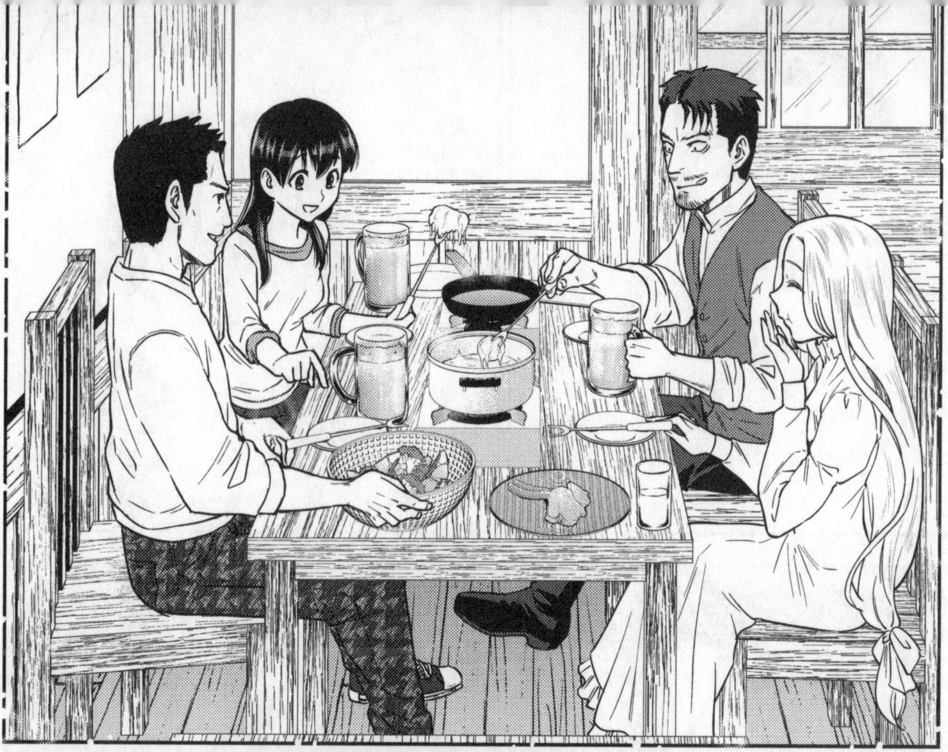

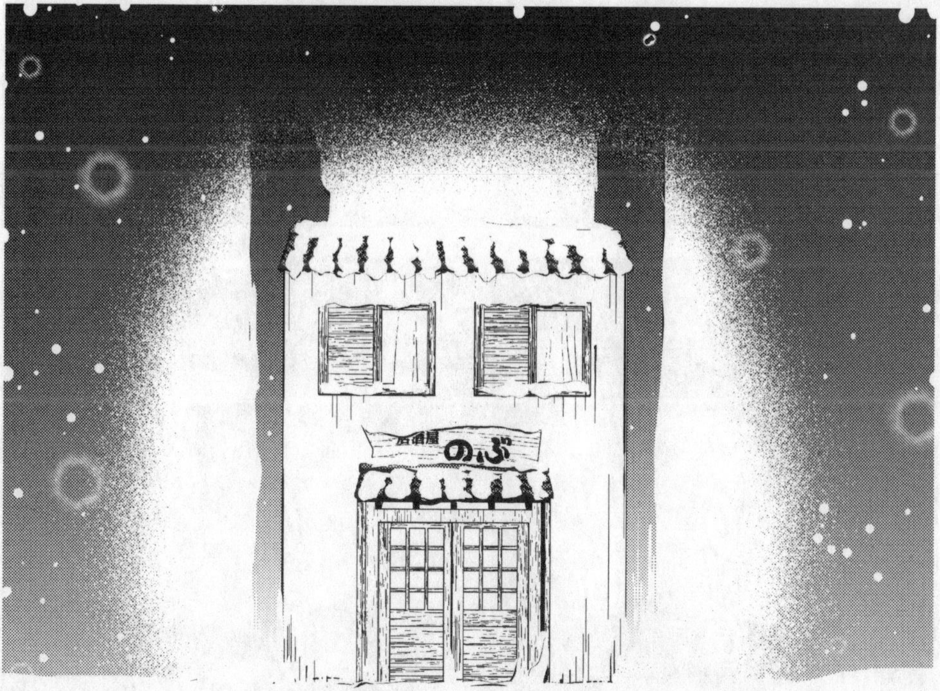
居酒屋 のぶ

COURSE 50 - CLOSING TIME

Cheese Fondue

M
E
N
U

FOOD VOCABULARY ENCOUNTERED IN THIS BOOK:
The fantasy world of "Nobu" brings together speakers of Japanese and German for a delicious cross-cultural exchange. Hans, Nikolaus, Chief, Shinobu, and the gang use a variety of foreign food vocabulary throughout, so here's a quick review of what came up in this volume!

JAPANESE

Ankake yudofu: boiled tofu topped with viscous ankake sauce

Atsukan: hot sake (served at about 50 degrees C)

Buri: yellowtail

Buridaikon: cooked yellowtail and daikon in a seasoned broth

Daikon: a type of large, Japanese radish

Donabedofu: homemade tofu, created by heating soy milk in a clay pot

Konabedate: food cooked and served in a small pot, meant for an individual

Ikameshi: squid stuffed with rice and cooked in dashi broth

Mochi: rice cake, made by pounding glutinous rice into a paste before shaping

Mochigome: especially sticky glutinous rice

Nihonshu: what is known in English as sake, or rice wine (literally, "Japanese alcohol")

Nikujaga: meat and potato stew

Nurukan: hot sake (served at about 40 degrees C)

Oden: a hot stew of fishcakes and root vegetables

Okaki: cracker-like fried pieces of mochi

Osechi-ryori: traditional Japanese New Year foods, such as datemaki, konbu, and toshikoshi soba

Oshibori: the hot, rolled towels provided to restaurant customers before the meal

Purin: a chilled, flan-like custard with a layer of caramel sauce

Reishu: sake served cold

Umeboshi: pickled Japanese plum

Yuba: skin of boiled soy milk

Yuzu: a small, yellowish-green citrus fruit

GERMAN

Alkohol: alcohol

Bohne(n): bean(s)

Brachsen: bream

Brot: bread

Fisch: fish

Fleisch: meat

Gemüse: vegetables

Kartoffel(n): potato(es)

Käse: cheese

Lachs: salmon

Meeresfrüchte: seafood

Milch: milk

Nudeln: noodles

Obst: fruit

Reis: rice

Schalentiere: shellfish

Suppe: soup

Tintenfisch: squid

Wurst: sausage

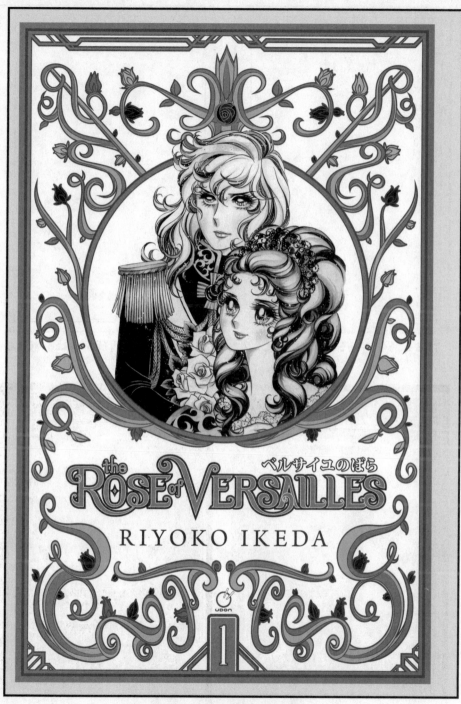

the ROSE of VERSAILLES
ベルサイユのばら
RIYOKO IKEDA
UDON
1

THE ROSE OF VERSAILLES VOL.1

ISBN-13: 978-1927925935

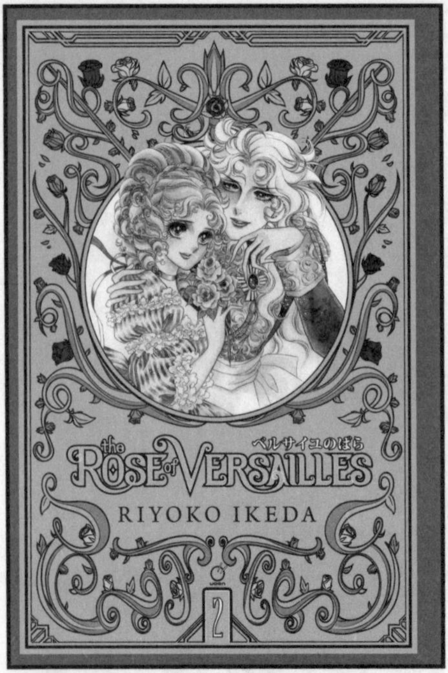
ベルサイユのばら
the ROSE of VERSAILLES
RIYOKO IKEDA
2

THE ROSE OF VERSAILLES VOL.2

ISBN-13: 978-1927925942

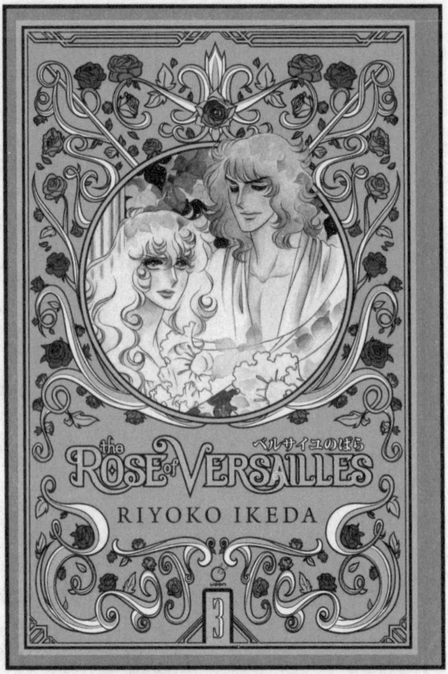
ベルサイユのばら
the ROSE of VERSAILLES
RIYOKO IKEDA
3

THE ROSE OF VERSAILLES VOL.3

ISBN-13: 978-1927925959

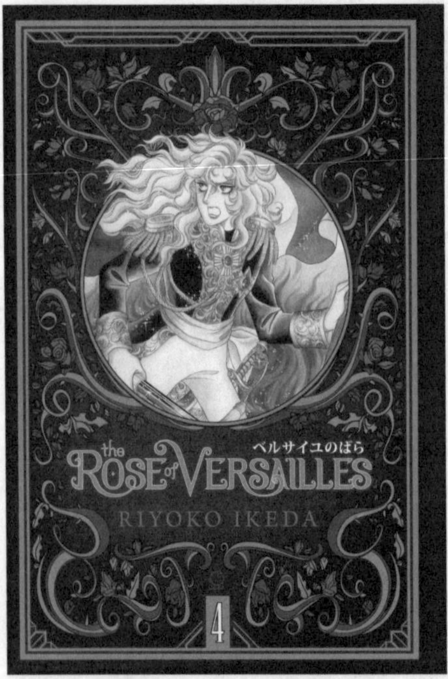
ベルサイユのばら
the ROSE of VERSAILLES
RIYOKO IKEDA
4

THE ROSE OF VERSAILLES VOL.4

ISBN-13: 978-1927925966

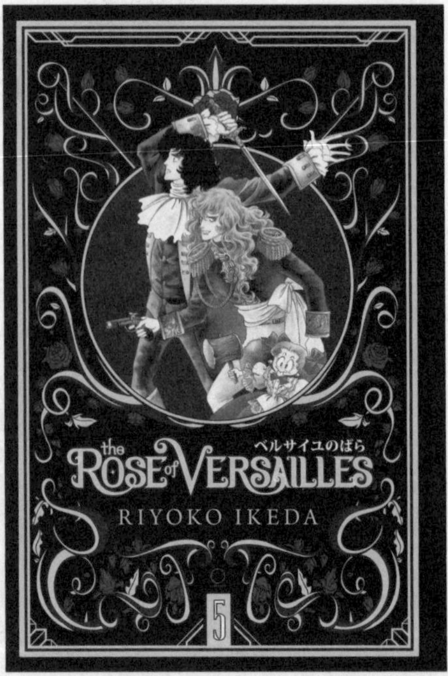
ベルサイユのばら
the ROSE of VERSAILLES
RIYOKO IKEDA
5

THE ROSE OF VERSAILLES VOL.5

ISBN-13: 978-1927925973

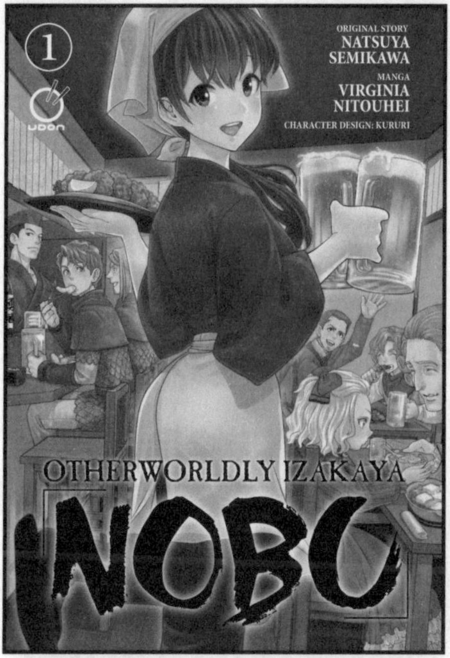
1
ORIGINAL STORY
NATSUYA SEMIKAWA
MANGA
VIRGINIA NITOUHEI
CHARACTER DESIGN: KURURI
UDON
OTHERWORLDLY IZAKAYA
NOBU

OTHERWORLDLY IZAKAYA NOBU VOL.1
ISBN: 978-1772940671

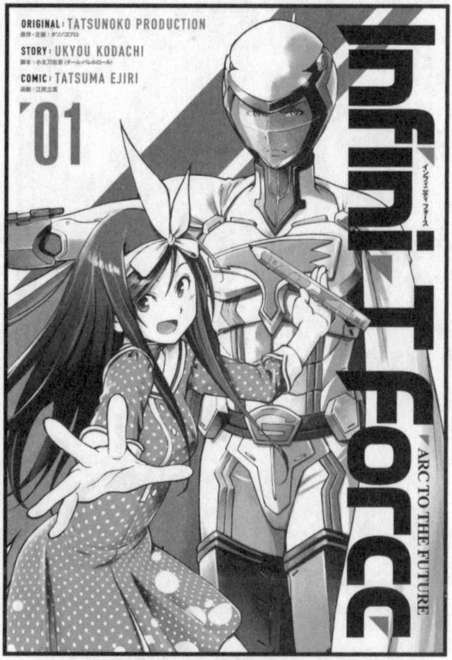
ORIGINAL: TATSUNOKO PRODUCTION
STORY: UKYOU KODACHI
COMIC: TATSUMA EJIRI
01
INFINi-T FORCE
ARC TO THE FUTURE

INFINI-T FORCE VOL.1
ISBN-13: 978-1772940503

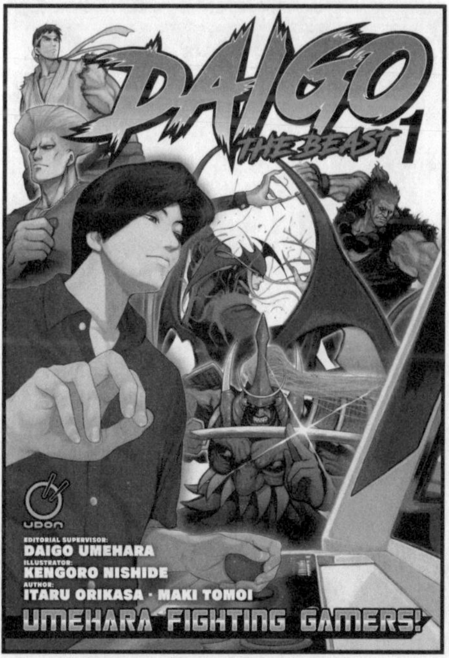
DAIGO THE BEAST 1
UDON
EDITORIAL SUPERVISOR:
DAIGO UMEHARA
ILLUSTRATOR:
KENGORO NISHIDE
AUTHOR:
ITARU ORIKASA · MAKI TOMOI
UMEHARA FIGHTING GAMERS!

DAIGO THE BEAST VOL.1
ISBN: 978-1772940572

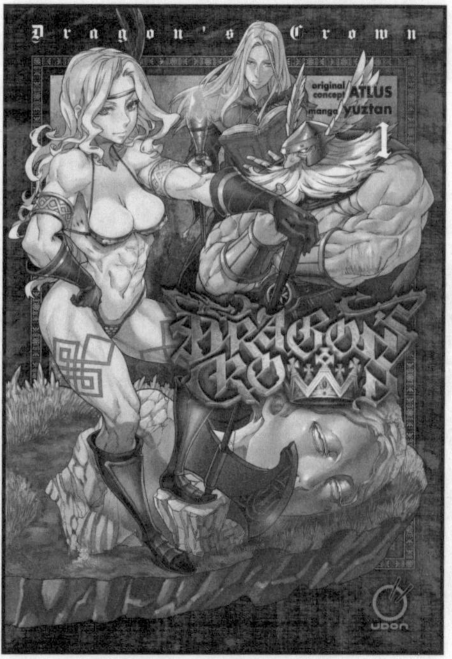
Dragon's Crown
original concept ATLUS
manga yuztan
1
UDON

DRAGON'S CROWN VOL.1
ISBN: 978-1772940480